MEXICO
FOR THE
GLOBAL
INVESTOR

ALSO BY TIMOTHY HEYMAN

La inversión en México (with Arturo León) (1981)
Inversión contra inflación (eds. 1986, 1987, 1988)
Investing in Mexico (1989)
Mexico: emerging from the lost decade (with Pablo Riveroll) (1991)
Inversión en la globalización (1998)

MEXICO
FOR THE
GLOBAL
INVESTOR

Emerging markets
theory and practice

Timothy Heyman

EDITORIAL MILENIO, S. A. DE C. V.

First edition, June 1999
Second impression, April 2002
Third impression, January 2012

All rights reserved © 1999
Editorial Milenio, S.A. de C.V.
Member of the Cámara Nacional
de la Industria Editorial Reg. Núm. 1659

Copyright © 1999, Timothy Heyman

Distribuited by
Editorial Milenio, S.A. de C.V.
Tel: (52) 5 203 7117
Email: milenio.editorial@gmail.com

ISBN 968-6141-10-3
Printed in Mexico / *Impreso en México*
Comments to author
Email: milenio.editorial@gmail.com

In memoriam
Sir Horace Heyman
1912-1998

For Malú

Contents in brief

Contents   IX

Introduction   XXI

1   Globalization: Mexico as an emerging market   1

2   Investment: emerging markets theory and practice   25

3   Country risk: Mexican debt and stocks   51

4   Cycles: the global long cycle, economic cycle,
    liquidity cycle and Mexico   71

5   Debt I: global and Mexican history and description   97

6   Debt II: analysis of Mexican debt securities   129

7   Stocks I: global and Mexican history and
    description   153

8   Stocks II: analysis of Mexican stocks   183

9   Derivatives: global and Mexican history, description
    and analysis   225

10 Irrationality: booms and crashes in the world and
    Mexico   255

11 Investors: individual and institutional investors in
    the US and Mexico   279

12 Management: five investment rules for Mexico   303

    Appendices A-E   321
    Glossary   357
    Bibliography   371
    Index of figures   377
    Index   383

Contents

Introduction   XXI

1 Globalization   1
1.1 CHANGE   1
1.2 GLOBALIZATION   4
   1.2.1 Globalization as a process between and within countries   5
   1.2.2 Aspects of globalization   5
     — Ideas   5
     — Information   5
     — Capital   7
     — Goods and services   7
     — People   7
   1.2.3 Causes of globalization   7
   1.2.4 History as globalization   9
1.3 EMERGING MARKETS   9
   1.3.1 Concept   9
   1.3.2 Capital flows   11
   1.3.3 Research   11
   1.3.4 Definition   11
   1.3.5 Economic and financial potential   13
   1.3.6 Prospects   15
   1.3.7 The emerging markets crisis 1997-99   15
1.4 MEXICO AND GLOBALIZATION   16
   1.4.1 The globalization process   16
   1.4.2 Globalization and Mexican markets   18
   1.4.3 Mexico as emerging market   19
     — Comparison with other emerging markets   19
     — International markets for Mexican securities   19
     — Financial intermediaries   21
1.5 THE FUTURE   21

2 Investment   25
2.1 INVESTMENT   25
   2.1.1 Definition   25
   2.1.2 Direct and portfolio investment   25
   2.1.3 Global investment   26
2.2 THE FOUR KEY INVESTMENT PARAMETERS   27
   2.2.1 Return   27
     — Definition   27
     — Reference currency   27
     — Time   28

2.2.2 Liquidity and organized markets in Mexico   29
— Marketplace   29
— Authorized intermediaries   29
— Rules   29
— Authorities   29
2.2.3 Term   30
2.2.4 Risk   32
2.3 RETURN RANKING IN MEXICO   32
2.3.1 The minimum return - inflation   32
2.3.2 The risk-free rate   33
— The real rate   33
— The real rate as an indicator of country risk   34
— Inflation-linked bonds   34
2.3.3 The rate of return with risk   35
2.3.4 Debt   36
— Term premium   36
— Company premium   36
2.3.5 Stocks   37
— Large company premium   37
— Medium-size company premium   37
2.3.6 Historical risk and return   37
2.4 VALUATION OF INVESTMENTS WITH RETURN AND RISK   38
2.4.1 Present value   38
2.4.2 An investment portfolio   40
— Modern Portfolio Theory   40
— Capital Asset Pricing Model   42
— Sharpe ratio   42
— Arbitrage pricing theory   43
2.5 THE EFFICIENT MARKET HYPOTHESIS   44
— The market is efficient   44
— The market is not efficient   45
— Empirical tests   45
— The efficiency of emerging markets   46
2.6 INVESTMENT STYLES   46
2.6.1 Passive management   46
2.6.2 Active management   49
— Market timing   49
— Selection   49
— Great investors   50

3 Country risk   **51**
3.1 INTRODUCTION   51
3.1.1 Definition of country risk   51
3.1.2 Return and country risk   51
3.2 COUNTRY RISK - DEBT   52
3.2.1 Debt ratings as a measure of country risk   52
3.2.2 Other techniques for measuring country risk   55
— Economic indicators   55
— Country risk ratings   57
— Real interest rate   58

CONTENTS

3.3 COUNTRY RISK - STOCKS   59
3.4 COUNTRY RISK – DEBT AND STOCKS   59
3.5 MEXICAN RISK IN A GLOBAL CONTEXT   60
    3.5.1 Research criteria   60
    3.5.2 Global debt and stock markets   61
    3.5.3 Debt   64
    3.5.4 Stocks   64
3.6 THE RISK OF MEXICAN INVESTMENTS   64
    3.6.1 Debt   64
    3.6.2 Stocks   66
    3.6.3 Risk and return for Mexican asset classes   66
3.7 THE PROBLEM OF TERM   67

4 Cycles   71
4.1 INTRODUCTION   71
4.2 THE KONDRATIEFF LONG CYCLE   71
4.3 THE ECONOMIC CYCLE   74
    4.3.1 The traditional US cycle   74
    4.3.2 The role of government   75
4.4 THE LIQUIDITY CYCLE   76
    4.4.1 The liquidity cycle and portfolio investments   79
    4.4.2 The liquidity cycle and emerging markets   81
    4.4.3 The liquidity cycle and interest rates   81
4.5 THE GLOBAL CYCLE AND MEXICO   83
4.6 THE MEXICAN CYCLE   83
    4.6.1 The economic cycle   83
    4.6.2 The role of government   84
    4.6.3 The liquidity cycle   85
    4.6.4 The investment cycle   86
4.7 ECONOMIC FORECAST FOR MEXICO   86
    4.7.1 Cycles   86
    4.7.2 Scenarios   88
    4.7.3 Techniques for generating scenarios   89
      — Quantity   89
      — Definition   89
      — Factors   89
      — Surprises   90
      — Probabilities   90
      — Use   91
4.8 AN EXAMPLE - SCENARIOS FOR MEXICO 1998   92
    4.8.1 The government scenario   92
    4.8.2 Consensus forecasts   93
    4.8.3 High growth   94
    4.8.4 Low growth   94
    4.8.5 Medium growth   95
    4.8.6 Probabilities   95
    4.8.7 The Mexican economy in 1998   96

5 Debt I   97
5.1 INTRODUCTION   97

5.2 HISTORY OF GLOBAL DEBT INSTRUMENTS   98
    5.2.1 Antiquity   98
    5.2.2 Middle Ages and Renaissance - Italy and Low Countries   99
    5.2.3 The XVIII century - England   102
    5.2.4 Spain   103
    5.2.5 XIX and XX centuries – England and United States   103
5.3 HISTORY OF MEXICAN DEBT INSTRUMENTS   104
    5.3.1 Precolonial and colonial period   104
    5.3.2 Independence   107
    — Foreign debt   107
    — The first bank   107
    5.3.3 The Porfirian Period   107
    — Foreign debt   107
    — Banking system   108
    5.3.4 The Revolution   108
    — Foreign debt   108
    — Banking system   109
    — Creation of Bank of Mexico and development banks   109
    5.3.5 The modern period   110
    — Foreign debt   110
    — Debt markets   111
5.4 TRADING AND ISSUE OF DEBT SECURITIES   112
    5.4.1 Peso securities   112
    5.4.2 Dollar securities   114
    5.4.3 Liquidity of debt securities   114
5.5 PRINCIPAL FEATURES OF DEBT SECURITIES   115
    5.5.1 Issuer (debtor)   115
    5.5.2 Security   115
    5.5.3 Amount   115
    5.5.4 Face value   116
    5.5.5 Rate of return   116
    5.5.6 Payments   116
    5.5.7 Term   116
    5.5.8 Amortization   116
5.6 GOVERNMENT PESO DEBT SECURITIES   117
    5.6.1 Cetes   117
    5.6.2 Bondes   118
    5.6.3 Ajustabono and Udibono   119
5.7 CORPORATE PESO DEBT SECURITIES   119
    5.7.1 Bank acceptances   119
    5.7.2 Commercial paper   120
    5.7.3 Medium term commercial paper   120
    5.7.4 Corporate bonds   121
    — Convertible bonds   121
5.8 DOLLAR DEBT SECURITIES   122
    5.8.1 Brady bonds and emerging markets debt   122
    5.8.2 Mexican Bradys   123
    5.8.3 Eurobonds   124
    — The international eurobond market   124
    — Mexican eurobonds   126

— Eurobond market securities   126

6 Debt II   129

6.1 INTRODUCTION   129
6.2 FOUR TYPES OF DEBT SECURITY   129
6.2.1 Zero coupon   129
6.2.2 Fixed rate   130
6.2.3 Floating rate   131
6.2.4 Real rate   132
6.3 INTEREST RATE FORECASTING   133
6.3.1 Forecasting techniques – inflation, real rate, and cycles   133
6.3.2 The yield curve   134
6.3.3 Empirical yield curves   137
6.4 DURATION   138
6.5 RETURN AND RISK OF PESO SECURITIES   140
6.5.1 Return ranking   140
6.5.2 Inflation   140
6.5.3 Country risk premium   140
6.5.4 Term premium   140
6.5.5 Company premium   141
— Rating agencies   141
— Indicators of credit quality   143
6.6 RETURN AND RISK OF DOLLAR SECURITIES   145
6.6.1 Return ranking   145
6.6.2 The base rate in US$ 146
6.6.3 Mexico country risk   146
6.6.4 Mexican sovereign eurobonds   146
6.6.5 Mexican Bradys   146
6.6.6 Mexico company risk   147
— The sovereign ceiling   147
— Credit quality   148
6.7 THE EXCHANGE RATE   148
6.7.1 Comparison between peso and dollar debt securities   148
6.7.2 Exchange rate forecasting   149
— Economic analysis – purchasing power parity   149
— Peso futures   151
— Return and risk   152

7 Stocks I   153

7.1 INTRODUCTION   153
7.2 HISTORY OF GLOBAL STOCK MARKETS   153
7.2.1 Introduction   153
7.2.2 The first exchanges   153
7.2.3 The first partnerships   155
7.2.4 Holland   156
7.2.5 England   156
— Sectoral booms   157
— Stock market development   157
7.2.6 United States   157
— Sectoral booms   157

— Stock market development   159
7.3 HISTORY OF THE MEXICAN STOCK MARKET   159
  7.3.1 Beginnings   159
  7.3.2 The second foundation   162
  7.3.3 Modern times   163
7.4 THE MEXICAN STOCK MARKET   164
  7.4.1 Size   164
  — Sectoral breakdown   166
  7.4.2 Growth   167
7.5 PRIMARY MARKET   167
  7.5.1 Primary and secondary market   167
  7.5.2 Main market   168
  7.5.3 Mexican medium-size company market (MMEX)   169
  7.5.4 International Quotation System (SIC)   170
7.6 FOREIGN INVESTMENT   171
  7.6.1 Stocks open to foreign investment   171
  7.6.2 ADRs   172
  7.6.3 Listing on foreign exchanges   175
  7.6.4 Listing of companies not listed in Mexico on foreign exchanges   175
7.7 SECONDARY MARKET   176
  7.7.1 Growth   176
  7.7.2 Concentration   176
  7.7.3 Liquidity   177
  7.7.4 MMEX   179
  7.7.5 Foreign markets   181

8 Stocks II   183
  8.1 INTRODUCTION   183
  8.2 BASIC CONCEPTS   183
  8.3 STOCK VALUATION TECHNIQUES   184
    8.3.1 The concept of multiple   184
    8.3.2 The price/value multiple   185
    — Book value   185
    — Replacement value   186
    8.3.3 The price/flow multiple   186
    — Net earnings   187
    — Cash flow   187
    — EBITDA   188
    8.3.4 Multiple expansion and contraction   188
    8.3.5 The problems with multiples   189
    8.3.6 The present value model   189
  8.4 RESEARCH APPROACHES - "TOP-DOWN" AND "BOTTOM-UP"   191
  8.5 MEXICAN MARKET VALUATION TECHNIQUES   192
    8.5.1 Liquidity cycle   192
    8.5.2 Historical comparisons   193
    8.5.3 International comparisons   194
    8.5.4 Problems with market valuation techniques   194
    8.5.5 Present value   195
    8.5.6 Stock index forecasting   196
    8.5.7 Comparison with the US stock market   197

8.6 MEXICAN SECTOR VALUATION   198
  8.6.1 The concept of sector   198
  8.6.2 The role of brokerage research departments   198
  8.6.3 Sectors of the Mexican stock market   200
  8.6.4 Sector analysis   202
    — Multiples   202
    — Sector rotation   204
    — International multiples   205
  8.6.5 Structural analysis of sectors   207
    — Market share   208
    — Activity chain   208
    — Service companies   209
  8.6.6 Other definitions of sector   210
    — Capitalization   210
    — Growth   211
    — Value   211
    — Yield   212
8.7 MEXICAN STOCK VALUATION   213
  8.7.1 Liquidity   213
  8.7.2 Allocation of stocks to sectors   216
  8.7.3 Multiples   217
  8.7.4 Earnings forecasts   218
    — Company information   218
    — Sales   219
    — Operating costs   219
    — Financial cost   219
    — Net earnings (profit)   220
    — Consensus forecasts   220
  8.7.5 Stock valuation   220
    — Present value model   220
  8.7.6 One year price targets   222

9 Derivatives   225
  9.1 INTRODUCTION   225
  9.2 HISTORY OF GLOBAL DERIVATIVES   227
    9.2.1 Origins   227
    9.2.2 The Chicago futures markets   229
    9.2.3 The introduction of financial derivatives   230
    9.2.4 Expansion and consolidation of derivatives markets   231
  9.3 STRUCTURE OF GLOBAL DERIVATIVES MARKETS   231
    9.3.1 Introduction   231
    9.3.2 Market, underlying asset, instrument and counterparty   232
  9.4 HISTORY OF MEXICAN DERIVATIVES   234
  9.5 STRUCTURE OF MEXICAN DERIVATIVES MARKETS   236
    9.5.1 International organized markets   236
    9.5.2 Mexican organized markets   237
      — Mexican Stock Exchange   237
      — MexDer   238
    9.5.3 Importance in relation to underlying market   238
  9.6 USE OF DERIVATIVES   238

9.7 FORWARDS AND FUTURES   239
   9.7.1 Definition   239
   9.7.2 Valuation   240
   9.7.3 Cost   242
   9.7.4 Payoff functions   242
9.8 OPTIONS   243
   9.8.1 Definitions   243
   9.8.2 Valuation   244
      — Intrinsic value and time value   244
      — Theoretical value   246
   9.8.3 Cost   247
   9.8.4 Option payoff functions   248
      — Call and put options   248
9.9 BASIC ELEMENTS IN THE USE OF DERIVATIVES   250
   9.9.1 Futures   250
      — Price trend of underlying asset   250
      — Potential profit and loss   250
      — Term   251
      — Cost   252
   9.9.2 Futures strategies   252
   9.9.3 Options   252
      — Trend and volatility of price of underlying asset   252
      — Potential profit and loss   252
      — Term   252
      — Cost   253
   9.9.4 A hedging strategy with put options   253

10 Irrationality   255
   10.1 RATIONALITY AND IRRATIONALITY   255
      10.1.1 The Wall Street tribe   255
      10.1.2 Beyond technique   255
   10.2 BOOMS AND CRASHES   257
      10.2.1 Financial crises and booms   257
      10.2.2 Historical booms   259
         — Tulipomania (Holland)   259
         — The Mississippi boom (France)   262
         — South Sea Bubble (England)   263
         — The crash of 1929 (US)   264
      10.2.3 Gold and silver   265
      10.2.4 Mexican stock market booms   266
         — 1979   266
         — 1984   266
         — 1987   266
      10.2.5 Mexican peso booms 1982 and 1994   268
   10.3 THE ANALYSIS OF IRRATIONALITY   269
   10.4 THE CLASSIC BOOM CYCLE   269
      10.4.1 The Minsky model   269
         — Displacement   269
         — Gradual growth   270
         — Increase in liquidity   270

— Entry of novices   271
— Euphoria   271
— Insider selling   271
— Crash   271
— Panic   271
— Rejection   272
10.4.2 Application of the Minsky model to Mexico   272
10.5   THE CAUSE OF BOOMS – GROUP PSYCHOLOGY   273
10.5.1 Investors as a group   273
10.5.2 The consequences of the collective mind   274
— The influence of the group   274
— The influence of the expert   275
— The fallibility of the expert   275
— Experts are also members of a group   275
10.5.3 Rules of contrary opinion   276
— Investment objectives   276
— Economic assumptions   276
— Specific investments   277
— Trading   277
10.6   INVESTMENT AS A LONELY ACTIVITY   277

11 Investors   **279**
11.1   INDIVIDUAL AND INSTITUTIONAL INVESTORS   279
11.2   THE INDIVIDUAL INVESTOR   280
11.2.1 Return and risk   280
— Risk tolerance   280
— Life cycle   282
11.2.2 Term and liquidity   283
— Term   283
— Liquidity   284
11.2.3 Taxes and inheritances   284
— Taxes   284
— Inheritances   284
11.3   TRENDS IN INDIVIDUAL INVESTMENT   285
11.3.1 United States   285
11.3.2 Mexico   286
11.4   INSTITUTIONAL INVESTMENT   287
11.4.1 Types of institutional investment   287
— Mutual funds   287
— Pension funds   288
— Charitable funds   288
— Insurance companies   289
— Other financial institutions   289
— Companies   289
11.5   TRENDS IN INSTITUTIONAL INVESTMENT   289
11.5.1 Global institutional investment   289
11.5.2 Institutional investment in the US   291
— History   291
— Recent growth   292
— Traditional institutional business   293

— Defined contribution pension plans   294
— Mutual funds   295
11.5.3 Institutional investment in Mexico   297
— History   297
— Afores and Sicfores   298
— The Chilean pension system   299
— The future of institutional investment in Mexico   300

12 Management   303
12.1 INVESTMENT MANAGEMENT   303
12.2 PLANNING   303
12.2.1 Formulation of objectives   303
12.2.2 Formulation of analysis techniques   303
12.2.3 Investment analysis   304
12.2.4 Portfolio construction   305
— Asset allocation   305
— Optimization of return-risk   305
— Benchmark selection   307
12.3 CONTROL   307
12.3.1 Performance measurement   307
12.3.2 Measurement of one asset class   308
12.3.3 Performance measurement of a portfolio with several asset
       classes   310
12.3.4 Revision of assumptions   311
12.4 SYSTEMS AND ORGANIZATION   312
12.4.1 Institutional investment   312
12.4.2 Individual investment   314
12.5 INVESTMENT ADVICE   314
12.6 FIVE INVESTMENT RULES   315
12.6.1 Term   316
12.6.2 Diversification   316
12.6.3 Discipline   316
12.6.4 Knowledge and understanding   316
12.6.5 Contrary opinion   316

Appendices   319

Appendix A Investment   321
A.1 GEOMETRIC AND ARITHMETIC MEAN   321
A.2 PRESENT VALUE   322
A.3 MODERN PORTFOLIO THEORY (MPT)   323
A.3.1 Measurement of return and risk of a single investment   323
A.3.2 Measurement of return of a portfolio   323
A.3.3 Measurement of risk for a portfolio of one risky and one risk-free
      investment   324
A.3.4 Measurement of risk for a portfolio of two risky investments   325
A.4 CAPITAL ASSET PRICING MODEL (CAPM)   326
A.5 ARBITRAGE PRICING THEORY   327

Appendix B Debt II   329
B.1 BASIC MEXICAN MONEY MARKET CALCULATIONS   329
B.1.1 Discount rate and price   329

CONTENTS

B.1.2 Rate of return   329
B.1.3 Rate of return with sale prior to maturity   330
B.2 REPOS AND EQUIVALENT RATES   331
B.3 BASIC UDIBONO CALCULATIONS   332
B.4 DURATION   333
B.5 BRADY BONDS: CALCULATION OF STRIPPED YIELD AND STRIPPED
    SPREAD   335

Appendix C Stocks I   337
C.1 INDICES OF THE MEXICAN STOCK MARKET   337
C.1.1 National indices   337
C.1.2 International indices   339
C.2 STOCK SYMBOLS OF ISSUERS ON MSE MAIN MARKET CLASSIFIED
    BY SECTOR 1998   341

Appendix D Stocks II   343
D.1 THE FORMULA OF PRESENT VALUE AND CONSTANT GROWTH   343
D.1.1 The dividend discount model (DDM)   343
D.1.2 The constant growth model   343
D.1.3 Combination of DDM and constant growth   344
D.2 APPLICATION OF THE PRESENT VALUE FORMULA TO MEXICAN
    MARKET VALUATION   345
D.2.1 Trailing earnings   345
D.2.2 Growth rates   346
D.2.3 The rate of return   346
D.2.4 Fair value estimates for the index   347
D.2.5 Weighting of the sale price in the fair value calculation   347
D.3 A TECHNIQUE FOR FORECASTING THE MEXICAN STOCK INDEX   349
D.4 PRESENT VALUE FORMULA FOR INDIVIDUAL STOCK VALUATION   350
D.5 PRICE FORECASTS FOR INDIVIDUAL MEXICAN STOCKS   350

Appendix E Derivatives   353
E.1 THEORETICAL OPTION VALUE: BLACK-SCHOLES MODEL   353
E.2 OPTIMAL COVERAGE RATIO WITH FUTURES AND THE CHANGE OF
    BETA IN A STOCK PORTFOLIO   354

Glossary   357

Bibliography   371

Index of figures   377

Index   383

Introduction

"Mexican stocks rose slightly on low volume, owing to a recovery in the Russian stock market."

Stock market fax (June, 1998)

During the 1990s, Mexico was an emerging markets pioneer in the globalization process. In the debt markets, Mexico was the first issuer of Brady bonds in 1990. In the equity markets, Telmex was the first important emerging markets issuer to have its ADRs listed on the New York Stock Exchange in 1991. In the Chicago futures markets, the first emerging markets derivatives were for the Mexican peso in 1995, and the Mexican market index (IPC) in 1996.

Mexico was also first to suffer the unexpected consequences of globalization, with the financial crisis which exploded in December, 1994. A relatively small devaluation of 15% unleashed a wave of speculation against all Mexican investment instruments traded both in Mexico and offshore. These investments, and investors, in the currency, stock, bond and derivative markets interacted to cause a crash: an irrational collapse of the peso, the stock market, and dollar denominated Mexican bonds.

However, the US government support package for Mexico in March 1995 would not have been possible without the globalization process symbolized by the North American Free Trade Agreement (NAFTA) implemented in 1994. This package facilitated the financial recovery in 1995, and the economic recovery in 1996. At the same time, the competitiveness of Mexican industry (that was the result of trade liberalization that had begun in 1986) facilitated the export boom that followed the 1994 devaluation and that was an important cause of the economic recovery in 1996.

I participated intensely in these processes as the chief executive in Mexico of an international brokerage house which was itself an emerging markets pioneer. In 1996, when the financial and economic storm had passed, I felt a growing need to broaden and deepen my understanding of what had happened, both in Mexico and the world. I could not help comparing the participants in emerging stock, bond and derivatives markets to those renaissance painters lying on their backs and painting their part of the church's ceiling, without being able to see the fresco as a whole.

The generous and imaginative offer by the Mexican Autonomous Technological Institute (*Instituto Tecnológico Autónomo de México - ITAM*) of a sabbatical year as visiting Professor of Finance encouraged me to climb down from the scaffolding, study the ceiling as a whole, and, if possible, describe it.

My original intention was to update an earlier book, *Inversión contra Inflación*, which had first been published in 1986 and which, with its subsequent editions (in 1987 and 1988) and its companion book *Investing in Mexico* (1989), reflected my dual role as an active participant in the Mexican financial system and part-time finance professor at the ITAM during the 1980s.

I arrived at the preliminary conclusion that the Mexican investment environment had changed owing to four main influences: globalization, modern financial theory, new information and operations technology in financial markets, and new techniques that combined theory, information and operations. Globalization, as a consequence of the collapse of communism in 1989 and the technological explosion of the 1980s, had created the phenomenon of emerging markets. As a result of the new technologies, emerging markets, including Mexico, were in a process of continuous transformation

With this initial framework, I realized that the original idea of updating my previous book would have to be discarded. In order to understand and describe the transformation process of Mexican investments, I would have to start afresh.

Two years later, after a sabbatical year and a year with my own Mexican institutional investment management company in this new investment environment, the result was *Inversión en la Globalización*, published in July, 1998.

The book's success led to demand for an English-language version. This I began in December, 1998, and finished in May, 1999. The English text has been modified to reflect changes since the publication of *Inversión en la Globalización*. First, there was the world markets crisis triggered by the Russian default of August 1998, and the Brazilian devaluation of January, 1999, which was nevertheless followed by an emerging markets recovery, and record levels for the US stock markets in the first quarter of 1999. Second, the original text, which reflected market facts and performance to the end of 1997, has been updated, where possible, to incorporate information to the end of 1998. On being forced to rethink the book through the act of translation, I was gratified that its conceptual thrust and structural framework proved quite robust in the face of the wrenching market movements of August and September 1998.

Chapter 1 begins with a detailed analysis of globalization in general, in its historical and geographical context: Mexico and its financial markets are recognized as pioneering participants in this process. In chapter 2, basic investment concepts (return, risk, term and liquidity), and the concept of net present value are updated with Modern Portfolio Theory, the Capital Asset Pricing Model (CAPM), the Efficient Market Hypothesis, and the concepts of active and passive investment management, all with special reference to emerging markets and Mexico. In chapter 3, modern investment theory is applied to the analysis of Mexico in space, comparing it to other countries through use of the concept of "country risk". In chapter 4, the problem of investment over time is analyzed, through the concept of investment "cycles", with specific application to Mexico and the development of economic scenarios for Mexico.

Chapters 5 through 9 cover the analysis of the main Mexican asset classes: debt, stocks and derivatives. For each asset class the analysis is divided into two parts: history and description, and analytic techniques with their application to the investment decision process. The in-depth description of the historical foundations of investment markets and instruments stems from two firm convictions. First, that all markets were "emerging" at some time or other, and, if they are now "developed", it is important and useful in an emerging markets context to see how, why and when the development occurred. Second, that in a time of rapid change, both global and in Mexico, it is important to understand that markets and instruments are not static and unchanging, but dynamic and flexible, a product of the capacity of market participants to react to new situations and opportunities.

Chapter 10 (on Irrationality) is the only chapter in this book that bears a strong resemblance to the chapter in *Inversión contra Inflación* that covers the same subject. This is due not only to the importance of psychology in investments, but also to a historical reality that is often forgotten in the dynamic world of financial markets: that, whereas technology might change, human nature remains immutable.

In chapter 11, different types of institutional and individual investor are analyzed, both globally and in relation to Mexico, with particular emphasis on the potential development of institutional investment in Mexico through the new pension fund system (the SAR). Finally, in chapter 12, the investment management process is described, for both institutions and individuals. The book closes with a summary of what I consider to be its most important lessons in five "investment rules" for emerging markets in general and Mexico in particular.

The book's structure reflects the logical process of investment analysis, which consists in the formulation of premises about the investor's objectives, the investment environment, and the investment instruments available in Mexico. The conclusion of these premises is an investment portfolio.

Ten years ago, it would have been very difficult to provide complete information on the premises for the investment environment and investment instruments. Now, with the explosion of information technology and electronic databases, the challenge is not so much to find the information as to select it and process it intelligently. This explains the inclusion of more than 200 tables and charts in the book, most of them with information up to December 31, 1998.

The book is written in a style which should make it accessible to anyone interested in Mexican, or emerging markets, investment. The only formula in the text is that of present value, applied to the different asset classes: this formula, developed in 1938, is the basis of modern financial analysis. For those readers who are interested, there are five technical appendices which contain explanations of other formulae I consider useful for the analysis of debt, stocks, and derivatives.

The investment analysis and management techniques presented in the book are self-sufficient for all Mexican investments currently available, with the exception of derivatives. This is for two reasons. The first is that the use of derivatives for Mexican investments is not very widespread, and a treatment as extensive as that for other asset classes might give a misleading idea of their current importance in the context of Mexican investment. The second is that, as the term implies, derivatives derive their value from an underlying asset, and the possible permutations and combinations of assets and strategies are literally unlimited. For that reason, I have preferred to introduce the reader to the main concepts of derivatives (futures and options) that are used for Mexican investments, with some specific and practical examples. For those who wish a more extensive treatment of the subject, I refer to more advanced books on derivatives in the footnotes to the derivatives chapter (9).

This is a Mexican investment book with a global focus. It therefore contains some general material on investment which is not Mexico-specific: for example, on investment concepts and theory (chapter 2), on investors (chapter 11), and on investment management (chapter 12). This material has been retained in the English version, as it shows how Mexican investment fits within a global investment framework. For readers already familiar with this general material, it will be obvious which sections can be safely skipped.

This book is being published at a difficult time for the Mexican market and emerging markets in general. Following the emerging markets boom between 1991 and 1994, there was the Mexican crisis in 1994-5, the Asian crisis in 1997-8, the Russian crisis in 1998, and the Brazilian crisis of January 1999. Although there has been an emerging markets recovery in the first months of 1999, mediocre, or negative, returns in these markets between 1995 and 1998 coincided with the most sustained boom in the US stock market in history between 1995 and 1999. The unfavorable comparison in terms of risk and return between developed and emerging markets over this period could appear to nullify the arguments presented in this book in favor of investment in emerging markets in general, and Mexico in particular.

My view is that the recent crises in emerging markets are an inevitable consequence of the process of adaptation to the new forces of globalization, and represent a necessary consolidation after a period of rapid growth and change. They do not imply a change in the justification for investment in emerging markets over the long term. The addition of three billion people to global markets is an irreversible process that offers unique opportunities for those markets - and for those who choose to invest in them.

****

Inversión en la Globalización was supported by three major Mexican institutions: the Mexican Stock Exchange (MSE – *Bolsa Mexicana de Valores*), the Mexican Financial Executives' Institute (*Instituto Mexicano de Ejecutivos de Finanzas - IMEF*), and the ITAM. The MSE is in the vanguard of emerging stock markets. The IMEF occupies a unique position in Mexico in the development of finance in all its aspects. The MBA and Finance programs at the ITAM are internationally recognized. I am grateful to all three institutions, none of which attempted to influence the book's content.

This work would not have been possible without the help and influence of family, friends, colleagues, clients and students. Arturo Fernández, Javier Chávez-Ruiz, Fernando Lifsic, and Mónica Sacristán provided at the ITAM an ideal physical and intellectual environment for starting this project. Eric Stevens was my guide to the most recent developments in financial theory and an inexhaustible source of ideas, techniques and information at all stages of the project. The help of Efrén

Bruciaga has been invaluable as first reader of many chapters, support in the more technical aspects of the book, and expert in the development of its final format. Catherine Mansell Carstens and Ricardo Peón supported the project from the beginning, and made a significant contribution in terms of both form and content.

Other friends have read drafts of the manuscript in whole or part, in Spanish and/or in English, offered conceptual or detailed commentaries, or technical or literary assistance: Adrian Beamish, Andrés Conesa, Angela Cozzini, Lucy Conger, John Dalle Molle, Maurice de Bunsen, Alfonso de Lara, Efrén del Rosal, Federico Estévez, Juan Fernández, Roxana Fuentes, Marc Gilly, Bernardo González Aréchiga, Martín Luis Guzmán, Clifford Haslam, Alfredo Hernández, Michael Howell, Emilio Illanes, Jorge Mariscal, José Luis Martínez, Susan Minushkin, Víctor Ortiz, Neil Perry, Agustín Polanco, Oscar Recio, Antonio Saldívar, Jorge Santiago, Jack Sweeney, Jeb Terry, José Miguel Torres, and Oscar Vera.

My thanks to them all. Any errors of fact or opinion that remain are of course my own responsibility. Finally, I dedicate this book to the memory of my father, who was an inspiration and guide to the very end of his life and happily lived to see the publication of *Inversión en la Globalización*, and, as ever, to my wife Malú.

TH
Mexico City
May, 1999

MEXICO
FOR THE
GLOBAL
INVESTOR

Notes to text

1. References
📖 refers to the book in general
📖 ch. 1: see chapter 1
📖 app. A: see appendix A
📖 1.2.4: see section 2.4 of chapter 1
📖 A.2: see section 2 of appendix A
figure 1-2: figure 2 of chapter 1
figure A-2: figure 2 of appendix A
equation 6-1: equation 1 of chapter 6

2. Currencies and numbers
$: Mexican pesos
US$: US dollars
m.: thousands (*miles*)
mn.: millions (*millones*)
bn.: billions (*miles de millones*)
trn.: trillions (*billones*)
rounding: some totals may not appear to reflect the sum of their parts owing to rounding.

3. Mexican companies listed on the Mexican Stock Exchange (MSE)
Companies listed on the MSE are referred to by their MSE code (*clave*).
Example: TELMEX (Teléfonos de México)

4. Glossary
The glossary contains definitions and Spanish translations of the main technical terms used in the book.

5. Bibliography
The bibliography includes all books, articles and websites (*páginas de Internet*) referred to in the text, in addition to other books, articles and websites which are not specifically referred to.

6. Spanish
The definition of the main technical terms in the text and glossary is accompanied by its Spanish translation, in italics.

7. Male/female
For practical purposes, groups or types of people are referred to as males.
Example: "the investor" refers to the universe of investors, both male and female.

Chapter 1
Globalization

"GLOBAL: I feel global. I see myself participating in global activities: sitting in jets, speaking to machines, eating small geometric snacks, and voting by telephone."

Rem Koolhaas

1.1 CHANGE

Over the last twenty years, returns from Mexican investments have been among the highest in the world. Between 1976 and 1998, the index of the Mexican Stock Exchange (MSE) rose 28 times in dollars, a compound annual return of 16.5%, compared to a compound return of 10.7% from the Dow Jones over the same period (figure 1–1).

Since its first appearance in January 1978 to the end of 1998, the Mexican 91 day Treasury Bill (*Cete*) has provided a compound annual return in dollars of 8.0%, compared to a return of 7.3% from US Treasury bills for the same maturity. Mexican Brady bonds[1] have

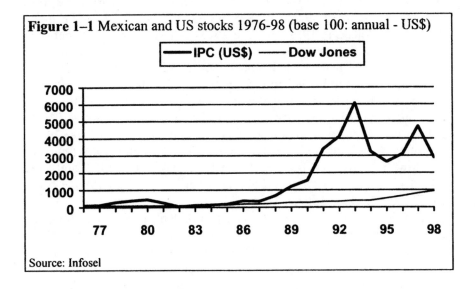

Figure 1–1 Mexican and US stocks 1976-98 (base 100: annual - US$)

IPC (US$) ——— Dow Jones

Source: Infosel

---

[1] glossary for definition of terms mentioned in the text.

Figure 1–2 91 day Cetes and Mexican inflation 1978-98 (monthly annualized rates - %)

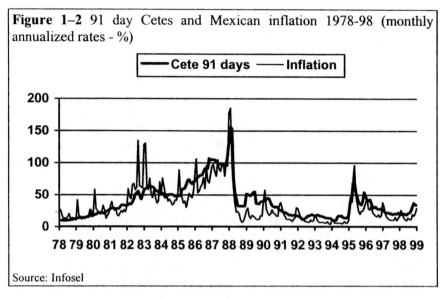

Source: Infosel

provided a compound annual dollar return of 14.6% since their appearance in 1991 to 1998, compared to a return of 10.4% for US Treasury bonds over the same period.[2]

But these returns have reflected a high level of risk, measured as the volatility of returns. Between 1976 and 1998, the peso depreciated from $0.0125 per dollar to $9.98 (in 1998 pesos), or 99.87%. The MSE index fell 87% in dollars in 1982 and rose 262% in 1983: it fell 74% between October and November 1987, and rose 100% in the first two months of 1988: it fell 66% between November 1994 and February 1995, and rose 134% between March 1995 and December 1997, to fall 40% in 1998.

The yields on 91 day Cetes were at 9.8% in January 1978, rose to 63% in May 1983, reached 155% in January 1988, fell to 10% in February 1994, rose to 71% in April 1995, and had fallen to 30% at the end of 1998, reflecting similar fluctuations in the inflation rate (figure 1–2). Growth in GDP fell from +8.1% in 1981 to -4.3% in 1983, and from +4.2% in 1993, to -6.2% in 1995, recovering to +5.2% in 1996, +7% in 1997, and +4.8.% in 1998.

This volatility reflected the most turbulent period for Mexican financial instruments and institutions in modern history. The banking system was nationalized in 1982, and reprivatized between 1991 and 1992 as part of a new system of "financial groups" (*grupos financieros*). Mexican brokers, which had enjoyed an extraordinary boom in the 1980s

---

[2] A.1 for measurement techniques for historical returns.

were absorbed by financial groups in the 1990s. However, by 1998, six years after the bank privatization, few groups were controlled by their original shareholders.

Foreign financial institutions, which had not participated directly in the Mexican financial system since the Revolution, now operate financial groups, banks, brokerages, and insurance companies in Mexico. The Bank of Mexico (*Banco de México*), Mexico's central bank, is now independent. There is a new pension system, the System of Savings for Retirement (*Sistema de Ahorro para el Retiro - SAR*), managed by new financial institutions, the Retirement Fund Managers (*Administradoras de Fondos para el Retiro - Afores*).

Petrobonds, the controlled exchange rate, *bibs*, *bondis*, *bores*, *caps*, *pagafes* and *tesobonos* are financial instruments that were created, traded for a few years, and have now disappeared from the Mexican financial markets. Meanwhile, other instruments and institutions have appeared: American Depositary Receipts (ADRs) of Mexican shares, inflation linked bonds (*udibonos* and *ajustabonos*), Brady bonds, rating agencies, stock index and peso futures, the Mexican medium-sized company market (*MMEX*), and warrants on Mexican shares.

At the end of 1998, 35% of the capitalization of the MSE was held by foreign investors. The traded or issued value of Mexican shares, debt or derivatives denominated in dollars was equal to, or greater than, that of the same instruments denominated in pesos.

Mexico is now called an "emerging market", and forms part of a new international asset class. In this context, the Fed funds rate in the US, or the index of the Sao Paulo Stock Exchange (*Bovespa*) could have more effect on the MSE than the result of a Cete auction, or the latest balance of payments figures in Mexico.

To sum up, the investor in Mexico has had the opportunity for extraordinary returns over the last twenty years, but with a high level of risk, the result of economic and financial changes without precedent in Mexico's modern history. It is reasonable to assume that similar or better opportunities will be available in the future. In order to take advantage of them, the investor will have to take three realities into account:

• the greater volatility (and therefore risk) of global investment, including Mexican investment,

• the growing range of instruments, markets and intermediaries for Mexican investments, both in and outside Mexico, and

• the fact that Mexico is now just one "emerging market" among the many that global investors can choose from.

The purpose of this book is to help the investor, both institutional and individual, domestic and foreign, to understand and benefit from the opportunities for investment in Mexico taking account of these new realities. A first step towards achieving this purpose, which will be covered in the rest of this chapter, is to understand how and why the Mexican investment environment has changed, and what are likely to be its future trends.

1.2 GLOBALIZATION

The change in the financial and economic environment in Mexico between 1976 and 1998 can be explained by internal and external factors. Among internal factors there are political and economic variables. In politics, these include the presidential cycle, the increasing competition between political parties, the changing role of the President, organized and spontaneous protest movements, and the tragic events of 1994 – all part of a process called the "transition" to a more open and competitive political system. In economics, we could include government policies over the last twenty years in relation to the budget, money supply, exchange rate, trade, and the financial system. These points will be covered in more detail in the context of "country risk" (⊞ ch.3) and "cycles" (⊞ ch. 4).

External factors which have affected Mexico's financial and economic environment over the last twenty years can be summarized in one word: "globalization" (*globalización*).

What is globalization? The relatively recent use of the word is proved by its dictionary definition as " the process of making global".[3] There is a broader definition in a book on sociology which analyzes the subject:

"a social process whereby the geographical limits on social and cultural arrangements diminish, and people are aware of this process."[4]

However, the problem with this definition is that there is no explicit mention of economic and financial aspects, which can be as important as social processes.

There is another definition in a magazine that specializes in world politics:

---

[3]Oxford English Dictionary.
[4]Waters, Malcolm, *Globalization* (Routledge, 1995), p. 3.

"the integration of national markets associated with innovation and deregulation during the postwar period, and evidenced by an increase in the flow of crossborder capital." [5]

But the problem with this definition is that it is only limited to finance.

1.2.1 Globalization as a process between and within countries

In the absence of a generally accepted definition of globalization, we offer our own. Globalization is: "the process of increasing interaction, both between and within countries, of ideas, information, capital, goods and services, and people".

We illustrate the globalization process, applied to Mexico, in figure 1–3. The concept of "interaction" covers multiple relationships between the five concepts (ideas, information, capital, goods and services, and people) both globally and nationally, between countries, and within countries.

1.2.2 Aspects of globalization

1.2.2.1 Ideas

It is clear that the collapse of the Berlin Wall on November 9, 1989, represented the final victory by the ideas of a market economy and democracy over the principal competing ideology, collectivism, in its two forms, totalitarian collectivism (or communism), and democratic collectivism (or socialism). These ideas are becoming continuously more global, or "globalized". Following the changes in Eastern Europe and the former USSR, there are few countries that still have a collectivist system. Even where they do, as in China, they attempt to maintain a collectivist political system with a capitalist economic system. The introduction (or reintroduction in many cases) of a capitalist system is reflected in economic liberalization, deregulation and privatization, and political democratization.[6]

1.2.2.2 Information

Information has become globalized owing to technological progress, principally in the areas of telecommunications (where satellites have

---

[5]Cohen, Benjamin J., "Phoenix Arisen: The Resurrection of Global Finance" (*World Politics 48*, January 1996), p. 269.

[6]Fukuyama, Francis, "The End of History?" (*The National Interest*, 1989), announced the victory of the XVIII century Enlightenment five months before the fall of communism, symbolized by the collapse of the Berlin Wall.

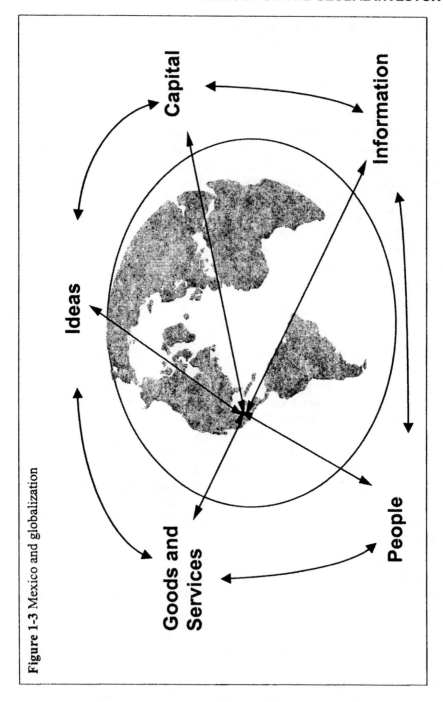

Figure 1-3 Mexico and globalization

revolutionized telephony and television) and computing (where computers have revolutionized the productivity of knowledge work and knowledge workers).[7] Multimedia systems and the Internet represent the increasing integration of information, telecommunications and media technologies.

1.2.2.3 Capital

Capital becomes globalized owing to the increasing technological capabilities of electronic transfers between countries and continents, and the increasing availability of complete and timely information (as well as systems to process it) about an increasing number of countries which offer possibilities for capitalist development. As capital (and investors) go global, so do companies with direct investments (multinationals), companies with portfolio investments (money managers) and the financial institutions that service them (commercial and investment banks and insurance companies).

1.2.2.4 Goods and services

Trade in goods and services was the first aspect of globalization that appeared following World War II, with the assumption by the US of world leadership and the establishment of organizations for the development of world trade such as GATT (now the World Trade Organization – *Organización Mundial de Comercio*). World trade grew 16 times between 1945 and 1996.

1.2.2.5 People

People become more global if they have more facilities for travelling. During the postwar period, this has occurred owing to the expansion of trade in goods and services, and the expansion of transport as a result of technological development of transport systems, principally air travel.

1.2.3 Causes of globalization

There are many theories about which of the five factors mentioned in the previous section was the principal cause of globalization. After World War II, international trade became the main dynamo of the world economy. The success of world trade demonstrated the superiority of the capitalist economic model, and provided the prosperity that led to technological development, which in turn resulted in the surprisingly peaceful collapse of collectivism. Despite the importance of trade in the globalization process, if we analyze the sequence of the most important

---

[7]See O'Brien, Richard, *Global Financial Integration, The End of Geography* (New York: Council on Foreign Relations, 1992).

Figure 1–4 Steps towards globalization: 1944-98

Year	Event	Aspect*
1944	Bretton Woods agreement for new financial order	C
1945	Foundation of United Nations, World Bank and International Monetary Fund (IMF)	C
1947	Foundation of GATT	G
1950	Foundation of Bank for International Settlements (BIS)	C
1950s	International expansion of US companies	G
1951	Establishment of European Coal and Steel Community (ECSC)	G
1957	Beginning of eurodollar market	C
1963	US Interest Equalization Tax (IET) on foreign bonds detonates eurobond market	C
1969	Neil Armstrong lands on Moon	IN
1972	Introduction of Boeing 747	P
1973	Flotation of principal world currencies	C
	Beginning of Internet	IN
	UK enters European Economic Community (EEC)	G
	Inauguration of options market (CBOE) in Chicago	C
	Publication of Black-Scholes option valuation model	C
	First oil crisis: Yom Kippur War	I
1974-76	Petrodollar recycling	C
1976	Invention of first personal computer (Altair)	IN
1978	Deng Xiao Ping introduces market economy in China	I
	Election of first Polish pope, John Paul II	I
1979	Revolution in Iran: second oil crisis	I
	Election of Margaret Thatcher in UK	I
1980	Election of Ronald Reagan in US	I
	Foundation of Solidarity Movement in Poland	I
1981	First privatizations in UK	I
1982	Mexican debt crisis	C
	Introduction of PC by IBM	IN
1983-90	Economic and financial boom of Asian countries	GC
1983-87	Derivatives boom in international markets	C
1984	Mikhail Gorbachev becomes President of USSR	I
	Breakup of ATT into ATT and seven "Baby Bells"	I,IN
1986	First placement of Emerging Markets Growth Fund	C
1987	New York stock market crash (October 19)	C
1989	Fall of Berlin Wall (November 9)	I
	Brady Plan for Mexico: end of debt crisis	C
	Free Trade Agreement between US and Canada	G
1991	Issue by Teléfonos de México on New York Stock Exchange	C
1991	Maastricht: agreement on common currency in European Union by 1999	C
1991-94	Emerging markets boom	C
1994	NAFTA between Mexico, Canada, US	G
	Mexican financial crisis: "tequila effect" on other emerging markets	C
	Invention of Hypertext and of Netscape browser: Internet boom	IN
1995	US led financial rescue operation for Mexico	C
1997-98	Emerging markets crisis	C
1998	Agreement on common currency (the euro) by 11 European countries	C
1999	Introduction of euro	C

*aspect: ideas (I), information (IN), capital (C), goods and services (G), people (P)

Source: Encarta (Microsoft, 1997), Grun, Bernard, The Timetables of History (Touchstone, 1982), author

events in the globalization process since 1944 in its different aspects (ideas, information, capital, goods and services, and people - figure 1-4), the complexity of the process becomes evident.

1.2.4 History as globalization

Globalization has in fact been a natural historical trend. Many empires expanded for commercial reasons (the Phoenicians, the Athenians, the British) which later brought ideological and technological progress. In the case of the Phoenicians, there is an interesting interaction between trade and information. After colonizing the Mediterranean between 1500 and 800 BC, the Phoenicians invented the first symbolic alphabet, clearly one of the most important advances in "information technology" in history, perhaps only equalled by the invention of the Arab-Indian numbers system in the IX century AD. [8]

The longest uninterrupted period of globalization began with the discovery of the Americas in 1492 AD and ended with the so-called Golden Age of capitalism at the end of the XIX century and the beginning of the 20th. This period ended with World War I in 1914 and victory of Communism in Russia in 1917, the introduction of protectionism in the 1930s, World War II, and the subsequent Cold War.[9]

From this perspective, the period between 1914 (World War I) and the collapse of collectivism (1989) merely represents an interruption in the process of globalization, which constitutes the "normal" condition of historical processes and the technological and economic progress of humanity.

1.3 EMERGING MARKETS

1.3.1 Concept

The aspect of globalization with most relevance to Mexico's economic and financial environment was the appearance of "emerging markets" (*mercados emergentes*) in the 1980s and 1990s.

The concept of "emergence" is passive, and reflects the free market ideas of Ronald Reagan and Margaret Thatcher during the 1980s, in contrast with the interventionist philosophy reflected in the word

---

[8]Bernstein, Peter, *Against the Gods, The Remarkable Story of Risk* (John Wiley, 1996), p. 33.

[9]Hale, David D., "The World Economy After the Russian Revolution, or Why the 1990s Could Be the Second Great Age of Global Capitalism Since the 19th Century" (Kemper Financial Companies, September 1991).

Figure 1–5 Principal emerging markets: 1986 and 1998

1986	1998				
Brazil	Argentina	Hong Kong	Morocco	Singapore
Chile	Bangladesh	Hungary	Pakistan	Sri Lanka
Jordan	Brazil	India	Peru	Taiwan
Malaysia	Chile	Indonesia	Philippines	Thailand
Mexico	China	Israel	Poland	Turkey
Philippines	Colombia	Jamaica	Portugal	Venezuela
S. Korea	Czech R.	Jordan	Russia	Zimbabwe
Thailand	Egypt	Malaysia	S. Africa	
	Greece	**Mexico**	S. Korea	

Source: IFC, CrossBorder Capital

"development" of the previous decades. Technically, an "emerging market" is "the capital market of a developing country in which financial investments can be made". However, this terminology has been extended to cover the countries themselves, even when they do not have a capital market (Haiti would be called an "emerging market").

The first use of the term "emerging markets" was in 1986, when the Emerging Markets Growth Fund Inc. was launched by the International Finance Corporation (IFC), the member of the World Bank group that invests in the private sector, and by the Capital Group, the largest manager of international equities in the US.[10] The Fund's investment objective was "to seek long term capital growth through investment in securities of developing countries". The Fund raised, with some difficulty, US$50mn. and in its prospectus management estimated that "it might take up to one year to invest the total amount of funds in securities of developing countries".

After the launch of this first fund, investment in emerging markets received a major impetus through the globalizing forces referred to in the previous section: ideas (the collapse of communism implies the incorporation of 3 billion additional producers and consumers into the global market) and information (the extension to emerging markets of specialized services such as Reuters, Bloomberg, and Dow Jones-Telerate)[11] – causing an ever increasing flow of capital, goods and services, and people to these countries.

---

[10]The term is attributed to Antoine van Agtmael, who was then an executive of the IFC, and is now a well known manager of emerging markets funds.

[11] Infosel, the Mexican financial information service, began operations in November, 1990.

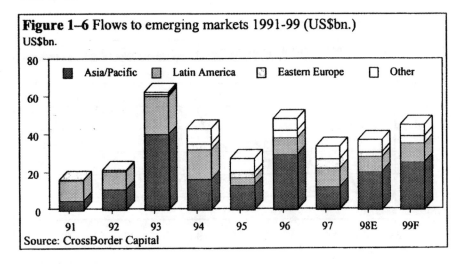

Figure 1–6 Flows to emerging markets 1991-99 (US$bn.)
US$bn.

Source: CrossBorder Capital

1.3.2 Capital flows

The number of countries considered "emerging" (that is, whose markets were considered investment targets by international portfolio investors) increased from 8 in 1986 to 34 in 1998 (figure 1–5).

This increase in the number of emerging markets reflects the enormous increase in capital flows towards emerging markets, both in Latin America and other regions of the world (figure 1–6). Similarly, over the long term, emerging markets returns have in general been higher than returns from stock markets in the US and developed countries (Europe, Australia and the Far East) in the aggregate[12] (figure 1–7).

1.3.3 Research

The flow of capital, and the development and revaluation of emerging markets have led investors and financial intermediaries to undertake detailed research of emerging markets: their definition, potential, and political, economic and financial prospects.

1.3.4 Definition

There is no generally accepted criterion to distinguish an "emerging" from a "developed" market.[13] Two qualitative criteria have been

---

[12]Returns in emerging markets were negatively affected in 1997-98 by the emerging markets crises in Asia, Russia and Brazil.

[13]See Heyman Timothy, "Is Mexico Still an Emerging Market?", (Baring Securities, May 1993).

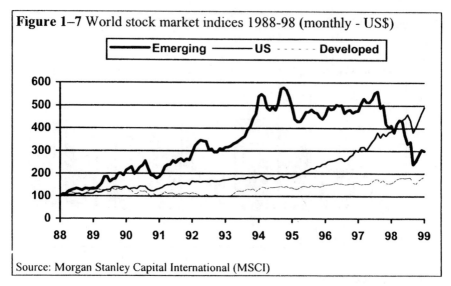

Figure 1–7 World stock market indices 1988-98 (monthly - US$)

Source: Morgan Stanley Capital International (MSCI)

suggested, by exclusion: non-membership of the OECD and non-issue of debt securities rated investment grade (*grado de inversión*) by international debt rating agencies (*calificadoras de valores*) such as Standard & Poor's and Moody's (🕮 3.2.1). However, Mexico, Portugal and Turkey are members of the OECD, but considered "emerging markets". Chile has issued debt securities with a BBB (investment grade) rating: but Chile is still considered an "emerging market".

The most durable criterion for an emerging market remains that of GNP (or GDP) per capita, utilized by the IFC. For the IFC, an emerging market has a GNP per capita less than US$8,625. GNP per capita can also be correlated with the stages of economic development identified by the US economist Walt Rostow (figure 1–8).

Rostow distinguished five stages of economic development: "before takeoff" (below US$400 per capita), "takeoff" (US$400-2,000 per capita), "industrialization" (US$2,000-8,000), "mass consumption" (US$12,000-22,000), and the "search for quality" (above US$22,000). Emerging economies are those with a GNP per capita between US$400 and US$8,000, the stages of takeoff and industrialization.

However, many analysts realize that the GNP per capita indicator can mask major variations within a country, as is the case of India (where among its 900 million inhabitants, approximately 150 million participate in the "market economy") and China (where the zones of Shenzen, in the South, and the port of Shanghai are considerably more prosperous than the rest of the country). For this reason, countries with levels of GNP per

Figure 1–8 The stages of economic growth 1995 (GNP/GDP per capita US$)

			mass
Stage 1	*before takeoff*	*Stage 4*	*consumption*
Nigeria	276	Ireland	12,358
China	326	N. Zealand	12,426
India	359	Spain	13,522
Pakistan	369	Hong Kong	13,952
		Singapore	15,435
Stage 2	*takeoff*	Australia	16,832
Indonesia	602	UK	17,641
Zimbabwe	665	Holland	19,024
Philippines	755	Germany	19,572
Jordan	956	Italy	19,835
Colombia	1,364	Belgium	20,030
Thailand	1,450	Austria	20,951
Turkey	1,940	France	21,011
		Canada	21,730
Stage 3	*industrialization*	US	21,961
Chile	2,191		
Malaysia	2,440		*search for*
Venezuela	2,544	*Stage 5*	*quality*
Mexico	2,814	Norway	24,777
Argentina	3,302	Finland	25,190
Brazil	3,328	Denmark	25,243
Portugal	5,717	Japan	27,141
Greece	6,582	Sweden	27,527
S. Korea	6,689	Switzerland	33,222
Taiwan	7,890		

Source: IFC, Rostow

capita below US$400 are also included in the category of "emerging markets".

1.3.5 Economic and financial potential

There is an enormous imbalance between the percentage represented by emerging markets of the world's population and surface, and its wealth as measured by GDP and market capitalization. In 1999, emerging markets represented 86% of the world's population and 76% of its surface, but just 21% of its GDP and 7% of the capitalization of its stock markets (figure 1–9).

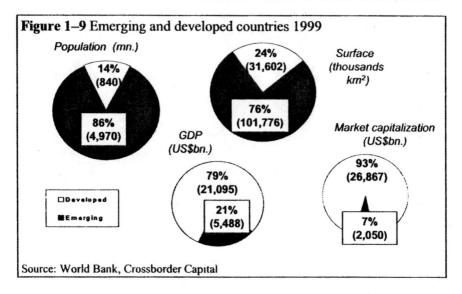

Figure 1–9 Emerging and developed countries 1999

Source: World Bank, Crossborder Capital

This imbalance has begun to be corrected in recent years with the higher rate of economic growth in emerging markets. Between 1975 and 1995, emerging markets economies grew at an average annual rate of 4.8%, compared with a figure of 2.7% for developed countries. Similarly, emerging stock markets increased their capitalization between 1980 and 1994 by 1272%, compared to 375% for developed markets.

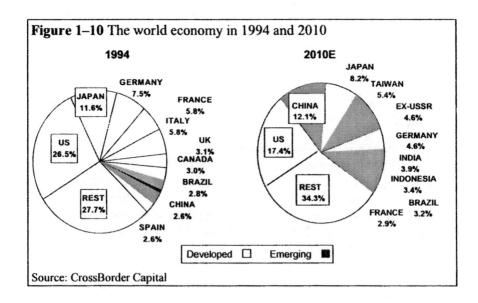

Figure 1–10 The world economy in 1994 and 2010

Source: CrossBorder Capital

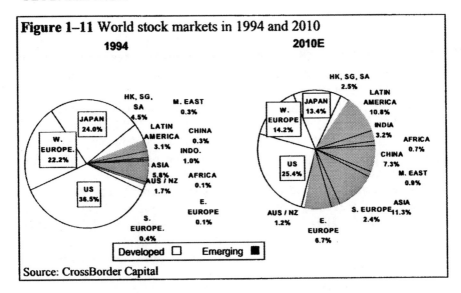

Figure 1–11 World stock markets in 1994 and 2010

Source: CrossBorder Capital

1.3.6 Prospects

Taking these facts into account, analysts made positive forecasts for the future of emerging markets. It was estimated that by the year 2010 (figure 1–10) 5 of the 10 largest economies in the world will be emerging markets (China, Taiwan, India, Indonesia, and Brazil), compared with two in 1994 (Brazil and China). Emerging markets will represent 45-50% of the capitalization of world stock markets, compared to their level in 1994 of 13% (figure 1–11).

1.3.7 The emerging markets crisis 1997-99

These forecasts were shaken by the 1997-99 emerging markets crisis which called into question the advantages of globalization described in previous sections:

- Free market ideas, without a strong financial and regulatory framework at the global and national level, could lead to market breakdowns, as occurred in the financial systems of many emerging markets, detonating a financial crisis at the global level.
- The existence of more countries (184 IMF members in 1999) and currencies than ever before, combined with the rapid movement of information and capital, increased the vulnerability of all countries, particularly emerging markets, to speculative capital flows.
- The shift from Cold War economies, combined with global liberalization of trade in goods and services, led to an

unprecedented supply of manufactured goods and raw materials, especially from the emerging markets. But the 1997-99 crisis revealed the need to seek ways of increasing demand from those markets, in order to avoid a deflationary spiral that could affect the global economy as a whole.

However, swift reaction by world financial leaders to contain the crisis led to a recovery in world markets in October 1998, containment of contagion to other markets from the Brazilian crisis of January 1999, and a recovery in emerging stock markets and the prospects for emerging markets in general in the first quarter of 1999.

These events reinforce the view that the recent crises in emerging markets are an inevitable consequence of the process of adaptation to the new forces of globalization, and represent a necessary consolidation after a period of rapid growth and change. They do not imply a change in the justification for investment in emerging markets over the long term.

1.4 MEXICO AND GLOBALIZATION

1.4.1 The globalization process

Mexico has been a participant and often a pioneer in the world's globalization process. It was the most important country in the globalizing thrust of the Spanish Empire which began in 1492, and the most important country to declare independence from Spain, in 1810. Its 1910 Revolution was a precursor of the Russian Revolution of 1917.

During the period following World War II, Mexico participated fully in the globalizing movement represented by the foundation of the World Bank and the International Monetary Fund in 1945. In the 1970s, as a result of the oil boom, Mexico was one of the most important recipients of "petrodollars" that were the product of the boom, and it was Mexico which detonated the debt crisis in 1982, and which was the first country to emerge from the crisis, with the announcement of the Brady Plan in March, 1989.

When the rhythm of globalization accelerated in the 1980s through the spread of the free market ideas of Thatcher and Reagan, Mexico began to apply policies of liberalization, deregulation, internationalization and privatization. The most important steps in this process were GATT (now the World Trade Organization - WTO) entry in 1986, the opening to foreign portfolio capital reflected in the establishment of the Nafin Trust (*Fondo Nafin*) in 1989, the privatization of TELMEX in 1990, and its subsequent public offering on the New

Figure 1–12 Mexico: steps towards globalization 1984-98

Miguel de la Madrid

1984 (Feb)	Reprivatization of non-bank assets
1986	Bankruptcy of Aeromexico
1986	Entry to GATT
1987 (Dec)	Economic Solidarity Pact

Carlos Salinas

1989 (Mar)	Plan Brady announced
1989 (May)	Neutral Fund of Nacional Financiera announced
1990 (May)	Bank reprivatization announced
1990 (Jun)	Beginning of NAFTA negotiations announced
1990 (Dec)	Sale of controlling block of shares in Telmex
1990	Permission for foreigners to invest freely in Cetes and Tesobonos
1991 (May)	Sale of Telmex block through NYSE
1991 (Jun)	First bank privatization (Multibanco Mercantil)
1992 (Apr)	Simultaneous IPO of ICA on MSE and NYSE
1993 (Nov)	Approval of NAFTA
1994 (Jan)	Implementation of NAFTA
1994 (Apr)	Support line agreed with US
1994 (Apr)	Entry to OECD

Ernesto Zedillo

1994 (Dec)	Mexican financial crisis: "tequila effect" on other emerging markets
1995 (Mar)	Financial rescue package organized by US
1997 (Jan)	Repayment of rescue package to US by Mexican government
1998 (Mar)	Oil agreement between Mexico, Saudi Arabia and Venezuela

Source: author

York Stock Exchange (NYSE) in 1991, and the privatization of the banks between 1991 and 1992 (figure 1–12).

A landmark in financial globalization was the simultaneous Initial Public Offering (IPO), both in Mexico and New York, of the shares of ICA, the largest Mexican construction company, in April, 1992. The globalization process was consolidated with the implementation of NAFTA in 1994, and entry by Mexico into the OECD in the same year.

One form of viewing the 1994 Mexican crisis is as a consequence of globalization. An apparently small stimulus (the increase, announced on December 20, of the upper parity of the flotation band by 15%) unleashed a wave of speculation in all Mexican investment instruments traded both in Mexico and offshore. These investments (and investors) in the currency, equity, debt and derivatives markets interacted to cause a financial crash: an irrational collapse of the peso, the stock market, and debt markets.

But the support package orchestrated by the US government in March 1995 would not have been possible without the greater degree of globalization (interdependence and interaction) implicit in NAFTA. This package facilitated Mexico's financial recovery in 1995, and its economic recovery in 1996, in the same way that the competitiveness of Mexican industry which was the result of trade liberalization between 1986 and 1994 facilitated the export boom following the 1994 devaluation, which was the major reason for the economic recovery in 1996. The success of the US rescue was confirmed by the final payment by the Mexican government to the US government on January 16, 1997, three years earlier than had been originally agreed.

1.4.2 Globalization and Mexican markets

The effects of globalization on Mexican securities markets can be observed in figure 1–13. The proportion of foreign investment in the stock market rose from 12% in 1990 to 27% in 1993, reaching 35% in 1998. In the debt market, the proportion of foreign investment rose from 11% in 1991 to 53% in 1993, falling to 7% in 1998, mainly as a result of the 1994 crisis. As a result of foreign participation, the capitalization of the market rose from US$32.7 bn. in 1990 to US$200.6 bn. in 1993, making Mexico, with Taiwan and Malaysia, one of the three largest emerging markets in the world in that year.

The market's valuation rose from a price/book value ratio of 1.4x in 1990 to 2.9x at the end of 1993, and daily trading rose from an average US$48 mn. in 1990 to US$336 mn. in 1994. This combination of factors

Figure 1–13 Mexico: development of capital and money markets 1990-98

	1990	1991	1992	1993	1994	1995	1996	1997	1998
Stock market									
Market capitalization (US$bn.)	32.7	98.7	138.7	200.6	129.9	90.9	106.8	156.2	92.0
Market cap./GDP (%)	13.9	34.6	41.8	54.4	34.4	36.4	31.9	39.3	24.1
Foreign investment (US$bn.)	4.0	18.5	28.7	54.6	34.4	24.5	31.0	49.0	32.6
Foreign investment/market cap. (%)	12.2	18.7	20.7	27.2	26.5	27.0	29.0	31.4	35.4
Stock issues (US$bn.)	0.2	5.1	4.5	4.3	2.7	0.0	0.6	1.1	0.0
Average daily trading value (US$mn.)	48.4	125.8	178.3	249.4	336.4	138.6	172.5	211.2	138.5
Price/earnings (:1)	11.9	14.5	13.5	18.8	18.9	20.6	13.5	17.9	16.2
Price/book value (:1)	1.40	2.47	2.25	2.87	2.39	1.85	1.76	2.32	1.61
Debt instruments (value outstanding US$bn.)									
Cetes		22.6	18.5	24.2	7.2	5.8	7.2	11.0	10.5
Bondes		18.7	12.0	5.4	1.6	5.9	8.6	10.1	14.4
Tesobonos		0.3	0.3	1.2	17.2	0.3	0.0	0.0	0.0
Ajustabonos/Udibonos		9.5	11.4	10.5	5.5	5.4	4.0	6.3	7.5
Total		51.1	42.1	41.4	31.5	17.3	19.8	27.5	32.4
Foreign investment (US$bn.)		5.5	14.2	21.8	17.2	3.3	3.4	3.4	2.4
Foreign investment/total debt (%)		10.8	33.7	52.7	54.6	19.0	17.2	12.4	7.4

Source: MSE, Ministry of Finance and Public Credit (SHCP)

Figure 1–14 Net balance of foreign debt Mexico 1990-98 (US$bn.)

	1990	1991	1992	1993	1994	1995	1996	1997	1998
Public sector	84.3	86.7	81.7	83.5	89.3	118.2	111.6	97.4	100.7
Private sector	22.5	30.3	34.8	47.0	50.5	47.4	45.6	52.2	60.6
Total	106.7	117.0	116.5	130.5	139.8	165.6	157.1	149.6	161.3

Public sector: includes Bank of Mexico debt
Private sector: includes bank debt
Source: SHCP

enabled the Mexican stock market to return to its primary function, the financing of Mexican industry, commerce and services, with a total placement of stock offerings of US$16.8 bn. between 1989 and 1994, a record for Mexico or any other emerging market.

Similarly, in the international debt markets, there was an important increase in financing for Mexico. Between 1990 and 1994, total external debt of the private sector rose from US$22.5 bn. to US$50.5 bn. (figure 1–14).

1.4.3 Mexico as emerging market

Despite the 1994 crisis, owing to the size and development of its national capital and money markets, the broad availability of investment and financing instruments in international markets, and the participation of foreign financial institutions in the Mexican financial markets, Mexico can be considered one of the most "globalized" emerging markets.

1.4.3.1 Comparison with other emerging markets

Among the principal emerging markets at the beginning of 1999 (figure 1–15) Mexico was 8th in size of population, 4th in GDP, and 8th in stock market capitalization.

While obviously size is not in itself a guarantee of attractiveness as an investment option, these numbers, combined with Mexico's recent economic and financial history, assure Mexico a prominent place within the emerging markets asset class.

1.4.3.2 International markets for Mexican securities

Mexico is unusual among major emerging markets in the fact that, for various important investment instruments, the value traded or stock outstanding outside Mexico is greater than that in Mexico itself (figure 1–16).

The first ADR (American Depositary Receipt) of a Mexican stock to be listed on the New York Stock Exchange was TELMEX, in May, 1991. At the end of 1998, Mexico had the largest number of ADRs

Figure 1–15 Emerging markets: comparative figures (February 1999)

	Population (mn.)	GDP 1997 (US$bn.)	GDP per capita (US$)	Equity market cap (US$bn.)	Equity market cap per capita (US$)
Argentina	35	324	9,334	41	1,191
Bangladesh	120	31	258	1	10
Brazil	159	777	4,878	105	662
Chile	14	73	5,166	48	3,398
China	1,200	919	766	61	51
Colombia	37	69	1,880	11	307
Czech Republic	10	48	4,609	15	1,432
Egypt	58	76	1,309	8	140
Greece	10	116	11,072	95	9,055
Hong Kong	6	173	27,947	317	51,176
Hungary	10	42	4,058	5	479
India	929	355	382	151	162
Indonesia	193	135	696	20	102
Israel	6	96	17,330	40	7,316
Jamaica	3	6	2,503	2	912
Jordan	4	7	1,674	3	783
Kuwait	2	30	18,157	19	11,118
Malaysia	20	71	3,513	98	4,880
Mauritius	1	4	3,472	2	1,458
Mexico	**92**	**394**	**4,294**	**89**	**970**
Morocco	27	33	1,237	6	218
Pakistan	130	57	437	6	46
Peru	24	64	2,672	9	394
Philippines	69	61	884	36	522
Poland	39	126	3,274	25	635
Portugal	10	98	9,838	64	6,424
Russia	148	437	2,946	25	170
Singapore	3	85	28,576	95	31,727
South Africa	41	122	2,948	175	4,215
South Korea	45	248	5,538	124	2,758
Sri Lanka	18	15	802	1	72
Taiwan	21	65	3,103	252	11,923
Thailand	58	102	1,754	34	589
Turkey	61	142	2,321	31	516
Venezuela	22	85	3,912	18	831
Zimbabwe	11	5	413	3	231
Total/average	**3,636**	**5,488**	**1,510**	**2,035**	**560**

Source: CrossBorder Capital

traded on the NYSE and other US stock markets of any emerging market (📖 7.6.2). The daily value traded in Mexican ADRs offshore was greater than that traded on the MSE (for the same stocks) during 1998. Similarly, the stock of debt denominated in dollars and held outside Mexico was much greater than the stock of debt denominated in pesos

Figure 1–16 National and international markets 1998			
	Total	National	International
Mexican stocks traded in foreign markets			
Average daily traded value (US$mn.)	228	88	140
Public and private bond			
Value outstanding (US$bn.)	111	42	69
Stock, currency, interest rate and index derivatives			
Value outstanding (US$mn.)	1,733	621	1,112
Source: MSE, SHCP, CME			

and issued in Mexico. Finally, trading in Mexican derivatives during 1998 was greater in Chicago than in Mexico.

1.4.3.3 Financial intermediaries

In December, 1998, more than 30 foreign financial institutions were authorized to trade in the Mexican financial markets (figure 1–17).

Banks controlled by foreigners represented 16% of total deposits, and banks with some foreign ownership represented a further 58% of deposits. At the same date, brokers controlled by foreigners represented 25% of total stock trading and 14% of total debt trading, four years after their entry into the market in November 1994.

1.5 THE FUTURE

At the end of the twentieth century, on the threshold of the third millennium, the globalization process is accelerating.[14] The economies of the emerging markets in aggregate have grown more than those of developed markets in the second half of the twentieth century, with generally positive long term consequences for their capital markets, and investment. Mexico is one of the most globalized emerging markets, due to its size, the sophistication of its financial markets, both inside and outside Mexico, and foreign participation in its financial markets.

It is reasonable to consider that these are long term trends.[15] It has been said that good futurologists do not "forecast" the future, but produce an accurate diagnosis of current trends. Once these trends have been diagnosed, forecasting consists in the extrapolation of these trends

---

[14]The complex social and political consequences of globalization are outside the scope of this book. See, for example, Dani Rodrick, "Has Globalization Gone Too Far?" (Institute for International Economics, 1996), and William Greider, *One World, Ready or Not* (Touchstone, 1998).

[15]📖 4.2 for an analysis of current trends in the context of the "long cycle" of Kondratieff.

Figure 1–17 Principal foreign financial institutions in Mexico 1998

	Country	Bank	Brokerage	Insurance	Financial group
ABN Amro	Holland	X			
American Bankers Insurance	US			X	
American International Group	US			X	
American Express	US	X			
Skandia	Sweden			X	
Bank of Boston	US	X			
Bankers Trust	US	X	X		
Bank of America	US	X			
Bank of Tokyo-Mitsubishi	Japan	X			
BBV	Spain	X	X	X	X
Chase-Chemical	US	X			X
Chubb	US			X	
Citibank	US	X			X
Colonial Penn Insurance Co.	US			X	
Combined Insurance Co.	US			X	
Deutsche	Germany	X	X		
Dresdner	Germany	X			
First Chicago	US	X			
Ford Credit	US				X
Fuji Bank	Japan	X			
GE Capital	US	X		X	X
Gerling America Insurance	Germany				
Goldman Sachs	US		X		
ING Barings	Holland	X	X	X	X
Merrill Lynch	US	X			
JP Morgan	US	X			X
Nationsbank	US	X			
Pioneer Financial Services	US			X	
Reliance Insurance	US			X	
Republic National	US	X			
Santander	Spain	X	X	X	X
Scotiabank	Canada	X	X	X	X
Société Générale	France	X			
Tokyo Marine	Japan			X	
Transocean	US			X	
Windsor Insurance Co.	US			X	
Zurich Insurance	Switzerland			X	

Source: MSE, author

into the future. [16] On this basis, if the trends outlined in this chapter bear some relation to reality, it is not difficult to forecast that:

---

[16]Drucker, Peter, *Managing in a Time of Great Change* (Butterworth, Heinemann, 1995).

- Emerging markets will become increasingly important within the universe of investment options. In the aggregate, they will offer greater returns, albeit with greater risks.
- Mexico will continue to be regarded as one of the most important emerging markets, for its size, sophistication, and financial internationalization.
- The Mexican financial system and its investment instruments, owing to their current and foreseeable level of internationalization, will grow increasingly close to those of developed financial systems.
- As an emerging market, with the development of its financial system, Mexico will provide increasing and better opportunities to the Mexican and global investor.

With the globalization of Mexican investments, the investor in Mexico will have to globalize his understanding of Mexico. It is hoped that this book will represent a contribution to this process.

Chapter 2
Investment

"When you invest money, the amount of interest you receive depends on whether you want to eat well, or sleep well."

J. Kinfield Morley

2.1 INVESTMENT

2.1.1 Definition

Investment (*inversión*) has two main meanings. The first is "the thing in which you invest" (e.g. "investments"); the second is "the act of investing". In this chapter, we analyze the second meaning.

One can invest resources of many kinds in an enormous variety of things or activities. One can invest money in a company, plant and equipment, stocks, Tbills, a shop, jewels, paintings, or real estate. Similarly, one can invest time or energy in a sport, a child, or a course of study.

What acts of investment have in common is "the application of resources to something to obtain a benefit". But application by itself could imply consumption, or immediate benefit. We could, for instance, apply resources to the purchase of a drink, but we would not call this "investment" but "consumption" (*consumo*). The difference between investment and consumption is that in consumption one expects an immediate benefit, while in investment one expects a future benefit.[1]

A definition of investment that would cover all the cases mentioned above would be "the application of resources to obtain a future benefit".

2.1.2 Direct and portfolio investment

There is a difference between direct investment (*inversión real*) and portfolio investment (*inversión financiera*). Direct investment involves investment in goods that can not be easily bought and sold. Normally, in the business context, such goods would include plant and equipment,

---

[1]The difference between investment and "savings" (*ahorro*) is that, while in investment one expects a future benefit, savings is the simple act of postponing consumption.

inventories, land, real estate, even an entire company. But one could also include in this category: paintings, horses, furniture or jewels.

Portfolio investment is investment in assets that can be easily bought and sold, that are "liquid" (*liquidos*). Normally, an asset's liquidity is a function of the existence of a "financial market" (*mercado financiero*), that is, an organized market, established precisely for that purpose. The markets for securities, currencies and derivatives are classic examples of financial markets according to this definition. So are the markets for hard commodities (*commodities duros²*), e.g. gold, silver, copper and non-ferrous metals, and soft commodities (*commodities blandos*) – e.g. sugar, cotton, orange juice, corn, soybeans. Even though they are physical, they become financial owing to the fact that they can be bought and sold at a moment's notice.

New financial instruments can appear for two main reasons. One reason would be because they are introduced into classical financial markets. For example, in May 1996, futures and options on futures of the MSE index were launched on the Chicago Mercantile Exchange (CME). The other reason would be because a way has been found to make liquid a hitherto illiquid product or commodity. This occurred in the 1970s when the price of oil suddenly soared, and an important oil spot and futures market was established on the Commodities Exchange (Comex), one of the commodities markets located in New York.

Taking into account the difference between direct and portfolio investment we can extend our definition of investment to a definition of "portfolio investment" as "the application of resources to an organized market to obtain a future benefit".

2.1.3 Global investment

Global investment offers four possibilities to the investor, which are reflected in figure 2–1: national and international investment, and portfolio and direct investment. In this book, we will focus on portfolio

Figure 2–1 Global investment

	Portfolio	Direct
National	Subject	
International	of this book	

²There is no Spanish translation for "commodities" (*mercaderías* are not just commodities).

investment, both national and international, that is, global portfolio investment, with specific reference to Mexico.

2.2 THE FOUR KEY INVESTMENT PARAMETERS

From the definition of financial investment, one can derive the four key parameters of investment. These parameters represent the objectives that any investor, institutional or individual, should define for himself, before undertaking an investment.

2.2.1 Return

2.2.1.1 Definition

"Benefit" is the first important word of the definition of "portfolio investment. In the investment context, the benefit of an investment is called "return" or "yield" (*rendimiento*).

The return from a portfolio investment is expressed as a percentage of the amount invested. If we invest 100 and earn 10, our return was 10%. Return can only be obtained from an investment through three mechanisms: interest, capital gain, and dividends, or some combination. Thus, return from investment in metals is through capital gains, return from a bank deposit is through interest, return from stocks is through a combination of capital gains and dividends, and return from bonds is through a combination of capital gains and interest (figure 2–2).

2.2.1.2 Reference currency

Return cannot be defined without a "reference currency" (*moneda de*

| Figure 2–2 Return from Mexican investments | | | |
Instrument	Interest	Dividends	Capital gains
Debt			
Bank deposit	Yes		
Cete			Yes
Bonde	Yes		Yes
Bank acceptance			Yes
Commercial paper			Yes
Ajustabono/Udibono	Yes		Yes
Corporate bond	Yes		Yes
Convertible bond	Yes		Yes
Medium term note	Yes		Yes
US$ bond	Yes		Yes
Brady bond	Yes		Yes
Stocks		Yes	Yes
Currencies			Yes
Commodities			⋅Yes
Derivatives			Yes

referencia): one has to add to a return figure of "10%" some currency, i.e. "10% in pesos", or "10% in dollars". The reference currency is the currency in which the investor chooses to denominate his return.

In the Mexican case, there are two main possibilities: the peso and the dollar. The investor uses the peso as reference currency if he intends in the short and the long term to spend and invest only in peso denominated assets. If he intends to spend or invest in assets not denominated in pesos, or if he wants to compare the returns on his peso investments with investments in other currencies, the dollar is the most logical reference currency. As it is the most commonly used currency for international financial and commercial transactions, the dollar is the reference currency for global investment managers. With the introduction of the euro as common currency for 11 members of the European Union (EU - *Unión Europea*) in 1999, it is possible that this new currency will begin to compete with the dollar's use as reference currency over the medium term.

2.2.1.3 Time

The return on an investment is normally expressed in terms of an annual (*anual*) percentage. If we invest $100 to receive $10 in six months, we have earned 10% in absolute or "simple" terms (*interés simple*). In annual terms, we can express our return in two ways. An "annualized" rate of return (*tasa anualizada*) would be 20% (twice 10%, as there are two six month periods in the year). A "compound" rate (*tasa de rendimiento compuesta*) would be 21%. This figure is calculated from the reinvestment of the first flow of $10 that we received after six months (10% on $110).

In the case of debt instruments, the compound rate of return is calculated on the basis of the "nominal rate" (*tasa nominal*). The nominal rate is the annualized rate paid on its nominal (or face) value by an investment instrument. An example would be a 3 month bank deposit with a nominal return of 10%. This rate consists of an annual rate (10%), divided into four periods, that is, 2.5%. On a compound basis, reinvestment of the three payments of interest made prior to maturity would produce a rate of 10.38%.[3]

There are many "rates of return". The reader might like to ask himself whether he can distinguish between the nine rates of return presented in

---

[3]Assuming that the reinvestment rate was also 2.5%, something that occurs only infrequently in real life.

Figure 2–3 Rates of return

Gross	Annual	Real
Net	Annualized	Positive real
Nominal	Compound	Negative real

figure 2–3 (📖 glossary for definitions of each rate and 📖 A. 1 for techniques for the calculation of geometric and arithmetic mean return).

2.2.2 Liquidity and organized markets in Mexico

The liquidity of an investment instrument depends on the existence of an organized market where it can be traded. To be "organized", a market must fulfill four basic conditions:

2.2.2.1 Marketplace

The marketplace can be physical, as in the case of the NYSE or the CME. But it can also be electronic, as in the case of the MSE and NASDAQ, the securities market of the National Securities Dealers' Association (NASD) in the US, or telephonic, as in the case of the eurobond market.

2.2.2.2 Authorized intermediaries

Intermediaries are institutions (or individuals) authorized to trade in the marketplace. Different kinds of entities are authorized to trade in different kinds of market: a broker or specialist in a stock market (e.g. MSE or NYSE), or a broker or a "local" in a commodities market (e.g. Comex).

2.2.2.3 Rules

For any given security or product, there are rules for the initial listing, setting of prices, payment (in the case of purchases), and delivery (in the case of sales), and for the distribution of information about the security itself or trading in the security.

2.2.2.4 Authorities

In an organized market, authorities supervise compliance with rules for the admission to the market of intermediaries or securities, for trading, settlement and information. Authorities may be chosen by intermediaries themselves (self-regulation), or by the government (legal or statutory regulation), or both.

The Mexican securities market is an example of an organized market that fulfills all the criteria mentioned above. There is an electronic marketplace administered by the MSE in Mexico City, where representatives of financial intermediaries are permitted to trade. The intermediaries (brokerages - *casas de bolsa*) are authorized to trade both by the MSE and the National Banking and Securities Commission (*Comisión Nacional Bancaria y de Valores - CNBV*). Trading rules are issued both by the MSE and the CNBV, through the mechanism of the Securities Market Law (*Ley del Mercado de Valores*), as well as a series of circulars issued by the CNBV to cover more detailed aspects of the market. The authorities in this case are the MSE, whose owners are the brokers themselves (self-regulation) and the CNBV, which is part of the Ministry of Finance and Public Credit, and which has as its responsibility the supervision of the Securities Market Law of 1975 (figure 2–4).

Another market organized in similar fashion is the NYSE which still has a physical floor, has authorized intermediaries, trading and other rules, and authorities – both the NYSE and the SEC (Securities and Exchange Commission), which was established to supervise the 1933 and 1934 Securities Laws (*Leyes de Valores*).

Markets can have different levels of liquidity depending on the extent to which they fulfill the basic conditions outlined above. Similarly, within each asset class traded in a financial market, different securities can have different levels of liquidity, depending on the level of supply and demand.

The level of liquidity of a market or instrument is one of the most important factors that an investor should take into account when he decides to invest. That is why a critical function of intermediaries and issuers of securities in financial markets is to maintain and increase the liquidity of the securities traded in the market (⌻ ch. 5-9 for details of the liquidity of Mexican markets and securities).

2.2.3 Term

"Future" is the third word of our definition of portfolio investment that requires explanation.

The concept of future implies some concept of "term" (*plazo*). This concept can vary depending on the investor and the investment environment. For a speculator, or any investor in a period of high inflation, "short term" (*corto plazo*) can be one day, "medium term" (*mediano plazo*) a week, and long term (*largo plazo*) a month

However, in Mexico there is a generally accepted definition of the different terms of investment: short – less than three months, medium – three months to one year, and long – more than one year. For developed markets, this definition would probably be extended, owing to the

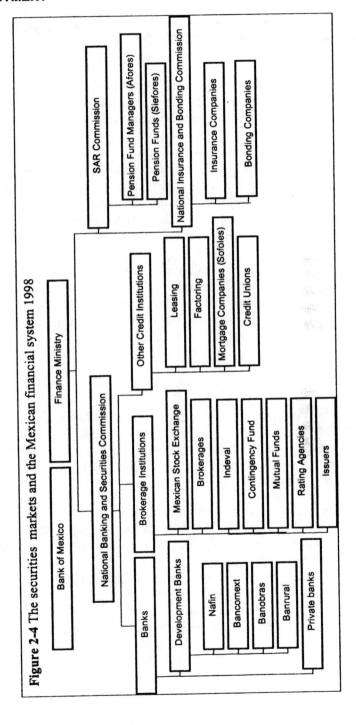

Figure 2-4 The securities markets and the Mexican financial system 1998

traditionally lower levels of inflation: short – less than a year, medium – one to five years, and long – more than five years.

2.2.4 Risk

Another implication of the word "future" is the concept of "risk" (*riesgo*). As the return expected from an investment is in the future, there always exists the possibility of not obtaining it. This possibility is called "risk".

Another definition of investment risk is the "variation" *(variación)*, or "volatility" (*volatilidad*) of returns. This definition implies the measurement of risk as the standard deviation (*desviación estándar*) of a normal distribution of returns over time. A calculation is made of the mean (*promedio*) and standard deviation of historical returns (📖 A.1). The higher the standard deviation, the higher the "risk" of the instrument.

Another definition of risk, derived from the previous one, is as the expected volatility of expected return. The estimation technique for risk according to this definition implies the estimation of an expected return (and its corresponding standard deviation) on the basis of historical data and the subjective expectations of the investor.

2.3 RETURN RANKING IN MEXICO

When he is planning an investment, the investor normally fixes a return target (or objective) in his reference currency, taking into account his risk tolerance (*tolerancia hacia el riesgo*) (📖 11.2.1.1). In any investment market there is a "return ranking" (*jerarquía de rendimientos*) between the different asset classes, with their corresponding risk, which the investor should match to his objectives of term and liquidity.

2.3.1 The minimum return - inflation

Investment is financed through savings. Savings are postponed consumption. But the saver requires a return that compensates the postponement of consumption.

Let us take an example. I need an automobile. Currently an automobile costs $50,000, and I estimate that, in three months, it will cost $55,000 (10% more). But the return on Cetes over the same period, on $50,000, is $7,000 (14%). On the basis of these calculations (if I am in no hurry to buy the automobile), I prefer to defer consumption, or save. Should the return on Cetes be less than 10%, it would be better to buy the automobile immediately.

In general, the return from a portfolio investment should be higher than the inflation rate over the same period. This difference between the rate of return and the rate of inflation is called the "real rate" (*tasa real*) and can be either "positive" (*positiva*) or "negative" (*negativa*).

2.3.2 The risk-free rate

2.3.2.1 The real rate

Given the foregoing, it is obvious that, to encourage savings, a country must offer a positive real rate of return on the investment instrument used as the benchmark for interest rates (*tasa líder*). Normally, this rate is the rate of a short term government debt instrument and it is fixed by supply and demand in the money market, which may itself be affected by the monetary policy of the country's monetary authority (📖 4.3.2). The fact that the government can influence the benchmark rate permits the market to react constantly and flexibly to changes in the inflation rate.

In Mexico, the benchmark rate is the 28 day yield on Treasury Bills (*Cetes*), which are the most liquid debt instrument and are guaranteed by the Mexican government. Therefore, this rate can be taken as the "risk-free rate" (*tasa carente de riesgo*) for the Mexican financial market.

Since its introduction in 1978, Cete yields have been very volatile, reflecting the volatility of inflation (figure 2–5). For this reason, investors demand a higher real rate (7.1% on average between 1983 and 1998) than for a country with more inflationary stability. In the US, the real interest rate has averaged 2.8% over the same period, with much

Figure 2–5 Real rate in Mexico 1983-98 (difference between Cete 28 days and monthly CPI - % annualized)

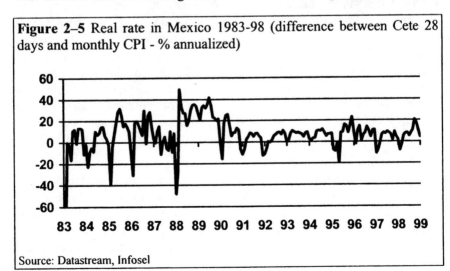

Source: Datastream, Infosel

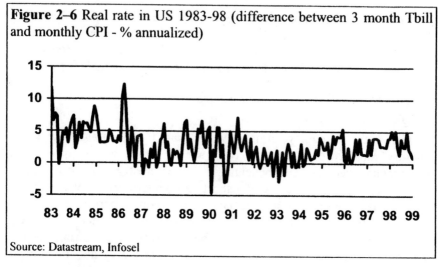

Figure 2–6 Real rate in US 1983-98 (difference between 3 month Tbill and monthly CPI - % annualized)

Source: Datastream, Infosel

lower volatility (figure 2–6).

In economic theory, there is no consensus on what the real rate of interest should be for a country. Perhaps the most logical view is that the real rate should be equivalent to the rate of long term growth of the economy, reflected in the real growth rate of its GNP. Another way of expressing this identity is that the "capital" of an economy (both direct and portfolio) should grow at the same rhythm as the economy itself

2.3.2.2 The real rate as an indicator of country risk

The risk-free rate of a currency is not risk-free for an investor whose return target is denominated in a different reference currency. For example, an investor whose reference currency is dollars runs a risk when he invests in the "risk-free rate" in pesos. We analyze this risk in detail in 📖 ch. 3 ("Country risk"). However, it is worth mentioning at this stage that one way of analyzing country risk is by comparing the real rate offered by one currency against another. The higher the real rate, the higher the country risk. In cases where the country issues foreign currency debt (e.g. in dollars) this facilitates comparison with other countries that have issued debt in the same currency (📖 3.1 and 3.2).

2.3.2.3 Inflation-linked bonds

A real rate guaranteed over a longer term offers more certainty to the investor than a real rate for a shorter term, whose level would depend on fluctuations in the level of inflation and the money markets. For this reason, several countries issue long term bonds with a guaranteed real rate, that is, at a premium over the inflation rate. Mexico first issued

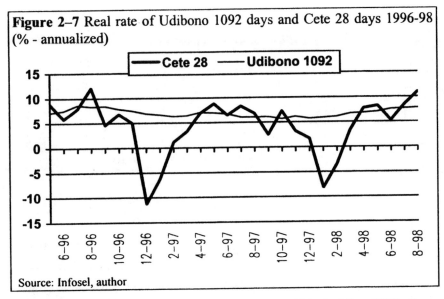

Figure 2–7 Real rate of Udibono 1092 days and Cete 28 days 1996-98 (% - annualized)

Source: Infosel, author

inflation-linked bonds (called *ajustabonos*) in 1989. In May 1996, these began to be substituted by a similar kind of inflation linked bond, the *Udibono*, which functions in a similar manner (📖 6.2.4 and B.3).

Historically, owing to their longer term, Udibonos have offered higher real returns than Cetes, with lower volatility (figure 2–7). During the period shown in the graph, the average real annualized return was 6.8% for 3 year (1092 day) Udibonos, compared to 5.3% for 28 day Cetes.

In Mexico, it would be logical for the long term investor to take the Udibono rate as his "risk-free rate" rather than the Cete rate.

2.3.3 The rate of return with risk

For a return higher than the risk-free rate, it is necessary to assume more risk, that is, a "risk premium" (*prima por riesgo*). The relationship between return and risk is intuitive, logical and empirically verifiable over time. Intuitively, it seems reasonable that the greater the risk of an investment, the greater the return, to compensate for the greater risk.

Logically, if there are two investments with the same estimated return but one is riskier than the other, the investor will sell the riskier investment to buy the less risky investment, until the return of the riskier investment increases to compensate the higher risk. Similarly, if there are two investments that are equally risky with differing expected returns, the investor will switch from the lower return investment to the higher

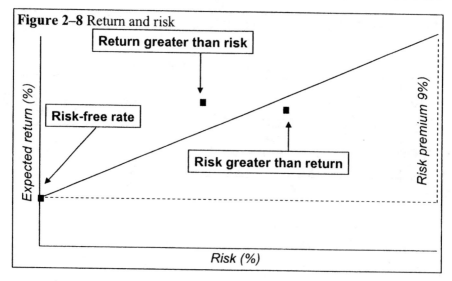

Figure 2–8 Return and risk

return investment, until the return on each investment is the same (figure 2–8).

Empirically, risk premiums (above the risk-free rate) have been identified for debt and stocks in the US.[4] In the following sections, we apply a similar methodology to Mexican instruments, denominated in both pesos and dollars (figure 2–9).

2.3.4 Debt

2.3.4.1 Term premium

The "term premium" (*prima por plazo*) is required by an investor in debt securities issued by both the government and corporate sector to compensate holding the security for a longer period than a short term instrument. Therefore, long term securities normally offer higher yields than short term securities (e.g. Mexican Udibonos and Cetes).

2.3.4.2 Company premium

In any currency, there is a greater risk of default on corporate instruments (because a company can fail) than government instruments. Therefore, normally corporate securities offer higher yields than government securities with the same maturity, e.g. Mexican corporate eurobonds compared to eurobonds issued by the Mexican government – United Mexican States (UMS).

---

[4]Ibbotson Associates, *Stocks Bonds Bills and Inflation 1996 Yearbook* (Ibbotson Associates, 1996), p. 161.

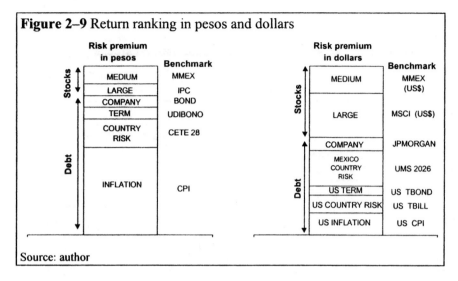

Figure 2–9 Return ranking in pesos and dollars

Source: author

2.3.5 Stocks

2.3.5.1 Large company premium

The risk premium for stocks (or "equity risk premium") reflects the premium that the investor requires from stocks because they are riskier than debt instruments. In Mexico, the index used for measuring the performance of large companies over time is the price index (*Indice de Precios y Cotizaciones* – IPC) of the main market (*mercado principal*) of the MSE (📖 C.1).

2.3.5.2 Medium-size company premium

The risk premium is higher for medium-size companies than for large companies owing to the greater volatility of earnings. In Mexico, medium-size companies are reflected in the index of the medium-size company market (MMEX- 📖 8.6.6.1).

2.3.6 Historical risk and return

Historical returns for different asset classes, reflecting different risk premiums, are shown in figure 2–10. It can be observed that, for a relatively long period, there is a correlation between return and risk (measured by standard deviation) in both US and emerging markets investments.

The riskiest investments in the sample (stocks) offered the highest return. Emerging stocks offered higher returns than US stocks, owing to higher country risk. Similarly, the least risky investments (US Tbills)

Figure 2–10 Historical risk and return 1945-95

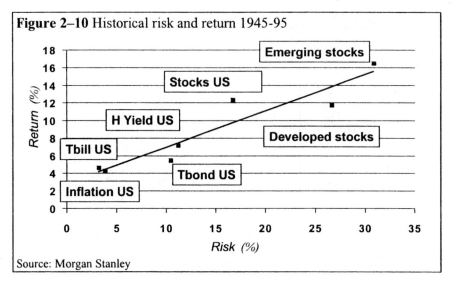

Source: Morgan Stanley

offered the lowest return, followed, as one would expect, by US Tbonds and by high yield bonds (*bonos de alto rendimiento*).

2.4 VALUATION OF INVESTMENTS WITH RETURN AND RISK

The investor must choose his investments according to his objectives of return, risk, liquidity and term. The concept of "present value" (*valor presente)* provides a tool that helps to compare portfolio investments with direct investments, and different asset classes with each other, according to risk and return.

2.4.1 Present value

The concept of present value (*valor presente*) is based on the reality that a peso tomorrow is worth less than a peso today.[5] More generally, any investment represents a series of future flows, discounted to the present at a rate of return[6]:

$$PV = \frac{F_1}{(1+R)^1} + \frac{F_2}{(1+R)^2} + \ldots + \frac{F_n}{(1+R)^n} \qquad (2\text{-}1)$$

The formula can be linked to the concepts of return and risk, and our definition of investment. Investment is the application of resources to

---

[5]It was introduced by John Burr Williams in his classic book, *The Theory of Investment Value* (Harvard University Press, 1938).

[6]📖 A.2 for a formal derivation of equation 2-1.

obtain a future benefit (📖 2.1.1). The "resources" represent our view of the present value (*PV*) of these benefits. The benefits represent the future flows (*F*) that we expect to receive from our investment over a predetermined term (*n* periods).

The concept of risk is managed through the rate of return (*R*). If we expect to reinvest our flows at the rate of inflation, or the risk-free rate, this is our *R*. If we expect that the reinvestment rate will be higher (owing to the riskiness of the flows) we utilize the total of the risk-free rate and the risk premium corresponding to the asset category.

With values assigned to all the variables in the formula, the "net present value" (*valor presente neto*) can be calculated. If the present value of estimated future flows less the application of resources (*A*) (net present value - *NPV*), is greater than, or equal to, zero, the investment fulfills the investor's objectives of return, risk and term. If not, not:

$$NPV = \frac{F_1}{(1+R)^1} + \frac{F_2}{(1+R)^2} + \ldots + \frac{F_n}{(1+R)^n} - A \qquad (2\text{-}2)$$

It is also possible to know what are the initial resources and estimate the future flows during a predetermined term. With values for these variables, the formula can be solved to determine that rate of return (*R*) which equates the initial resources with future flows. This rate is called "the internal rate of return" - IRR (*tasa interna de rendimiento - TIR*). If the IRR is estimated to be greater than, or equal to, the investor's target return, whether it be inflation, the risk-free rate, or a rate that includes a risk premium, the investment is worth making: if not, not.

The concept of present value was developed for direct investments: a company, or a product. Positive and negative flows are calculated to arrive at net flows, and they are discounted during the useful life of the project at a rate of return to reach a net present value. Alternatively, knowing the flows and the initial investment, the IRR is calculated as explained in the previous paragraph. This activity is non-trivial, as the projection of flows for any business or project can be complex.

For portfolio investment, net present value is used to compare asset classes, or, within asset classes, different instruments (📖 8.7.5.1 for an adaptation of this technique to stock valuation). However, it has a significant drawback. It takes no account of a portfolio (*cartera*) of investments, each of which might imply a different level of risk, which would require different levels of return to discount future flows.

Portfolios can consist of different asset classes (e.g. debt and stocks) or different instruments within an asset class (e.g. stocks of different sectors of the stock market).

A portfolio can have a different risk profile from its individual components, because the risks implicit in each investment may be more or less correlated (*correlacionados*). They can even be negatively correlated. Modern Portfolio Theory (*Teoria Moderna de Portafolios*), or MPT, addresses the problem of calculation of return and risk of combinations (or portfolios) of investments.

2.4.2 An investment portfolio

2.4.2.1 Modern Portfolio Theory

The objective of MPT, pioneered by Harry Markowitz[7], is to obtain the best combination of return from different investments, for a given level of risk. The method focuses on the search for investments whose expected returns are negatively correlated. Therefore, the key components of MPT are: the expected return and risk of each investment, and the estimated correlations of their returns.

There are three extreme forms of correlation between two investments. A perfectly positive correlation (measured as 1) implies that the return of two investments rises on average by the same proportion. A perfectly negative correlation (-1) implies that the return on an investment diminishes on average in the same proportion as the return of another investment increases. A zero correlation (0) implies that there is no way of relating the average return of one investment with the average return of another (figure 2–11).

The concept of correlation permits the investor to ensure with

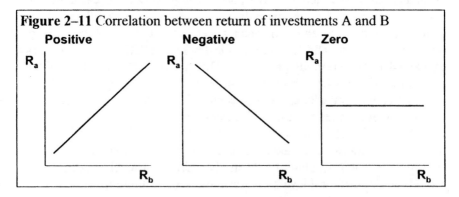

Figure 2–11 Correlation between return of investments A and B

7Markowitz, Harry M., "Portfolio Selection" (*Journal of Finance*, 1952).

combinations of investments what he can do intuitively with individual investments:

1. That for an expected level of return there is no portfolio with a lower expected risk.

2. That for an expected level of risk, there is no portfolio with a higher expected return.

The return on a portfolio of investments is measured as the weighted average of the expected returns of its component investments. The risk of a portfolio is measured as the standard deviation of its expected returns. The formula for the standard deviation of a portfolio takes account of the riskiness of each investment, and their mutual correlations.[8] The lower the correlation between different components of a portfolio, the lower the risk of the overall portfolio.

In figure 2–12 we show examples of different portfolios, with different levels of risk, all of which are on the "efficient frontier" (*frontera eficiente*), that is, which offer the highest level of return for the corresponding risk.

The major theoretical advance of MPT was not just the insight that a combination of investments could be less risky than an individual investment, but also the provision of mathematical tools for the calculation of risk and return.

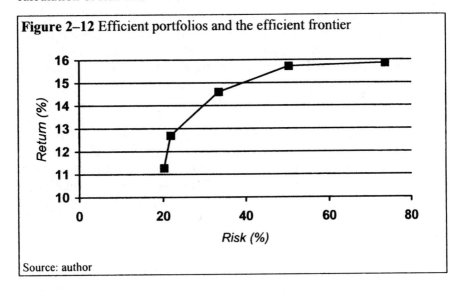

Figure 2–12 Efficient portfolios and the efficient frontier

Source: author

---

[8] A.3 for formulas for the calculation of return and standard deviation for investment portfolios.

2.4.2.2 Capital Asset Pricing Model

MPT can be applied both to portfolios of different asset classes (such as debt, stock or real estate) and to portfolios of one asset class (e.g. stocks).[9] However, there is a major problem in its practical application: the calculation of correlations between a large number of investments (above all, stocks), to determine the risk of a portfolio.

The "Capital Asset Pricing Model" (known as "CAPM" in both English and Spanish) developed by William Sharpe[10] simplifies this problem. An assumption is made that there is a common element in the return of all stocks, which is reflected by the relevant stock market index. Subsequently, the relation of each stock with the index is calculated, to determine whether it is more or less volatile. The measure of relative volatility is called "beta" (represented by the Greek letter β).[11] If the relative volatility is greater than the index (>1), the stock will make the portfolio riskier: if its volatility is lower, it will make it less risky. The overall risk of the portfolio is calculated as the weighted average of the betas of its components.

Studies to determine the number of stocks required for an adequate level of diversification (*diversificación*) in a portfolio indicate that between 8 and 12 stocks are sufficient to achieve a level of diversification equivalent to the market as a whole.

2.4.2.3 Sharpe ratio

Professor Sharpe also developed a method for measuring the "efficiency" (*eficiencia*) of investments, defined as the way in which, for any level of risk, a specific investment (or a portfolio) offers the optimal level of return. This method is called the "Sharpe ratio".

For explanatory purposes, we show in figure 2–13 the efficient frontier for a series of portfolios composed of just one risk-free and one risky asset. The figure shows, for each unit of risk (horizontal axis) the additional expected return above the risk-free rate of 10% (vertical axis). C is the portfolio containing only the risk-free asset, and I is the portfolio containing only the risky asset: the portfolios containing a mixture of the two kinds of asset are located on the line between C and I, or CI (📖 A.3.3).

---

[9]In its original formulation it was applied only to stocks.

[10]Sharpe, William F., "A Simplified Model for Portfolio Analysis" *(Management Science* Vol. 9, pp. 277-293, 1963). Sharpe was awarded the Nobel Economics Prize for his contributions to financial theory.

[11]📖 A. 4 for the mathematical expression of β.

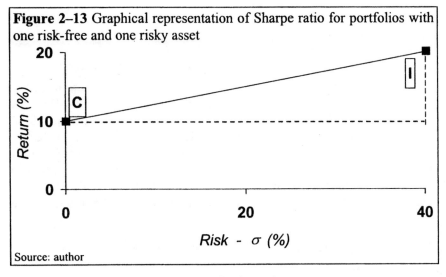

Figure 2–13 Graphical representation of Sharpe ratio for portfolios with one risk-free and one risky asset

Source: author

The slope of CI is described by the formula:

$$P = \frac{I - C}{\sigma}$$

using the numbers in figure 2-13:

$$= \frac{20 - 10}{40} = 0.25$$

Any portfolio above the line is positive, and any portfolio below the line is negative. We will see the practical application of this formula when we discuss "performance measurement" (*evaluación del desempeño*) of Mexican mutual fund portfolios in 📖 12.3.2.

2.4.2.4 Arbitrage pricing theory

Arbitrage Pricing Theory (APT), developed by Stephen Ross[12], is based on the view that, in the case of stocks, CAPM is not an adequate reflection of the complexity of the factors which can affect stock prices. Therefore, expected stock returns are correlated not only with the expected return of the market (represented by a market index) but with unanticipated changes in a series of factors, including[13]:

---

[12]Ross, Stephen A., "The Arbitrage Theory of Capital Asset Pricing" (*Journal of Economic Theory*, 1976).
   [13]Nai-fu Chen, Richard Roll and Stephen A. Ross, "Economic Forces and the Stock Market (*Journal of Business*, July 1986).

- industrial production
- inflation
- the default premium on corporate bonds
- the difference in yield between short and long term bonds.[14]

To calculate expected returns on stocks, risk premiums are added to the risk-free rate related to each of the factors, which could affect the expected return of the stock. Similarly to calculate the risk of a portfolio of stocks, betas are calculated for each stock in relation to each factor. As there are only approximately 10 factors (in the most complex models), the calculation of betas for stocks, although more complex than the CAPM model, is much less complex than the calculation of individual correlations between 100 stocks that had to be made before the introduction of CAPM.[15]

2.5 THE EFFICIENT MARKET HYPOTHESIS

2.5.1.1 The market is efficient

The historical analysis of investments in previous sections indicates that investment returns tend to reflect investment risk. This reality appears to prove one of the important hypotheses of MPT, the "efficient market hypothesis" (hipótesis del mercado eficiente).

The efficient market hypothesis states that, in an efficient market, expected return reflects the level of risk. Abnormal (or excessive) returns are those that more than compensate the level of risk, and do not last long owing to the phenomenon of "arbitrage" (arbitraje). Arbitrage is the process whereby investors buy or sell investments above or below the efficient market line.

In terms of the net present value formula, a formal definition of efficient market would be "a market where a net present value higher than zero cannot be consistently obtained through trading in the secondary market". In terms of the formula:

$$NPV = \frac{F_1}{(1+R)^1} + \frac{F_2}{(1+R)^2} + \dots + \frac{F_n}{(1+R)^n} - A \qquad (2\text{-}3)$$

R always reflects accurately the risk premium.

There is a close relation between the concepts of risk, "uncertainty" (incertidumbre) and "information" (información). Risk is correlated with

---

[14] A.5 for the APT formula.

[15] BARRA, a US company, has a complete information and analysis system for the management of US and international stock portfolios according to APT.

uncertainty. Uncertainty (and, therefore, risk) increases or decreases according to the availability of information. In an efficient market, there are no barriers to the spread and use of information. In other words, all publicly available information is already included or "discounted" (*descontada*) using the terms of net present value, in the price of an investment. In an efficient market, only "new" information (news - *noticias*) should affect the price of investments.

It seems reasonable that, on these terms, markets are efficient. Specialized financial institutions employ large numbers of professional experts with access to the same information, the same techniques for processing the information, and the same tools for acting on the basis of their analysis, i.e. trading in the markets (📖 8.6.2).

2.5.1.2 The market is not efficient

Despite the rationality of the efficient market hypothesis, there are two logical and one empirical argument against market efficiency.[16] If everyone believed that markets were efficient, nobody would analyze them and they would become inefficient. Markets could only be efficient if information had no cost. As information does have a cost (though it might be small) markets tend to be inefficient, to a greater or lesser degree.

The other logical argument is that all investors who participate actively believe that they are good investors. But not all participants are good, and bad investors become the "victims" of good investors. This implies that one of the premises of an efficient market, that it is peopled by "experts" with the same information and analysis techniques, does not reflect reality.

The empirical argument is that, in practice, arbitrage (which supposedly maintains a constant balance between risk and return) is neither easy nor cheap. There are practical and institutional barriers, and transaction costs, which imply that theory and reality do not always coincide.

2.5.1.3 Empirical tests

Exhaustive studies of market efficiency, mainly on US stocks, have tested whether information (specifically news) affects stock prices.

The results of these studies are not conclusive. Most probably, domestic markets (i.e. within a country) are generally efficient, that is, investment prices respond to new information, expected returns reflect

---

[16]See Ibbotson, Roger G., Gary P. Brinson, *Global Investing* (McGraw-Hill, Inc., 1993), pp. 39-41.

expected risk, and prices are fair. The only way to beat the market is either with inside information (*información privilegiada*) or specialized information (*información especializada*).

2.5.1.4 The efficiency of emerging markets

We emphasize that markets are probably quite efficient at the domestic level. It is less probable that markets are efficient internationally – that expected returns from similar investments in different countries adequately reflect the corresponding risk. This is for three main reasons. There is less comparative information, there are fewer analysis techniques, and arbitrage is less developed and therefore more expensive.

This last possibility explains in theoretical terms the opportunities and risks of emerging markets. As they are less efficient than developed markets, they offer higher returns, but, owing to the lower availability of information, and of qualified people and technologies to process it, they imply higher investment risk than developed markets.

2.6 INVESTMENT STYLES

The "investment style" (*estilo de inversión*) adopted by an investor depends on his attitude towards market efficiency. If he thinks markets are efficient, he will adopt a "passive" style (*estilo pasivo*) of investment management. If he thinks he can "beat" the market, he will adopt an active style (*estilo activo*).

2.6.1 Passive management

If an investor thinks that the market is efficient, his investment analysis will consist in updating the risk-reward line shown in figure 2–10, with historical and estimated data. Because there are many experts who do this, there is little chance of finding anomalies, above or below the line. In this case, the investment management activity consists in the estimation of expected returns from the major asset classes (e.g. debt and stocks) and the establishment of an "investment policy" (*política de inversión*) determining the optimum "asset allocation" (*asignación de activos*) according to their proportion of the investment universe.

Studies on the importance of asset allocation have shown that 91.5% of yields of a sample of pension fund portfolios is explained by asset

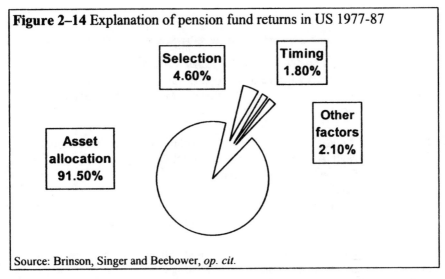

Figure 2–14 Explanation of pension fund returns in US 1977-87

Selection 4.60%

Timing 1.80%

Other factors 2.10%

Asset allocation 91.50%

Source: Brinson, Singer and Beebower, *op. cit.*

allocation, 4.6% by the selection of investments within each asset class, 1.8% by market timing, and 2.1% by other factors (figure 2–14).[17]

These studies, based on efficient market theory and the increasing availability of computing muscle, have led many investors to passive investment management. The goal of passive investment management is not to outperform (*superar*) but to track (*igualar*) the average performance of the asset classes chosen for the portfolio.

The average performance of an asset class is measured by benchmarks (*estándares*), which are normally indices. The best known indices for stock markets are the IPC for the MSE and the Dow Jones and Standard & Poor's indices for the US stock markets. But there are also international indices for stocks and bonds of developed and emerging markets outside the US. We provide a list of the principal indices used in this book in figure 2–15 (also 📖 C.1).

Many institutional investors have adopted a passive management style (📖 11.4). Their performance is measured against indices, and they are happy to match them. In fact, in any given year, less than 50% of invested funds can outperform the relevant benchmark. As in the aggregate they represent the market, it is logically impossible that, after costs (which are never included in indices) more than 50% could outperform any index.

---

[17]Brinson, Gary P., Brian D. Singer, Gilbert L. Beebower, "Determinants of Portfolio Performance II: an Update" (*Financial Analysts' Journal*, May/June 1991), pp. 40-48.

Figure 2–15 Principal stock and bond indices used in this book

Stocks

National	Index	Source
US	Dow Jones 30 Industrials	Dow Jones (DJ)
	Standard & Poor's 500	Standard & Poor's (S&P)
Mexico	IPC	Bolsa Mexicana de Valores (BMV)
	Inmex	Banamex
Global		
MSCI	World	Morgan Stanley Capital Internatio-
	North America	nal (MSCI)
	Europe Australia Far East (EAFE)	
	Emerging Markets (EMI)	
FT-Goldman	World	Financial Times, Goldman
Emerging		
IFC	By region and country	International Finance Corporation
MSCI	By region and country	MSCI

Bonds

Global		
JP Morgan	Developed and emerging	JP Morgan
Salomon	Developed and emerging	Salomon

Source: author

In an extreme case, one could imagine a global passive portfolio. The total value of world stocks is US$X bn. and of world bonds is US$Y bn. The passive investor allocates his assets in relation to the world, individual countries and individual assets, according to their weighting as a proportion of world assets.

It seems unlikely that anyone would invest using this strategy on a global scale. The reason for this is that so far there is no global investor whose necessities reflect a global portfolio. Any investor has a bias towards a certain country. In fact most investors tend to invest a disproportionate amount of their portfolios in their own countries (this phenomenon is called "home country bias"- *sesgo hacia su país de origen*), not only because their future cash necessities are denominated in that country's currency, but also because they have more information on their own financial markets or investment instruments.

Our conclusion is that passive investment management implies matching the benchmark of an asset class, whether it be domestic or international. But neither domestic nor international asset allocation reflects accurately the weighting of the asset class as a proportion of total assets, either domestically or internationally. The main reasons for this are the difficulty of measuring the investment universe, and the differing needs of both individual and institutional investors.

To summarize, allocation between asset classes is rarely passive, while passive allocation between instruments within an asset class is quite common.

2.6.2 Active management

Active investment management implies that the investor believes that there are anomalies in investment markets and that he can beat the market. In more formal terms, he believes that he can generate positive net present value through the selection of investments. These anomalies can exist between markets (📖 ch. 3), between asset classes, and within asset classes. There are two relevant concepts for active investment management: "market timing" (*elección del momento oportuno*) and "investment selection" (*selección de la inversión dentro de una categoría*).

2.6.2.1 Market timing

This concept normally refers to timing of entry into (or exit from) a particular national market, or a particular asset category within that national market. The analytical techniques most frequently used as a basis for this investment style are country risk analysis (📖 ch. 3) and analysis of cycles (long cycles, economic cycles, and liquidity cycles - 📖 ch. 4).

The concept of "top-down investing" (*inversión de arriba para abajo*) is a form of market timing (📖 8.4). It implies the analysis of macroeconomic and financial factors in order to evaluate a country or an asset class.

As we discussed in the previous section, at both the international and national level, practically every investor is a market timer, as his asset allocation hardly ever coincides with the "world portfolio", or even the "national portfolio". However, within an asset class, there is an important difference between an active and a passive management style.

Speculation (*especulación)* is also a form of market timing, as it implies purchase and sale of an investment over a very short time period.

2.6.2.2 Selection

Within an asset category, it would appear reasonable and normal to believe that one investment is better than another, and to make an effort to outperform the relevant benchmark. This investment style is also called "bottom-up" (*de abajo para arriba*). It is different from top-down investing because the merits of an individual investment are analyzed for the medium and long term, and the investor is not influenced by short term fluctuations in market prices. This investment style implies a less volatile asset allocation, and is often contrasted with a market timing approach. It is also called "investment", as opposed to "speculation" in order to emphasize its long term focus.

The analysis techniques implicit in this investment style are described in 📖 ch. 5-9 (Debt, Stocks and Derivatives).

2.6.2.3 Great investors

All famous investors are "active", because they have outperformed the major market indices over time.[18] However, their investment styles differ. George Soros owes his success to massive bets on currencies (e.g. the pound), or asset classes (stocks, bonds or real estate) and could be characterized as a "top-down market timer". Carlos Slim, the Mexican owner of Grupo Carso and Grupo Inbursa, and Warren Buffett, who have spent their careers looking patiently for undervalued and undermanaged assets, could be characterized as bottom-up investors.

These investors have become famous (and rich) because their returns have consistently outperformed the major indices. This consistency has been taken as proof of the inefficiency of markets: or of their efficiency, because they are such rare exceptions that they prove the rule of market efficiency.

---

[18]See Lowenstein, Roger, *Buffett, The Making of an American Capitalist* (Random House, 1995), Soros, George, *Soros on Soros* (John Wiley, 1995), Train, John, *The Money Masters* (Harper & Row, 1980), and *The New Money Masters* (Harper Perennial, 1989).

Chapter 3
Country risk

"It seems a truism to say that no lender to a country can be safe unless he knows something about that country. But in practice it is a paradox. We lend to countries of whose conditions we do not know and whose want of civilization we do not consider and, therefore, we lose our money."

Walter Bagehot (1826-1877)[1]

3.1 INTRODUCTION

3.1.1 Definition of country risk

A first application of the investment concepts presented in the previous chapter is a risk-return analysis of Mexican investments compared to those of other countries. A useful tool for this activity is the concept of "country risk" (*riesgo país*). If risk is "the possibility of not achieving an expected return", "country risk" would be "the possibility of not achieving an expected return in a specific country".

3.1.2 Return and country risk

The minimum expected return from a country would be its risk-free rate (*R*), in the terms of the previous chapter:

$$PV = \frac{F_1}{(1+R)^1} + \frac{F_2}{(1+R)^2} + \ldots\ldots + \frac{F_n}{(1+R)^n} \qquad (3\text{-}1)$$

Each country has its risk-free rate, at different levels depending on country risk. The key to the selection between countries lies in the estimation of greater than generally expected flows (*F*), or less than generally expected risk (*R*). As risk decreases and uncertainty diminishes, there is also the possibility of increasing the time horizon of the investment, discounting more periods (*n*), and increasing present value (*PV*).

---

[1]Cited in Howell, Michael J. ed., *Investing in Emerging Markets* (Euromoney Books, 1994), p. vi.

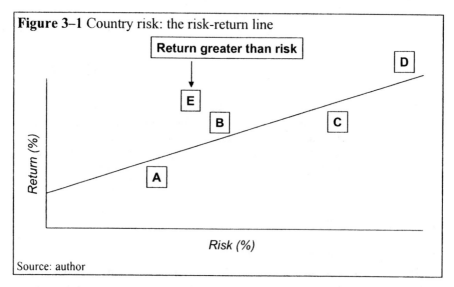

Figure 3–1 Country risk: the risk-return line

Source: author

We show this graphically in figure 3–1. Countries A, B, C and D are on the risk-return line. A passive investor can choose any of these countries, depending on his attitude towards risk. If he is an active investor, he tries to find country E, which offers a higher return than its corresponding risk would imply.

In terms of 📖 2.2.4, risk is defined as the volatility of historic returns, and is used as the basis of estimation of the volatility of future returns (measured by their standard deviation). According to this definition, we could analyze country risk (in our case, Mexico) through statistical analysis of historical risk-return, to make projections into the future, both for debt and stocks.

However, before doing this, it is important to point out that there is another definition of "country risk" related to debt securities, and country "sovereign debt ratings" (*calificaciones de la deuda soberana*). In 📖 3.2, we analyze the concept of country risk in relation to sovereign debt. Subsequently, we relate this concept to the definitions of risk presented in 📖 2.3. Finally, utilizing these concepts, we analyze risk and return of Mexican investments comparing them with those of developed and emerging markets, and with each other.

3.2 COUNTRY RISK - DEBT

3.2.1 Debt ratings as a measure of country risk

Many countries issue sovereign debt denominated in dollars, where "sovereign risk" (*riesgo soberano*) is defined as the risk of the country's

	Moody's	Standard & Poor's	ordinal scale
Figure 3–2 Rating scales (above default) of principal rating agencies			
Investment grade			
Highest quality	Aaa	AAA	1
High quality	Aa1	AA+	2
	Aa2	AA	3
	Aa3	AA-	4
Strong payment capacity	A1	A+	5
	A2	A	6
	A3	A-	7
Adequate payment capacity	Baa1	BBB+	8
	Baa2	BBB	9
	Baa3	BBB-	10
Speculative grade			
Payment probable, but uncertain	Ba1	BB+	11
	Ba2	BB	12
	Ba3	BB-	13
High risk	B1	B+	14
	B2	B	15
	B3	B-	16
Ratings outlook			
Positive	possibility of upgrade		
Negative	possibility of downgrade		
Under development	possibility of upgrade or downgrade		
Stable	no change anticipated		
"+/-" relative strength of security within its grade			
Source: Moody's, S&P			

government. This debt can be ranked according to its level of yield (or return), and compared with some measurement of risk. For debt securities, the ratings produced by specialized "rating agencies" (*agencias calificadoras de deuda*) are frequently used to measure risk.

Rating agencies rate debt securities according to consistent and comparable criteria, in order to facilitate their initial placement and subsequent trading in financial markets. The two principal agencies, Moody's and Standard & Poor's (S&P), have similar rating systems, each with 16 different grades, but with different rating symbols. These grades can also be nuanced with four levels of "outlook" (figure 3–2). These ratings, which are revised periodically, are used for debt securities

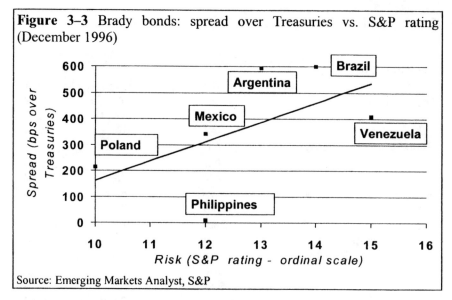

Figure 3–3 Brady bonds: spread over Treasuries vs. S&P rating (December 1996)

Source: Emerging Markets Analyst, S&P

issued by both the public and private sector in the US and in international capital markets.[2]

To compare yields over time, one does not take the absolute yield of the debt securities of a given country, but the spread (*spread* or *diferencial*) between the yield on the security and the yield on US government debt (Tbonds or Tbills) for the same term.

In figure 3–3, we show spreads and risks for 6 countries at a specific date (December 1996). Spread is measured as the difference in basis points (bps - *puntos base*[3]) between the stripped spread of each country's Brady bond and the Tbond of the same term. Brady bonds are used because they have approximately the same term (with maturities between 2019 and 2024) and the same methodology for calculation of the spread.[4] Risk is measured as the S&P rating, on an ordinal scale (figure 3–2).

There is a positive correlation between spread and risk. However, there are anomalies at each extreme: the risk of the Philippines does not correspond to its spread, and the spreads of Argentina and Brazil do not correspond to their risk. There are at least three possible explanations for

---

[2]When a rating agency operates in a national market, it issues ratings for debt securities denominated in the national currency. S&P purchased Calificadora de Valores, S. A. de C. V. ("Caval"), one of four Mexican rating agencies, in 1993 (📖 6.5.5.1).

[3]Basis points are hundredths of one per cent (e.g. 371 bp = 3.71%).

[4]📖 5.8.1, 6.6.5 and B.5 for a detailed analysis of Brady bonds.

these anomalies: market imperfections, the possibility that the market is expecting something that is not in the chart (e.g. that S&P intends to upgrade the Philippines) – or that, in fact, Argentine and Brazilian bonds are undervalued and Philippine bonds are overvalued.

There is a practical problem in the broad use of debt ratings to measure country risk. Despite the continuous growth of international debt markets, as not all the 184 countries that are IMF members have issued dollar denominated debt, ratings from internationally recognized rating agencies are not available for all countries. It is therefore necessary to look at other forms of measuring country risk.

3.2.2 Other techniques for measuring country risk

3.2.2.1 Economic indicators

One way to measure country risk would be for the investor to replicate the analysis of the rating agencies, and produce his own rating system. However, the rating agencies, although they list the factors they take into account when they produce a rating, do not reveal how they quantify them and weight them to reach their final rating decision.

An independent study of Moody's and S&P ratings has been able to isolate the factors determining their ratings, through the relatively simple technique of running statistical correlations between ratings for specific countries and their principal economic and financial indicators.[5]

The study covers 49 developed and emerging countries, which were rated by the two agencies at a specific date, September 29, 1995 (figure 3–4). Using a multiple regression technique, the study found that five factors explained 90% of the two agencies' rating decisions: per capita income, the level of external debt, inflation, debt payment history, and the level of economic development.[6]

The authors point out that two factors, which could seem important, are not significant: the government balance and the current account balance (🕮 4.3.2). They conclude that the reason for this apparent anomaly is that many countries with a high level of country risk (i.e. low grade) may have relatively healthy indicators for these two categories because they are trying to improve their rating, and their country risk

---

[5]Cantor, Richard, and Frank Packer, "Determinants and Impacts of Sovereign Credit Ratings", (Federal Reserve Bank of New York, Research Paper #9608, April 1996).

[6]Of the 49 countries, the two agencies had the same rating for 28 countries: 12 were rated higher by S&P, and 9 higher by *Moody's*. In the 21 countries where there was disagreement, 14 differed by one grade and 7 by two grades.

Figure 3–4 Ratings of 49 developed and emerging countries 1995

Developed countries	Moody's	S&P	Emerging countries	Moody's	S&P
Australia	Aa2	AA	Argentina	B1	BB-
Austria	Aaa	AAA	Brazil	B1	B+
Belgium	Aa1	AA+	Chile	Baa1	A-
Bermuda	Aa1	AA	China	A3	BBB
Canada	Aa2	AA+	Colombia	Baa3	BBB-
Denmark	Aa1	AA+	Czech Republic	Baa1	BBB+
Finland	Aa2	AA-	Greece	Baa3	BBB-
France	Aaa	AAA	Hong Kong	A3	A
Germany	Aaa	AAA	Hungary	Ba1	BB+
Iceland	A2	A	India	Baa3	BB+
Ireland	Aa2	AA	Indonesia	Baa3	BBB
Italy	A1	AA	Malaysia	A1	A+
Japan	Aaa	AAA	**Mexico**	**Ba2**	**BB**
Luxembourg	Aaa	AAA	Pakistan	B1	B+
Malta	A2	A	Philippines	Ba2	BB
Netherlands	Aaa	AAA	Poland	Baa3	BB
New Zealand	Aa2	AA	S. Africa	Baa3	BB
Norway	Aa1	AAA	S. Korea	A1	AA-
Portugal	A1	AA-	Slovak Republic	Baa3	BB+
Singapore	Aa2	AAA	Thailand	A2	A
Spain	Aa2	AA	Turkey	Ba3	B+
Sweden	Aa3	AA+	Uruguay	Ba1	BB+
Switzerland	Aaa	AAA	Venezuela	Ba2	B+
Taiwan	Aa3	AA+			
UK	Aaa	AAA			
US	Aaa	AAA			

Source: Cantor and Packer

ranking. Mexico's current account balance in 1995 could serve as an example. The current account balance improved considerably compared with 1994, but its country risk rating had deteriorated owing to the 1994 crisis.

One implication of the study is that the analyst can perform his own risk analysis, basing himself on the five factors mentioned above. This would permit him to broaden his coverage beyond the 49 countries covered by the rating agencies. In fact, one of the main activities of financial intermediaries that specialize in debt is to evaluate yields on

Figure 3–5 Country risk analysis services

Supplier	Product
Bank of America World Information Services	Country Outlooks
	Country Data Forecast
	Country Risk Monitor
Business Environment Risk Intelligence, S. A.	FORCE Country Reports
	Political, operations, and remittance/repatriation risk indices
Control Risks Information Services	On-line country information services
	Travel security guide
	Security Risk ratings and forecasts
Economist Intelligence Unit	Repayment risk measure
	Regional and Country Reports
Euromoney	Risk Assessment Index
Institutional Investor	Country Credit Rating Index
Moody's Investors Services	Sovereign Foreign Currency Debt Ratings
	Credit Opinions for Governmental Bodies
Political Risk Services: ICRG	Country Risk Ratings
Political Risk Services - Coplin - O'Leary rating	Country Risk Ratings: International Business Climate Index
Standard & Poor's Ratings Group	Sovereign Credit Ratings
	Local and foreign currency debt ratings
	Regional and local government debt ratings
	Sovereign-supported debt ratings
	Multilateral institution debt ratings
	International structured financing ratings

Source: Erb, Harvey and Viskanta

debt securities and analyze whether they reflect the risk, as defined by the rating agencies.

3.2.2.2 Country risk ratings

There are country risk analysis services, which are not tied to specific debt securities (figure 3–5). Normally, they analyze the same qualitative and quantitative factors covered by Moody's and S&P, and provide their own rating system with their own weightings.

Among the most frequently used country risk services are those of Institutional Investor (II), a magazine targeted towards the US and global institutional investor, and of International Country Risk Guide (ICRG), a publication of *Political Risk Services*. A study of II and ICRG has found a high level of correlation between them (a correlation coefficient of

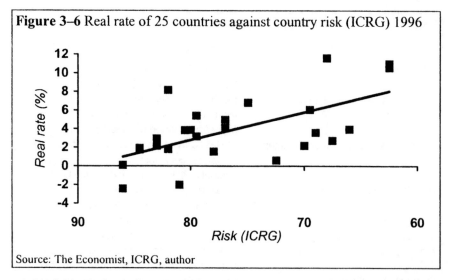

Figure 3–6 Real rate of 25 countries against country risk (ICRG) 1996

Source: The Economist, ICRG, author

0.88).[7] Similarly, it found a high correlation between the two debt rating services (Moody's and S&P), and between them and the two country risk rating services: II (0.95) and ICRG (0.87).

What this implies is that the investor can theoretically expand his universe from the 49 countries covered by the debt rating agencies to the (approximately) 130 countries covered by ICRG – II covers approximately 120 countries.

3.2.2.3 Real interest rate

Having found a broader system of country risk measurement than the debt rating agencies, the investor must then look for an equally broad system of measurement of country return, as not all the countries analyzed issue debt securities denominated in dollars.

We mentioned in 📖 2.3.2.2 that a country's risk-free real rate in its own currency could provide a measurement of country risk. Uncertainty about future real rates could be the result of uncertainty about interest rates or inflation rates. This uncertainty (and therefore risk) should be reflected in the level of the country's real interest rate.

This hypothesis is supported by figure 3–6. Real interest rates were plotted against risk measures from 25 developed and emerging countries, on the basis of real return data published in *The Economist* (which publishes weekly information on interest and inflation rates for

---

[7]Erb, Claude B., Campbell R. Harvey, Tadas E. Viskanta, "Political Risk, Economic Risk and Financial Risk" (www.duke.edu, 1996).

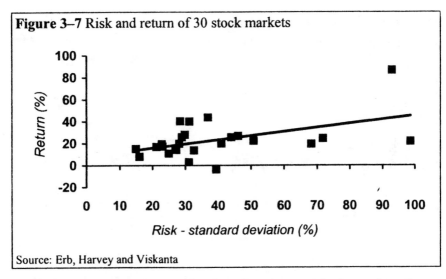

Figure 3–7 Risk and return of 30 stock markets

Source: Erb, Harvey and Viskanta

developed and emerging markets) and country risk data taken from ICRG. The results show a clear inverse correlation. The higher the rating (the country with the higher rating has the lower country risk) the lower the real rate. In the most extreme cases, Singapore and Hong Kong, real rates are actually negative. The correlation between the two variables is minus 0.62.

3.3 COUNTRY RISK - STOCKS

We saw in 📖 3.1.2 that, in the stock market, country risk would be defined as the volatility of returns of a stock index of the relevant country measured by their standard deviation. In the study mentioned in the previous section, a positive correlation was found between historic return and risk measured in this way[8] (figure 3–7). The chart appears to confirm the hypothesis about different asset classes presented in 📖 2.3, not only about the correlation between risk and return, but also about the possibility of finding anomalies, above all in global investments (📖 2.5.1.3).

3.4 COUNTRY RISK – DEBT AND STOCKS

A study of the relationship between stock risk, measured as the standard deviation of returns, and country risk applied to debt, measured by the ICRG ratings, shows a positive correlation (figure 3–8).

---

[8]Erb, Harvey & Viskanta, *op. cit.*

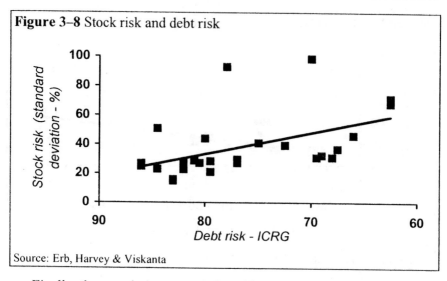

Figure 3–8 Stock risk and debt risk

Source: Erb, Harvey & Viskanta

Finally, the correlation was analyzed between risk measurements and the valuation measures most commonly used for stocks: multiples of price/book value, price/earnings, and the ratio of dividend/price.[9] The multiple with the highest correlation to the risk measures was the multiple of price/book value, where an inverse correlation was found: the higher the multiple, the lower the risk.

3.5 MEXICAN RISK IN A GLOBAL CONTEXT

3.5.1 Research criteria

To analyze Mexican risk within a global context, global investments were divided into equity and debt for three main regions: US, developed markets[10], and emerging markets. This implies six asset classes: equity and debt for the US, developed markets, and emerging markets.

Historical monthly series were analyzed from 1991. This year was taken as the base date for two main reasons. The first is that foreign investment in the Mexican stock market (and in emerging markets in general) only began seriously in 1991, owing to the catalytic effect of the listing of TELMEX ADRs on the NYSE in May of that year (📖 1.4.1). The second is that Brady bonds were exchanged for Mexican bank debt in 1990, and the Brady bond index (which includes Mexican bonds and those of other countries) only begins in 1991.

---

[9] 📖 8.3 for a detailed explanation of these valuation ratios.

[10] Including the markets of Europe, Australia and Far East, measured by the EAFE index of MSCI.

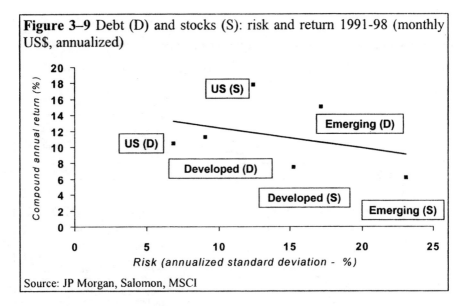

Figure 3–9 Debt (D) and stocks (S): risk and return 1991-98 (monthly US$, annualized)

Source: JP Morgan, Salomon, MSCI

3.5.2 Global debt and stock markets

Our analysis for the years 1991-8 indicates that the hypothetical risk-return ranking presented in ☐ 2.3 is not supported by the evidence during the period analyzed (figure 3–9):

- US stocks have produced higher returns than emerging stocks, with less risk,
- the debt of developed and emerging markets has produced higher returns than their stock markets, with less risk.

These apparent paradoxes are the result of several extraordinary factors:

- the extraordinary performance (in a historical context) of US stocks, above all in the years 95-98,
- the negative effect of the slump in the Japanese stock market on the aggregate stock index for developed markets during the 1990s,
- the negative effect of the Asian and Russian crises in 1997–98 on the emerging stock index,
- the positive effect on the Brady bond index of the overall undervaluation of Brady bonds when they were first issued in 1991.

In the following sections, we analyze in more detail debt and equity performance for Mexico in the context of emerging markets as a whole, and Latin America.

Figure 3–10 Mexican debt in a global context 1991-8 (monthly)

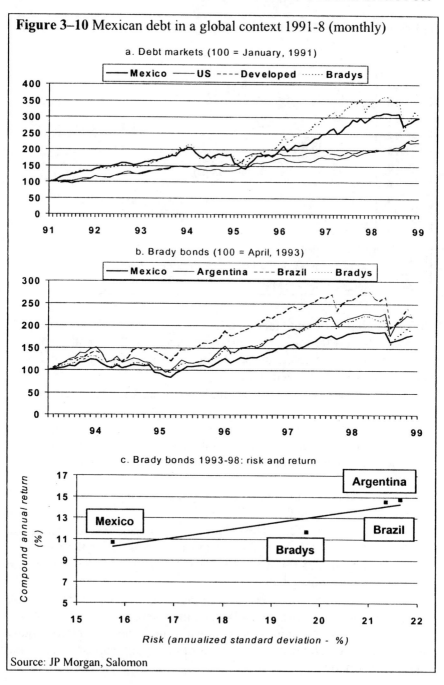

a. Debt markets (100 = January, 1991)

b. Brady bonds (100 = April, 1993)

c. Brady bonds 1993-98: risk and return

Source: JP Morgan, Salomon

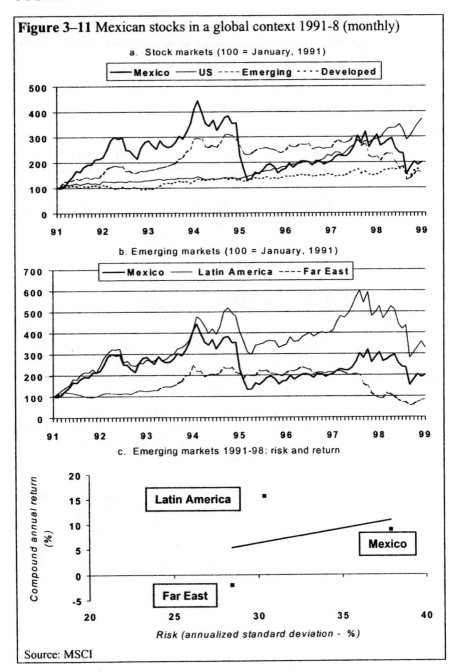

Figure 3–11 Mexican stocks in a global context 1991-8 (monthly)

a. Stock markets (100 = January, 1991)

b. Emerging markets (100 = January, 1991)

c. Emerging markets 1991-98: risk and return

Source: MSCI

3.5.3 Debt

In spite of the 1994 crisis, Mexican Brady bonds produced higher returns than US and developed country bonds (figure 3–10a). However, as a result of the crisis, Mexican Brady bonds produced lower returns than Argentina, Brazil and the general Brady index[11], although with lower risk (figure 3–10b and figure 3–10c).

3.5.4 Stocks

Owing to the Asian and Russian crises of 1997-98, returns of emerging stock markets in the aggregate, despite higher risk, have been lower than those for the US and Mexico (figure 3–11a). The only reason they outperformed developed markets was the underperformance of the Japanese market during the period analyzed. Among emerging markets, the return on the Mexican market underperformed the Latin American average, but outperformed the Far East, although with more risk (figure 3–11b and c).

3.6 THE RISK OF MEXICAN INVESTMENTS

3.6.1 Debt

S&P rated Mexican dollar denominated debt for the first time in 1992. The rating was BB+, with a stable outlook (📖 3.2.1). The highest point for Mexico's rating was November 1993, when it reached the level of BB+ with a positive outlook, and this rating was reflected in the level of spread for Mexican sovereign debt (figure 3–12).

When NAFTA was implemented in January 1994, and Mexico joined the OECD in the same year, it seemed likely that Mexico would be rated "investment grade" (minimum BBB-) within twelve months. However, following the troubled political events in 1994, Mexico's spread returned to early 1993 levels: subsequently, successful presidential elections in August 1994 and the apparently smooth presidential succession in December 1994 encouraged the belief that Mexico would reach investment grade during 1995.

This prospect had to be drastically modified as a result of the December 1994 crisis. Mexican debt was downgraded from BB+ with a "positive outlook" to BB with a "negative outlook", in January 1995, and Mexican spreads reached levels above 1600 bps in March 1995.

---

[11]In December 1998, 89% of the Brady bond index was represented by Latin American bonds (📖 5.8.1).

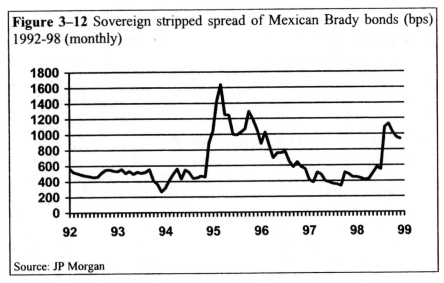

Figure 3–12 Sovereign stripped spread of Mexican Brady bonds (bps) 1992-98 (monthly)

Source: JP Morgan

After that date, the sovereign spread showed a practically continuous downward trend until the 1997 emerging markets crisis. Mexico's debt rating was improved from "negative outlook" to "stable outlook" in September 1996, and the spread had almost reached November 1993 levels in September 1997, just before the Asian crisis of October 1997. In 1998, once the crisis had passed, there was again talk of Mexico reaching investment grade within "a reasonable period", but this became

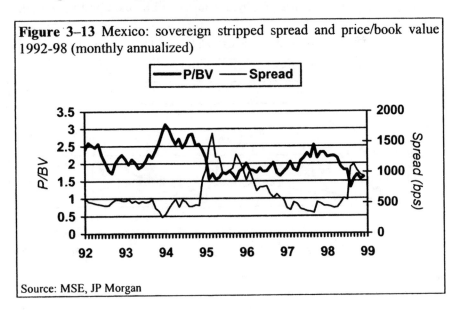

Figure 3–13 Mexico: sovereign stripped spread and price/book value 1992-98 (monthly annualized)

Source: MSE, JP Morgan

less likely following the Russian crisis of August 1998.

3.6.2 Stocks

The lower the country risk, the higher the average stock market multiple (📖 3.4). The inverse correlation between the price/book value multiple and measures for country risk also exists in the Mexican case (figure 3–13): the correlation coefficient is –0.63.

3.6.3 Risk and return for Mexican asset classes

Although they share the same country risk, returns on Mexican asset classes should reflect different risk levels, related to their intrinsic characteristics as debt or equity – owing to the concept of return ranking (📖 2.3).

Statistical analysis of risk and return for major Mexican asset classes during the period 1991-98 only partially reflects the theory implicit in the return ranking. Brady bonds produced the highest return (figure 3–14), but with the lowest risk (figure 3–15).

There is no complete explanation for the abnormal returns of Brady bonds, in relation to their risk. The most convincing explanations are: a) they were new securities in 1991, and b) they are dollar denominated. As they were new (and unknown) when they were first issued, they were offered to investors at very attractive prices in 1990. As they are dollar denominated, they fell less during the exchange rate crisis of 1994-95 than peso denominated securities (Cetes and stocks). We would expect that, as these securities mature, their returns will be more in line with the

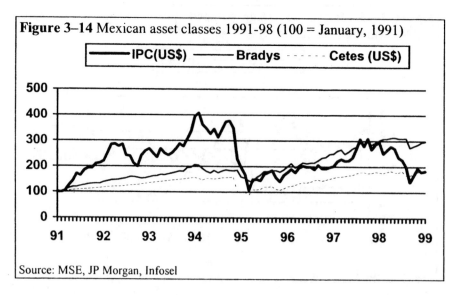

Figure 3–14 Mexican asset classes 1991-98 (100 = January, 1991)

IPC(US$) ——— Bradys ····· Cetes (US$)

Source: MSE, JP Morgan, Infosel

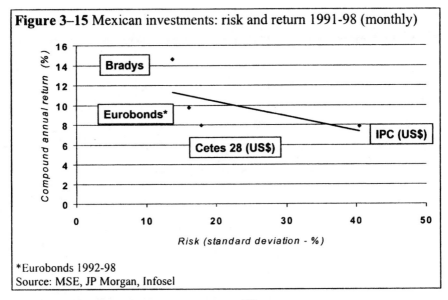

Figure 3–15 Mexican investments: risk and return 1991-98 (monthly)

*Eurobonds 1992-98
Source: MSE, JP Morgan, Infosel

theoretical return ranking explained in 📖 2.3.

3.7 THE PROBLEM OF TERM

It is obvious that the results presented in previous sections were heavily influenced by the period chosen for the analysis - 1990-98, and the factors listed in 📖 3.5: the outperformance of US stocks and Brady bonds, and the underperformance of the stock markets of Asia and Japan.

To understand better the sensitivity of risk and return to the period of analysis which is chosen, we analyzed the longest series of financial indicators we could find for Mexico and the US: the stock market indices of Mexico (in US$) and the US for the period 1918-1998 (figure 3–16), subdividing the long period into three shorter periods (1950-98, 1976-98, 1990-98).[12]

In figure 3–16, it can be observed that over the whole period the Dow Jones has outperformed the Mexican market index. At first sight, this appears to conflict with the return ranking, whereby the higher risk of an emerging market should be rewarded with higher return.

However, if we consider that the Mexican economy was "premodern" before the 1940s, this result is not surprising. If we take 1950 as the base

---

[12]For figure 3–16 the logarithmic scale is used to highlight the volatility of the index over time.

Figure 3–16 Mexico and the US: stock markets 1918-98 (annual US$ - logarithmic scale)

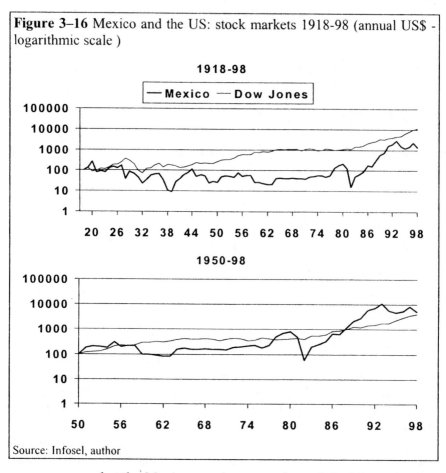

Source: Infosel, author

year, we note that the Mexican market outperformed the US market for the period 1950-98.

Risk-return analysis for the four periods (figure 3–17) shows that Mexico offered higher returns for 1950-98 and 1976-98 (although with a significantly higher risk), but not 1990-98. This leads us to suspect that the period 1990-98 which was used in previous sections of this chapter for reasons explained in 📖 3.5.1 could have been atypical (although unavoidable).

Another interesting conclusion of our analysis over the longer term is that, even though return varies significantly for different terms, the level of risk remains surprisingly constant, both for Mexico and the US. This is consistent with what occurred in the 1990s, when, in spite of the 1994 crisis, there was no change in the BB rating for Mexican country risk.

Figure 3–17 Mexican and US stocks: risk and return for different terms

	Mexico		US	
	Return[1]	Risk[2]	Return[1]	Risk[2]
1918-98	3.3	56.8	6.1	19.4
1950-98	8.6	54.9	8.1	13.2
1976-98	16.5	70.5	10.7	13.9
1990-98	8.1	54.6	16.9	10.7

[1] Return: compound annual rate (%)
[2] Risk: standard deviation of annual returns (%)
Source: author

Similarly it matches our intuition, that the periods of good and bad returns in Mexico can be relatively short, while the problem of risk is longer term.

We turn to the analysis of cycles, of different terms, in the next chapter.

Chapter 4
Cycles

"A study of economics usually reveals that the best time to buy anything was last year."

Marty Allen

4.1 INTRODUCTION

A useful tool for the choice of the right moment to invest in a country or an asset class is the concept of cycles (*ciclos*). The word "cycle" is derived from the almost identical Greek word κυκλοσ, a wheel (hence a *bi*cycle, or two wheels). A cycle can be defined as "a repetitive pattern" and the concept has been applied to all aspects of human activity: political, economic, and social.

As we noted in chapter 2, the activity of investment, by definition, implies the concept of time. If we can detect patterns in the factors which affect investments (or in the investments themselves) this will help us to forecast future returns.

In more formal terms, we return to the basic formula for any investment, direct or portfolio:

$$PV = \frac{F_1}{(1+R)^1} + \frac{F_2}{(1+R)^2} + \ldots + \frac{F_n}{(1+R)^n} \qquad (4\text{-}1)$$

In chapter 2, we sought to understand the concept of R, and in chapter 3 we attempted to quantify it in relation to Mexico. To reach a more precise estimate of PV (present value), we need to know for how many periods in the future we can predict, i.e. some value for the variable n (number of periods). In addition it would be useful to know if the flows derived from our investment (F) and the rate of return (R) bear any relation to a repetitive process (i.e., a cycle), and therefore if this process can be explained and predicted.

In this chapter, we analyze three kinds of cycles: long cycles, economic cycles, and liquidity cycles, for the world and for Mexico.

4.2 THE KONDRATIEFF LONG CYCLE

In its simplest form, the economic cycle is represented as the percentage rise and fall in economic activity (normally represented by

Figure 4–1 Original Kondratieff cycles

Cycle	trend	dates
First long cycle	rise	1780s - 1810/17
	fall	1810/17 - 1844/51
Second long cycle	rise	1844/51 - 1870/75
	fall	1870/75 - 1890/96
Third long cycle	rise	1890/96 - 1914/20
	fall	1914/20 - ?

Source: The New Palgrave: A Dictionary of Economics (The Macmillan Press Limited, 1987)

Gross Domestic Product - GDP, or Gross National Product - GNP) of a country, a group of countries, or the world as a whole (understood as the aggregate of developed and emerging countries).

Over the very long term, cycles have been detected in relation to important world events: wars, voyages of exploration, or technological inventions. Various names have been applied to these cycles: long cycles (*ciclos largos*), major cycles (*ciclos mayores*), long waves (*ondas largas*), secular trends (*tendencias seculares*).

The economist who pioneered the study of long cycles is the Russian Nikolai Kondratieff (1892-193?) [1], who in 1925 published an important study of long cycles. He discovered three long cycles since 1780, each with a duration of between 50 and 70 years (figure 4–1).

The common factors in each cycle are:

• There are more prosperous years during the "up" stage, and more recessive years during the "down" stage.

• Inventions are developed during the "down" stage and applied during the "up" stage.

• The total market is extended through the incorporation of new markets at the beginning of the "up" stage.

• Wars and revolutions occur towards the end of the "up" stage.

Analysts subsequent to Kondratieff have updated his research to the period following World War I, adding two further cycles (figure 4–2). Thus, in the most recent (fifth) cycle, the microchip was developed in the "down" stage and now, at the beginning of the change of trend, we are seeing its massive adoption (through multimedia and the Internet). Similarly, the broadening of world markets is consistent with the current development of emerging markets (⊞ 1.3).

---

[1] Kondratieff, Nikolai, "Major Economic Cycles" (*Voprosy kon'iunktury I*, 28-79, 1925). The exact date of his death, in Siberia, is unknown.

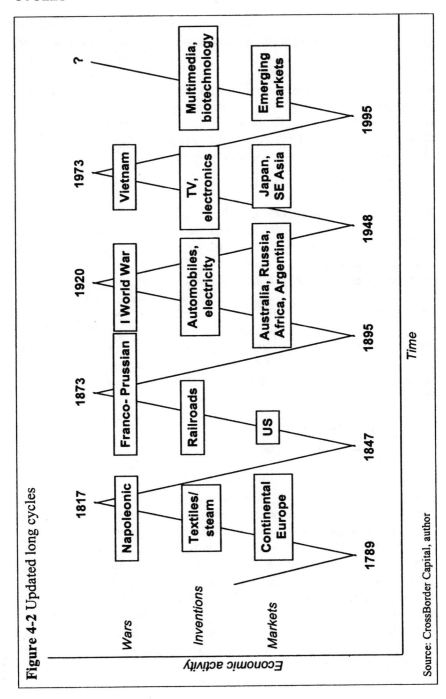

Figure 4-2 Updated long cycles

Source: CrossBorder Capital, author

There is controversy about the empirical regularity of each cycle, and the events, and sequence of events, which should be included. For example, in figure 4-2, World War II is not included, although it was clearly more important than the Vietnam War. Even so, it is generally accepted that long cycles exist at a global level, with important geopolitical and technological discontinuities, which affect economic activity. In this context, figure 4-2 tends to reinforce the conclusions about long term globalization trends suggested in 📖 ch. 1, above all those relating to technology, and emerging markets.

4.3 THE ECONOMIC CYCLE

4.3.1 The traditional US cycle

The classic economic cycle began to be used as a forecasting tool in the US in 1923, when the National Bureau of Economic Research was established as a center for economic research for the private sector.

It was discovered that economic activity, as measured by GNP, tends to rise and fall according to a cyclical pattern, normally between 4 and 6 years. Other indicators also vary according to the same pattern: indicators of production, investment, consumption, inflation, money supply, and interest rates. However, some move before, others at the same time, and others after the GNP indicator: leading, coincident and lagging indicators (*indicadores de previsión, coincidentes, y de secuencia*). Of these indicators, some have a positive correlation with GNP (e.g. production and employment) and others a negative correlation (e.g. inflation - figure 4–3).

The duration of economic cycles in the US corresponds approximately to the planning and execution of major capital projects which serve as the motor of economic development in any country. Normally, the planning of a major building, real estate complex or microchip plant lasts between one and two years. Similarly, the construction period is of approximately the same duration.

The pattern of the cycle corresponds to periods of underutilized and excess capacity of productive plant. At the beginning of the cycle, there is excess capacity, and unemployment. With low interest rates, businessmen begin to invest in their own businesses, as they observe that real returns from direct investment are likely to be higher than returns from financial investments. As these direct investments are made, employment, consumption and production increase, to the point that excess production capacity is fully utilized.

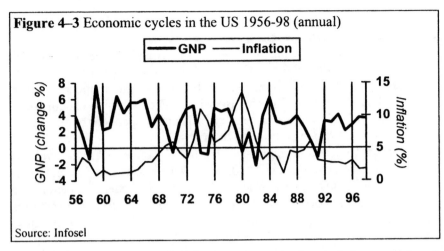

Figure 4–3 Economic cycles in the US 1956-98 (annual)

Source: Infosel

As this capacity is utilized, there is more demand than supply of goods and services, inflation rises, and, with it, interest rates. As capacity becomes scarce, businessmen begin to expand their plants. Until new plant comes online, the inflationary spiral (prices and wages) continues, with a corresponding rise in interest rates. As purchasing power decreases with inflation, consumer demand also decreases: similarly, as interest rates and the cost of capital rises, investment decreases.

As consumer demand falls, unemployment increases, and demand falls even more. Meanwhile, new investment projects that were planned at the height of the economic expansion begin to come onstream, increasing even further the level of supply, but with no corresponding increase in demand. The inflation rate begins to fall, and interest rates with it - until they reach the level when the cycle begins all over again.

4.3.2 The role of government

The objective of any government in relation to the economic cycle is to maintain a growth rate sufficient to improve the standard of living of its population (measured by an increase in GNP or GDP per capita) compatible with price stability, that is, a minimal level of inflation.

The two kinds of tool available to governments to achieve this objective are fiscal and monetary. The fiscal tool permits it to influence production through taxes (varying spending and investment by the private sector) or through public spending (with a direct effect on the economy).

The monetary tool (control of the money supply) permits the government to influence the economy by injecting liquidity into the system when the economy appears to be stagnating, and removing liquidity when the economy appears to be overheating, and that inflation could reach undesirable levels.

In the US, the "government" (that is, the President, the Secretary of the Treasury, and the Director of the Office of Management and Budget, balanced by the Congress) controls the fiscal tool. The monetary tool is controlled by the Federal Reserve Board, or "Fed" – which is equivalent to the Central Bank in another country. It is an independent body, whose main mission is to control the level of prices.

It can be observed in figure 4–3 that the objective of growth without inflation was achieved in the 1950s and 1960s. However, in the 1970s, this was not achieved, due to a combination of exogenous factors, of which the most important was the rise in the oil price (from US$3/barrel in 1973 to US$35 in 1981), combined with the Fed's inability to adjust its monetary policy to these new circumstances.

It was only after a determined policy of money supply control at the beginning of the 1980s by the then Fed Chairman Paul Volcker that inflation began to be controlled. Healthy macroeconomic policies, along with a major thrust by the Reagan government towards deregulation and liberalization (📖 1.2.2.1), resulted in a renewal of growth, with lower inflation, in the 1980s.

These policies have been continued in the 1990s, despite the victory in 1992 of a Democratic President, whose party is normally identified with expansionist fiscal policies. In the 1996 presidential campaign, won for a second time by President Clinton, some attributed the success of his economic policy to the combination of a Republican fiscal policy and the sensible monetary policy of Alan Greenspan, Chairman of the Fed.[2]

4.4 THE LIQUIDITY CYCLE

The cycle described in the previous section, both its "natural" part, and the participation of the government, represents a simplification of a very complex process with different phenomena, and different sequences of phenomena, occurring in each cycle. More importantly, the globalization of trade and capital (through both direct and portfolio investment) has made what was previously an individual country cycle interact with processes and phenomena in other countries. For example, a lack of production capacity in the US can now easily be compensated by production in other countries. Similarly, as industrial capacity

---

[2]In the US, when there is economic growth higher than the previous year during an electoral year, the party in power normally wins (see the four year electoral cycles in figure 4–3).

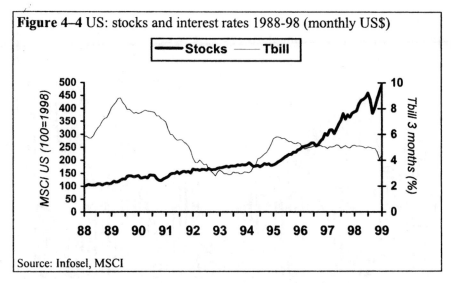

Figure 4–4 US: stocks and interest rates 1988-98 (monthly US$)

Source: Infosel, MSCI

increases outside the US (e.g. the recent increase in Asia of production facilities for computer DRAMs) this can affect prices and supply in the US.

Owing to the cycle's complexity and its globalization, investment strategists have attempted to focus on the aspects of the cycle that have most effect on portfolio investment. It is obvious from the net present value formula that the factor that most affects portfolio investments is the interest rate, because it is the most important ingredient of the rate *R* which is used to value any kind of investment.

To take an example, there is a clear inverse correlation between the US interest rate and the stock market. When the rate falls, the market index rises: when the rate rises, the market index stops rising, or falls (figure 4–4). This relationship reflects the inverse correlation observed in figure 4–3 between GNP (which has a high correlation with corporate profits) and inflation (which has a high correlation with interest rates).

To anticipate movements in interest rates (and GNP) an analysis is made of the supply and demand for money (or liquidity), which determines interest rates, and represents the response of monetary authorities to their perception of the economic cycle.[3] Liquidity is measured as primary money creation (primary liquidity – *liquidez*

---

[3]CrossBorder Capital has pioneered the systematic analysis of the liquidity cycle (*ciclo de liquidez*), as well as its practical application to investment decisions: it produces two monthly publications, one for developed and the other for emerging markets (www.liquidity.com).

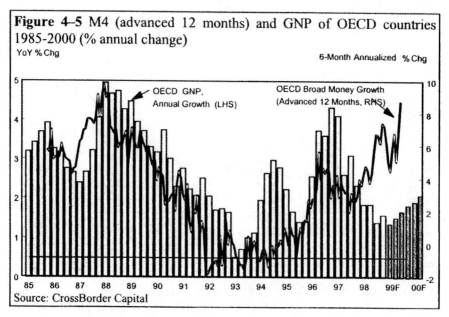

Figure 4–5 M4 (advanced 12 months) and GNP of OECD countries 1985-2000 (% annual change)

Source: CrossBorder Capital

primaria) of OECD member countries. This liquidity goes directly towards financial assets, i.e. portfolio investment. Money deposited in the banking system (secondary liquidity – *liquidez secundaria*) affects the real economy. Normally, the expansion of primary liquidity anticipates the expansion of the real economy by a period of between 12 to 18 months (figure 4–5).

We have measurements of the primary liquidity cycle between 1969 and 1998 (figure 4–6). There was an important reduction in liquidity (measured as M4, the broadest definition of money supply) at the beginning of each decade. These liquidity "squeezes" (*contracciones*) are caused by restrictive monetary policy of the central banks in the face of an increase in the rate of inflation. The result is an "absolute" global recession (a recession where the economy decreases in absolute terms for two consecutive quarters).

In the middle of each decade, approximately 4 or 5 years after these squeezes, there are shorter and more abrupt contractions in liquidity. These contractions are not so much the product of inflation as monetary policy errors by central banks, who have emerged from the previous recessions with an excessively cautious attitude towards monetary policy. These contractions in liquidity end quickly when central banks realize their mistake and begin to inject more liquidity into the system. They are different from the longer 9-10 year cycles because: 1) they do

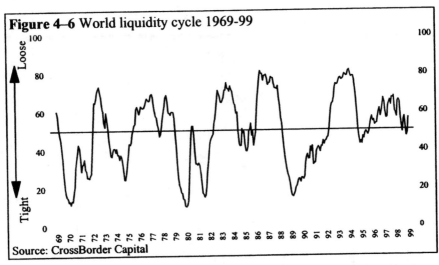

Figure 4-6 World liquidity cycle 1969-99

Source: CrossBorder Capital

not last as long, nor are they as severe, 2) they are not related to inflation, and 3) they cause "growth recessions" (i.e. with a reduction in the rate of growth, in contrast to an "absolute recession", with negative growth).

4.4.1 The liquidity cycle and portfolio investments

Different portfolio investments are appropriate at each stage of the liquidity cycle (figure 4-7). In stage VI, when liquidity is at its low point, cash (*efectivo*) is appropriate. It is uncertain whether liquidity may not be tightened even further, pushing interest rates even higher, and that is why short term debt instruments are recommended (📖 6.3.2).

As liquidity begins to increase (stage I), interest rates begin to fall, and bonds become attractive (*bonos*). As liquidity continues to increase (stage II), an economic recovery looks probable, along with a continuation of the fall in interest rates: bonds continue to be attractive, and stocks, or equities (*acciones*), become interesting. As liquidity peaks (stage III), interest rates stop falling, and bonds become less attractive, but equities continue attractive owing to the prospect of an increase in economic activity. In stage IV, liquidity falls, either because central banks see an increase in inflation, or because they fear that it will occur: some stocks continue to be attractive, but, with the increase in inflation, assets that benefit from inflation are also attractive: real estate (*bienes raices*) and commodities (*commodities*). As liquidity is squeezed further, and inflation peaks (stage V), stocks are no longer attractive, although real estate and commodities are still attractive – until in stage VI the cycle begins again with cash.

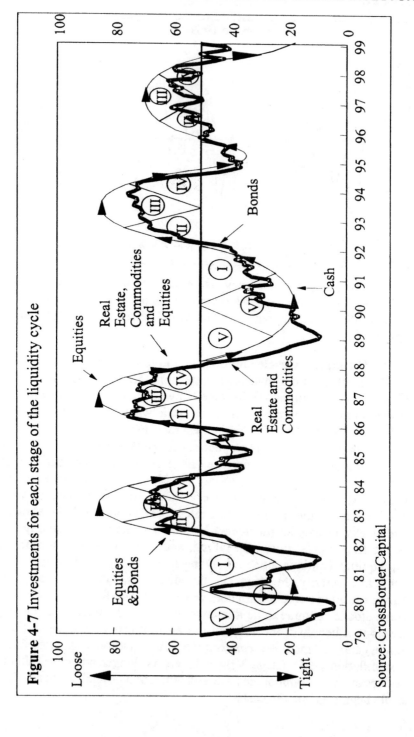

Figure 4-7 Investments for each stage of the liquidity cycle

Source: CrossBorderCapital

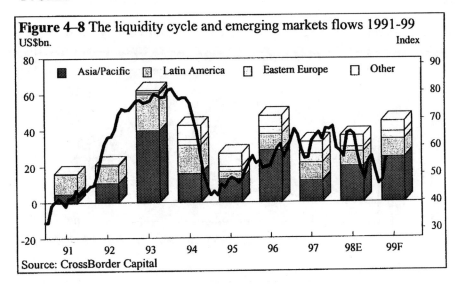

Figure 4–8 The liquidity cycle and emerging markets flows 1991-99

US$bn.   Index

Source: CrossBorder Capital

4.4.2 The liquidity cycle and emerging markets

Since the end of the 1980s, when emerging markets began to be attractive, there has been a correlation between flows to emerging markets and the global liquidity cycle. The year of the highest liquidity, 1993, corresponds with the highest flow towards emerging markets, and the years when flows decline, 1994 and 1995, correspond with the decrease in world liquidity (figure 4–8).

The general conclusion is therefore that the stages of the global liquidity cycle when emerging markets are attractive are III and IV, i.e. following stage II, when developed country and US equities are attractive.

4.4.3 The liquidity cycle and interest rates

The liquidity cycle is a fundamental determinant of the returns on portfolio investments in both developed and emerging markets. This is the reason for the attention which is given by global investors to the monetary policy of the Fed.

The mechanism for managing liquidity in the US is the deposit rate offered by the Fed on reserves deposited with it by US banks ("Fed funds rate"). This rate is fixed eight times a year by the Federal Open Markets Committee (FOMC), whose members are the governors of the

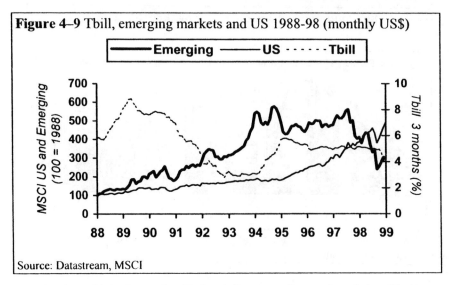

Figure 4–9 Tbill, emerging markets and US 1988-98 (monthly US$)

Source: Datastream, MSCI

12 banks which form the Federal Reserve System[4] and its Chairman (currently Alan Greenspan). To determine the rate, the Committee takes account of multiple indicators of the level of consumer and producer inflation, and the growth rate of GNP. If they feel that there is risk of an increase in the inflation rate (owing to an excessive rate of economic growth), a rate increase is possible, to cool down the economy. If, on the other hand, they think that the economy is too stagnant, and that it is suffering from excess capacity, they might decide to lower the rate, to reactivate it. If they feel that the economy is growing at an adequate rate, and that inflation is under control, they decide to leave the rate unchanged.

Fed members, economists, investment strategists, and those who specialize in Fed activities ("Fed-watchers") have access to the same information about the state of the US economy. However, interpretations of the data can vary considerably. For example, it is well known that the Fed's main concern is the price level of goods and services in the real economy. However, in 1999, owing to the boom in the prices of financial assets[5], there was a question about the extent to which the Fed was

---

[4]The regional banks of the Fed system are independent, with commercial banks as shareholders, and function like "branches" of a central bank.

[5]In the years 1995-98 the Dow Jones index rose by 139%.

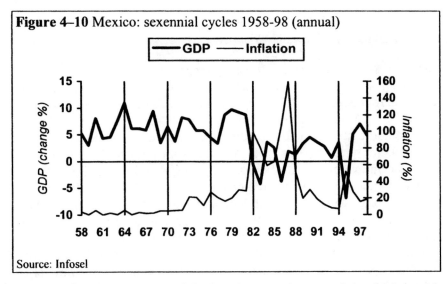

Figure 4–10 Mexico: sexennial cycles 1958-98 (annual)

Source: Infosel

concerned with the price of financial assets (e.g. stocks) which could eventually affect the prices of goods and services.[6]

4.5 THE GLOBAL CYCLE AND MEXICO

The long (Kondratieff) cycle tends to confirm the argument presented in 🕮 ch. 1 that Mexico as an emerging market should, *ceteris paribus*, be a more attractive investment candidate than developed markets. Similarly, as a result of globalization, the global liquidity cycle has an important effect on flows to emerging markets and, therefore, to Mexico. This was the lesson of the rate increases beginning in February 1994, and decreases in 1998 (Sep – Nov) which affected both developed and emerging markets (figure 4–9).[7]

4.6 THE MEXICAN CYCLE

4.6.1 The economic cycle

In Mexico, the economic cycles of the 1950s and 1960s (the period of "stable development" - *desarrollo estabilizador*) do not seem so clearly marked as in subsequent years. GDP growth was relatively constant, with low inflation (figure 4–10). Since 1970, the beginning of the *sexenio* (6 year presidential term) of President Luis Echeverría, the

---

[6]In 1997, when the economy seemed to be well balanced, "neither too hot nor too cold", it was called the "Goldilocks economy", after the fairy tale.

[7]There is a divergence between the Dow and emerging markets, owing to the "tequila effect" in December 1994, and the Asian crisis in 1997.

economic cycle is clearly related to the presidential cycle, and the role of the government in the economy.

In the *sexenio* of President José López Portillo (1976-1982), GDP rose 3.5% in 1977, and 8% on average during the next 4 years. Following the 1982 economic crash, it fell to –0.8% in that year, and even more negative (-4.3%) in the first year of the next President, Miguel de la Madrid, recovering to 3.6% in 1984.

The traditional "parabolic" pattern began to be broken in 1985, when the economy grew by less than 1984 (2.8%), owing to the problems of the price and volume of oil exports which began in June, and the Mexico City earthquake, which occurred on September 19, 1985. In 1986, owing to the oil price collapse, growth turned negative again (-3.8%), but there was a recovery (1.9%) in 1987. A greater recovery in 1988 was frustrated by the stock market crash of October 1987 (📖 10.2.4.3), followed by the devaluation of November in the same year. These two factors caused a rise in inflation, owing to the deliberate one time price adjustment that was an important component of the first Economic Solidarity Pact that was signed in December 1987 in a (successful) attempt to reduce the inflation rate. The resulting high level of interest rates slowed growth in 1988 to a level of just 1.25%.

In the *sexenio* of President Carlos Salinas (1988-1994), the rate of GDP growth picked up: 3.4% in 1989, 4.4% in 1990, and 3.6% in 1991, slowing in 1992 and 1993 (2.8% and 0.6%) owing to uncertainty about the passage of NAFTA (negotiations had begun in 1990), and the restructuring of Mexican industry as a result of the liberalization of trade and investment. Finally, there was a recovery of 3.5% in 1994 (despite the political problems of that year), owing to investment that had been postponed the previous year, and the increase in government spending in an electoral year.

In 1995, GDP growth touched its lowest level (-6.2%) since 1932, owing to the double blow of the devaluation of December 1994, and the austerity plan introduced by the administration of President Ernesto Zedillo in March 1995, but there was a significant recovery in 1996 (5.2%), 1997 (7%) and 1998 (4.8%).

4.6.2 The role of government

Just as in the US, the Mexican government has fiscal and monetary tools to control the economy. After the two *sexenios* of stable development (1958-1970), there is general agreement that under Luis Echeverría (1970-76) the government began to misuse its fiscal and monetary tools to force economic growth and redistribute income, resulting in the devaluation of 1976, the first since 1954.

In the following *sexenio* of President José López Portillo, economic mismanagement took another form. With windfall profits from the rise in oil prices, major public spending projects were undertaken, which were partially financed by excess foreign credit. When oil prices fell in 1982, and credit dried up, there was another devaluation crisis at the end of 1982.

During the *sexenio* of Miguel de la Madrid there was an attempt to solve the legacy of twelve years of misguided economic policies, with macroeconomic stabilization, and microeconomic liberalization, following the international trends of privatization, deregulation, and internationalization (📖 1.4). Despite the earthquake in 1985, the oil price collapse in 1986 and the market crash in 1987, following the success of the Economic Solidarity Pact in 1988[8] it was possible for the administration of President Carlos Salinas to continue the economic policies set by the previous President with positive results in the macroeconomy (GDP and inflation) and the microeconomy (privatization, deregulation and internationalization).

In this context, an important reform was the independence of the Mexican Central Bank (*Banco de México*) which became effective in April 1994, and gave it explicit responsibility for the control of inflation through control of the money supply. However, owing to globalization (📖 1.4.1) there was an increasing dependence on foreign capital, combined with a lack of understanding about the size and scope of financial markets for Mexican instruments outside Mexico, and the possible interaction between them. The result was that, in the face of political destabilization in 1994, and the realities of an electoral year, it was impossible to maintain an independent and coherent monetary policy. The result was the devaluation crisis of 1994.

4.6.3 The liquidity cycle

As in the US, there is a clear relationship between interest rates and stock prices (figure 4–11). This reflects the inverse correlation between inflation and GDP mentioned in the context of the Mexican economic cycle (figure 4–10).

It is for this reason that liquidity in the Mexican economy is monitored, as a way of forecasting movements in interest rates and GDP.

---

[8]See Heyman, Timothy, *Investing in Mexico* (Editorial Milenio, 1989), pp. 33-38.

Figure 4–11 Mexico: stocks and interest rates 1988-98 (monthly)

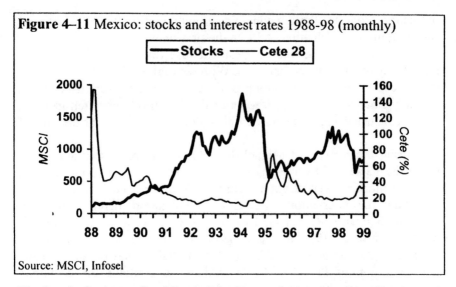

Source: MSCI, Infosel

The level of primary liquidity in Mexico can be measured as the rise and fall of real M4, the broadest definition of the money supply. Based on quarterly data, liquidity tends to forecast economic activity with a shorter lead time than the world cycle (12-18 months), of approximately two quarters (figure 4–12).

4.6.4 The investment cycle

There is no "Mexican investment cycle" similar to the global investment cycle described in figure 4-7. The main reason for this is that Mexico does not at the present time (December, 1998) have a major asset class: long term fixed rate debt denominated in pesos – owing to the high volatility of the inflation rate which has inhibited the development of a long term debt market (📖 5.6).

However, the Mexican liquidity cycle does have an effect on the Mexican stock market. When liquidity expands, the stock market tends to rise, and when it contracts, the stock market tends to fall (figure 4–13).

4.7 ECONOMIC FORECAST FOR MEXICO

4.7.1 Cycles

It will have become apparent from previous sections that cycle analysis (whether it is of long cycles, economic cycles or liquidity cycles) is an imprecise activity – as in any other branch of the social sciences.

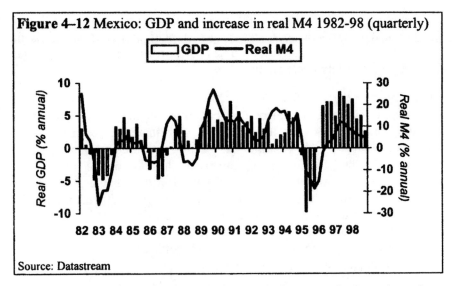

Figure 4–12 Mexico: GDP and increase in real M4 1982-98 (quarterly)

Source: Datastream

Even so, useful conclusions can be drawn from previous sections that can help us in our analysis of Mexico. The most important can be summarized as follows:

- Mexico, as an emerging market, was, at the end of 1998, at a positive stage of the long cycle.
- The global liquidity cycle has an important effect on emerging capital markets.
- In Mexico, there is an economic cycle, which corresponds to the

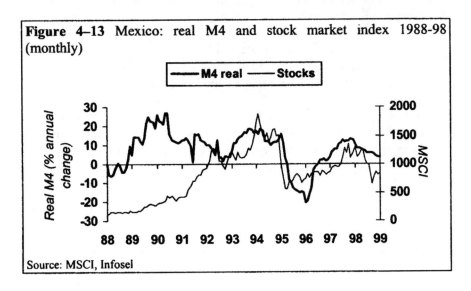

Figure 4–13 Mexico: real M4 and stock market index 1988-98 (monthly)

Source: MSCI, Infosel

cycle of each presidential administration (*sexenio*). On a short term basis, it is possible to forecast interest rates and rises and falls in GDP, two very important variables for portfolio investment, on the basis of liquidity cycle analysis.

4.7.2　Scenarios

Despite the foregoing, there is a general problem with the application of the concept of cycles to economic and financial forecasting for Mexico. Owing to the volatility of recent cycles, there is no reliable statistical method for forecasting either the duration or the intensity of any given cycle. In terms of the graphs used in this chapter, there is no way to extrapolate the line that represents the cycle, either horizontally or vertically, with an acceptable level of confidence.

We believe that the concept of "scenarios" (*escenarios*) can be useful in the forecasting process. In the words of Peter Schwartz, a recognized expert in scenario analysis, scenarios are

"stories that describe different but credible futures. Taken together, they represent a tool for ordering our perceptions about alternative future environments, which will affect the consequences of decisions taken today."[9]

The first person to use scenarios for strategic planning purposes was Herman Kahn, the father of "futurology" (*futurología*) – the forecast of the future. As part of his consulting activity with the US Air Force in the 1960s, Kahn used scenarios to anticipate the actions of potential enemies. In the private sector, a pioneer of scenarios was Pierre Wack, Planning Director at Royal Dutch Shell, the largest oil company in the world, who adapted the concept to his company's needs, and, as a consequence, was able to anticipate and benefit from the oil crises of the 1970s. More recently, Peter Schwartz himself is the man who has developed and marketed scenario methodology as a tool for strategic planning.

In developed countries, scenarios are normally used for the long term, i.e. more than one year. Owing to the uncertainty, and intensity, of recent cycles in Mexico, there is an argument for applying scenario analysis in Mexico to the medium term, i.e. for periods of up to one year.

---

[9]Schwartz, Peter, "The Art of the Long View, User's Guide" (www.gbn.org).

4.7.3 Techniques for generating scenarios

As the purpose of scenarios is to exercise the imagination about the future, it can be counterproductive to over-"mechanize" the process of scenario generation. However, there are certain key elements that it is useful to bear in mind, which can facilitate the scenario generation process.

4.7.3.1 Quantity

The quantity of scenarios generated should be sufficient to exercise the imagination, without overwhelming it. For the purposes of planning portfolio investments over a one year time frame, three scenarios are sufficient: one scenario reflects a favorable investment environment, another a negative environment, and a third (normally the most complex) a "mixed" environment, with elements of each of the other two.

4.7.3.2 Definition

There is always a temptation to define scenarios as "good" and "bad": it would appear logical to call a favorable scenario "good" or "optimistic". However, this kind of labeling can inject too much subjectivity into the process. What is good for one investor can be bad for another, depending on how he has invested. In our view, it is therefore better to describe each scenario by its salient features, rather than qualify it.

In the case of portfolio investment planning, in earlier sections we analyzed the investment cycle as a key determinant of returns for different asset classes. The variables which can best be used to describe the investment cycle are: GDP growth, and inflation. In addition, historically, there has been an inverse correlation between these two variables (figure 4–3 for the US and figure 4–10 for Mexico). Therefore, investment scenarios can be defined in terms of:

1. High growth, low inflation.
2. Low growth, high inflation.
3. Moderate growth, moderate inflation.

4.7.3.3 Factors

The factors that determine scenarios can be deduced from the graphs describing global and national cycles presented in previous sections. These figures show the global liquidity cycle, which depends mainly on the US economic cycle, the fiscal policy of the Treasury and Congress and the monetary policy of the Fed. The national liquidity cycle reflects global trends, and the fiscal and monetary policy of the Mexican

Ministry of Finance and Public Credit, and Bank of Mexico, respectively.

4.7.3.4 Surprises

Surprises are probably the most important element in scenario development. As most economic forecasts are extrapolations of historic data, the main reason for producing scenarios is to imagine surprises, or, as Peter Schwartz says

"Can you imagine events and situations that are 'unthinkable' in your vision of the future?"[10]

International surprises can be classified in several ways, including: geopolitical (e.g. the Kuwaiti invasion in 1990), political (the Kennedy assassination in 1963), economic (the US rate hike in February 1994), financial (the New York stock market crash in 1987), or natural (*El Niño* in 1997-98).

At the beginning of 1998, it was not difficult to imagine "surprises" both for the world and for Mexico. A useful tool for surprise generation is a calendar of events programmed for the year for which the forecast is being made (figure 4–14). In the calendar for 1998, it was clear that two important political events were the federal elections in Germany in September and the congressional elections in the US in November. Similarly, a major financial event was the decision by member countries about participation in the European Monetary System, and adoption of its new currency, the euro, to be taken in May 1998. In Mexico, ten gubernatorial elections were programmed for 1998, beginning in the month of July, each of which could cause "surprises".

4.7.3.5 Probabilities

Once the scenarios have been described, it is important to give some weighting to the probability of their occurrence. Owing to the complexity of the combination of external and internal factors, and of positive and negative surprises, it is practically impossible to apply a probability based on historical observations. It is therefore necessary to use "a priori" probabilities, based on a subjective appreciation of external and internal variables. In an activity as important as forecasting, it is worth remembering that "it is better to be roughly right than precisely wrong".

---

[10]*ibid.* p. 2.

Figure 4–14 International calendar for 1998

January	Ramadan begins
	UK presidency of EU begins
	World Economic Forum in Davos
February	Winter Olympics in Japan
	Carnival in New Orleans, Rio de Janeiro, Venice
	Kim Dae Jung becomes President of South Korea
March	Change of Prime Minister in China
	Presidential elections in Indonesia
	Meeting of members of EU in London to discuss possible expansion
	Oscars in Hollywood
April	Summit of the Americas in Santiago (Chile)
	Deregulation of financial markets (Big Bang) in Japan
May	Decision by members of EU on membership of monetary union (euro)
	Meeting of G7 (plus Russia) in UK
	50 year anniversary of WTO in Geneva
	50 year anniversary of Israel
	Presidential elections in Colombia, Ecuador, Paraguay, Philippines
June	UN special assembly on drug trafficking
	Announcement of new governor of European Central Bank
	Soccer World Cup
July	Austrian presidency of EU begins
August	Accession of Presidents of Colombia and Ecuador
September	Elections for chancellor in Germany
	Annual Meeting of World Bank and IMF in Washington
October	Presidential elections in Brazil
	Nobel Prizes in Stockholm
November	Congressional elections in US
	Iberoamerican summit in Portugal
December	Presidential elections in Venezuela
	50 year anniversary of signature of Universal Declaration of Human Rights

Source: The Economist, January 1998

4.7.3.6 Use

International brokers target their research efforts towards major international investment managers. Competition between these brokerages for investment managers' business is based on who offers the "best" top-down and bottom-up research (📖 2.6.2. and 📖 8.6.2). Brokers believe that if they are paid "to be right" the idea of producing three or four scenarios could appear too "lukewarm", even if they assign them a probability. That is why, for the most part, even if they have considered various scenarios, they prefer to present just one, the most probable, without giving it an explicit probability.

However, one way of incorporating scenarios into a forecast is to produce an explicit mention of "Risks" which specifies all those events that could occur that would nullify the forecast which has been selected for presentation. A leading investment strategist at one of the most important international brokerages publishes in January of each year a

Figure 4–15 The ten surprises of 1998

1   Long term interest rates in US fall to 5% in first semester, to later rise to 7% in
    second semester
2   Dow Jones pierces 9,000 in first quarter, falls to 7,000 in second quarter
3   Change of international leaders. Kohl loses German elections. Netanyahu
    resigns in Israel. Yeltsin resigns for reasons of ill-health in Russia. Hashimoto
    resigns in Japan
4   Rumors of sale of nuclear arsenal in ex-USSR. Problems of international
    security in Middle East, India, Asia
5   Brazil and South Korea reap benefits of economic reforms of 1997. Their stock
    markets rise
6   Owing to investigation of campaign finance, Vice President Albert Gore announces
    his retirement from presidential race in US for 2,000
7   Owing to Asian crisis, Japanese corporate profits outlook worsens, and Nikkei index
    falls to 10,000
8   Tech stocks rise again, owing to recovery in Asian sales
9   US corporate profits not affected by Asian crisis as much as expected. Operating
    profits for Dow Jones and S&P 500 rise 10% over 1997
10 Reduction in flows to US mutual funds

Source: Morgan Stanley, January 1998[11]

list of the surprises, which he could envisage during that year (figure 4–
15 for 1998). His definition of "surprise" is a "probability of occurrence
that is less than 33% for the typical investment manager, but higher than
50% for our investment strategist".

4.8 AN EXAMPLE - SCENARIOS FOR MEXICO 1998

4.8.1 The government scenario

The starting point in developing scenarios for Mexico for 1998 were
the government programs for fiscal and monetary policy, and their
subsequent modifications.[12] In May 1998, the government forecast for
1998 was GDP growth of 5.2% and inflation of 12%. It based this
forecast on moderate fiscal and monetary policies, and the expectation of
favorable global liquidity conditions. After the oil price fall in the first
quarter of 1998, the forecast for the average oil price for the year had
been downgraded from US$15.5 to US$12.5.

---

[11]Based on Wien, Byron, "The Ten Surprises of 1998" (Morgan Stanley,
January 1998).

[12]Secretaría de Hacienda y Crédito Público (www.shcp.gob.mex) and Bank
of Mexico (www.banxico.org.mx).

Figure 4–16 Consensus forecast: average of five economic forecasts

	GDP (%)		Inflation (%)		Current account balance (US$bn.)		Cete 28 (% average)		Peso/dollar (annual average)	
	1998	1999	1998	1999	1998	1999	1998	1999	1998	1999
ASESORIA	4.0	4.5	13.9	11.9	-13.5	-17.5	17.5	15.0	8.8	9.5
CAIE	4.7	4.9	14.3	12.2	-15.6	NA	17.7	15.2	8.6	9.6
CIEMEX	5.9	6.1	13.2	10.5	-12.4	-15.4	15.9	15.0	8.6	9.3
GEA	5.5	NA	13.1	NA	-9.5	NA	18.8	NA	9.1	NA
B.METRICA	4.5	4.0	13.9	11.5	-16.4	-21.6	17.5	13.5	8.8	9.9
Average	4.9	4.9	13.7	11.5	-13.5	-18.2	17.5	14.7	8.8	9.6
30 days ago	4.8	4.8	13.7	11.1	-13.1	-17.5	17.5	14.4	8.8	9.5
60 days ago	4.8	4.8	13.8	10.9	-12.3	-16.6	17.3	14.4	8.8	9.7

Source: SHCP (May 1998)

4.8.2 Consensus forecasts

A large number of analysts prepare forecasts on key economic indicators for Mexico. The average of some, or all, of these forecasts, is called the "consensus". Various organizations collect these forecasts to produce "consensus forecasts" (*estimaciones consenso*)[13].

In figure 4–16, we provide consensus forecasts for 1998 of five forecasting services for Mexico, collected by the Ministry of Finance and Public Credit. It is unsurprising that the consensus estimate for 1998 was quite close to the government forecasts, with average estimated GDP growth at 4.9%, and average inflation at 13.7%. For the investor, the main use of consensus forecasts is to see which are the most extreme

Figure 4–17 Scenarios for 1998

Indicators	1997	Government	Consensus	Growth high	medium	low
GDP (%)	7.0	5.2	4.9	6.0	4.8	3.5
Inflation (%)	15.6	12.0	13.7	12.0	14.0	18.0
Current account (US$bn.)	-7.3	-10.8	-13.5	-15.0	-13.0	-11.5
Cete 28 (annual average %)	20.6	NA	17.5	15.5	17.5	20.0
Peso/dollar (average)	7.95	NA	8.79	8.60	8.80	9.10
External variables						
Libor US$ (%)	6.0	NA	NA	5.5	6.3	7.0
Oil price (US$)	14.0	12.5	NA	14.0	12.5	10.0
Probability				25%	50%	25%

Source: SHCP, Bank of Mexico, author

---

[13]See Porvenir Online (www.porvenir.com) for 3 consensus forecasts: SHCP, Bank of Mexico, and the University of Arizona.

forecasts (i.e. the furthest from the consensus) to understand the premises (or surprises) which they imply, and thus test his own forecast.

4.8.3 High growth

After analyzing the government scenario and the consensus scenario, the investor should formulate his own scenarios, beginning with a high growth scenario. At the beginning of 1998, what were the conditions that would produce GDP higher than that estimate (for example, 6% in the high growth scenario)? An important precondition was a benign international investment environment (figure 4–17). In this case, the most favorable environment for Mexico was one of falling interest rates in the US, with the possibility of continuing capital flows towards the country. Another possibility was that the price of oil, having fallen during the first quarter, would stabilize, and perhaps even show a slight recovery in the second half of the year, without affecting the level of inflation, and hence interest rates, in the US. In Mexico, an important condition for the positive scenario was the fulfillment of fiscal and monetary policies announced by the government.

Another condition was the absence of negative surprises globally and in Mexico. Globally, a positive surprise would be that the Asian crisis had touched bottom, and that there would be no further surprises either in China (a renminbi devaluation), or in Japan.

In Mexico, the Mexican electoral process had been broadly studied and commented on. A positive surprise in this case would be not so much the results of the ten gubernatorial elections, as the absence of problems in the electoral and postelectoral process.

4.8.4 Low growth

What were the conditions which would produce a lower GDP than the official forecast? Globally, there was the possibility of a rise in US interest rates, induced by the Fed, owing to fear of inflation caused either by the tight employment situation, or by the continued rise in the prices of stocks and real estate. A rise in dollar interest rates could reduce the flow of capital to Mexico to cover the current account deficit. This could in turn cause a further depreciation of the peso, with pressures on the inflation rate and interest rates. Another negative global factor would be a further fall in the oil price, say, to an average level of US$10 per barrel in 1998, which could have a similar effect on the peso and interest rates. In a worst case, one could not discard a combination of these two events (although it was not very probable, as a fall in the price of oil would normally be positive for US inflation).

In Mexico (independently of what could happen globally) there was the possibility that in spite of expressed intentions, there could be greater public expenditure than programmed, owing to the pressure of gubernatorial elections, causing greater than expected inflation, with negative consequences for interest rates and growth

The low growth scenario also implied the possibility of other negative surprises. Globally, there was the possibility of a geopolitical surprise (Asia, China, Russia or the Middle East) or a financial surprise (a collapse of the New York Stock Exchange, after the most extended rise in its history). Any of these shocks could affect capital flows to emerging markets, and therefore Mexico.

In Mexico, negative surprises were possible in the elections, both in the electoral process, and in the electoral results, and reactions to the results. There were also unresolved problems, whose lack of resolution could affect the investment environment during 1998: Chiapas, drug-trafficking, and the restructuring of the banking system.

4.8.5 Medium growth

The conditions for medium growth would lie somewhere between the previous two scenarios. The global environment could remain stable, or deteriorate slightly. In Mexico, fiscal and monetary policy could be implemented as planned.

There could be both positive and negative surprises globally and in Mexico. However, for a medium growth scenario, positive surprises would be offset by negative surprises, in such a way that, through a combination of spurts and stumbles, the medium growth scenario would eventually play itself out by the end of 1998.

4.8.6 Probabilities

The global environment had been very positive for portfolio investment during the three previous years, and therefore some event which could alter this situation was not improbable. There were two main risks. The possibility of an interest rate hike in the US, and the possibility of a further deterioration of the Asian situation, with competitive devaluations and a consequent disinflation (or even deflation) on a global basis: falling interest rates and zero or negative economic growth.

Similarly, in Mexico, owing to ten important gubernatorial elections, it was impossible to discard the possibility of negative political surprises. However, these could be offset by positive economic surprises – just as occurred in 1997 with the surprisingly positive level of GDP growth of

7%, higher than anyone was forecasting at the beginning of that year. For these reasons, a 50% probability was assigned to the medium growth scenario.

Despite the possibility of a reversion in international dollar interest rates, it was also well understood that global structural change was only at the beginning of the stage referred to in 📖 ch. 1. In addition to this, the possibility of a repetition of the positive economic surprises of 1997 in Mexico was not totally discarded for 1998. Finally, there was the possibility that while there could be negative political surprises, a growing political maturity in Mexico would be reflected in a gradual separation between economic and political processes. Therefore, a probability of 25% was assigned to the high growth scenario.

There is always a natural tendency to hope that changes of trend – for instance in the global environment - occur gradually. However, usually they occur suddenly. The low growth scenario implied sharp surprises, either globally, or in Mexico. It was given a probability of 25%.

4.8.7 The Mexican economy in 1998

In 1998, Mexican GDP grew by 4.8%, with inflation at 18.6%, and the current account deficit at US$15.8bn. The average Cete rate was 24.5% and the average exchange rate was $9.15/US$. The Libor US$ 3 month rate averaged 5.6% and the Mexican average oil price (for the different grades of oil) was US$10.2 for the year.

The outturn for the Mexican economy in 1998 demonstrates the usefulness of scenario development, because none of the major variables fell broadly outside the parameters of the three scenarios. The most probable GDP figure (4.8%) was achieved. However, the sharp deterioration in the oil price (US$10/bbl. from the low growth scenario) led also to inflation indicators (18.6%) and an average peso ($9.15) close to those of the low growth scenario (18% and $9.1 respectively). Meanwhile, as a result of the collapse in the oil price, combined with higher than expected growth, the current account deficit (US$15.8bn.) deteriorated to a figure close to that estimated for the high growth scenario (US$15 bn.).

Chapter 5
Debt I

*"As an alternative to agriculture, you could try the merchant
fleet, if it were not such a dangerous activity, or money
lending, if it were not so dishonorable...Our ancestors
considered moneylenders much worse than thieves..."*
Cato the Elder (234-149 BC)

5.1 INTRODUCTION

Debt securities (*instrumentos de deuda*) have three features that
distinguish them from other investments. They offer a predetermined
return, principal amount, and term.[1]

These features are related to the fact that a debt security is a loan that
the lender (or investor) makes to the issuer (*emisor*) of the instrument.
The investor lends a principal amount (*valor nominal* or *valor principal*)
for an agreed term (*plazo*), or maturity (*vencimiento*), and receives in
exchange a predetermined return, plus, at the end of the period (or in
installments during the life of the loan) the principal amount (or
"predetermined" amount, where relevant).

Debt (or credit) is probably the oldest mechanism of financial
exchange – older even than currency.[2] Its development globally and in
Mexico has reflected political, social, economic and financial currents,
and can help us understand its current features and future trends.
Therefore, before describing Mexican debt markets and securities
currently available in this 📖 ch. 5, we analyze the historical
development of debt securities globally and in Mexico. In 📖 ch. 6, we
describe techniques for the analysis of Mexican debt securities.

---

[1]They are also called "fixed income" securities, to distinguish them from
"variable income securities" (stocks), because historically debt securities
provided fixed interest payments, while stocks provided variable dividend
payments. However, currently there are debt securities that offer variable
interest rates (e.g. floating, or indexed, rates). We therefore consider it more
accurate to call them debt securities than fixed income securities.

[2]The first coins were minted in the VII century BC, in Asia Minor.

5.2 HISTORY OF GLOBAL DEBT INSTRUMENTS

5.2.1 Antiquity

Credit, with interest, began when man settled down from a nomadic life to the cultivation and harvest of grain. When a neolithic farmer lent seed to his neighbor during the sowing season and hoped for its repayment (with a premium) after harvest, he had created a loan.

The legal history of many great civilizations begins with the regulation of credit.[3] The first known formal legal code is that of King Hammurabi of Babylon in 1800 BC. Among its most important provisions were those that regulated the creditor-debtor relationship. Interest rates were set at a maximum level of 33 1/3% annual for grain loans, and 20% for silver loans (figure 5–1). Loans were documented before official witnesses with written contracts. If an interest rate was charged above the official maximum, and discovered, the principal amount was cancelled. Land and furniture could be pledged, as well as the person of the debtor, his wife, his concubine, his children or his slaves. However, personal slavery to settle a debt was limited to a maximum term of three years.

Figure 5–1 Interest rates in antiquity (%)

Century	Sumeria and Babylon	Greece	Rome
BC			
3000-1900	20-25		
1900-700	10-25		
600	10-20	16-18	
500	10-20	10-12	8 1/3+
400	40?	10-12	8 1/3+
300	40?	6-12	8 1/3
200		6-9	6-8 1/3
100		6-12	4-12+
AD			
100		8-9	4-12
200			6-12
300			12+?
400			12 1/2+?

Source: Homer, op. cit

---

[3]Homer, Sidney, *A History of Interest Rates* (Rutgers University Press, 1963), pp. 3-4. Mr. Homer, a partner of Salomon Bros. and Hutzler (predecessor of Salomon Inc.), brings the experience and rigor of modern debt markets to the historical analysis of interest rates.

The legal history of Athens began 1,200 years later, in 600 BC, with the Laws of Solon. In contrast to the Code of Hammurabi, the Laws of Solon removed limits on interest rates, reduced or cancelled many debts, and permitted mortgages, but prohibited personal slavery. These laws lasted for several centuries, and provided the foundation for Athens' subsequent prosperity.[4]

The legal history of Rome also includes laws on credit. The Twelve Tables, of 450 BC, are more similar to the Code of Hammurabi than to the Laws of Solon. They fixed a maximum interest rate of 8 1/3%, and slavery was permitted to cover debts, although the physical person of the slave was protected.

The main difference between ancient and modern credit was its lack of institutionalization. Credit was contracted between individuals, or, at best, between groups of individuals. There were no "states" (governments), or large companies that issued debt. There were no institutionalized banks as lenders that acted as intermediaries between creditor and debtor - although private bankers did exist. Similarly, there was no organized debt market to mobilize resources between sources of funds (or creditors) and users of funds (debtors) – although there is evidence of an informal secondary market in both Athens and Rome.

5.2.2 Middle Ages and Renaissance - Italy and Low Countries

One of the most important aspects of the so-called "Dark Ages" in Europe (500 AD to 1000 AD) was the collapse of the rule of law and the civilized conditions necessary for organized financial activity. The only institution that preserved civilization was the Christian church. But Christian doctrine, since the first major Church assembly, the Council of Nicaea in 325 AD, prohibited "usury" (*usura*), defined as a process where "more is requested than is given". This prohibition had an important influence on the development of credit until the Middle Ages.

The prohibition of usury also had etymological consequences. To justify a loan, the theory was developed that compensation for a loan did not represent a profit for the lender (which would be usury), but compensation for a loss. The Latin verb *interesse* means "to lose", and *interest* means "it is lost".

---

[4]See also Edward E. Cohen, *Athenian Economy & Society: a Banking Perspective* (Princeton University Press, 1992).

Figure 5–2 History of global debt: important dates

BC	
XVIII	Laws of Hammurabi (Babylon)
VI	Laws of Solon (Athens)
450	Twelve Tables (Rome)
AD	
325	Prohibition of usury by clergy at Council of Nicaea
IX	Prohibition of usury by the Capitularies of Charlemagne
IX-XI	Arab hegemony of Mediterranean
1096	First crusade establishes control of Mediterranean for Italy
XII	First foreign currency promissory notes discounted in Italy
1164	First loan to city of Genoa
1174	Forced loan (*prestito*) to the city of Venice
XIII	First deposit and lending banks (Italy)
1262	Consolidation of debt securities and market in Venice
	Prosperity of Bruges (Flanders) as "Venice of the North"
1270	Last crusade by Louis XII of France
XIV	Suspension of payments by Kings of England and France
	causes bankruptcy of many Italian banks
	Foundation of Stock Exchange in Bruges
XV	
1430-80	Boom of Medici bank in Florence (bankrupt in 1494)
1461	First pawnshop established in Perugia, Italy
1482	Venice begins new series of *prestiti*
	Antwerp substitutes Bruges as financial center of Northern Europe
XVI	
	Martin Luther (1483-1536) attacks usury, defends payment of interest
	John Calvin (1509-1564) defends reasonable usury and payment of interest
1500	Development of market for state debt in Holland
1531	Stock exchange in Antwerp
1546	Boom of bank of Anton Fugger and Nephews in Augsburg (Germany)
	King of Spain and Netherlands largest debtor in Europe
	Payments suspension by the Spanish crown (1552, 1557, 1597)
1570	Amsterdam takes over financial leadership, on payments suspension by Antwerp
	Issue of permanent bonds by Republic of Genoa
	Genoa becomes banker of Spanish crown, replacing Dutch and German bankers
XVII	Suspension of payments by Spanish crown (1606, 1627, 1647, 1686)
	Fugger bankruptcy owing to loans to Spain
1609	Foundation of Amsterdam Wisselbank
1618	Pawnshop system organized in Netherlands
1624	Issue of permanent bond by Lekdyk Bovensdams Company
	(still paying interest in 1957)
1639	French government loans traded on new Paris Stock Exchange
1656	Foundation of Riksbank of Sweden
1661	Riksbank issues first paper money
1668	Riksbank passes to public ownership, becoming first central bank in world
1672	Government debt traded on Amsterdam Stock Exchange
1675	The Africa Company issues public debt in England
1688	William of Orange (William III) accedes to English throne

Figure 5–2 (cont.)

1692	First issue of long term debt by English government
1695	Bank of England begins operations (January 1)
	Bank of England discounts commercial paper (bills)
XVIII	Development of long and short term debt markets by Bank of England
	Canal bonds in England
1700	Payments suspension by Spanish crown
1724	French stock market begins operations in government paper
1747	Amsterdam Stock Exchange trades 25 government and state bonds,
	3 Dutch stocks, 3 English stocks, and 4 English bonds
1749	Issue of consolidated English debt (Consols), permanent and still outstanding
1773	Jonathan's Coffee House is called the "Stock Exchange"
1775	London Clearing House
XIX	Payments suspension by the Spanish crown (1820, 1837, 1851, 1873)
1802	English Stock Exchange builds own building
1818	English financial market begins to trade foreign loans and bonds
1840	Railway bonds
1844	Bank of England given monopoly for note issue
1860s	Expansion of joint stock banks
1877	First issue of Treasury Bills in England
XX	
1913-19	Establishment of Federal Reserve System in US
1963	US Interest Equalization Tax (IET) on foreign bonds launches eurobond market
1972	Inauguration of options market (CBOE) in Chicago
1973	Flotation of dollar, beginning period of currency and interest rate instability
1975	Introduction of first interest rate futures contract in Chicago
1977	Boom of syndicated credits in eurodollars
1980s	Boom in interest rate futures and futures exchanges
	(e.g.. London International Financial Futures Exchange (LIFFE))
1982	Mexican debt crisis
1989	Brady Plan for substitution of bank debt of indebted countries with tradeable
	bonds (Brady bonds)
1990	Issue of first Brady bonds, by Mexico
1991-4	Development of emerging markets eurobond market
1996	Derivatives of Brady bonds

Source: Homer, Kindleberger, author

It was not until the XII century, 700 years after the fall of Rome in 452 AD, that debt instruments and markets resumed their development in the merchant cities of Italy (principally Venice and Genoa) as the result of the development of trade with the Arab world and the Far East (the Silk Route), and the financing and provisioning of the Crusades.

To finance fleets and wars, Italian cities pioneered the issue of debt securities to their citizens, known as government bonds (*prestiti*), a critical invention in the development of debt, finance and the history of the State. Cities that were "Republican", or institutionalized (i.e. governed by their citizens, such as Venice and Genoa) were better credits than cities governed by a prince or a dynasty that was not institutionalized (e.g. the Medici in Florence). Similarly, it was in Venice and Genoa that durable banking institutions developed, as well as a secondary market for government debt.[5]

The Italian inventions[6] of banking and state finance subsequently migrated to Northern Europe, and were developed in the cities of Bruges, Antwerp and Amsterdam, which became commercial and financial centers. A Stock Exchange started in Bruges in the XIV century, in Antwerp in 1531, and in Amsterdam in 1613, with the Amsterdam Wisselbank (predecessor of its Central Bank) being formed in 1609.[7] In 1618, a system of official pawnshops (*montes de piedad*) was established in the Netherlands, and, in 1624, a perpetual corporate bond was issued by the Lekdyk Bovensdams Company, which was still paying interest in 1957.

5.2.3   The XVIII century - England

England was transformed both financially and politically by the Revolution of 1688, when King William III of Orange (Holland) was invited to govern the country. The fact that he was a constitutional king, and his Dutch origins, contributed to the establishment of the credit of the English crown, and the development of financial institutions on the Dutch model. From 1692, the government began to issue a series of loans to finance the war against France. In 1694, investors who subscribed to a new loan received the additional right, with maximum subscriptions of £20,000, to incorporate themselves as the "Governor and Company of the Bank of England", which began operations in 1695.

With the influence of the Dutch and the wealth generated by the British empire in the XVIII century, the new Bank of England began to offer a wide range of new securities, accepting deposits, issuing paper money, trading currencies and metals, and discounting commercial paper.[8]

---

[5]The Bank of Venice was established in 1157, the Bank of St. George (Genoa) in 1407, and the Bank of Rialto (Venice) in 1587.

[6]Also in Italy, in 1494, Fra Luca Pacioli of Florence published the first book on double entry bookkeeping, *Summa de Arithmetica*.

[7]The Swedish Riksbank, founded in 1656, was the first issuer of paper money (1661), and, on being nationalized in 1668, became the first central bank in the world.

[8]The landed gentry opposed the financial innovations of the Bank – the Tory party against the Whigs. They denounced financial activity and the increase in

Subsequently, during the same century, practically all the major financial instruments currently in use were either developed or refined in England. These securities included: government bonds (including Consols, permanent debt that still exists), and long term corporate bonds (for the canals): the money market (organized by the Bank of England): companies with traded shares, and stock exchanges for trading stocks and debt securities ([ ] 7.2 for the history of global stock markets): private deposit and mortgage banks; and an insurance market (Lloyd's), and insurance companies.

5.2.4 Spain

During the expansionary period of the European empires, Spain stayed outside the mainstream of financial development in Northern Europe. There were three main reasons for this:

- The discovery of the Americas provided an apparently unlimited supply of wealth (gold and silver) and, therefore, the illusion of self-sufficiency.
- The Counterreformation of Catholicism against Protestantism exacerbated the prejudice against usury.
- The expulsion of the Arabs and the Jews caused a significant loss of commercial and financial talent.

Owing to the absence of an efficient system of domestic financial intermediation, the kings of Spain, beginning with Charles V, had to seek finance from international bankers (principally Genoese and Germans), guaranteeing it with the flow of metals from the Americas.[9] However, owing to the instability of metals flows and prices, the Spanish crown suspended payments on foreign debt 12 times between the XVI and XIX centuries.

5.2.5 XIX and XX centuries – England and United States

In the XIX century, the English financial system developed even more, keeping pace with, and contributing to, the development of the Empire. In the first half of the century, after the end of the Napoleonic Wars, the English market opened for loans to other governments (including the recently independent countries of Latin America), a

---

government debt (with the consequent transference of power from the country to the city) as "Dutch finance".

[9]Carande, Ramón, *Carlos V y Sus Banqueros* (Sociedad de Estudios y Publicaciones, 1965), pp. 262-264.

building was constructed for the Stock Exchange, company formation was encouraged, and the expansion of the railways was financed.

In the second half of the century, the formation of joint stock banks (*sociedades anónimas bancarias*) was permitted, and the first issue of Treasury bills (*certificados de tesorería*) was made for the British government. British financial development was transferred to the rest of Europe, to the United States and other countries around the world (Latin America, India, South Africa, Australia and Canada) - the so-called "golden age" of world capitalism.

Following the end of the Civil War in the US (1865), a determining event in its consolidation as a nation, its stock and bond markets developed rapidly, as a means of financing the expansion of the new railway, steel and other industrial companies.

With World War I, the Russian Revolution, and the protectionism of the 1930s, financial market expansion slowed, or (in the case of Communist countries) stopped. With the resumption of globalization after World War II, debt securities and markets were expanded to the largest number of countries (called also "emerging markets" - 📖 1.3) in human history.

Few new debt securities were "invented" following their original introduction in England in the XVIII century. However, the great innovation of the 1970s was the "unbundling" (*desarticulación*) of the different risks implicit in debt securities, facilitated by advances in financial theory and technology (📖 2.4.2). The result was a proliferation of derivatives traded on specialized exchanges (e.g. Chicago Board of Trade, Chicago Mercantile Exchange) or stock markets (📖 9.2).

5.3 HISTORY OF MEXICAN DEBT INSTRUMENTS

5.3.1 Precolonial and colonial period

The Aztecs are known to have used credit as debts existed between them. Their laws included punishments of prison and slavery for insolvent debtors.[10] After the Conquest, Hernán Cortés contracted personal debt for 4 thousand pesos and merchandise debts for the same amount, guaranteeing them with his properties and Indian slaves. The Indians had Community Chests (*Cajas de Comunidades*), but they were badly managed and did not develop.

---

[10]Lagunilla Iñarritu, Alfredo, *Historia de la Banca y Moneda en México* (Editorial Jus, 1981), pp. 29-63.

Figure 5–3 History of debt in Mexico: important dates

1536	First mint of the Americas founded in Mexico
1775	Monte de Piedad (pawnshop) founded by Pedro Romero de Terreros
XIX	
1824	First debt issue by Mexican government in London
	(Debt suspensions 1827, 1832, 1838, 1846, 1847, 1861)
1830	Banco de Avío para Fomento de la Industria Nacional founded
1842	Banco de Avío liquidated by General Antonio López de Santa Anna
1864	Bank of London, Mexico and South America founded by Englishmen
1884	Banco Nacional Mexicano merges with Banco Mercantil Mexicano
	to form Banco Nacional de México
1884	Commerce Code (*Código de Comercio*) includes first banking legislation
1889	Renegotiation of foreign debt, resumption of foreign borrowing
1897	First Banking Law (Ley Bancaria) defines issuing, mortgage and industrial banks
1895	First Stock Exchange (Bolsa de Valores)
XX	
1907	Second Bolsa foundation
1922	De la Huerta-Lamont Treaty for foreign debt
1924	First National Banking Convention (*Convención Nacional Bancaria*)
	Creation of National Banking Commission (*Comisión Nacional Bancaria*)
1925	Bank of Mexico (Banco de México) founded
1926	Banco Nacional de Crédito Agrícola (now Banrural), first development bank, founded
1927	Pani Amendment for foreign debt
1931	Montes de Oca-Lamont Agreement for foreign debt
1932	First Law of Credit Institutions (Ley de Instituciones de Credito)
1933	Banco Nacional Hipotecario, Urbano y de Obras Públicas (Banobras) founded
1934	Nacional Financiera (*Nafin*) founded
1935	Banco Nacional de Crédito Ejidal (now *Banrural*) founded
1937	Banco Nacional de Comercio Exterior (*Bancomext*) founded
1942-6	Suárez-Lamont Agreements for foreign debt
1946	National Securities Commission (*Comisión Nacional de Valores*) founded
1973	Explosive growth of foreign debt begins
1975	First Securities Market Law (*Ley del Mercado de Valores*)
1977	Petrobonds (*petrobonos*), securities linked to oil price, introduced
	Unsecured bonds (*obligaciones quirografarias*) introduced
1978	First issue of Certificados de Tesorería (*Cetes*)
1978-81	Oil boom causes petrodollar recycling to Mexico
1980	Commercial paper (*papel comercial*)
1981	Bank acceptances (*aceptaciones bancarias*)
1982	Promissory notes (*pagarés fiduciarios*)
1982	Crisis of foreign bank debt
	Bank nationalization
1983	Bank indemnity bonds (*bonos de indemnización bancaria - BIBs*)
1984	Fixed income mutual funds (*sociedades de inversión de renta fija*)
1985	Bank development bonds (*bonos bancarios de desarrollo*)
1986	Urban renovation bonds (*bonos de renovación urbana - BOREs*)
	Dollar-denominated promissory notes (*pagafes*)
1987	Convertible subordinated bonds (*obligaciones subordinadas convertibles*)
	Development bonds (*bonos de desarrollo - Bondes*)
1989	Plan Brady to convert public sector bank debt to bonds agreed

Figure 5–3 (cont.)	
1989	Mexico returns to international capital market for first time since 1982
	Adjustable bonds (*bonos ajustables del gobierno federal - ajustabonos*)
	Treasury bonds (*bonos de la tesorería del gobierno federal - tesobonos*)
1990	First rating agency, Calificadora de Valores (*Caval*)
	Conversion of bank debt to Brady par and discount bonds
1991-1994	Eurobond boom for public and corporate borrowers
1994	Permission for foreign banks and brokers to operate in Mexico (NAFTA)
1995	Mexico returns to international capital markets after 1994 crisis
1996	Udibonds (*bonos de desarrollo del gobierno federal denominados en UDIs - Udibonos*)
1997	Futures on Cetes and TIIE on Chicago Mercantile Exchange
1998	Mexican derivatives market (MexDer) begins trading Cete, TIIE, UDI futures
Source: author	

However, during the 300 years of the Spanish Empire (1521-1821) and the first period of Mexican Independence (1821-1864), there was no institutionalized credit in Mexico. An important factor was the absence (📖 5.2.4) of a developed financial system in Spain. At a time when the Italians, and subsequently the countries of Northern Europe, had developed money, capital and credit markets, Spain was backward, and this backwardness was transmitted to its Colonies.

"What can be considered an incipient banking activity remained in the hands of the clergy and of individuals, who, without a legal concession, or regulations beyond those dictated by their own interest, made bank loans and guaranteed loans, issuing in some cases securities of limited circulation, which can be considered the embryonic beginnings of an issuing banking system".[11]

The only lasting financial institution of the Empire (*virreinato*) was established in February 1775, 254 years after the fall of Tenochtitlán. It was the *Monte de Piedad de Animas* (pawnshop), based on a similar institution that had been founded in 1702 in Madrid. It was founded by Pedro Romero de Terreros, a mining baron, the first Count of Regla, and the richest man of his time, as a way of helping the needy. It received royal patronage, with a Board formed by the Viceroy and its founder. It functioned for 46 years during the colonial period (1775-1821), and made 35,000 loans of a total value estimated between 400 and 600 thousand pesos.

---

[11]Lagunilla, citing Enrique Creel de la Barra, *op. cit.* p. 38. See also Luis Cerda, *Historia Financiera del Banco Nacional de México* (Fomento Cultural Banamex A. C., 1997), pp. 45-46.

5.3.2 Independence

5.3.2.1 Foreign debt

Owing to the absence of a domestic financial market, the new Mexican state contracted its first loans in London, in 1824 and 1825, for £16 millions. These loans were part of the first international loan boom in the London capital market following the Napoleonic Wars (📖 5.2.5).[12]

However, the conditions of the loan were tough, and debt service was difficult almost from the date of signature. Just three years after contracting its first loan, the Mexican government, following the long tradition of the Spanish crown, declared its first moratorium on foreign debt service. In the first 50 years of Mexican foreign debt, there were 6 payments suspensions (in 1827, 1832, 1838, 1846, 1847, and 1861).[13] The two main reasons were the Mexican government's inability to manage its finances to cover its debt obligations, and the inability of creditors to adjust their requirements to the government's ability to pay.

5.3.2.2 The first bank

In 1830, the government created the *Banco de Avío* (with the full name of the *Banco de Avío para Fomento de la Industria Nacional*), with a Board composed of three members, presided over by the Minister for Foreign Relations. The bank made loans to textile companies located in Tlalnepantla, Tlaxcala and Puebla. However, civil war began in Veracruz in 1832, and, after various attempts at normal operation, the bank was dissolved in 1842 under orders from General Antonio López de Santa Anna.

5.3.3 The Porfirian Period

5.3.3.1 Foreign debt

Mexico's external credit rating recovered as a result of economic and political stabilization during the Porfirian period (*porfiriato*). After the

---

[12]Secretaría de Hacienda y Crédito Público, *Deuda Externa Pública Mexicana* (Fondo de Cultura Económica, S. A. de C. V., 1988), pp. 12-15.

[13]George White, representative of Baring Brothers, the English bank, arrived in Mexico in 1862 to analyze the feasibility of repayment of the sovereign debt, of which Barings was the bondholders' representative in London. After one year, he returned to England, without success. The letters (which offer a prototype of "country risk analysis") and watercolor paintings produced by White during his stay in Mexico are still preserved in the head office of Barings (now ING Barings) in London.

conversion of existing debt negotiated by Manuel Dublán in 1889, foreign debt increased by 300% in foreign exchange terms between 1890 and 1911 (from $52.5 to $441.5 millions in pesos).

5.3.3.2 Banking system

Just as Holland had imported financial technology from Italy, and England from Holland, Mexico imported its first modern bank from England, at practically the same time as the joint stock bank boom in London (📖 5.2.5). In July 1864, at the beginning of Maximilian's "empire", the Bank of London, Mexico and South America (now *Banca Serfin*), was founded by Messrs. William Newbold and Robert Geddes, who had been granted a concession by the Board of Directors of the Bank of Mexico and South America Limited. The bank continued to operate following the fall of Maximilian and restoration of Republican government in 1867.

There was a banking boom during the *porfiriato*. The Banco de Santa Eulalia was founded in 1875, Banco Mexicano in 1878 and the Banco Minero de Chihuahua and Banco Mercantil Mexicano in 1882. In 1881, a French financial group was granted a concession to found the Banco Nacional Mexicano, with special powers to lend to the government and issue paper money. In 1884, as a result of a financial and monetary crisis that caused the bankruptcy of the Monte de Piedad, this bank was merged with the Banco Mercantil Mexicano to form the "Banco Nacional de México".

The Commerce Code (*Código de Comercio*) of 1884 was the result of the banking crisis of that year, and included the first banking legislation.[14] The first Banking Law (of 1897) defined three kinds of bank: issuing banks (*bancos de emisión*), mortgage banks (*bancos hipotecarios*), and industrial banks (*bancos refaccionarios*). By the end of the XIX century, there were 23 banks in Mexico.

5.3.4 The Revolution

5.3.4.1 Foreign debt

The Revolution interrupted the recovery of Mexico's external debt rating that had occurred during the *porfiriato*, and Mexico did not issue voluntary foreign debt between 1911 and 1946. However, the value of its foreign debt increased five and a half times, owing to the compounding of unpaid debt service. There were three efforts to resolve the foreign debt problem during this period: the De la Huerta-Lamont Treaty in

---

[14]Cerda, *op. cit.*, pp. 60-62.

1922, the Pani Amendment in 1927 and the Montes de Oca-Lamont Agreement in 1931. However, none was successful, and definitive agreement was only reached between 1942 and 1946, with the Suárez-Lamont Agreements.

5.3.4.2 Banking system

When the Revolution broke out in 1910, there were 24 banks. However, in June 1914, following the removal of President Huerta, the new government of Venustiano Carranza ordered banks to replenish their reserves, which had fallen owing to the Revolution. Fifteen banks could not comply with the order, and were forced into liquidation. Several years of crisis and reconstruction followed.

The first National Banking Convention (*Convención Nacional Bancaria*), in January 1924, had four important consequences for the development of the credit system:

- A new General Law of Credit Institutions (*Ley General de Instituciones de Crédito*) modifying the 1897 Law to take account of new conditions,
- The creation of a National Banking Commission (*Comisión Nacional Bancaria*),
- The foundation of a new central bank, the Bank of Mexico *(Banco de México)*, and
- The foundation of the first development bank, the National Bank of Agricultural Credit (*Banco Nacional de Crédito Agrícola*).

5.3.4.3 Creation of Bank of Mexico and development banks

The Bank of Mexico was founded as the only bank authorized to issue currency on September 1, 1925. An important precedent had been set by the formation of the Federal Reserve System in the US in 1913. Another had been the establishment of central banks in Bolivia, Colombia and Uruguay in previous years.[15]

As part of the same thrust, state development banks were established during the 1920s and 1930s: the National Bank of Agricultural Credit (*Banco Nacional de Crédito Agrícola* - now *Banrural*) in 1926, the National Mortgage Urban and Public Works Bank (*Banco Nacional Hipotecario, Urbano y de Obras Públicas* - now *Banobras*) in 1933, Nacional Financiera in 1934, the National Bank of Ejido Credit (*Banco Nacional de Crédito Ejidal* - now also *Banrural*) in 1935, and the

---

[15]Chile established its central bank almost simultaneously and Argentina, Ecuador and Peru a few years later.

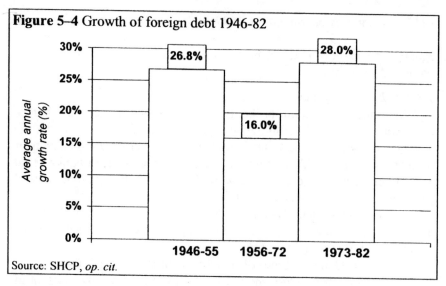

Figure 5–4 Growth of foreign debt 1946-82

Source: SHCP, *op. cit.*

National Bank of Foreign Trade (*Banco Nacional de Comercio Exterior*) in 1937.

5.3.5 The modern period

5.3.5.1 Foreign debt

After the 1946 agreement, Mexico's foreign debt increased continuously and rapidly, from 1% of GDP in 1946 to 35.9% in 1982. However, its growth during the period was uneven (figure 5–4). The greatest increase occurred between 1973 and 1982, beginning with the deficit budgets of Luis Echeverría, and culminating in the oil and credit spiral of José López Portillo. In contrast to the 1994 crisis, which was a crisis of foreign debt contracted on the international capital markets, 1982 was a crisis of foreign debt contracted with foreign banks.

The voluntary return of the Mexican government to the international capital markets for the first time since 1982 was marked by the issue, seven years afterwards in 1989, of a eurobond (by the National Bank of

Figure 5–5 Mexican foreign debt: net value 1990-98 (US$bn.)

	1990	1991	1992	1993	1994	1995	1996	1997	1998
Government	84.3	86.7	81.7	83.5	89.3	118.2	111.6	97.4	100.7
Corporate	22.5	30.3	34.8	47.0	50.5	47.4	45.6	52.2	60.6
Total	106.7	117.0	116.5	130.5	139.8	165.6	157.1	149.6	161.3

Government: includes Bank of Mexico debt
Corporate: includes bank debt
Source: SHCP

Foreign Trade). Brady bonds were exchanged for bank debt in 1990. With the relaxation of regulations on foreign portfolio investment in 1989 (🕮 1.4.1) and the emerging stock market boom of the early 1990s, there was also a boom in Mexican foreign debt issues for both public and private sectors between 1990 and 1994. After the crisis of December 1994, the flow of foreign debt to Mexico was renewed in July 1995, just seven months later (figure 5–5).

5.3.5.2 Debt markets

The development of a domestic debt market in parallel with the banking system began with the first Securities Market Law (*Ley del Mercado de Valores*) of 1975. The Law laid the foundations for the development of the stock market with the institutionalization of brokerage houses and a comprehensive regulation of the MSE, financial intermediaries, and issuers.

Petrobonds and unsecured corporate bonds were introduced in 1977. A key event for the development of the debt markets was the introduction in 1978 of Treasury Bills (*Certificados de Tesorería - "Cetes"*), as the basis for a money market and a mechanism for monetary policy. As an extension of the money market, commercial paper was introduced in 1980 and bank acceptances in 1981.

Figure 5–6 Main Mexican debt securities 1998		
	Government	*Corporate**
Pesos		
Money market	Cetes	Bank acceptances
	Bondes	Commercial paper
	Bondes 91	
	Udibonos	
Long term		Bank bonds
		Corporate bonds
		Commercial paper
Other currencies		
Money market		Commercial paper
Long term	Eurobonds	Eurobonds
	Brady bonds	
* includes financial institutions		
Source: author		

Figure 5–7 Mexican securities market trading 1991-98

(US$ bn.)	1991	1992	1993	1994	1995	1996	1997	1998
Stocks	39.4	50.6	64.3	89.2	35.7	43.8	55.5	37.1
Long term debt	7.6	11.4	17.5	15.0	7.7	2.8	1.0	0.9
Money market	1682.7	3534.8	4550.4	4011.2	721.0	908.1	1820.3	1268.5
Total	1729.7	3596.8	4632.2	4115.4	764.4	954.7	1876.7	1306.6
(percentage)								
Stocks	2.3	1.4	1.4	2.2	4.7	4.6	3.0	2.8
Long term debt	0.4	0.3	0.4	0.4	1.0	0.3	0.1	0.1
Money market	97.3	98.3	98.2	97.5	94.3	95.1	97.0	97.1
Total	100.0	100.0	100.0	100.0	100.0	100.0	100.0	100.0

Source: MSE

To extend Cetes' maturities, development bonds (*Bonos de Desarrollo - Bondes*) were introduced in 1987. Following a decade ravaged by inflation and to encourage longer term savings, index-linked inflation bonds (*bonos ajustables - ajustabonos*) were introduced in 1989, to be replaced by "Udibonos" in 1996. "Tesobonos" were introduced in 1989 as a form of dollar-denominated Cetes: they became very popular during 1994 owing to exchange rate uncertainty, and were withdrawn from circulation in 1995, as a result of the 1994-95 crisis.

5.4 TRADING AND ISSUE OF DEBT SECURITIES

The main Mexican debt securities (figure 5–6) can be classified by issuer (government or corporate), currency (peso or other), and maturity (money market or long term).[16]

5.4.1 Peso securities

In 1998, debt trading valued at US$1,269 bn. represented 97.1% of all MSE trading by value, compared with 2.8% for stocks (figure 5–7). Corporate debt accounted for US$379.4 bn., or 29.9%, of all debt trading. This implies that government securities accounted for 70.1% of debt trading.

The breakdown of trading between different government securities has fluctuated over the last seven years (figure 5–8). In 1991 and 1992, trading in Cetes, the traditional money market instrument, dominated. In 1993, the importance of Bonde trading increased owing to brighter longer term prospects for the economy: this trend was reversed in 1994. In 1994, owing to exchange rate uncertainty, there was an increase in tesobono trading. In 1995, trading in tesobonos increased even more (reflecting their withdrawal from circulation) and Cete trading fell:

---

[16]Despite their maturities (from 3 to 5 years), ajustabonos and Udibonos are classified as "money market" owing to the way in which they are traded.

Figure 5–8 Main Mexican debt securities: value traded 1991-98

	1991	1992	1993	1994	1995	1996	1997	1998
Public (US$bn.)								
Cetes	1533.1	3283.4	456.8	3600.3	215.8	175.2	717.8	481.8
Bondes	38.6	77.8	3896.1	173.9	229.7	263.9	484.8	207.3
Tesobonos	0.3	2.8	2.0	35.7	42.0	0.0	0.0	0.0
Ajustabonos	88.8	154.1	178.7	187.9	206.7	449.2	152.7	24.5
Udibonos						0.1	344.3	175.4
Subtotal	1660.8	3518.1	4533.6	3997.8	694.2	888.4	1699.6	889.0
(percentage)								
Cetes	92.3	93.3	10.1	90.1	31.1	19.7	42.2	54.2
Bondes	2.3	2.2	85.9	4.3	33.1	29.7	28.5	23.3
Tesobonos	0.0	0.1	0.0	0.9	6.1	0.0	0.0	0.0
Ajustabonos	5.3	4.4	3.9	4.7	29.8	50.6	9.0	2.8
Udibonos						0.0	20.3	19.7
Total	100.0	100.0	100.0	100.0	100.0	100.0	100.0	100.0
Corporate (US$bn.)								
Highway indemnity bonds								84.0
Bank acceptances				0.0	0.0	0.1	13.4	19.1
Bank promissory notes				0.5	0.0	0.0	65.2	218.1
Bank bonds				0.0	0.0	1.4	2.0	18.0
Medium term notes						0.4	2.2	2.3
Commercial paper				13.4	26.8	17.7	37.5	34.7
Other				0.3	0.0	0.1	0.4	3.3
Total	0.0	0.0	0.0	14.3	26.8	19.7	120.7	379.4
(percentage)								
Highway indemnity bonds				0.0	0.0	0.0	0.0	22.1
Bank acceptances				0.1	0.0	0.6	11.1	5.0
Bank promissory notes				3.4	0.1	0.1	54.0	57.5
Bank bonds				0.1	0.0	7.2	1.7	4.7
Medium term notes				0.0	0.0	2.0	1.8	0.6
Commercial paper				94.2	99.8	89.8	31.1	9.1
Other				2.2	0.0	0.3	0.4	0.9
Total				100.0	100.0	100.0	100.0	100.0

Source: MSE

Bonde trading increased, reflecting the desire by the government to lengthen the term structure of its domestic debt. In 1996, tesobonos had disappeared, Cete trading fell, and ajustabono and Bonde trading rose, owing to the outlook of falling interest rates from very high levels and above all owing to repo operations (*reportos* - 📖 B.2) by financial intermediaries. In 1997, there was an important increase in Cete and Bonde trading, along with a gradual substitution of ajustabonos by Udibonos. In 1998, the rise in Cete trading (compared to Bondes) was due to the rise in interest rates during the year.

Figure 5–9 Traded debt: value outstanding 1998 (US$bn.)			
	Government*	Private**	Total	%
Pesos	32.4	9.2	41.6	37.6%
Dollars	51.9	17.2	69.1	62.4%
Total	84.3	26.4	110.7	
%	76.2%	23.8%		

* In pesos, domestic traded debt: in dollars, bonds in international markets
** In pesos, debt securities placed on the MSE: in dollars, eurobonds
and commercial paper on international markets
Source: MSE, SHCP

5.4.2 Dollar securities

Main dollar debt securities are Brady bonds issued by the Mexican government in 1990 to replace foreign bank debt, and eurobonds issued on the international capital market both by the government and by corporate issuers, since the market reopened for Mexican issuers in 1989.

As there is no "stock exchange" in the international capital market where trades are registered and measured, trading is either telephonic or screen-based, and therefore there are no reliable statistics for trading in Mexican dollar debt securities traded offshore. [17] However, at the end of 1998, there were statistics on their value outstanding, which can be compared with the value outstanding of peso securities (figure 5–9).

The value outstanding of dollar denominated securities was larger (62%) than that of peso securities (38%) (📖 1.4.3.2). Of total value outstanding, government securities represented 76% and private sector securities 24%. Of private sector traded debt (US$26 bn.) 65% was in dollars and 35% in pesos.

5.4.3 Liquidity of debt securities

The conclusion of the previous sections is that the most liquid (*bursátil*) peso debt securities are Cetes, Bondes and Udibonos, and dollar securities are Brady bonds and eurobonds. As Mexico's inflation rate falls (and, therefore, the cost of money), its economy recovers, and institutional investment develops (through Afores and mutual funds - 📖 11.5.3), it is probable that the availability of private sector peso debt securities with longer maturities will increase. For this reason, in the following sections and in 📖 ch. 6, we provide descriptions and analysis

---

[17]In 1997, some government dollar debt securities were admitted to the MSE, but trading was low (US$30.8 mn. in 1997 and US$127.2 mn. in 1998).

techniques not only for securities that are currently liquid, but also for those whose liquidity might increase in the future.

5.5 PRINCIPAL FEATURES OF DEBT SECURITIES

All debt securities have certain common features. These features reflect the fact that debt securities represent a loan (*préstamo*) by the investor to the debtor (*deudor*), or issuer (*emisor*). Therefore, evaluation of these securities is similar to the credit analysis performed by a bank, a company that offers credit to its clients, or an individual who lends money to a relative or friend.

The eight main features of debt securities are:

5.5.1 Issuer (debtor)

There are two kinds of issuer: the government and the private sector (which includes both financial institutions and companies). The government borrows in the domestic market mainly through Cetes, Bondes, and Udibonos, and in the international market through eurobonds.[18] Financial institutions borrow in the domestic securities markets through bank acceptances or bonds, and in the international markets through eurobonds. Companies borrow in the domestic securities markets through commercial paper, medium term notes and bonds, and in the international capital market through eurocommercial paper and eurobonds.

5.5.2 Security

If the government (or a parastatal organization like Nacional Financiera, or Petróleos Mexicanos) is the issuer, there is normally no specific security (*garantía*) for the issue.[19] If a company is the issuer, there may be security (mortgage bond), or not (commercial paper, unsecured bond or eurobond).

5.5.3 Amount

In the case of issues by the government, there is no practical limit[20] for individual issues of Cetes, Udibonos or eurobonds: the amount depends on the government's needs and its borrowing capacity in each market. Bank securities have regulatory limits related to the level of

---

[18]Brady bonds reflect the conversion of bank debt: eurobonds are new debt.

[19]The US loan to Mexico following the 1994 financial crisis was secured on Mexican oil exports.

[20]There is, however, an overall limit for government borrowing approved annually by Congress.

capital and reserves of each bank issuer. In the case of companies, there is no formal limit on the amount of an issue in the domestic or international markets.

5.5.4 Face value

In the case of traded debt securities, the total amount of an issue is divided into securities of a lower denomination, in order to facilitate secondary market liquidity. For example, the "face value" or "nominal value" (*valor nominal*) of Cetes is $10 and of commercial paper is $100. In the international market, the face value of eurobonds is US$1,000: for Bradys, the minimum amount is US$250,000 with subsequent increments of US$1,000.

5.5.5 Rate of return

The rate of return can be expressed in two ways. In the money market, it is quoted as a "discount rate" (*tasa de descuento*), from which a "rate of return" or "yield" (*tasa de rendimiento*) is derived for the relevant maturity. In the case of peso and dollar bank securities and longer term traded securities, the rate of return is expressed as an interest rate or coupon (*cupón*), which can be either fixed (*fija*) or floating (*flotante*). The floating rate is set, for peso securities, at a premium over the rate for government or bank securities, and, for dollar securities, at a premium over US$ LIBOR or the US government Tbill or Tbond rate.

5.5.6 Payments

Payments representing the returns on a debt instrument can be made at maturity (in the case of the money market), or at regular intervals, either monthly, quarterly, semiannually or annually (in the case of other securities).

5.5.7 Term

The term of an instrument can vary from one day (money market) to 30 years (Brady bonds or eurobonds).

5.5.8 Amortization

Amortization (*amortización*) can occur at maturity (money market) or in installments at regular intervals prior to maturity. Similarly, there can be "call or put options" (*derechos de compra o venta anticipada*) that permit redemption either in whole or in part before maturity.

Figure 5–10 Main government debt securities

	Cete	Bonde	Ajustabono	Udibono
Issuer	government	government	government	government
Guarantee	no	no	no	no
Amount	without limit	without limit	without limit	without limit
Face value	$10	$100	$100	100 UDIs
Rate of return	discount	Cetes or UDIs	real rate	real rate
Payments	sale or maturity	28 days	quarterly	semiannual
Term	7-728 days	1-3 years	3, 5 years	3, 5 years
Amortization	maturity	maturity	maturity	maturity

Source: author

5.6 GOVERNMENT PESO DEBT SECURITIES

5.6.1 Cetes

The Certificado de Tesorería ("Cete") was first issued, for a term of 91 days, in January 1978.[21] It was the first instrument consciously designed for the securities market, as the foundation for the development of a money market.

Cetes are issued through an auction system managed by the Bank of Mexico. Every Friday, the Bank announces amounts and maturities of the Cetes to be issued the following Thursday to financial institutions (brokerages, banks and insurance companies) permitted to buy Cetes directly from the Bank through the auction mechanism. Before 13:30 PM the following Tuesday, participants in the auction must send to the Bank bids (*posturas*) for amounts, maturities and discount rates, along with a "guaranteed" amount (*monto asegurado*), i.e., the amount they are prepared to accept at the blended rate for all the bids received for the relevant instrument. On the same Tuesday, at 15:00 PM, the result of the auction is announced in terms of the amount issued and its average (blended) discount rate.

---

[21]The 28-day Cete was first issued in August 1982.

On the Thursday, i.e. the issue date, the financial institution credits the Bank with the funds, which represent its total purchase price for each issue. Meanwhile, the Bank registers the number of Cetes sold with the name of each institution that has purchased them, and publishes in the newspapers of the same day the official announcement of the issue (or issues, where relevant) with their corresponding term, weighted average discount rate and rate of return to maturity.

The Bank has auctioned issues with maturities from 7 days (in periods of high inflationary uncertainty), to 728 days (in periods of greater calm). In 1998, there were issues between 28 and 364 days. There are times when the Bank is unable to place all the Cetes on offer, for lack of demand, or because it does not consider the bids "adequate". In these cases, the Bank can also sell Cetes in the secondary market.

The importance and popularity of the Cete is due to its high liquidity, security (owing to the explicit backing of the Federal Government) and the possibility of performing repo (*reporto*) operations (📖 B.2). We provide a guide to the most useful calculations for Cetes and other money market securities (bank acceptances and commercial paper) in 📖 B.1.

5.6.2 Bondes

The Bono de Desarrollo del Gobierno Federal (*Bonde*) was first introduced in October 1987 as an instrument with a longer term than the Cete, but that could be traded as a money market security.

Bondes are issued for a minimum maturity of 364 days and a maximum (so far) of 3 years. Interest payments are on a 28 day basis. The rate is set every 28 days as the greater of the yield on 28 day Cetes and one month bank promissory notes (*pagarés bancarios a un mes*). In October 1997, inflation indexed Bondes were introduced with a three year maturity, and yields linked to 91 day Cetes, or inflation (measured by the increase in value of the UDI), whichever is higher.

Bondes are issued in the same way as Cetes, through an auction managed by Bank of Mexico and, like Cetes, they are settled each Thursday. Similarly, bids are placed at a discount to face value, and Bondes are allocated to the bidder who offers the lowest discount.

Owing to the discount mechanism through which they are issued, Bondes offer a higher yield than Cetes, owing to their longer term. Like Cetes, they are traded in the money market and can be used for repos.

5.6.3 Ajustabono and Udibono

The *Bono Ajustable del Gobierno Federal* (*ajustobono*) was first issued in 1989, and was discontinued in 1996 owing to the introduction of a very similar instrument, the *Bono de Desarrollo del Gobierno Federal denominado en Unidades de Inversión* (UDIs), or "Udibono", which was first issued in May 1996.[22]

The Udibono offers the investor a rate fixed above the inflation rate. It is denominated in UDIs, which are *unidades de inversión* (investment units) whose value increases (and is published) daily according to the inflation rate measured by the Consumer Price Index (*Indice Nacional de Precios al Consumidor - INPC*). It is issued through auctions managed by Bank of Mexico every two weeks at a real interest rate payable semiannually, for maturities of 3 and 5 years.

For the investor, the importance of the Udibono is that it provides him with the opportunity of receiving a guaranteed real rate (above inflation), and therefore it represents the long term "risk-free rate" of the Mexican financial market (📖 2.3.2). It can also be used for repos, which implies increased liquidity both for investors and for financial intermediaries.

While the Udibono concept is simple, techniques for calculating price and yield for trading purposes are relatively complex. We provide an explanation in 📖 B.3.

5.7 CORPORATE PESO DEBT SECURITIES

5.7.1 Bank acceptances

Bank acceptances (*aceptaciones bancarias*) were first issued in 1981, as a complement to the other options available in the money market: Cetes (1978), and commercial paper (1980). Acceptances are loans made by the bank to a company and documented through a bill of exchange "accepted" by the bank. This bill (or acceptance) is then traded (or discounted) in the money market through one or several financial institutions. Even though the borrowing company uses the funds, the risk for the investor is on the accepting bank. However, the bank funds itself not through deposits, but the money market.

Acceptances normally have terms similar to those of Cetes. The yield is set through a negotiation between the accepting bank and the issuing

---

[22]The main differences between the ajustabono and the Udibono are:
- the ajustabono pays interest quarterly, the Udibono semiannually, and
- the real rate of the ajustabono is fixed in relation to the Mexican CPI, while for the Udibono it is fixed in relation to the UDI.

Figure 5–11 Main corporate debt securities

	Bank acceptances	Commercial paper	Medium term commercial paper	Corporate bond
Issuer	bank	corporate	corporate	corporate
Guarantee	no	possible	possible	possible
Amount	proportion of capital and reserves	no specific limit	no specific limit	no specific limit
Face value	$100	$100	$100	$10
Rate of return	discount	discount	or multiples interest rate	or multiples interest rate
Payments	sale or maturity	sale or maturity	quarterly semiannual	quarterly semiannual
Term	up to 182 days	up to 91 days	up to 5 years	variable
Amortization	maturity	maturity	prior to or at maturity	prior to or at maturity

Source: author

house, in relation to the expected yield of the next Cete issue. As the bank is a private company, it is perceived as riskier than the government and therefore acceptances are issued at a higher yield than Cetes.

Yield calculations for acceptances are the same as those for Cetes, the main difference being that the face value of acceptances is $100, compared to a face value of $10 for Cetes (📖 B.1).

5.7.2 Commercial paper

Commercial paper (*papel comercial*) was first issued in 1980. It takes the form of a promissory note (*pagaré*) issued by a company (whose stock may or may not be listed on the MSE). Maturity is normally 91 days, and the yield is set through a negotiation between the issuing house and the company.

Commercial paper has a face value of $100 and price, discount and yield calculations are the same as for Cetes (📖 B.1).[23]

5.7.3 Medium term commercial paper

Medium term commercial paper (*pagaré a mediano plazo*) is the equivalent of short term commercial paper, but issued at terms between 3 and 5 years. It has a face value of $100, and its interest rate, payable

[23]Since 1990, rating agencies have rated commercial paper, medium term commercial paper, and bonds issued in pesos in Mexico. We provide an explanation of their rating systems in 📖 6.5.5.

quarterly or semiannually, is set at a premium above a reference rate (normally that for government or bank securities).

5.7.4 Corporate bonds

Corporate bonds (*obligaciones corporativas*) are long term debt securities issued by companies (industrial, commercial, financial and services) and listed on the MSE. They offer a yield through interest payments, normally either quarterly or semiannual. Amortization of principal is either in installments, or a bullet payment at maturity.

Prior to 1977, the company that issued most bonds was TELMEX, which made regular issues of mortgage bonds (guaranteed by the assets of the company). In 1977, a new kind of bond was authorized, the unsecured bond (*obligación quirografaria*), so called in Spanish because the only guarantee was the signature (*quirógrafo*) of authorized signatories of the company.

Bonds have provided returns in different ways over time, depending on economic conditions in Mexico. When the inflation rate was relatively low and stable (prior to 1976), TELMEX mortgage bonds were issued at a fixed rate, in pesos. When inflation became more volatile (after 1976), bonds began to be issued at floating rates, revised quarterly, at a premium over a reference rate, usually of government or bank securities.

The most recent innovation is the issue of bonds denominated in UDIs, with a similar structure to government Udibonos. The principal amount is fixed in UDIs, with a value that increases daily according to the estimated inflation rate. The instrument pays a real interest rate (quarterly or semiannual), that is applied to the value of the instrument in UDIs on the date of payment. The real rate of interest payable by the issuer is fixed at a premium over the real rate paid by government Udibonos at the time of issue, owing to the higher risk of a corporate borrower compared to the government.

5.7.4.1 Convertible bonds

Convertible bonds (*obligaciones convertibles en acciones*) have the same basic features as corporate bonds: a principal amount (which can also be denominated in UDIs), interest rates linked to market rates (Cetes or bank deposits) or real rates (in the case of UDIs), and principal payment normally at maturity. The important differences between convertibles and straight bonds are:

- the option they provide the bondholder to convert them into shares of the issuing company after an agreed term and according to an agreed formula, and
- the option they provide the issuer of forcing conversion, also according to conditions agreed in the original terms of issue of the bond.

The advantage of convertibles for the issuer is that it normally pays a lower interest rate than for straight bonds, in exchange for the conversion feature. Similarly, the investor has the advantage of an agreed yield through interest payments, plus a possible capital gain, because the price of the bond rises in line with the price of the issuing company's stock. Since the 1994-5 banking crisis, several financial institutions have issued subordinated convertible bonds to strengthen their capital base, which was depleted by losses in their credit portfolios.

5.8 DOLLAR DEBT SECURITIES

5.8.1 Brady bonds and emerging markets debt

Brady bonds are bonds issued by sovereign governments in substitution for bank debt. They are called "Brady" bonds owing to the "Brady Plan", a plan for restructuring Mexican debt that was announced on March 10, 1989, when Nicholas Brady was Secretary for the Treasury of the United States. By December 1998, the scheme originally applied to Mexican debt had been extended to more than 10 countries that had exchanged their bank debt for Brady bonds.

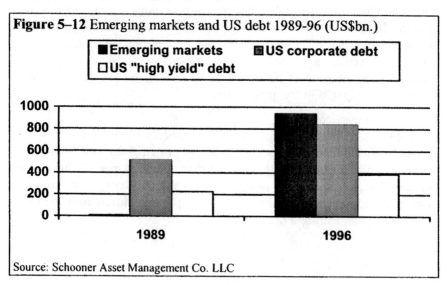

Figure 5–12 Emerging markets and US debt 1989-96 (US$bn.)

■Emerging markets   ▨US corporate debt
□US "high yield" debt

1989   1996

Source: Schooner Asset Management Co. LLC

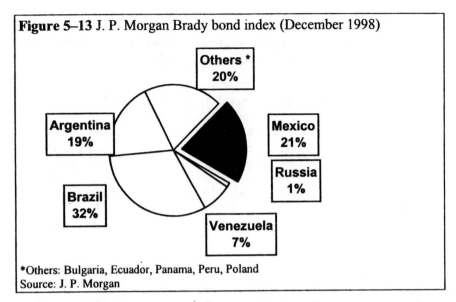

Figure 5–13 J. P. Morgan Brady bond index (December 1998)

*Others: Bulgaria, Ecuador, Panama, Peru, Poland
Source: J. P. Morgan

Brady bonds (or "Bradys") formed the base for a new asset class, emerging markets debt (*deuda de mercados emergentes*) which had a similar issued value to the total of US corporate debt (figure 5–12). More than eight years since the first issue of Bradys, Mexico represented, at the end of 1998, 21% of a Brady index (figure 5–13)

5.8.2 Mexican Bradys

In March 1990, Mexico, following negotiation with its bank creditors, converted a significant percentage of its total bank debt into two types of bond:

- US$11.5 bn. of discount bonds (*bonos de descuento*), at a discount of 35% to its previous face value, with a variable interest rate set at 13/16% over LIBOR, revised on a semiannual basis,
- US$17.9 bn. of "par bonds" (*bonos par*), without a discount, and at a fixed interest rate of 6.25%.

The two bonds were issued for a 30 year term, maturing on December 31, 2019. There were two kinds of guarantee: one guarantee in cash on 18 months of interest payments (or three interest coupons), and the other on the principal amount, with coverage worth US$7.1 bn. in US Treasury zero coupon bonds, with a matching 30 year maturity. The bonds also give their holders Value Recovery Rights (VRRs - *derechos de recuperación de valor*), represented by warrants on the price of Mexican oil, so that, should the oil price exceed a certain level, bondholders could participate in profits arising from an increase in the oil price (📖 9.4).

Figure 5–14 Main Mexican US$ government debt securities 1998

Issuer	Brady par	Brady discount	UMS 2026
	government	government	government
Guarantee	USTB zero coupon principal amount 3 interest coupons	USTB zero coupon principal amount 3 interest coupons	no
Amount: issued	US$17.9 bn.	US$11.5 bn.	US$1.75 bn.
outstanding	US$15.5 bn.	US$7.6 bn.	US$1.75 bn.
Face value	US$250,000 min.	US$250,000 min.	US$1,000
Rate of return	6.25%	LIBOR + 13/16%	11.50%
Payment	semiannual	semiannual	semiannual
Maturity	12/31/19	12/31/19	5/15/26
Amortization	maturity	maturity	maturity

Source: author

In the case of Mexico, there is another bond issue, which is comparable and trades in the same market as Bradys (figure 5–14). The UMS (*United Mexican States*) eurobond was issued in 1996 as a sign of Mexico's recovery following the 1994-5 crisis, with no guarantee of either interest or principal, in an amount of US$1.75bn., for a 30 year term, and with a fixed interest rate of 11.5%.

5.8.3 Eurobonds

5.8.3.1 *The international eurobond market*

Eurobonds (*eurobonos*) are bonds (also known as "debentures") issued by public and private sector borrowers, and denominated in "eurocurrencies" (*eurodivisas*). A eurocurrency is a currency traded or deposited outside its country of issue. The most common eurocurrency is the "eurodollar" (*eurodólar*) which is a dollar deposited outside the US, its country of issue.[24]

---

[24]With the entry of the euro, the common currency of 11 countries of the European Union, in 1999, this terminology will become complicated. The winning proposal of a competition organized by the *Economist* magazine for a new name for "eurobonds" was "xenobond", from the Greek ξενοσ - foreign.

"This market began in the 50s when the Soviet Union had substantial dollar deposits in New York banks, used to finance imports, mainly of grain. Faced with the political embarrassment of "lending" money to the capitalist enemy and with the reasonable fear that, if the Cold War worsened, the US could freeze or confiscate these dollar deposits, the Soviet Union preferred to transfer them to Europe. One of the French-Soviet banks where the Soviets deposited their dollars...was the Banque Commerciale d'Europe du Nord, whose cable address...is Eurobank." [25]

The eurobond market is an extension of the eurodollar market. The value of dollars deposited in European banks began to increase not only because of Russian imports but also because of the US trade deficit. As the US imported more, the export of dollars increased. But the holders of dollars preferred to deposit them outside the US, in European banks. The value in circulation of eurodollars increased enormously with the oil booms of 1973 (the Arab boycott) and 1979 (the Iranian revolution), and through the process of "petrodollar" recycling.

Eurobond issuance began formally in 1963, when the US imposed the "Interest Equalization Tax" (IET - *impuesto para igualar intereses*) on bonds. This tax was levied on loans to foreign borrowers contracted in the US money and capital markets (▢ figure 1-4). The result was that, with the ever-increasing flow of dollars outside the US, the issuers (frequently US multinationals) decided to issue bonds for longer terms, outside the US, with European banks, and denominated in eurodollars. In a short time, issue structures for eurobonds evolved, with investment banks and underwriting syndicates similar to structures that already existed for bond issues in US markets.

In contrast with domestic bond markets (above all, in the US) the international eurobond market is not an "organized market" according to the definitions used in ▢ 2.2.2. There is no physical trading floor, as all trading is performed by telephone. There are no officially "authorized" intermediaries, as the market itself decides who is permitted to trade. There are no formal rules for inscription, operation, payment or information[26], but the market itself determines them. Finally, there is no formal authority for the market.

---

[25]Mansell Carstens, Catherine, *Las Nuevas Finanzas en México* (Editorial Milenio, S. A. de C. V., 1992), p.183. See pp.180-194 for a description of the eurocurrency markets.

[26]Many issues are listed on stock exchanges like Luxembourg, owing to their relatively flexible regulations.

However, the eurobond market could not exist without domestic markets with their more formal organization, because most of the financial intermediaries and issuers that participate in the eurobond market already have a long tradition in their domestic markets, and a history of meeting trading and information requirements. It is this experience that permits them to participate in the "international capital markets", of which the eurobond market represents an important part.

5.8.3.2 Mexican eurobonds

In the 70s when the "euromarkets" *(euromercados)* began to assume importance, Mexico's main source of external credit was bank loans, both to the public and the private sector. The oil and petrodollar boom between 1977 and 1981 provided a major impetus to this process. In the 80s, the so-called "lost decade" (*década perdida*) for Mexico, banks spent most of their time rescheduling debt outstanding of the public and private sectors. Following the announcement of the Brady Plan in March 1989, the eurobond issue by the National Bank of Foreign Trade (Banco Nacional de Comercio Exterior) in July 1989 signified the formal end of the "debt crisis" that began in 1982, because it represented the voluntary return of Mexico to international capital markets.

In the 90s, the convergence of various factors led to a boom in eurobond issues for Mexican public and corporate borrowers: the resurgence of emerging markets following the collapse of the Berlin Wall in 1989, the increase in international investment by developed country mutual funds, and the appreciation by international investors of Mexico's efforts at economic modernization (liberalization, deregulation, privatization, and internationalization).

At the end of 1998, the total issued value of Mexican eurobond issues was estimated at US$45 bn., US$28 bn. for the government and US$17 bn. for the private sector.

5.8.3.3 Eurobond market securities

There are three main types of security in the eurobond markets: floating rate notes (*euronotas con tasa flotante*), straight bonds (*eurobonos normales*), and convertible bonds (*eurobonos convertibles*):

- Floating rate notes (FRNs)

FRNs offer a yield that consists of a fixed premium (spread), measured in basis points, over a market rate. The most frequently used market rate is the three or six month rate for eurodollars in the London Interbank Market (LIBOR - London Interbank Offered Rate).

- Eurobonds

Most eurobonds are traditional bonds with a principal amount, payable either at maturity or in installments, and a yield, which is received through the mechanism of fixed interest payments during the life of the bond.

- Convertible eurobonds

There are few convertible eurobonds issued by Mexican borrowers. However, they offer interesting investment possibilities. They have the same general features as eurobonds: a principal amount, the payment of a fixed interest rate, and repayment of the principal amount at maturity. Like peso convertible bonds (📖 5.7.4), they offer the bondholder the right to convert them into shares of the issuing company after a defined term and according to a defined conversion formula, and the issuer the right to force conversion, again according to terms and conditions defined in the issue document.

The important difference between peso and dollar convertible bonds is that dollar bonds offer a fixed dollar yield through the mechanism of interest payments, but the terms for conversion into shares depend not only on the share price of the issuer, but also on the exchange rate at the time when the investor wishes to exercise his conversion right.

Chapter 6
Debt II

"The advanced reader, who skips parts that appear too elementary, may miss more than the less advanced reader, who skips the parts that appear too complex."

G. Polya (1954)

6.1 INTRODUCTION

In 📖 ch. 5 we presented a brief history of debt globally and in Mexico, and a description of Mexican peso and dollar debt securities.

In this chapter, we present techniques for the valuation of Mexican debt securities. We begin with the application of the basic present value formula to the four types of debt security. In the context of the price sensitivity of debt securities to the level of interest rates, we present the concepts of yield curve and duration. Using the concept of return ranking, we analyze the relationship between risk and return for peso and dollar securities. Finally, we present techniques for selecting between peso and dollar securities.

6.2 FOUR TYPES OF DEBT SECURITY

There are four types of debt security, whatever their currency of issue: zero coupon, fixed rate, variable (or floating) rate, and real rate. In this section, we adapt the basic present value formula to each type of security.

6.2.1 Zero coupon

Most money market securities (Cetes, bank acceptances, and commercial paper in Mexico, Treasury bills and commercial paper in the US) do not offer interest payments, but are quoted at a discount to face value. Their price is calculated from this discount, and the difference between the purchase price and face value at maturity reflects the return on the security. Similarly, in the US there are longer term bonds which do not make regular interest payments but are quoted at a discount to face value, and are called "zero coupon bonds" (*bonos cupón cero*).

All zero coupon securities are valued the same way. Let us take the example of a debt security with a face value of 10 and one year maturity, yielding 20%. According to the valuation formula, the price is calculated as follows:

$$P = \frac{F_n}{(1+R)^n}$$ (6-1)

where:
P = price
F = flow (in this case face value at maturity)
R = return (yield) to maturity
n = number of periods
Resolving the equation for the above-mentioned security:

$$P = \frac{10}{\left(1+\frac{20}{100}\right)^1} = 8.333$$ (6-2)

This equation, and calculation, is the basis of all money market calculations – in the case of Mexico, for Cetes, bank acceptances, and commercial paper. We provide a guide for basic money market calculations (discount rate, price, yield, repos and equivalent rates) in 📖 B.1 and B.2.

6.2.2 Fixed rate
In countries with relatively stable inflation rates, most debt securities with maturities longer than one year are issued with fixed interest rates. To calculate the price, the basic valuation formula is used:

$$P = \frac{F_1}{(1+R)^1} + \frac{F_2}{(1+R)^2} + \ldots + \frac{F_n}{(1+R)^n}$$ (6-3)

Where:
P = price
F = cash flow (coupons and amortizations)
R = rate of return (yield) to maturity
n = number of periods
Knowing R and F, one can solve the equation for P. Similarly, knowing P and F, one can solve for R. In figure 6–1 we show the calculations for a bond with a coupon of 7%, semiannual payments, and amortization at maturity, to see the effect on P of changes in R and n.

Figure 6–1 Price calculation for bond with semiannual coupon (%)

Coupon   7.0%

Return	Maturity-years (amortization at maturity)									
	1	*2*	*3*	*4*	*5*	*6*	*7*	*8*	*9*	*10*
6.0%	100.95	101.86	102.71	103.51	104.26	104.97	105.64	106.28	106.87	107.43
6.5%	100.48	100.92	101.34	101.74	102.10	102.45	102.77	103.08	103.36	103.63
7.0%	100.00	100.00	100.00	100.00	100.00	100.00	100.00	100.00	100.00	100.00
7.5%	99.53	99.09	98.68	98.30	97.95	97.62	97.32	97.03	96.77	96.53
8.0%	99.06	98.19	97.38	96.64	95.95	95.31	94.72	94.18	93.67	93.21
8.5%	98.59	97.30	96.10	95.00	94.00	93.07	92.21	91.42	90.70	90.03
9.0%	98.13	96.42	94.85	93.41	92.09	90.89	89.78	88.77	87.85	87.00
9.5%	97.67	95.55	93.61	91.84	90.24	88.77	87.43	86.21	85.11	84.09
10.0%	97.22	94.69	92.39	90.31	88.43	86.71	85.16	83.75	82.47	81.31

Source: author

There are two clear and interrelated facts, which are the logical consequences of the valuation formula:

1. When the yield is less than the coupon, the price is above par, and the longer the term, the higher the price.

2. When the yield is greater than the coupon, the price is below par, and the longer the term, the lower the price.

6.2.3 Floating rate

In Mexico, most debt securities with maturities longer than a year have been issued at a floating rate (*tasa flotante*), at a fixed premium or "spread" (reflecting the level of risk of the security and the issuer) above a floating reference rate (*tasa de referencia*). The reference rates used can be Cetes, or the Interbank Equilibrium Interest Rate (*Tasa de Interés Interbancaria de Equilibrio* – TIIE). The main reason for the dominance of this type of security in Mexico has been the high level and volatility of the inflation rate (and therefore of interest rates) since 1976. Therefore, neither borrower nor lender have wanted to assume the risk (implicit in a fixed rate security) of a drastic change in its borrowing cost, or lending rate.

In the eurobond market, floating rate notes (*euronotas con tasa flotante*) account for more than 20 percent of the total issued value.[1] The reason for this has been to protect both issuers and investors from sudden changes in the level of interest rates.

---

[1]Solnik, Bruno, *International Investments* (Addison Wesley Publishing Company, 1996), p. 336.

Theoretically, the valuation formula for a floating rate note is the same as that for a fixed rate bond:

$$P = \frac{F_1}{(1+R)^1} + \frac{F_2}{(1+R)^2} + \ldots + \frac{F_n}{(1+R)^n} \qquad (6\text{-}4)$$

In a fixed rate security, the problem is the variability of R, which causes changes in the price P (depending on maturity), as we saw in figure 6–1. In a floating rate security this problem is avoided, because at the beginning of each period, F is adapted to R: i.e., the rate paid by the security adapts to the general level of interest rates.

This concept, applied to each flow, can be demonstrated more easily with the last flow. The last flow (F_n) consists of a coupon C and the amortization of the note at 100%. But by definition, at the moment $n\text{-}1$ (the beginning of the last period), the coupon will have been fixed in relation to R. This implies, that at the moment $n\text{-}1$, the price is also 100%:

$$P_{n\text{-}1} = \frac{100\% \ast (1 + R_{n\text{-}1})}{(1 + R_{n\text{-}1})} = 100\% \qquad (6\text{-}5)$$

However, the level of interest rates can vary between the dates when the coupon is changed (reset dates). In this case, the security behaves like a debt security with the term corresponding to the frequency of coupon payments (normally between three months and one year). For example, a floating rate note with semiannual coupons behaves like eurocommercial 182 day paper. The longer the term, the more the price of the security can vary between payment (or reset) dates. Logically, the moment of greatest price sensitivity to interest rate changes is the moment when maturity is longest, i.e. just after the reset date.

6.2.4 Real rate
In Mexico, inflation-indexed securities are ajustabonos, and Udibonos. In the US, there are inflation-indexed bonds, which have a similar structure to ajustabonos.

This security is a hybrid between a fixed interest security, because the real interest rate is fixed, and a floating rate security, because the basis for calculation of the overall yield (i.e, inflation) is variable. The nominal rate is variable, but the real rate is fixed.

The most liquid security in this asset class in Mexico is the Udibono, and there are two techniques for valuing it. One technique implies the assumption that the real rate of reinvestment remains fixed throughout the life of the security. The security is valued like a fixed rate security, and any change of R affects the price of the security, denominated in UDIs. The other technique implies that the real rate of reinvestment varies during the life of the security. Owing to the difficulty of estimating the real rate of reinvestment, the first technique is used more frequently. We describe the methodology for both techniques in 📖 B.3.

In the case of any debt security, three variables (F, R, and n) determine its present value, or price. The F of debt securities are predetermined on issue. Therefore, debt security analysis has two fundamental aspects:
- Forecast of the level of R, that is, the general level of interest rates.
- The sensitivity of the price P to changing values for F, R, and n.

In the following sections, we present techniques for the forecast of interest rates, and the concept of "duration" (*duración*), which provides a way to measure the sensitivity of debt security prices to the changes in F, R and n.

6.3 INTEREST RATE FORECASTING

6.3.1 Forecasting techniques – inflation, real rate, and cycles
In previous chapters of the book, we have presented three techniques

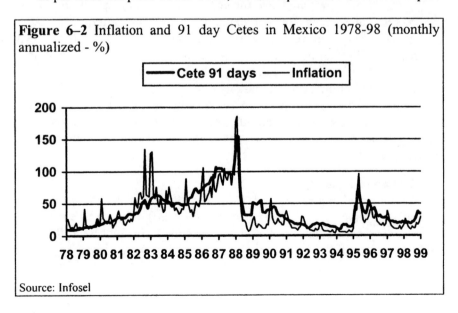

Figure 6–2 Inflation and 91 day Cetes in Mexico 1978-98 (monthly annualized - %)

Source: Infosel

Figure 6–3 Inflation and 91 day Tbills in the US 1983-98 (monthly annualized - %)

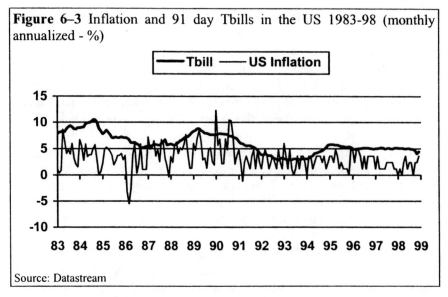

Source: Datastream

for forecasting interest rates:

1. In 📖 2.3.2, we analyzed the relation between a country's inflation rate and its risk-free interest rate. If the risk-free rate is not positive (higher than inflation), there is no incentive to save in that currency. In both Mexico and the US, there is a close relationship between inflation and interest rates (figure 6–2 and figure 6–3).

2. In 📖 3.2.1, we analyzed the concept of country risk in relation to interest rates. This concept explains the premium required above inflation, i.e. the real rate for different countries in their own currency. Furthermore, it explains the interest rate in an international currency (normally the dollar) paid by securities issued by countries in the international capital markets.

3. In 📖 4.4.3, we saw the relationship of interest rates to the economic cycle and the liquidity cycle, globally and for Mexico.

All these techniques are relevant to the forecasting of interest rates, globally and for Mexico.

6.3.2 The yield curve

Another technique, derived from the debt markets themselves, is called the "yield curve" (*curva de rendimiento*). The yield curve is a graphic representation of the yields provided by debt securities for different maturities of the same issuer (normally the government, that is

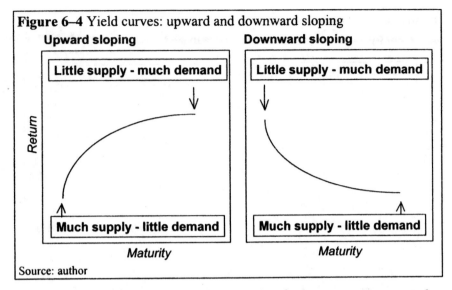

Figure 6–4 Yield curves: upward and downward sloping

Source: author

the issuer of lowest risk in a given country).[2] The curve represents the "term structure" (*estructura por plazo*) of interest rates at a specific moment in time.

In 📖 2.3.4, we commented that the investor requires a term premium in debt securities, to compensate for lower liquidity at longer maturities. If an investor has to sell a debt security before maturity, there is always the risk of not receiving the yield to maturity expected at the time of purchase: this risk is compensated for by the term premium.

The term premium implies that the "normal" yield curve has an upward sloping trend (figure 6–4). In any market, it is theoretically possible (but practically very difficult, because it changes according to circumstances) to analyze what this normal curve should be. If the curve is steeper (*más inclinada*) than normal, one can apply classic yield curve analysis in order to draw conclusions about interest rate expectations implicit in the curve. Similarly, if the curve is not upward sloping, but downward sloping (figure 6–4), horizontal, or even "humped" (*jorobada*) (figure 6–5), the same analysis techniques can be applied to the yield curve.

The yield curve reflects market expectations about interest rate trends in the following way. If the curve is upward sloping, short-term rates are below long term rates. This upward sloping line implies that the market expects rates to rise.

---

[2]See Mansell Carstens, Catherine, *op. cit.*, pp. 201-205.

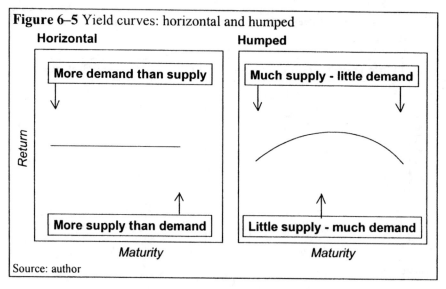

Figure 6–5 Yield curves: horizontal and humped

Source: author

The reasoning behind this conclusion is as follows. If investors think that interest rates will rise, they prefer to invest short term, because if they invest long term they lose the opportunity to invest at higher rates at a later date. Therefore, there is a large supply of money to be invested short term. However, there is little demand for funds by the borrower, because he prefers to borrow longer term, as he also thinks that rates will rise in the future. If, for the short term, there is much supply and little demand, the price of money (that is, the interest rate) falls. Similarly, if, for the long term, there is much demand and little supply, the interest rate rises.

When the yield curve is downward sloping, the same phenomenon occurs in reverse. As they expect a fall in rates, investors want to invest long term to assure a high interest rate over the longest possible term. Similarly, the borrower, if he thinks rates will go lower in the future, prefers to borrow short term. The result is a large supply of long term funds, but little demand, which results in low long term rates. Meanwhile, investors do not want to lend short term, but the borrower prefers short term money. This combination of little supply and much demand results in high short term rates.

There are other possible yield curves, or combinations of yield curves (figure 6–5). A "horizontal" curve would imply the expectation that rates will fall, because downward pressure on rates is greater than the natural upward trend of the yield curve (due to liquidity preference). A

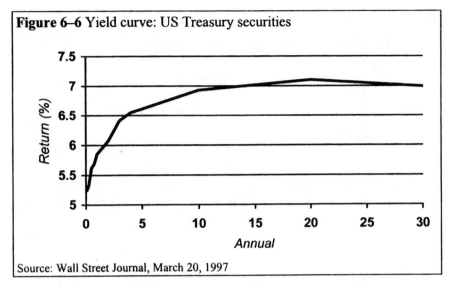

Figure 6–6 Yield curve: US Treasury securities

Source: Wall Street Journal, March 20, 1997

"humped" curve implies that, over the medium term, a rise in rates is expected, but that, over the long term, they are expected to fall again.

6.3.3 Empirical yield curves

Yield curves can be for maturities from one day to a hundred years, depending on the inflationary and financial stability of a country and the investor's focus.[3] In the US, the yield curve of government securities (Treasury bills and bonds) normally goes from one month to 30 years, the longest maturity currently available (figure 6–6). In the figure, the curve is upward sloping, with some parts steeper than others. This could have been the result of temporary imperfections in the market, or because at that moment the market was expecting an interest hike from the Fed.[4]

In Mexico, owing to inflationary instability since December 1994, there have been no long term peso debt issues by the government. Therefore the yield curve can only be drawn with maturities up to one year, on the basis of equivalent yields of Cetes (☐ B.2) at 28, 91, 182 and 364 days (figure 6–7). In the example, the curve was practically

---

[3]In the US and Japan, there have been debt issues with maturities up to 100 years. In England, in the XVIII century, the government issued "permanent" debt (the famous "Consols").

[4]There was a rate increase of 0.25%, from 5.25% to 5.50%, on March 25, 1997.

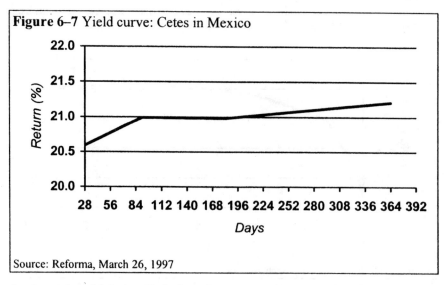

Figure 6–7 Yield curve: Cetes in Mexico

Source: Reforma, March 26, 1997

horizontal, which implied that the expectation was that interest rates would fall, which is what actually occurred in 1997.

6.4 DURATION

The duration of a debt security is its "average maturity" (*vencimiento promedio*). It represents a method of capturing the price sensitivity of the security to its cash flows (consisting of coupons and amortizations - (*F*)), different levels of interest rates (*R*), and different maturities.[5]

In 📖 B.4 we provide the explanation and derivation of the concept of duration. In figure 6–8, we provide calculations of duration for different terms (*n*) and coupons (*F*), at five levels of interest rates (*R*) from 6 to 16%, in increments of 2%. Several aspects of duration can be observed which can help us in the management of debt securities, and which amplify the conclusions of figure 6–1:

- Longer term securities have greater duration than shorter term securities, at the same coupon level.
- Securities of the same maturity have a shorter duration with a higher coupon, and a longer duration with a lower coupon.
- Securities of the same maturity and coupon have a shorter duration with a higher interest rate and a longer duration with a lower interest rate.

---

[5]Duration has come to replace the traditional concept of "average life" (*vida promedio*) for debt securities, because average life only takes account of amortizations (but not coupons), and does not apply a discount rate to them.

Figure 6–8 Calculation of duration for different levels of F, R and n (annual payments)

Maturity (n years)	Coupon (F) 6% R =	8% 12%	10%	12%	14%	16%
1	1.00	1.00	1.00	1.00	1.00	1.00
5	4.38	4.24	4.13	4.03	3.95	3.87
10	7.21	6.83	6.54	6.32	6.14	6.00
	R =	14%				
1	1.00	1.00	1.00	1.00	1.00	1.00
5	4.35	4.21	4.10	3.99	3.91	3.83
10	7.01	6.62	6.33	6.11	5.94	5.80
	R =	16%				
1	1.00	1.00	1.00	1.00	1.00	1.00
5	4.32	4.18	4.06	3.96	3.87	3.79
10	6.80	6.41	6.12	5.91	5.74	5.60

Source: author

We show in graphical form the relation between maturity, duration, yield and volatility (standard deviation) of the yields for four representative Mexican eurobonds in figure 6–9.

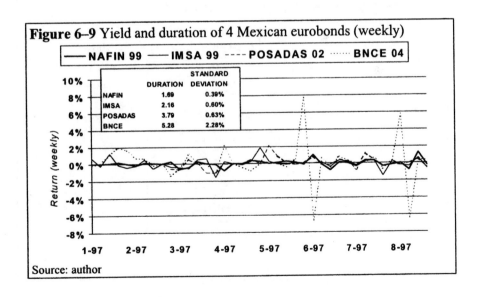

Figure 6–9 Yield and duration of 4 Mexican eurobonds (weekly)

Source: author

6.5 RETURN AND RISK OF PESO SECURITIES

6.5.1 Return ranking

In 📖 2.3, we presented the concept of "return ranking" according to the risk levels of different debt and equity securities. Applying the ranking to peso debt securities described in 📖 ch. 5, there are four levels of return, with their corresponding level of risk (figure 6–10).

6.5.2 Inflation

This is the minimum return required from savings in a given currency. If a currency does not provide a return above estimated inflation, it is illogical to save in that currency.

6.5.3 Country risk premium

The country risk premium is reflected in the real interest rate, which represents the rate above inflation offered by government debt securities in their own currency.

6.5.4 Term premium

As was mentioned in the previous section, securities with longer duration have a greater sensitivity to changes in interest rates, and, therefore, greater risk than securities of shorter duration. As normally

---

Figure 6–10 Return ranking: peso debt securities

Risk premium in pesos	Benchmark
CORPORATE	BOND
TERM	UDIBONO
COUNTRY RISK	CETE 28
INFLATION	CPI

Source: author

duration is highly correlated with the term of debt securities, longer term securities offer a premium for higher implicit risk. Between May 1996 and September 1997, 28 day Cetes offered a nominal cumulative return of 35.92%, and three year Udibonos 39.97%.

6.5.5 Company premium

There is a higher risk of default in corporate debt securities (because a company can fail) than on government securities. Therefore, there is normally a higher yield on corporate securities than government securities for the same term.

In Mexico since 1982, owing to the high level of inflation and the changing nature of financial securities during the period, there is no index for securities with a term greater than one year, either for government or corporate securities. However, there is a time series for short term securities, of yields on Cetes since 1991, and for corporate commercial paper from the same date (figure 6–11). It can be observed that commercial paper offered a higher yield than Cetes.

6.5.5.1 Rating agencies

Just as in the case of country risk (📖 3.2), bond rating agencies (*calificadoras de valores*) provide risk ratings for corporate debt securities. In Mexico, the ratings agencies are: Calificadora Duff & Phelps de México, S. A de C. V., Fitch IBCA México, S. A. de C. V, and Standard & Poor's, S. A de C. V. A debt rating is:

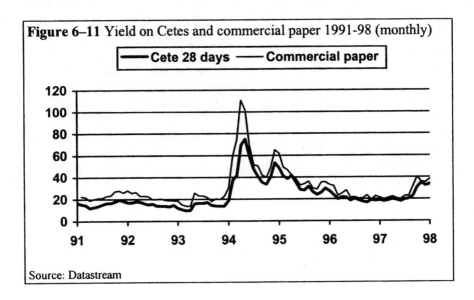

Figure 6–11 Yield on Cetes and commercial paper 1991-98 (monthly)

Cete 28 days —— Commercial paper

Source: Datastream

Figure 6–12 Standard & Poor's: rating scale

Maturity more than one year		Maturity less than one year	
Ratings	Payment capacity	Ratings	Payment capacity
	Investment grade		
mxAAA	substantially strong	mxA-1	strong
mxAA	very strong	mxA-2	satisfactory
mxA	strong	mxA-3	adequate
mxBBB	adequate		
	Not investment grade		
mxBB	possibility of default	mxB	uncertain
mxB	greater possibility of default	mxC	doubtful
mxCCC	identified possibility of default	mxD	default
msCC	high probability of default		
mxD	default		

Ratings outlook (for maturities more than one year)
Positive   possibility of upgrade
Negative   possibility of downgrade
Under development   possibility of upgrade or downgrade
Stable   no change anticipated

"+"   relative strength of security within grades A-B

Source: Standard & Poor's

"the expression of an opinion about the probability and relative risks of the capacity and intention of the issuer of a debt security… to effect payment in full at the agreed term."[6]

Company rating systems are similar to those used for countries.[7] In figure 6–12 we provide the rating system of Standard & Poor's for debt securities with maturities longer than one year, and less than one year. For maturities longer than one year, mxAAA is the highest rating, with a minimal risk of default, and mxAA represents a slightly lower rating. MxA and mxBBB represent a middle rating. These four grades, mxAAA to mxBBB, are considered "investment grade" (*grado de inversión*). Securities below these four grades (i.e., from mxBB to mxD) are considered of high risk or "not investment grade" or speculative (*de alto riesgo* or *de "no inversión"*). For securities with a term of less than one year (figure 6–12), the ratings (from mxA-1 to mxD) are similar, although there is no explicit distinction between investment and non-investment grade.

---

[6]Standard & Poor's Caval, "Calificaciones y Comentarios" (July 1997).
[7]In fact, rating systems were originally developed to rate companies, and were subsequently adapted to rate countries.

Figure 6–13 Standard & Poor's: selected long and short term ratings (July 1997)

	Type*	Rating	Outlook	Special review
Long term ratings				
Grupo Bimbo, S. A. de C. V.	CRC	mxAAA	stable	
Teléfonos de México, S. A. de C. V.	MP	mxAAA	stable	
Tablex, S. A. de C. V.	LP	mxAA+	stable	
Grupo Carso, S. A. de C. V.	MP	mxAA	stable	
Sanborn Hermanos, S. A. de C. V.	MP	mxA+	stable	
Factoraje Serfin, S. A. de C. V.	LP	mxA	negative	
ICA Inmobiliaria, S. A. de C. V.	MP	mxBBB+	stable	
Artes Gráficas Unidas, S. A. de C. V.	MP	mxBBB	stable	
Situr Desarrollos Turísticos S. A. de C. V.	LP	mxCCC		negative
Olimex, S. A. de C. V.	MP	mxCC		
Fábricas de Calzado Canadá, S. A. de C. V.	LP	mxD		
Short term ratings				
Ford Credit de México, S. A. de C. V.		mxA-1+		
Grupo Carso, S. A. de C. V.		mxA-1		
El Palacio de Hierro, S. A. de C. V.		mxA-2		
Compañia Hulera Euzkadi, S. A. de C. V.		mxA-3		
Grupo Synkro, S. A. de C. V.		mxC		negative

*CRC: credit risk
 MP: medium term commercial paper or promissory note
 LP: long term corporate bonds
Source: Standard & Poor's

Just as in the case of country risk, there is a refinement in long term ratings called "Outlook" (*Perspectivas*). "Positive" indicates that the rating can rise, "negative", that it can fall, "stable", that no changes are foreseen, and "under development", that it can rise or fall. An issue can be considered "under special review", to indicate that a specific short term event deserves special observation. The concept of "special review" includes three indicators of potential trend similar to those mentioned above: "positive", "negative", and "under development". In the two scales (long and short term), a plus sign (+) distinguishes the relative position of an issue's rating within its grade.

In figure 6–13, we show the application of the CAVAL scale to selected long and short term ratings.

6.5.5.2 Indicators of credit quality

Although the rating agencies perform an important role in rating risk and return for debt securities, investors normally do not rely only on ratings for their decisions to invest in debt securities, for two reasons. First, not all securities traded in securities markets are rated.[8] Second, a debt security can have its rating changed, either positively (upgrade) or negatively (downgrade): any investor who can anticipate a rating change can increase his potential return or reduce his potential loss. Therefore, it is important to understand the criteria used for rating debt securities by rating agencies.

There are four main indicators of corporate credit quality:

- Interest coverage

The most important indicator of credit quality is the level and trend of profits before interest, taxes, depreciation and amortization (EBITDA or UAFIDA - *utilidades antes de financiamiento, impuestos, depreciación y amortización*) compared with the level of interest payments. This indicator is called "interest coverage" (*cobertura de intereses*).

- Debt in relation to net worth or total assets

A second indicator is the level of total debt of a company in relation to its net worth or total assets (debt to equity or debt to assets – *deuda/capital contable o deuda/activos totales*).

- Working capital/long term debt or cash/total debt

A third indicator is the current or expected situation of corporate liquidity. Two ratios used for this measure are those of net working capital to long term debt (*capital de trabajo neto en relación con deuda a largo plazo*) and cash to total debt (*efectivo en relación con deuda total*).

- Competitive situation

Finally, the size and competitive situation of a company within its industry are important factors in determining its long term future. Clearly, a company with a dominant market share in its industry has a greater possibility of long term continuity than a company with a lower market share.

The relevance of these indicators can be seen in figure 6–14, with two extreme cases, BIMBO and SYNKRO. It can be observed that BIMBO

Figure 6–14 Application of credit quality indicators

	Caval	EBITDA/ Interest	Debt/ Mkt. Cap	Cash/ Debt	% Market
Grupo Industrial Bimbo, S. A. de C. V.	mxAAA	9.05	21.44%	8.02%	80%
Grupo Synkro, S. A. de C. V.	mxC	0.16	209.00%	0.03%	50%
Source: Standard & Poor's Caval, author (July 1997)					

---

[8]Certain types of investor can be legally prohibited from investing in unrated securities – for example, the Afores - 📖 11.5.3.

has an interest coverage ratio of more than 9 times, compared to SYNKRO (0.16 times), and that it has a ratio of debt to capitalization of 21%, compared to 209%. The ratio of cash to total debt for BIMBO is 8% compared with .03% for SYNKRO. The market position of the two companies is not a useful criterion for explaining the difference in ratings of the two companies, as the two are leaders in their respective main markets (bread for BIMBO and pantyhose for SYNKRO).[9]

6.6 RETURN AND RISK OF DOLLAR SECURITIES

6.6.1 Return ranking

The difference between the return ranking for peso and dollar securities is that the "risk-free rate" for dollar securities is a dollar denominated rate, whose level depends on the United States. Therefore, the return ranking has to be modified from the structure reflected in figure 6–10 to that reflected in figure 6–15.

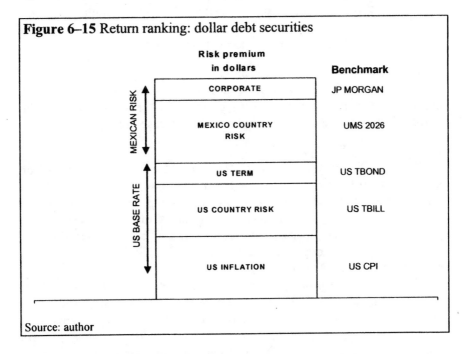

Figure 6–15 Return ranking: dollar debt securities

Source: author

---

[9]However, in September 1997, when this section was written, SYNKRO's market position was significant, because it assured its survival as a company through the restructuring of its debt, with its creditors taking control of the company.

6.6.2 The base rate in US$

The base rate in US$ consists in the combination of the expected inflation rate, the real rate and the term premium offered by US government debt securities. We provide the tools for analyzing these elements in 📖 4.4.3, where we underline the importance of analyzing the liquidity and economic cycles to understand interest rate trends in the US.

6.6.3 Mexico country risk

The country risk premium represents the additional rate offered by Mexican government (or "sovereign") debt securities (📖 3.2.1). The way in which the "country risk premium" (*prima por riesgo país*) is expressed for Mexican dollar debt securities is as a spread (*diferencial*) over the US government debt security for the same maturity (e.g. spread over Treasuries), expressed in basis points (*puntos base*), that is, hundredths of a percent.

The two dollar securities that reflect Mexican country risk are sovereign eurobonds (issued by the Mexican government, or *paraestatal* entities, which reflect the same risk level) and Bradys.

6.6.4 Mexican sovereign eurobonds

In figure 6–16, we show spreads over Treasury for some Mexican eurobonds. It can be observed that the longer the term, and therefore the duration, the wider the spread, owing to the increase in risk.

6.6.5 Mexican Bradys

Bradys offer only a partial reflection of Mexico risk, owing to the guarantees on the principal amount and on 3 coupons (18 months) of interest payments. The principal amount, owing to the zero coupon Treasury bond guarantee, reflects the credit of the US Treasury. The partially guaranteed interest payments represent a mix of credit risk, between the three coupon guarantee (which is US risk) and the other coupons (which are Mexico risk).

To calculate the proportion of the yield on Brady bonds that reflects Mexico risk, and the proportion that reflects US Treasury risk, it is necessary to strip out the effect of the guarantees on principal and interest. This yield is called the "stripped yield" (*rendimiento sin colateral*). Similarly, the differential between the stripped yield and the Treasury bond yield is called the "stripped spread" (*diferencial sin colateral*). We provide in 📖 B.5 a technique for calculating the stripped yield and stripped spread for par and discount Bradys.

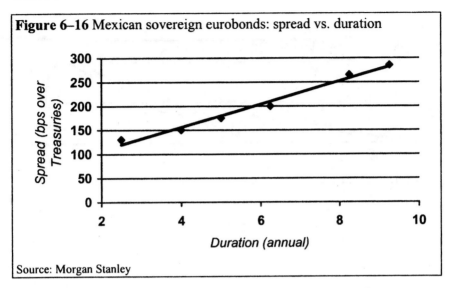

Figure 6–16 Mexican sovereign eurobonds: spread vs. duration

Source: Morgan Stanley

6.6.6 Mexico company risk

6.6.6.1 The sovereign ceiling

The minimum yield offered by any Mexican dollar debt security issued by a corporate borrower is the yield offered by a sovereign debt security for the same maturity, and is called the "sovereign ceiling" (*techo soberano*). The sovereign ceiling exists because all government and corporate issuers from a given country are subject to the same macroeconomic and political factors, i.e. the same country risk. Therefore, it is impossible for a corporate issuer to have a better risk rating than its own government.[10] Corporate eurobonds offer a higher yield than sovereign eurobonds (figure 6–17).

---

[10]This "ceiling" can be broken in the case of securities whose main source of payment is insulated from country risk:
- there are Mexican companies that derive a high percentage of income from sources outside Mexico (e.g. GRUMA),
- there are securities issued by Mexican companies whose main source of repayment is derived from accounts receivable from exports of tradeable goods (e.g. oil, copper, telephone receipts), which are collected outside the country, and deposited in a trust established offshore for the specific purpose of debt servicing.

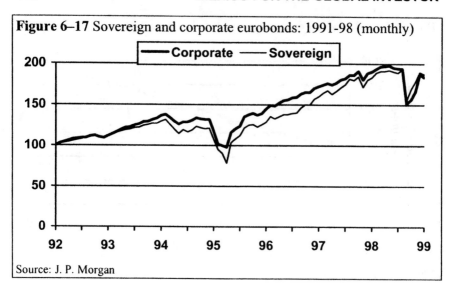

Figure 6–17 Sovereign and corporate eurobonds: 1991-98 (monthly)

Source: J. P. Morgan

6.6.6.2 Credit quality

Mexican eurobonds are rated in the same way as peso debt securities. Many eurobond issues are rated by the main rating agencies, and normally their yields reflect their ratings. As in the case of sovereign eurobonds, yields on corporate eurobonds are expressed as spreads over Treasuries for the same maturity (figure 6–18).

Credit analysis of corporate eurobonds is performed in the same way as that for peso debt securities, using techniques described in 📖 6.5.5. The correlation between the most important financial ratios, debt ratings and spreads over Treasuries can be observed in figure 6–18.

6.7 THE EXCHANGE RATE

6.7.1 Comparison between peso and dollar debt securities

How does the investor decide between Mexican peso and dollar debt securities?

The question can be answered with an example. In the month of July 1997, the one year Cete yielded 22%, and a one year Mexican sovereign eurobond yielded 7.5% in dollars. This implied that, for the two yields to be equivalent, the dollar would have to revalue against the peso for the one year period by the following amount:

$$Rev = \frac{1.22}{1.075} - 1 = .1349 = 13.5\% \qquad (6\text{-}6)$$

Figure 6–18 Corporate eurobonds: spreads over Treasuries, ratings, and financial ratios 1997

Issuer	Maturity	Term	Coupon	Dura-tion	Price 9/23/97	YTM	YTM Tbond	Spread over Tbond
		years	%	years	%	%	%	bps
CEMEX	09/20/01	3.99	9.50	3.43	105.63	7.83	5.94	189
EMPRESAS ICA	05/30/01	3.68	11.88	3.03	111.75	8.11	5.92	219
GIDUSA	08/03/01	3.86	12.63	3.18	114.13	8.26	5.93	233
GRUPO ELEKTRA	05/15/01	3.64	12.75	2.94	112.10	8.80	5.92	288

	Spread over Tbond	S&P	Moody's	Ratios EBITDA/ interest	Debt/ Equity	Cash/ Debt
	bps			:1	%	%
CEMEX	189	BB	B1	2.39	48.87	9.07
EMPRESAS ICA	219	BB-	B1	0.69	51.20	43.79
GIDUSA	233	BB-	B1	1.88	50.41	16.87
GRUPO ELEKTRA	288	B		6.5	26.94	23.01

Source: Standard & Poor's Caval, Moody's, author

The investor should then ask the question: how probable is it that the dollar will revalue against the peso by 13.5% over a one year period?

6.7.2 Exchange rate forecasting

There are two main techniques for exchange rate forecasting: economic analysis, and peso futures (*futuros del peso*).[11]

6.7.2.1 Economic analysis – purchasing power parity

Exchange rate forecasting based on economic analysis normally begins with "purchasing power parity" (*paridad de poder de compra*). The concept of purchasing power parity is simple. Let us imagine that in year 1 the value of the peso was exactly one dollar. Similarly the price of a chocolate bar in Mexico is one peso, and that of an identical bar (let us say a Hershey's bar) in the US is one dollar. In the period between year 1 and year 2, the increase in the price of chocolate (reflecting the general inflation level) is 15% in Mexico and 3% in the US. This implies that the price of chocolate in Mexico is $1.15 and in the US is US$ 1.03.

Now if the exchange rate remained constant between the two countries, and there were a free market for the import and export of chocolate between the two countries, no one would buy Mexican chocolate because it costs 11.6% more than in the US ($1.15 against US$1.03). To avoid the bankruptcy of the Mexican chocolate industry, it

---

[11]See also Mansell Carstens, *op. cit.*, pp. 112-124.

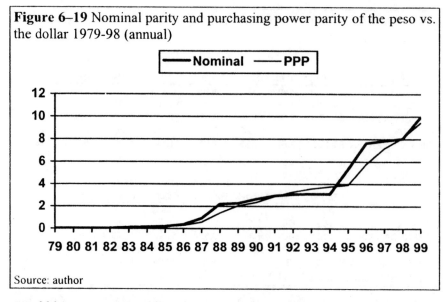

Figure 6–19 Nominal parity and purchasing power parity of the peso vs. the dollar 1979-98 (annual)

Source: author

would be necessary to align the two exchange rates by ensuring that the dollar revalue against the peso by exactly the 11.6% mentioned in the previous sentence. This 11.6% represents the differential between the US inflation rate and the Mexican inflation rate, or

$$Rev = \frac{1.15}{1.03} - 1 = .1165 = 11.6\%$$ (6-7)

By revaluing the dollar against the peso (or devaluing the peso against the dollar[12]) we would be restoring the "purchasing power parity" of the peso against the dollar.

The problem with the concept of purchasing power parity is that, although it works over the long term, it does not work over the short term (figure 6–19).[13] In figure 6-19, it can be observed that there is a long period of overvaluation (1991-1994), and an equally long period of undervaluation (1995-1997).

---

[12]The peso devaluation would be 10.4%, as the dollar value of each peso would fall from 1 dollar per peso to 1/1.1165, or 89.6 cents per peso.

[13]The British magazine, *The Economist*, uses the concept of PPP for its regular analysis of exchange rates in various countries according to the price of the "Big Mac" hamburger, which, owing to its homogeneity across countries, produces interesting results.

Figure 6–20 Peso futures and interest rates 1997-98						
A	B	C	D	E	F	G
peso/US$	9/12/97	7.78		Annualized	Annualized	Simple
Future	US$/peso	peso/US$	% diff.	Cete	Tbill	% difference
Dec-97	0.12337	8.105698	4.19%	21.19%	5.13%	3.96%
Mar-98	0.11882	8.416092	8.18%	21.98%	5.36%	8.09%
Sep-98	0.11172	8.950949	15.05%	21.71%	5.59%	15.27%
Source: The Economist, Wall Street Journal, author						

For these reasons, economists have used more complex models of fundamental analysis, taking into account not only comparative inflation levels, but the many factors which affect inflation in a given country. However, despite their greater complexity, these models suffer from the same defect. They work over the long term, but do not work for practical forecasting purposes over the short term.

6.7.2.2 Peso futures

Peso futures are traded in the Chicago Mercantile Exchange (CME), and reflect the opinion of the market about the price of the peso over 3, 6, and 12 months.

Foreign exchange theory implies that the "forward premium" on the currency (*prima adelantada*) should equate the difference between the interest rate on the domestic currency and the foreign currency (📖 9.7.2), or:

$$PA = \frac{F-S}{S} = \frac{1+R_d}{1+R_e} - 1 \qquad (6\text{-}8)$$

where:
PA = forward premium
F = peso future exchange rate
S = peso spot exchange rate
R_d = domestic interest rate
R_e = foreign currency interest rate

In figure 6–20 we show peso futures for September 12, 1997, compared with spot levels for the same day, and the rates for Cetes and Tbills for similar maturities.

It can be observed that the market functions according to the theory. The difference between the peso future and spot price (column D) is very similar to the difference between the rates for Cetes and Tbills for the same maturity (column G).

Even so, in terms of the decision between peso and dollar securities with which we began this section, peso futures only repeat the question.

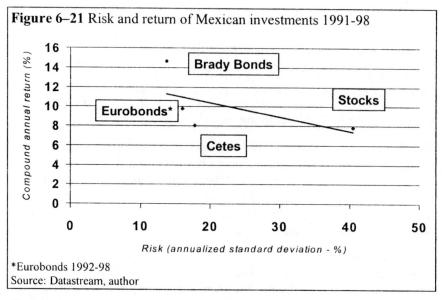

Figure 6–21 Risk and return of Mexican investments 1991-98

*Eurobonds 1992-98
Source: Datastream, author

They represent the difference between two interest rates. However, we are attempting to decide between a Mexican interest rate in pesos, and in dollars.

6.7.2.3 Return and risk

To make the decision between pesos and dollars, it might be more useful to use the graphs of return and risk. In 📖 3.6.3, we analyzed both Mexico country risk, and the return-risk features of the main Mexican asset classes. It can be observed in figure 6–21 that Cetes have offered a lower return (calculated in dollars) than eurobonds, with greater risk, and that stocks have offered a similar return (with much higher risk). However, it is important to emphasize that these numbers are historic and only provide one source of information for future estimates. This implies that, ultimately, the decision between pesos and dollars depends on where the investor wishes to place himself on the return-risk curve, and his reference currency. We will cover this issue in the practical context of portfolio management in 📖 12.3.3.

Chapter 7
Stocks I

"If you have a minute, I'll tell you how to make money in stocks. Buy low and sell high. Now, if you have five or ten years, I'll tell you how to know when stocks are high and low."

JRL (1966)

7.1 INTRODUCTION

Stocks are probably the most visible investment of all those currently available in financial markets. This is why there is an almost total identification in Mexico between "Stock Exchange" and stocks. In daily language, everyone understands the question "How's the market?" to mean "How are stocks?" – without realizing that in 1998 stocks only represented 2.8 percent of all trading by value on the MSE. Similarly, in other countries (like the US) "How's the market?" is also understood to refer to stocks, not Treasury bonds, or oil futures.

As with debt, we have split our treatment of stocks into two parts. In this 📖 ch. 7, we outline the historical development of global stock markets, followed by the history and current situation of the Mexican market. In 📖 ch. 8, we present techniques for stock valuation in relation to the Mexican market as a whole, stock sectors, and individual stocks, with examples of their practical application.

7.2 HISTORY OF GLOBAL STOCK MARKETS

7.2.1 Introduction

The early history of stock markets has two main threads (figure 7–1). The first is the history of exchanges (*Bolsas*), which were not originally established for the trading of stocks, so much as merchandise in general. The second is the legal development of systems of corporate organization (e.g. "corporations" and "companies"). Stock markets have developed through the interaction between these two processes.

7.2.2 The first exchanges

The origins of the first exchange, and even of the word "Bolsa", are obscure. The first exchanges probably began with medieval fairs, where

Figure 7–1 Global stock market history: important dates

XIV	First exchanges in Bruges, Antwerp
XVI	1553 The Muscovy Company formed in England
	1581 The Levant Company formed in England
XVII	1600 The East India Company formed in England
	1602 Vereenigde Oostindische Compagnie formed in Holland
	1613 Amsterdam Stock Exchange building inaugurated
	1637 Tulipomania in Holland
	1657 The East India Company becomes permanent
	1688-95 100 new companies formed in England
XVIII	1720 Compagnie d'Occident (Mississippi) crashes in France
	1720 South Sea Company crashes in England (South Sea Bubble)
	1758-1803 165 canal construction companies formed in England
	1773 Jonathan's Coffee House called "Stock Exchange" in London
	1794 Canal crash in England (canal manía)
	1792 New York Stock Exchange founded
XIX	Development of English stock market
	1802 Stock Exchange building inaugurated in London
	1808 42 companies formed, including 7 breweries, 5 wineries, 4 distilleries, insurance, coal, wool, copper, paper, textile companies
	1827 Liverpool Stock Exchange
	1830 Manchester Stock Exchange
	1827-37 81 railway companies formed
	1844-47 630 railway companies formed
	1847 Railway crash (railway mania)
	1856 New company law includes limited liability
	1862 Limited liability extended to insurance companies
	1860s Expansion of "joint stock banks", with limited liability
XX	1914 I World War: stock markets closed
	1920s Boom of white goods, radio, auto companies in US
	1929 New York Stock Exchange crash
	1933-34 Securities laws in US: Securities and Exchange Commission (SEC)
	1939-45 II World War: stock markets closed
	1960s Boom of computer, office equipment companies in US
	1980s Asian stock market boom
	1987 New York Stock Exchange crash
	1989 Fall of Berlin Wall
	1990-4 Boom and expansion of emerging markets
	1992- Boom of high tech companies in US
	1994-5 Tequila effect on emerging markets
	1997 Crisis of Asian emerging markets
	1998 Russia crisis
	1999 Brazil crisis

Source: Kindleberger, author

all kinds of articles were traded, principally commodities. These fairs boomed in the XIV century, when the financial center of gravity began to shift from the cities of Italy to the Low Countries, specifically the cities of Antwerp and Bruges.

The story is told that, around the year 1360, the people of Bruges used to hold their fair in the main square of the town, in front of the house of the Chevalier van der Beurse (knight of the purses). His coat of arms were three purses (Beurse - *bolsas*) carved on the façade of his house. The expression "to go to the purses" became popular among local residents, not so much as a description of the place, as of the type of gatherings that were held there, i.e. trading of goods. This activity spread not only in Flanders, but to other countries as well.[1]

7.2.3 The first partnerships

The first systems of business organization were partnerships (*sociedades*) where the partners provided capital or services, or both. These systems were developed in the XIV and XV centuries for the financing of commercial voyages. In England, they were extended to the formation of partnerships for the export of wool, leather, tin and lead in the XIV century, and for finished products like cloth in the XV and XVI century.

With the discovery of the Americas in 1492, technologies for ship construction and navigation were given a boost, and made longer voyages possible in the XVI century. The need arose for more capital, and a more permanent legal structure. The concept of a "partnership" evolved to that of a "company" (*compañía*), which received the trading rights for a certain region of the world, but whose capital could be liquidated and renewed after each voyage. In England, The Muscovy Company was formed in 1553 for the Russia trade, and The Levant Company in 1581 for trade with the Ottoman Empire.

The East India Company (*Compañía de Indias*) received its authorization from Elizabeth I of England in 1600, for just one voyage. Gradually, its organization became more elaborate, and its monopoly was consolidated. In 1613, funds were collected for four voyages: in 1617, when funds were collected for seven voyages, the company already had 36 ships and 934 stockholders. In 1657, the company

---

[1]Heyman, Timothy and Arturo León y Ponce de León, *La Inversión en Mexico* (Universidad del Valle de Mexico, 1981), pp. 84-5.

became more "permanent", with a duration for its constitution specified in its statutes.[2]

7.2.4 Holland

The pioneers in both legal structures and stock market development were the Dutch, who inherited financial leadership from the Flemish of Bruges and Antwerp in the XVI century (📖 5.2.2). When the Vereenigde Oostindische Compagnie (VOC – United Company of the East Indies - *Compañía Unida de las Indias Orientales*) was formed in 1602, it already had a durable constitution, and its stocks were traded informally among Dutch merchants.[3] The first exchange building in the world, the Amsterdam Stock Exchange, was constructed in 1613, principally to formalize the informal trading in stocks of the VOC. This combination of legal form (the company), and market structure (the Stock Exchange) made the Amsterdam Stock Exchange the first organized stock market in the world.[4]

7.2.5 England

As in the case of debt instruments, England benefitted from Dutch financial innovation in the XVII century, and became the center of global stock market development during the following two centuries. The Glorious Revolution of 1688, when King William of Orange was invited to rule the country, had the same effect on the stock market as on debt markets (📖 5.2.2). Between 1688 and 1695 (the date of the foundation of the Bank of England), 100 new companies were formed in England.

In 1711, The South Sea Company (*Compañía del Mar del Sur*) was formed with the exclusive concession to exploit South America. Intense speculation developed in the stocks of this new company, with the consequent formation of 195 more companies between September 1719 and August 1720. The price of the company's stock rose from £100 in 1719 to a peak of £1,000 in the month of July 1720. But the collapse of some fraudulent companies, and the example in France of a similar company, the Compagnie d'Occident (the Western Company - *Compañía del Occidente*), triggered a fall in the price of the stock, with the price reaching £160 in December 1720. As it caused the collapse of

---

[2]Keay, John, *The Honourable Company, A History of the East India Company* (HarperCollins, 1993).

[3]The first Dutch deposit bank, the Amsterdam Wisselbank, modeled on similar banks in Genoa and Venice, was started in 1609.

[4]It was also in Holland that the great tulip mania occurred, in 1637 (📖 10.2.2).

the government of the period, the South Sea Bubble (*Burbuja del Mar del Sur*) became a historic event, as the first stock market boom (and crash) with political consequences (10.2.2).

The subsequent history of the English stock market in the XVIII and XIX centuries is of successive booms in different sectors of the economy, in parallel with the continuous development of both the physical and legal infrastructure of the market.

7.2.5.1 Sectoral booms

For the effective and economic transport of coal (an indispensable fuel for steam engines) in the first half of the XVIII century, a system of canals was developed. Between 1730 and 1790 the coverage of the canals doubled, to 2,200 miles, and, between 1758 and 1803, 165 canal companies were formed, with the highest concentration between 1791 and 1794, when 81 were formed.

During the Napoleonic Wars, in 1808, 42 companies were formed in different industries (beer, wine, distilleries, insurance, coal, wool, copper, paper and clothing). In 1823, after the formation of the Alliance Insurance Company, there was a boom in insurance companies.

The first railway was built in England between Stockton and Darlington in 1825. Between 1827 and 1837, 81 railway companies were formed, most of which were financed through provincial stock exchanges. Between 1844 and 1847, there was another railway boom, and 630 railway companies were formed. The sector crashed in 1847.

7.2.5.2 Stock market development

Meanwhile, the stock market continued its development as an institution. In 1773 Jonathan's Coffee House began to be called "The Stock Exchange", and in 1802 the London Stock Exchange completed construction of its first permanent home. However, most new companies were financed, and operated, outside London (in "the provinces"). In the second quarter of the XIX century, these markets began to be formalized with the foundation of the Liverpool Stock Exchange in 1827, and the Manchester Stock Exchange in 1830. The number of provincial stock exchanges increased with the railway boom. There were 12 in 1885, and 22 in 1914.

7.2.6 United States

7.2.6.1 Sectoral booms

The New York Stock Exchange was founded in 1792. However, the country received its first great economic and financial impetus following the end of the Civil War in 1865. An infrastructure of companies, intermediaries, and information was established which began to rival that of London.[5] Exhausted by the military, political and economic cost of World War I, the British Empire lost its economic and financial leadership, which was taken over by the US.

The first generalized boom in the New York stock market occurred in the 1920s. The prosperity of the period following the I World War coincided with a boom in industries based on the new electrical and automotive technologies. The boom culminated in the crash of October 1929 ([10.2.2), and the Dow Jones industrial index (DJIA) did not reach its level of 1929 in nominal terms until 1954 (figure 7–2). The second great boom occurred in the 1960s, again as a consequence of new technologies, such as computing (IBM, DEC) and office equipment (XEROX). It ended with the oil shock of 1973, with its resulting inflation, and, with the second shock in 1979, the 1970s were the worst decade for the US stock market since the 1930s.

The month of August 1982 marked the end of the inflationary period, and was followed by a sustained boom in the US stock market, until the crash of October 1987, the biggest one day fall in the history of Wall Street. However, the importance of the crash was not its severity, but the speed of the subsequent recovery. The stock boom was slowed by the invasion of Kuwait by Saddam Hussein in August 1990, and the ensuing

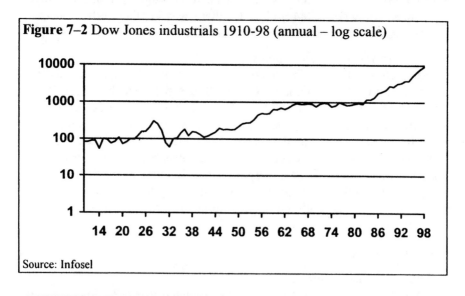

Figure 7–2 Dow Jones industrials 1910-98 (annual – log scale)

Source: Infosel

---

[5]The stock ticker was introduced in 1867, and the telephone in 1878. The Federal Reserve System (*Fed*), the US central bank, was founded in 1913.

recession which caused the Republican party to lose the White House in 1992.

The generalized stock boom which continued with the election of President Clinton to the White House was the product of three classic processes of the Kondratieff cycle (📖 4.2): the end of the Cold War, the opening of new markets and the maturation of the new technologies of computing, telecommunications, media, and biotechnology. There was a generalized effect on the existing sectors of the stock market, and the new high technology sectors ("high tech"). Between the end of 1994 and 1998, the Dow Jones rose by 139%.

7.2.6.2 Stock market development

Owing to its common language and culture, the US stock market initially followed English best practices. After the 1929 crash, and in order to prevent its recurrence, the Securities Laws of 1933 and 1934 were passed, and the Securities and Exchange Commission (SEC) was established as an independent organization to supervise the securities markets, intermediaries and issuers. The other four major contributions of the US to global stock market development in the XX century were:

- The extension and diffusion of a stock market "culture", with the result that more than 40% of US households became direct or indirect investors in stocks (📖 11.3.1),
- The development of institutional investment (mutual funds, pension funds, insurance companies - 📖 11.4),
- The development of derivatives linked to stock markets (options on individual stocks and indices, and futures on indices - 📖 9.2), and
- The application of the technologies of computing and telecommunications to the finance industry (📖 1.2.2).

7.3 HISTORY OF THE MEXICAN STOCK MARKET

7.3.1 Beginnings

Stock market activity began in Mexico around 1880 with informal trading in stocks. It was the result of four main factors:

- The economic and financial stabilization begun by the government of Porfirio Díaz in 1876,
- The establishment of a banking system, with the foundation of the Bank of London, Mexico and South America in 1864, and its strengthening in 1884 with the formation of the Banco Nacional de México as a deposit and issuing bank (📖 5.3.3),

Figure 7-3 Mexican stock market history: important dates

1824- Stock issues by European and US companies with Mexican operations
1880- Informal trading in Plateros street
1890s Mining stock boom
1895 Bolsa de México, S. A. founded
1896 Bolsa de México, S. A. closed
XX
1900- Mexican securities listed on European and North American stock exchanges
1907 Bolsa Privada de México, S. C. L. founded
1910 Bolsa renamed Bolsa de Valores de México, S. C. L
1920s Oil stock boom
1932 Law of Credit Institutions and Auxiliary Organizations (*Ley de Instituciones
        de Crédito y Organizaciones Auxiliares*) includes chapter on Stock Exchanges
1946 National Securities Commission (*Comisión Nacional de Valores*)
1975 First Securities Market Law (*Ley del Mercado de Valores*)
1976 Merger of Guadalajara and Monterrey with Mexico City stock exchange, and
        change of name to "Bolsa Mexicana de Valores, S. A. de C. V."
1978-9 Stock market boom: 56 new issues
1978 Securities Deposit Institute (*Instituto de Depósito de Valores - INDEVAL*)
1979 Stock Market Law Academy (*Academia de Derecho Bursátil, A. C.*)
1980 Mexican Brokerage Houses Association (*Asociación Mexicana de Casas de Bolsa, A. C.*)
1981 First issue of Mexico Fund (*Fondo México*)
1982 Bank nationalization: Bolsa closed (September 2-19)
1987 Stockmarket boom: 41 new issues
        Market crash: index falls 74% in 28 days (October 6 to November 17)
1989 Announcement (May) and implementation (November) of Nafin Trust (*Fondo Nafin*)
1989-94 Foreign investment boom
1990 New Stock Exchange (*Centro Bursátil*) inaugurated in Mexico City
1991 Issue of Telmex ADRs on NYSE
1992 Simultaneous IPO of ICA on MSE and NYSE
        First derivatives issue (warrants) on MSE
1993 Intermediate market (now *Mercado para la Mediana Empresa Mexicana-MMEX*)
1994 First foreign brokerage begins operations on MSE
1997 International Quotations System (*Sistema Internacional de Cotizaciones-SIC*)
1998 MexDer (derivatives exchange) begins operation
1999 Electronic trading begins on MSE

Source: Lagunilla, author

- The example of Mexican debt and equity securities that were traded on European and US stock markets[6], and
- The example of other stock exchanges in Latin America: the Rio de Janeiro stock exchange was founded in 1850, Buenos Aires in 1854, and Santiago in 1892.

Trading took place in the street of Plateros (now avenida Madero), and (as in the case of Jonathan's Coffee House in London in the XVIII century) eventually it centered on the cakeshop (*pastelería*) of Señora Filomena Mayeu, also known as "the widow of Genin" (*viuda de Genin*). The business, especially in mining stocks, grew to such a size that a

---

[6]Companies were formed outside Mexico to operate in Mexico. For example, the Anglo Mexican Mining Company was established in London in 1830.

group of brokers, who were now beginning to be called "kiters" (*jinetes*) and "scalpers" (*coyotes*), decided to set up a trading floor, with its own rules and procedures.

On September 2, 1895, the statutes of the "Bolsa de México, S. A." were registered in the Public Register for Property and Trade (*Registro Público de la Propiedad y del Comercio*). The Bolsa itself was inaugurated on October 21 of the same year. In his inaugural speech, Lic. Manuel Nicolín y Echanove, Chairman of the Exchange, compared it to the foundation of other stock exchanges:

"I am sure that the stock exchanges which are now the most famous in the world...were born in even more modest cradles than this....Trading on what is now called the Paris Stock Exchange began in the streets of that city...as it did in ours..."[7]

In the same speech, Lic. Nicolín also expressed a prophetic wish:

"I hope that...we will have the fortune to see this new institution move from these modest premises to a splendid building such as those now occupied by the...great exchanges of London, Paris, Berlin, Madrid and others..."[8]

But the inauguration of the new stock exchange coincided with a collapse in the price of mining stocks:

"The building (stock exchange) has been launched at a time when previous disasters have created among buyers a visceral fear that deters them like the plague from anything related to investments of this kind. Doubtless this fear will pass, and people will be attracted to the stock exchange to invest in this kind of business..."[9]

In addition, the trading system was less flexible than the one they had used in the street, and the brokers were not stockholders of the stock exchange. The result was that, in April 1896, not a single trade was registered on the exchange, and it was forced to close.

---

[7]Daily bulletin of "La Bolsa de Mexico", November 1895, quoted in Lagunilla Iñarritu, Alfredo, *La Bolsa en el Mercado de Valores de Mexico y su Ambiente Empresarial, 1895-1933* (Bolsa de Valores de Mexico, S. A. de C. V, 1976), pp. 316-319.

[8]*ibid.*, p. 317.

[9]*La Semana Mercantil*, quoted in *ibid.*, p. 40.

Meanwhile, informal trading continued. In 1906, according to a contemporary newspaper, there was trading in 70 mining companies, 20 industrials and 30 banks.[10]

7.3.2　The second foundation

In 1907, a new stock exchange was formed, called "Bolsa Privada de México", with offices inside the building of the Compañía de Seguros La Mexicana, located in the callejón de la Olla. The boom in all kinds of securities which occurred during the last years of the *porfiriato* (rule of Porfirio Díaz – 1876-1911) is reflected in price quotations in 1911 for Mexican securities on the stock exchanges of Europe (Amsterdam, Basle and Zurich, Brussels, Frankfurt and Berlin, Genoa, London, and Paris) and North America (Montreal and New York).

In 1910 the name of the Bolsa was changed to "Bolsa de Valores de Mexico, S. C. L.", and its location to Number 209 of calle 5 de Mayo. In 1916, it moved again to Isabel la Católica 33, to move subsequently in 1921 to Number 51 in calle de Uruguay, and then to number 68 in the same street. In April 1990, it moved to a new building in Paseo de la Reforma 255, where it is currently located.

The level of stock market activity declined substantially, owing to the Mexican Revolution (1910) and World War I. When the War ended in 1918, there was a boom in mining companies, and some oil stocks were registered on the exchange. During the War, Mexican oil had become an important fuel for the British fleet, and, in 1921, with a daily production of 500,000 bbl., Mexico was the second largest oil producer in the world.

However, during the 1920s, Mexico, owing to its own internal process of political consolidation, did not participate in the stock market boom of its northern neighbor. In 1931, there was practically no trading, and the number of operations reached its lowest point since 1907.[11]

In 1932, the government recognized the importance of the securities market by including in the new Law of Credit and Auxiliary Institutions (*Ley de Instituciones de Crédito y Auxiliares*) a special chapter on "Stock Markets", and by granting a concession to the institution which in 1933 changed its name to "Bolsa de Valores de Mexico, S. A. de C. V." In 1946, following the example of the SEC in the US, the National

---

[10]*Boletín Financiero y Minero de Mexico.*

[11]Krayer & Asociados, Jorge Fernández Font, Gabriela Breña Valle, *Historia de la Bolsa Mexicana de Valores* (Bolsa Mexicana de Valores, S. A. de C. V., 1996).

Securities Commission (*Comisión Nacional de Valores*) was created to supervise stock market activity.

7.3.3 Modern times

In 1975, the first Securities Market Law *(Ley del Mercado de Valores)* recognized the importance of the securities market in the economic development of the country, provided a clear definition of the responsibilities of authorities, stock exchanges, intermediaries and issuers, and promoted the institutionalization of brokerage houses. As a consequence of the Law, the exchanges of Guadalajara and Monterrey merged with Mexico, and its name was changed to "Bolsa Mexicana de Valores, S. A. de C. V." Between the years 1978-1980, the market's infrastructure was strengthened with the Securities Deposit Institute (*Instituto del Depósito de Valores – INDEVAL*) for the centralized and computerized custody of securities, the Academy of Stock Market Law (*Academia de Derecho Bursátil*), and the Mexican Association of Brokerage Houses (*Asociación Mexicana de Casas de Bolsa*).[12]

The greatest stock market boom since the beginning of the century occurred during the *sexenio* of José López Portillo. It was the result both of the impetus given to the market by the 1975 Law, and of the oil boom that occurred during the period. The result was an unprecedented boom in new issues (23 in 1978 and 33 in the first 5 months of 1979) and the consolidation of brokerage houses as financial intermediaries.

Subsequently, the market reflected the economic collapse of the last year of the López Portillo *sexenio*, falling in August 1982 (just before the nationalization of the banks) to a level similar to that reached at the time of the oil nationalization in 1938 (figure 7–4). In the 1980s, the market reflected the economic and financial recovery of the years following the 1982 crisis, and there was another boom in 1987, this time mainly of financial stocks (banks and brokers): there were 41 new issues in that year. While the Mexican crash which began on October 6, 1987, was aggravated by the New York Stock Exchange crash of October 19, it followed its own dynamic, falling by 74% in US$ in the 28 trading days between October 6 and November 17, 1987 (📖 10.2.4).

The next stock market boom came with the liberalization of foreign investment. The Nafin Trust (*Fondo Nafin*) was implemented in November 1989 to facilitate foreign investment in stocks, and the stocks of TELMEX were registered as American Depositary Receipts (ADRs)

---

[12]Now the Mexican Association of Stock Market Intermediaries (*Asociación Mexicana de Intermediarios Bursátiles, A. C. - AMIB*).

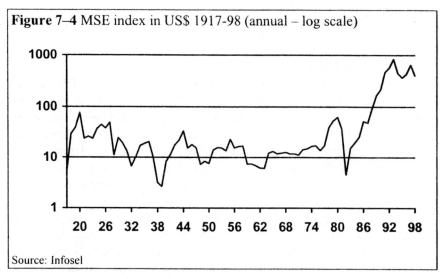

Figure 7–4 MSE index in US$ 1917-98 (annual – log scale)

Source: Infosel

on the NYSE in May 1991. These two events unleashed a foreign investment boom in the stock market. The stock index reached an all-time peak (in dollar terms) on February 8 1994, with market capitalization reaching US$222 bn., compared to US$2 bn. in 1982. That same year, average daily trading reached a record level of US$336 mn., and, between 1991 and 1994, the value of new issues also reached a record level, of US$16.6 bn.

Other important institutional advances during the 1990s were: the inauguration of the new Stock Exchange Center (*Centro Bursátil*) in 1990, the introduction of the first derivatives (*warrants*) in 1992 (📖 9.4), the establishment of the Intermediate Market (*Mercado Intermedio*) in 1993, the opening of the MSE to foreign intermediaries as part of NAFTA in 1994, the registration of the first foreign companies through the International Quotation System (*Sistema Internacional de Cotizaciones - SIC*) in 1997, the launching of the Mexican Derivatives Market (MexDer) in 1998, and the switch to electronic trading in 1999.

7.4 THE MEXICAN STOCK MARKET

7.4.1 Size

The Mexican stock market was the second largest in Latin America and ranked among the top ten emerging markets in terms of market capitalization (US$92bn.) on December 31, 1998.

Figure 7–5 Emerging stock markets: basic statistics (February 1999)

	Population (mn.)	GDP 1997 (US$bn.)	GDP per capita (US$)	Equity market cap (US$bn.)	Equity market cap per capita (US$)	Equity market cap/ GDP (%)
Argentina	35	324	9,334	41	1,191	13
Bangladesh	120	31	258	1	10	4
Brazil	159	777	4,878	105	662	14
Chile	14	73	5,166	48	3,398	66
China	1,200	919	766	61	51	7
Colombia	37	69	1,880	11	307	16
Czech Republic	10	48	4,609	15	1,432	31
Egypt	58	76	1,309	8	140	11
Greece	10	116	11,072	95	9,055	82
Hong Kong	6	173	27,947	317	51,176	183
Hungary	10	42	4,058	5	479	12
India	929	355	382	151	162	42
Indonesia	193	135	696	20	102	15
Israel	6	96	17,330	40	7,316	42
Jamaica	3	6	2,503	2	912	36
Jordan	4	7	1,674	3	783	47
Kuwait	2	30	18,157	19	11,118	61
Malaysia	20	71	3,513	98	4,880	139
Mauritius	1	4	3,472	2	1,458	42
Mexico	**92**	**394**	**4,294**	**89**	**970**	**23**
Morocco	27	33	1,237	6	218	18
Pakistan	130	57	437	6	46	11
Peru	24	64	2,672	9	394	15
Philippines	69	61	884	36	522	59
Poland	39	126	3,274	25	635	19
Portugal	10	98	9,838	64	6,424	65
Russia	148	437	2,946	25	170	6
Singapore	3	85	28,576	95	31,727	111
South Africa	41	122	2,948	175	4,215	143
South Korea	45	248	5,538	124	2,758	50
Sri Lanka	18	15	802	1	72	9
Taiwan	21	65	3,103	252	11,923	384
Thailand	58	102	1,754	34	589	34
Turkey	61	142	2,321	31	516	22
Venezuela	22	85	3,912	18	831	21
Zimbabwe	11	5	413	3	231	56
Total/average	**3,636**	**5,488**	**1,510**	**2,035**	**560**	**37**

Source: CrossBorder Capital

One measure of stock market development is the ratio between stock market capitalization and GDP (figure 7–5). In February 1999, the ratio for Mexico (23%) was below the average of 37%, owing to effect of the Russian crisis of 1998.

7.4.1.1 Sectoral breakdown

In December 1998, there were 156 companies listed on the main market (*mercado accionario principal*), with 296 stock series, divided into seven main sectors according to the classification of the National Institute of Statistics, Geography and Information (*Instituto Nacional de Estadística, Geografía e Información – INEGI*).

There was no direct representation of two sectors of GDP in the stock market (see figure 7–6): Livestock, Forestry and Fishing, and Electricity, Gas and Water. The Construction sector was over represented in the stock market compared to GDP. In the stock market, the "Miscellaneous" sector included holding companies, which would probably be included in the Manufacturing sector of GDP. Despite these differences, there is a certain correlation between the sectoral breakdown of the stock market and GDP.

The main sectoral categories can be understood better by analyzing the more detailed classification of the MSE (figure 7–7). Within the seven categories, there were 26 sectors covering the 156 companies listed on the main market. The largest sectors were Food, Tobacco and Beverages (*Alimentos, Tabaco y Bebida*) - 22 companies, Financial Groups (*Grupos Financieros*) - 21, Conglomerates (*Controladoras*) - 16, and Stores (*Casas Comerciales*) - 21. There is a table of all listed companies, with their MSE codes, in 📖 C.2.

Figure 7–6 Main market and GDP: sectoral breakdown (1998)

Stock market sectors	Mkt. Cap. US$mn.	%	GDP sectors %
Agriculture, Cattle, Forestry and Fishing	NA	NA	5.40
Mining	3,040	3.31	1.48
Manufacturing	25,007	27.19	21.93
Construction	8,458	9.20	4.52
Electricity, Gas and Water	NA	NA	1.18
Commerce, Restaurants and Hotels	14,615	15.89	20.90
Transport, Storage andCommunications	22,355	24.30	11.08
Finance, Insurance andReal Estate Services	9,798	10.65	13.25
Communal, Social andPersonal Services	NA	NA	21.75
Miscellaneous	8,705	9.46	NA
Less: Imputed Banking Services	NA	NA	-1.50
Total	91,978	100.00	100.00

Source: MSE, INEGI

Figure 7-7 Main market sectors (December 1998)

Sector	# Firms	Sector	# Firms
I. Extractive	4	15 Housing	3
1 Mining	4	**IV. Retail**	21
II. Manufacturing	46	16 Retail stores	21
2 Chemical	2	**V. Communications and transport**	11
3 Pulp and paper	3	17 Transport	2
4 Printing and publishing	1	18 Communications	9
5 Steel	5	**VI. Services**	43
6 Metals	4	19 Insurance	3
7 Machinery and transportation equipment	4	20 Financial Groups	21
8 Food, beverages and tobacco	22	21 Commercial Banks	9
9 Textiles, apparel and leather	3	22 Brokers	2
10 Non-metallic mineral products	1	23 Other credit institutions	1
11 Other manufacturing industries	1	24 Other services	7
III. Construction	14	**VII. Miscellaneous**	17
12 Construction	5	25 Holding companies	16
13 Cement	4	26 Others	1
14 Building materials	2	**Total**	**156**

Source: MSE

7.4.2 Growth

From 1976 to 1998, the Mexican stock market produced some of the highest returns in the world. The price index (*Indice de Precios y Cotizaciones - IPC*)[13] rose 28 times in dollar terms, i.e. at an annual average compound growth rate of 16.5%, compared to an equivalent rate for the DJIA of 10.7% over the same period (figure 7-8).

7.5 PRIMARY MARKET

7.5.1 Primary and secondary market

The "primary market" (*mercado primario*) is the market where new securities issued are placed through the Initial Public Offering (IPO – *Oferta Pública Inicial*) of the stock of a company, i.e., the "issuer" (*emisora*) of stock. This IPO also implies that the stock obtains a listing (*se inscribe*).[14] on the exchange. An essential condition for listing is that the offer be "public", according to criteria provided by the exchange in terms of the percentage of the company's capital on offer, and the

---

[13] C.1 for a comparative analysis of two national and four international indices of the Mexican stock market.

[14] The terms "register" (*registrar*) and "list" (*listar*) are also used: they are synonyms for "obtain a listing".

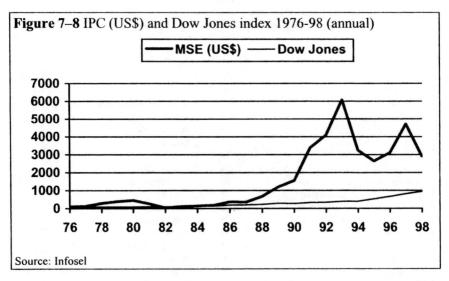

Figure 7–8 IPC (US$) and Dow Jones index 1976-98 (annual)

Source: Infosel

number of investors. If the offer is not public, there is no guarantee of its liquidity, and therefore no market.[15]

After the initial offering, a company can issue stock through subsequent offerings. A "primary offering" (*oferta primaria*), or "capital increase" (*aumento de capital*), implies that the company is selling stock and that the funds raised will go towards financing the company. A "secondary offering" (*oferta secundaria*) implies that a stockholder is selling a "block" (*paquete*) of stock, and that the funds to be received from the offering do not go to the company, but to the selling stockholder. There are also offerings that are "mixed" (*mixta*), where part goes to the company and part to the selling stockholder. The "secondary market" (*mercado secundario*) is the market where stocks are traded after their initial public offering (📖 7.7).

7.5.2 Main market

There are two stock markets in Mexico (with primary and secondary markets) both traded through the MSE: the "main market" (*mercado principal*) and the "Mexican medium-size company market" (*mercado para la mediana empresa mexicana - MMEX*).

The principal requirements for listing on the main market are:

---

[15]In the 1990s, the number of "private equity funds" for Mexico has increased dramatically. These are equity funds which invest in "private equity" (*acciones privadas*), whose aim is to realize a profit when the private equity becomes public, i.e. obtains a listing.

Figure 7–9 Stock markets: main listing requirements		
	Main market	Mid-size market
Operating history	3 years	
Minimum net worth	UDIs 125 millions	UDIs 20 millions
Average net profit (last three years)	positive	
Minimum percentage of capital to place	15%	30%
Number of investors	200	100
Information	Audited financial statements (3 years) Fixed assets valued by authorized valuer	
Source: CNBV		

- Minimum net worth: 125 million UDIs,
- Minimum equity to be placed: 15%
- Minimum number of investors: 200 (figure 7–9).

For an MSE listing, a company must receive the approval both of the MSE and the National Banking and Securities Commission (*Comisión Nacional Bancaria y de Valores - CNBV*).

There have been three new issue booms in the main market in modern times: 1978-79 (56 new issues), 1987 (41), and 1991-94, when the total value of new issues was US$16.6 bn., a record not only for Mexico but for any emerging market (figure 7–10).

7.5.3 Mexican medium-size company market (MMEX)

The Mexican medium-size company market (*mercado para la mediana empresa mexicana - MMEX*)[16] was founded in March 1993, to encourage listings by medium and small companies at an important stage of their development, with the possibility of later "graduating" to the main market. The difference between the MMEX and the main market is in the size of the company and listing requirements. Minimum net worth is 20 million UDIs, and 30% of total capital should be placed among minimum 100 investors (figure 7–9). This market has also been used to "reclassify" (*reclasificar*) companies, which no longer meet the listing criteria of the main market.

The first company to list on the MMEX was COFAR, a subsidiary of NADRO, which is listed on the main market. There was a surge of

---

[16]It was originally called the "Intermediate market" (*Mercado Intermedio*). Its name was changed to "Market for the medium-size Mexican company" (*Mercado para la Mediana Empresa Mexicana*) in August 1996.

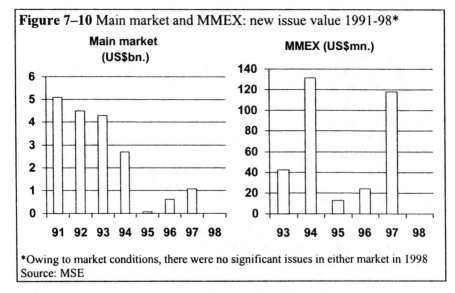

Figure 7–10 Main market and MMEX: new issue value 1991-98*

*Owing to market conditions, there were no significant issues in either market in 1998
Source: MSE

offerings on this market in 1994, but only one in 1995. The number of offerings rose again in 1996 and 1997 (figure 7–10).

At the end of 1998, there were 39 companies with 62 stock series listed on the MMEX. To the end of 1998, there had only been one "promotion" from the MMEX to the main market, that of CIE, which occurred in 1997. However, following the boom in new issues in 1997, more promotions can be expected from this mechanism which could become an important motor not only for the stock market, but also the Mexican economy.

7.5.4 International Quotation System (SIC)

The International Quotation System (*Sistema Internacional de Cotizaciones - SIC*) is a mechanism designed to list and trade on the MSE securities that are listed in another market recognized by the CNBV. The aims of the SIC are to offer Mexican investors the possibility of investing in foreign stocks, and provide the foundations for a financial center for other Latin American countries. The SIC began operating in April 1997, and at the end of 1998 included 4 Argentine issues (IRSA, TEAR2, TECO2, YPF), all of which were also listed on the NYSE.

7.6 FOREIGN INVESTMENT

7.6.1 Stocks open to foreign investment

Until 1989, there was little foreign investment on the MSE. Most companies had at least one stock series open to foreign investment. But these stocks were normally owned by an industrial joint-venture partner which did not want to lower its participation in the company's capital (e.g. CARBIDE, CELANES, KIMBER), and therefore the stocks were illiquid. The only cases of stocks open to foreign investment that were also liquid were: CEMEX B, CIFRA B, LIVEPOL, PEÑOLES B, TAMSA, and TELMEX.[17]

This situation changed radically with the implementation in November 1989 of the Nacional Financiera (Nafin) Trust, which represented a watershed for foreign stock market investment in Mexico. The purpose of this trust (also called *Fondo Nafin* or *Fondo Neutro*) was to decouple a stock's "corporate right" (*derecho corporativo*), to vote, from its "property right" (*derecho patrimonial*), to participate in the net worth and dividends of the company.

Through the Trust, a brokerage buys on behalf of a foreign buyer a stock that forms part of a stock series not open to foreign investment. This stock is deposited in the Trust, which issues an "ordinary participation certificate" (*certificado de participación ordinaria - CPO*) in the Trust, which is the security held by the foreign buyer. This CPO gives the foreign investor the property right of the underlying stock. The corporate right is exercised by the trustee (Nafin) who votes the stock according to the majority vote of the relevant stock series.

When the Nafin Trust mechanism was implemented, it became clear that corporate rights did not worry foreign investors, so much as property rights. If they disapprove of a company's management, they can always sell its stock. Therefore, based on the experience of the Nafin Trust, other classes of stock were introduced that opened stock investment even more to foreign investors. In 1990, CIFRA introduced successfully "C" series stock (non-voting), which offered property rights without corporate rights. In 1991, TELMEX introduced "L" stock (with limited votes): these stocks offer property rights, with corporate rights limited to cases such as the sale, liquidation or change of activity of the company. The reason for the introduction of "L" stock of TELMEX was their

---

[17]Heyman, Timothy, *Investing in Mexico* (Editorial Milenio S. A. de C. V., 1989), pp. 165-175.

listing on the NYSE, which does not accept non-voting stock, but does accept limited voting stock.

As a result of the developments described in previous paragraphs, at the end of 1998, there were three main classes of stock open to foreign investment:

- "Free" stock. Stock series open to foreign investment according to the company's statutes (e.g. CEMEX B, TAMSA).
- Ordinary Participation Certificates (CPOs) backed by stock in the Nafin Trust. Although these certificates do not offer voting rights, in many cases, owing to foreign investment, they are more liquid than the underlying stocks (e.g. CEMEX CPO compared to CEMEX A).
- Stocks with limited vote (L). After the TELMEX issue, this mechanism has become popular, above all with companies that wish to obtain a listing on foreign stock exchanges.

7.6.2 ADRs

The American Depositary Receipt (ADR) is a receipt that covers the purchase of stocks open to foreign investment (free stocks, CPOs, or L stocks). It is issued against shares deposited with a custodian (*custodio*) or depositary (*depositario*), normally an international bank that specializes in this activity (e.g. Bank of New York or Citibank). ADRs can be issued on the initiative of the listed company, in which case they are "sponsored" (*patrocinados*), or on the initiative of investors, in which case they are "unsponsored" (*no patrocinados*). After the initial issue, they can be traded on the secondary market, either over-the-counter (OTC – *en forma extrabursátil*), or on a stock exchange (e.g. NYSE).

The advantage of ADRs for the foreign investor is that he is buying a security similar to those in his own market, in his own currency, through his own broker. Before foreign investment liberalization in 1989, most ADRs were unsponsored, i.e. a US intermediary decided to issue ADRs against the deposit of stock without the agreement of the issuing company. If demand for a certain stock was detected among investors (e.g. TELMEX), no permission was required from the company to buy stocks on the MSE, deposit them with a US depositary and issue ADRs against them.

Following foreign investment liberalization in 1989, the US intermediary (who can be either a depositary or a broker) now prefers the ADR program to be set up with the approval of the company (i.e. sponsored) as it is felt that there will be little demand for an ADR which

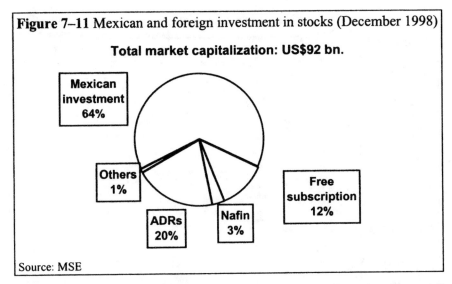

Figure 7–11 Mexican and foreign investment in stocks (December 1998)

Total market capitalization: US$92 bn.

Mexican investment 64%

Others 1%

ADRs 20%

Nafin 3%

Free subscription 12%

Source: MSE

does not enjoy the backing of the issuing company in terms of information and investor relations.

There are three levels of ADRs:

• Level 1 ADRs imply minimal listing requirements and are traded on the OTC market in the US.

• Level 2 ADRs are subject to stricter registration criteria from the US SEC and can be traded both on the OTC market and on an authorized exchange in the US.

• Level 3 ADRs are subject to the strictest registration and information criteria and can be used to obtain new money.

In April 1990, the SEC adopted rule 144A (*regla 144A*) which permits US institutional investors (QIBs - qualified institutional buyers) to invest in foreign debt and equity securities on the basis of information provided to their domestic markets, without the requirement of SEC registration. Under this mechanism, companies without ADRs can be traded through the PORTAL system in the US and SEAQ in London. These are automated systems for over-the-counter trading between institutional investors.

At the end of 1998, total foreign investment through the above described mechanisms in the Mexican stock market accounted for 36% of total market capitalization of US$92 bn., i.e. US$32.6 bn., divided between ADRs (20%), free stocks (12%), Nafin Trust (3%), and others (1%) (figure 7–11).

Figure 7–12 Main Mexican stocks traded abroad (December 1998)

Issuer (MSE symbol)	Series	ADR	GDR	144A	REGS	LEVEL I	NYSE	OTC	AMEX	NASDAQ	PORTAL	SEAQ	BERLIN	FRANKFURT	MUNICH	HAMBURG	Ratio stocks/ADR
ACERLA		X						ACLOF									5
AHMSA		X					IAM										5
ALFA	A		X	X	X			AFAAF				ALFPP					1
APASCO		X						AASAY									5
ARA				X	X			CNRUF									10
ATY		X					ATY				CSRAYP						10
BACHOCO	UBL	X					IBA					GCEA					6
BEVIDES	B	X						FRBNY									2
BIPER	B	X								BIPRY							50
BQ	L	X								QDRMV							1
BUFETE	CPO		X				GBI					BUFDS					3
CEMEX	A		X					N.D.			CMXOF						2
CEMEX	B	X			X			CMXBY				CMDR			CEX		2
CEMEX	CPO	X						CMXSY				CMXDS					2
CERAMIC	UB	X	X					ICDCY									1
CERAMIC	ULD	X					ICM										5
CIFRA	C	X						CFRCY									1
CIFRA	V	X						CFRVY				CFRD					10
COMERCI	UBC		X				MCM	CRRXY									20
CONTAL		X						GPOCY									10
DESC	C		X				DES	N.D.							DSC		20
DINA			X				DIN										4
DINA	L	X					DINL										4
ELEKTRA	CPO		X				EKT										10
EMPAQ	B		X					EPQRY									25
FEMSA	UBD		X	X			FMX										10
GACCION	B			X	X						GACNYP						10
GBMATLA	L		X	X		X		GGBMY			GGDSF	GBMS					4
GCARSO	A1	X	X					GPOVY			GPOOY	GPCDR			GRU		2
GEO	B			X	X			CVGEY									4
GFB	B	X		X	X			GFNSY			GFNBY	GFGDS					20
GFBITAL	L	X						GFBLY									10
GFESA	B	X						GPOFY									25
GFINBUR	B	X										GFIUY					5
GIDUSA	A	X					GID					IDDS					2
GIGANTE	B		X	X							GPGTY						10
GMD	B	X					GMDB					GRMB	GMD				1
GMD	L	X					GMD					GRML					1
GRUMA	B	X	X				GMK					GRUD					4
GSERFIN	L	X					SFN					GSNA					4
HERDEZ	B	X						GUZBY									25
HILASAL	A	X						HLMXY									20
HOGAR	B	X		X	X			CSHHY			HGARYP						10
HYLSAMX	BCP	X		X		X		HLETY			HLEXY	HYDS					6
ICA		X					ICA					ICADS			ICS		6
IEM	B			X				HEMYEY			IEMSY						1
IMSA	UBC	X					IMY										9
IUSACEL	D	X					CELD					IUSD					10
IUSACEL	L	X					CEL					IUSL			IUSL		10
KIMBER	A	X						KCDMY									5
KOF	L		X				KOF					CCLDS			CFSL		10
LIVEPOL	C-1		X								ELPLF	EPLDS					20
MASECA	B	X					MSK										15
MINSA	C			X	X	X		GPMNY			GMINYP						10
MODERNA	A		X				ELM					MODDS					4
NADRO	B			X				NADBY									15
NADRO	L			X				NADLY									15
PEPSIGX	CPO		X				GEM					PPGD					6
POSADAS	A			X							GRPAYP						20
POSADAS	L			X							GRPYP						20
PYP	B	X						GPPSY									2
RCENTRO	CPO	X					RC								RCT		9
SANLUIS	CPO		X	X	X			CILEY			SLRPP	CISD					6
SEARS	B1	X	X	X							N.D.	SRKDS					2
SEGCOAM	B			X								SCAS					1
SIDEK	B	X						GPSBY									4
SIDEK	L	X						GPSAY				GSDD					4
SIMEC	B	X							SIM								20
SITUR	B	X						GPSRY				GPSDS					10

Figure 7–12 (cont.)

Issuer (MSE symbol)	Series	Program Type					Market and symbol										Ratio stocks/ ADR
		ADR	GDR	144A	REG-S	LEVEL 1	NYSE	OTC	AMEX	NASDAQ	PORTAL	SEAQ	BERLIN	FRANKFURT	MUNICH	HAMBURGO	
SYNKRO	A	X						GPSYY									1
TAMSA		X							TAM								1
TELECOM	A1			X				CGTVY			CGTVF						2
TELMEX	A	X								TFONY							1
TELMEX	L	X					TMX							TDM		TMX	20
TLEVISA	CPO		X	X			TV				GRPFF	GTGDS	TLV				2
TMM	A	X					TMMA										1
TMM	L	X					TMM										1
TRIBASA		X					GTR							GRTDS	GTRS		2
TTOLMEX	B2	X					TLMXY										10
TVAZTCA	CPO	X					TZA							TVAD	TVA		16
VALLE	B	X								JUVAY							5
VIDEO			X									N.D.					20
VITRO	A	X					VTO										3

Source: MSE

7.6.3 Listing on foreign exchanges

The ADR mechanism facilitates trading in Mexican stocks for US investors, as they are denominated in US$ and traded through their own broker. Listing on one of the three main US exchanges (NYSE, American Stock Exchange - Amex, or NASDAQ), provides the investor with an additional level of comfort, as it implies that the company has complied with the same disclosure (*revelación*) and information requirements as US companies.

Listing on any of the US exchanges also implies registration with the SEC, in the same way as listing on the MSE implies registration with the National Banking and Securities Commission (CNBV). As SEC registration implies a similar level of disclosure and financial information for any of the three US exchanges, most Mexican companies that list in the US have chosen the NYSE, owing to its status as the exchange with the highest capitalization, the highest trading volume and the most prestige in the world.

At the end of 1998, there were 28 companies with ADRs listed on the NYSE, 2 companies with an ADR listed on the Amex, 18 companies with stocks traded under rule 144A on the PORTAL system in the US and/or SEAQ in Europe, and 4 companies traded over-the-counter (OTC) in the US through the mechanism of level 1 ADRs (figure 7–12).

7.6.4 Listing of companies not listed in Mexico on foreign exchanges

A company with operations in Mexico can list on a foreign exchange, without being listed on the MSE (as occurred in the XIX century - 📖 7.3.1). This is the case of many multinational companies with major operations in Mexico but even more important operations in other

Figure 7–13 Daily average trading value (US$mn.) and IPC (US$) 1978-98 (annual)

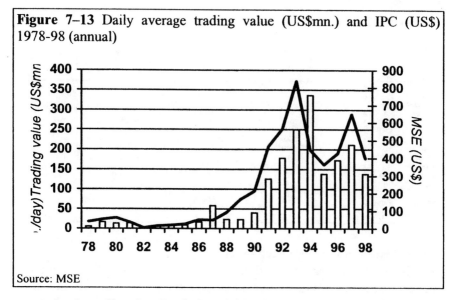

Source: MSE

countries (e.g. Chrysler, Ford, General Motors, Nissan and Volkswagen). However, there are other companies with major operations in Mexico, who have chosen to list on another stock exchange. One is PANAMCO, with important beverage operations in Mexico, which is listed on the NYSE. Another is ELAMEX, a company with important in-bond (*maquiladora*) operations, which is listed on the Amex.

7.7 SECONDARY MARKET

7.7.1 Growth

The secondary market for stocks in Mexico has grown explosively since the 1975 Securities Market Law.

Daily trading value has risen from an average level of US$5 mn. in 1978 to a peak of US$336 mn. in 1994, and US$138.5 mn. in 1998. Trading value has a high correlation with market performance for the obvious reason that there is more trading in a bull market than a bear market (figure 7–13).

7.7.2 Concentration

The 10 principal stock series (figure 7–14) represented 52% of the total trading value of the stock market in 1998 compared to 46% in 1997. This increase in concentration reflected the "flight to quality" (higher capitalization stocks) that was a reflection of the strong market decline in 1998.

Figure 7–14 Trading value of 10 top stock series 1997-8

	1997 Annual trading value (US$ mn.)	% of total		1998 Annual trading value (US$ mn.)	% of total
Issuer			*Issuer*		
1 TELMEX L	6,736	12.8	1 TELMEX L	4,887	14.1
2 ALFA A	2,721	5.2	2 FEMSA B	1,805	5.2
3 FEMSA B	2,552	4.8	3 EMPREXB	1,627	4.7
4 GCARSO A1	2,383	4.5	4 CEMEX CPO	1,624	4.7
5 CEMEX B	2,040	3.9	5 BANACCI B	1,439	4.2
6 CEMEX CPO	1,832	3.5	6 CEMEX B	1,423	4.1
7 CIFRA V	1,689	3.2	7 GCARSO A1	1,409	4.1
8 KIMBER A	1,644	3.1	8 ALFA A	1,364	3.9
9 BANACCI B	1,628	3.1	9 CIFRA V	1,291	3.7
10 CIFRA C	1,269	2.4	10 KIMBER A	1,222	3.5
Subtotal	24,495	46.4	Subtotal	18,090	52.2
Others	28,301	53.6	Others	16,539	47.8
Total	**52,796**	**100.0**	**Total**	**34,629**	**100.0**

Source: MSE

Despite the annual variation, these levels of concentration are normal in emerging markets: in fact, they are a symptom of their "emerging markets" status. However, if we compare Mexico with other emerging markets, we note that the percentage of total capitalization of the top ten companies (another indicator of concentration), was relatively lower (i.e. more favorable) at the end of 1996 (figure 7–15).

7.7.3 Liquidity

In 1989, a "liquidity index" (*índice de bursatilidad*) (see also 📖 2.2.2) was introduced for stocks. This index is calculated for each stock series listed on the MSE, and is published each month in the monthly MSE report. Four criteria are used to calculate the index:

- Traded value (column A): the number of stocks traded multiplied by the trade price for each trade.
- Number of transactions (B): number of trades for each stock.

Figure 7–15 Percentage of total capitalization (%) represented by top 10 companies: Latin American markets 1993-6

	1993	1994	1995	1996
Argentina	65.7	41.7	47.5	50.0
Brazil	36.3	34.5	37.1	37.4
Chile	48.3	46.4	40.4	39.8
Colombia	69.6	61.2	39.4	44.1
Mexico	**36.4**	**33.8**	**36.5**	**33.3**
Venezuela	55.7	73.8	63.0	70.7
Average	52.0	48.6	44.0	45.9

Source: Emerging Markets Analyst

- Market capitalization (C): number of stocks in issue multiplied by price of each stock.
- Volume traded (D): number of stocks traded by volume.

The universe of listed stock series is divided into 4 levels of liquidity: high, medium, low, and minimal. In August 1997, there were 21 series with high liquidity, 34 medium, 61 low, and 70 minimal.

In figure 7–16, we present for explanatory purposes stock series of high liquidity as at August 1997. The importance of the four criteria can be observed:

- The fact that a stock series has a high market capitalization does not necessarily imply a high value of trading (e.g. APASCO).
- A high value of trading does not imply a large number of transactions (e.g. TELECOM A1): just one trade could be for a very high value.
- Similarly, a relatively small volume of stocks traded can result in a

Figure 7–16 Liquidity index: stock series with "high" liquidity (August 1997)

Column Code	A Mar-Aug Amount ($mn)	B Mar-Aug transac- tions (#)	C Market capitalization Aug-27 ($mn)	D Mar-Aug volume ('000)	Liquidity index Aug
1 TELMEX L	24,539	17,617	117,837	1,360,626	9.89
2 GFB B	4,942	20,939	14,019	1,268,177	9.64
3 GCARSO A1	9,179	22,699	51,727	176,847	9.37
4 FEMSA B	8,893	17,695	30,750	190,189	9.24
5 CEMEX CPO	7,436	17,881	16,745	222,479	9.23
6 BANACCI B	5,792	18,077	16,718	281,360	9.21
7 CIFRA C	4,800	16,547	11,584	379,030	9.19
8 CEMEX B	7,488	15,588	20,449	202,466	9.15
9 KIMBER A	7,183	14,483	26,118	212,103	9.10
10 GFB A	1,764	11,337	8,162	682,576	9.08
11 ALFA A	7,806	13,714	37,860	148,169	9.05
12 CIFRA B	4,388	12,698	17,875	325,846	9.00
13 MASECA B	2,362	10,630	3,770	279,920	8.83
14 VITRO	3,360	11,770	12,816	119,677	8.78
15 APASCO	3,681	11,328	16,453	66,683	8.72
16 BBVPRO B	659	6,181	2,003	536,419	8.72
17 COMERCI UBC	1,763	7,940	2,558	253,898	8.66
18 AHMSA	2,251	9,851	8,350	118,794	8.61
19 GMODELO C	3,142	8,795	10,975	55,271	8.54
20 ICA	3,033	8,059	14,223	61,653	8.48
21 TELECOM A1	3,062	7,401	28,916	105,084	8.47

Source: MSE

high value traded, owing to a relatively high price for the stock (e.g. GMODELO C).

The IPC contained at the end of 1997 21 stock series with high liquidity and 14 with medium liquidity, while the INMEX contained 19 stocks of high liquidity (owing to its limitation of having only one series per issuer - 📖 C.1), and just two with medium liquidity.

7.7.4 MMEX

The stocks listed on MMEX are classified in two ways:

• Stocks which have been offered through an IPO and whose first listing on a stock exchange was through the MMEX.

• Reclassified stocks, i.e. stocks whose listing has been switched from the main market normally owing to lack of liquidity.

Total trading value has grown continuously since the beginning of 1995, rising from US$62.5 mn. in 1995 to US$157 mn. in 1998 (figure 7–17). This last figure is the equivalent of an average of US$0.62 mn. per day, 12% of the daily average value of US$5.4 mn. traded on the main market in 1978.

From figure 7–17, it can be observed that the traded value of new stocks is much higher than the value of reclassified stocks. This situation is logical, because these stocks have been reclassified precisely because of their lack of liquidity, while the new stocks have been placed among investors who have bought them because of their novelty. However,

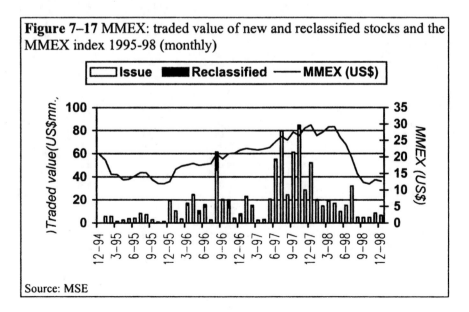

Figure 7–17 MMEX: traded value of new and reclassified stocks and the MMEX index 1995-98 (monthly)

Source: MSE

Figure 7–18 Traded value of stocks offshore and on the MSE 1998

(US$m.) Issuer	Traded value offshore	Traded value on MSE	Total value	% trading offshore	% trading MSE
AHMSA*	2,462	99,964	102,427	2.40	97.60
APASCO*	15,230	383,534	398,764	3.82	96.18
ATY*	98,136	44,306	142,442	68.90	31.10
BACHOCO UBL	38,258	75,596	113,854	33.60	66.40
BIPER B	199	39,640	39,838	0.50	99.50
BQ L	17,349	3	17,352	99.98	0.02
BUFETE CPO	57,884	7,323	65,206	88.77	11.23
CEMEX B	1,152,879	1,422,550	2,575,429	44.76	55.24
CEMEX CPO	203,800	1,624,249	1,828,049	11.15	88.85
CERAMIC ULD	8,463	4,786	13,249	63.88	36.12
CIFRA C	422	1,062,553	1,062,975	0.04	99.96
CIFRA V	1,056,255	1,291,327	2,347,583	44.99	55.01
COMERCI UBC	69,965	312,290	382,255	18.30	81.70
CONTAL *	37	88,559	88,596	0.04	99.96
DESC C	506,510	106,040	612,550	82.69	17.31
DINA*	28,003	9,738	37,741	74.20	25.80
DINA L	14,562	5	14,567	99.97	0.03
ELEKTRA CPO	144,731	395,617	540,348	26.78	73.22
FEMSA UBD	588,528	1,804,502	2,393,030	24.59	75.41
GCARSO A1	310,238	1,408,562	1,718,800	18.05	81.95
GFB B	374,198	1,013,506	1,387,704	26.97	73.03
GFINBUR B	6,066	118,963	125,029	4.85	95.15
GIDUSA A	27,268	33,774	61,042	44.67	55.33
GIGANTE B	58	94,476	94,535	0.06	99.94
GMD B	313	12	325	96.37	3.63
GMD L	743	NOT TRADED	743	100.00	
GRUMA B	2,601	114,246	116,847	2.23	97.77
GSERFIN L	28,781	12,352	41,133	69.97	30.03
HERDEZ B	1	70,333	70,333	0.00	100.00
HYLSAMX BCP	4,962	222,109	227,071	2.19	97.81
ICA*	556,561	388,189	944,751	58.91	41.09
IMSA UBC	93,563	59,420	152,983	61.16	38.84
IUSACEL D	20,658	231	20,888	98.90	1.10
IUSACEL L	111,111	2,288	113,399	97.98	2.02
KIMBER A	101,630	1,221,972	1,323,602	7.68	92.32
KOF L	883,169	58,893	942,062	93.75	6.25
MASECA B	112,087	115,727	227,814	49.20	50.80
MINSA C	4,270	14,182	18,453	23.14	76.86
MODERNA A	179,714	833,097	1,012,811	17.74	82.26
PEPSIGX CPO	240,211	171,326	411,538	58.37	41.63
RCENTRO CPO	101,587	19,601	121,188	83.83	16.17
SIDEK B	23	851	875	2.64	97.36
SIDEK L	127	64	190	66.58	33.42
SIMEC B	4,117	13,045	17,161	23.99	76.01
SITUR B	3	2,333	2,336	0.12	99.88
SYNKRO A	3	885	888	0.37	99.63
TAMSA*	850,309	371,140	1,221,449	69.61	30.39
TELECOM A1	49,644	474,484	524,128	9.47	90.53
TELMEX A	100,930	35,601	136,531	73.92	26.08
TELMEX L	21,820,961	4,887,348	26,708,309	81.70	18.30
TLEVISA CPO	3,625,189	588,583	4,213,772	86.03	13.97
TMM A	38,437	15,827	54,264	70.83	29.17
TMM L	78,236	3,196	81,432	96.07	3.93
TRIBASA*	200,201	135,694	335,895	59.60	40.40
TTOLMEX B2	578	5,880	6,466	8.94	91.06
TVAZTCA CPO	802,325	359,854	1,162,179	69.04	30.96
VALLE B	103	13,769	13,872	0.74	99.26
VITRO A	282,761	267,714	550,475	51.37	48.63
TOTAL	**35,017,410**	**21,922,119**	**56,939,529**	**61.50**	**38.50**

Source: MSE

another factor that should be taken into account in the annual statistics for traded value is that they include both primary and secondary market operations. New stocks are not only more liquid owing to their intrinsic novelty, but also because they include (for the year when they were issued) the value of the issue itself.

7.7.5 Foreign markets

None of the previous statistics takes account of the liquidity of stocks traded outside Mexico. To analyze the liquidity of a Mexican stock, one should add the value of trading on foreign markets to the value of trading on the MSE.

In figure 7–18 we show the value traded in 1998 of Mexican stocks traded both in Mexico and offshore. The value of trading offshore represented more than half (61.5%) of total trading value (📖 1.4.3.2).

Chapter 8
Stocks II

"The expectation of an event creates a much deeper impression upon the Exchange than the event itself."
Joseph de la Vega (1688)

8.1 INTRODUCTION

In the previous chapter, we provided an institutional description of the Mexican stock market, its history in a global context, its size, its growth, and its primary and secondary markets.

In this chapter, we present a system of analysis for Mexican stocks. This includes the presentation of valuation techniques, and subsequently, of examples of their practical application to the valuation of the overall market, of stock market sectors, and of individual stocks.

8.2 BASIC CONCEPTS

Stocks have also been called "variable income securities" (*valores de renta variable*), because they do not incorporate the three predetermined features of debt securities: value, yield and maturity.

The "face value" of a debt security, which is defined in its issue document, represents the value that the issuer promises to pay on maturity. The "book value" (*valor contable*) of a stock[1] represents the total net worth of the company divided by the number of stocks in issue. This value varies depending on the valuation of the company's assets (including its reinvested profits), less its liabilities.

Also in contrast to debt securities, the "yield" on stocks, traditionally provided by dividends, can vary for two main reasons: the variability of profits, and of the decision on dividends taken at the stockholders' meeting.

---

[1] The "par value" of a stock represents an arbitrary value determined when the company is formed to fix the number of stocks in issue. For example, a company with stockholders' capital of $10,000 and a par value per stock of $100 has 100 stocks in issue. After the company is formed, the par value of its stock has little or no relationship to its book value. Companies can be formed with stocks of no par value.

Finally, a stock's "maturity" is not determined, because the period of ownership of a stock is not limited by the maturity of the security (as in the case of debt), but by the decision of the stockholder to hold it, or sell it, depending on the circumstances.[2]

Owing to these differences between debt securities and stocks, valuation techniques are also different:

- Valuation ratios, or "multiples", compare the price of a company's stock to its value, or the flows that it generates.
- The present value formula used for debt valuation can be adapted to the flows generated by the company.[3]

8.3 STOCK VALUATION TECHNIQUES

8.3.1 The concept of multiple

Both the concept of "ratio" (*razón*) and that of "multiple" (*múltiplo*) imply a fraction, i.e., the division of one number (the "numerator" - *numerador*) by another (the "denominator" - *denominador*). The difference between the two concepts is that while ratio normally emphasizes the concept of division, i.e. the denominator, multiple emphasizes the concept of multiplication, i.e. the numerator.

The multiple is used in stock valuation for comparing the price of a stock with its value and with the flows it generates. In relation to value, it represents a way of analyzing the "backing" (*respaldo*) in net assets for each stock. In relation to flows, it is derived from the concept of "payback" (*devolución de la inversión*) in project valuation, which estimates the recovery period of the initial investment.

For example, if a project is forecast to cost 100 pesos per share and generate 25 pesos per share annually, it has a payback of four years. If the project were the whole company, it would have an "estimated multiple" (*múltiplo estimado*) of 4 "times earnings" (4x or *cuatro veces utilidades*).

In both cases, as the multiple's numerator is the price of the stock, the multiple represents the market's "verdict" on the denominator, i.e. its

---

[2]Theoretically, a stock can "mature" if its statutes contain a fixed duration for the company, as occurred in the case of the first companies in the XV and XVI centuries (□ 7.2.3). However, at the present time, there is a custom that, if a company is successful, its term is renewed automatically, and, therefore, in practical terms, stocks do not have a fixed maturity.

[3]To benefit fully from the following sections, basic knowledge of financial statement analysis is assumed.

valuation of the market, sector, or individual stock. The challenge for the analyst is to decide whether this verdict is correct, or not: in other words, if the price implies "overvaluation" (*sobrevaluación*), "undervaluation" (*subvaluación*), or "fair value" (*valor justo*).

8.3.2 The price/value multiple

The two most frequently used concepts of value for the price/value multiple are "book value" (*valor contable*) and "replacement value" (*valor de reposición*).

8.3.2.1 Book value

Book value per stock (*BV*) is the total book value of the company divided by the number of stocks in issue. In comparing the price (*P*) of a stock to its book value per stock, the multiple of price/book value measures the stock's backing in net assets:

$$\frac{P}{BV}$$

The first book of stock analysis, written by Benjamin Graham and David Dodd and published in 1934, focuses on "fundamental analysis" (*análisis fundamental*), i.e. analysis of the financial statements of listed companies.[4] Its main focus is on identifying stocks whose price is not only below book value per share, but net working capital per share - a much stricter criterion. Graham's technique is called "value investing" (*inversión en valor*).

The problem with this technique is that it places too much emphasis on a company's tangible assets, reflecting the very depressed period (the 1930s) when it was developed. Sixty years later, many companies need few tangible assets to generate important profits: service companies (e.g. retail, financial or technology companies) normally do not need the same values of fixed assets as manufacturing companies. There are also companies with intangible assets (e.g. trademarks and patents), that are not valued in financial statements, or are difficult to value.[5]

---

[4]Graham, Benjamin, David Dodd, Sidney Cottle, Charles Tatham, *Security Analysis, Principles and Techniques, 4th edition* (McGraw-Hill Book Company, 1962).

[5]Warren Buffett, a disciple of Graham and the most successful living "value investor", extended this technique to intangible values not always recognized in traditional financial statements – hence his investments in companies like Coca-Cola and Disney, for the value of their trademarks (🕮 2.6.2.3).

8.3.2.2 Replacement value

One solution to this problem is to value a company according to "replacement value" (*valor de reposición*). Replacement value per share (*RV*) of a company reflects the cost per share of replacing its assets. The "q ratio" (*razón q*)

$$\frac{P}{RV}$$

was developed by an economist, James Tobin, to value the total stock market against some parameter from the real economy, e.g. the value of the assets that it represents. Applied to the valuation of an individual company, the q ratio forces the analyst to make a more complete valuation of a company's book value, including both tangible and intangible assets.

Even with this adaptation of the concept of book value, any valuation method based on value per share has a fundamental problem. The measurement of value should be based not only on historic cost, but also on a company's capacity to generate flows for its stockholders in the future.

8.3.3 The price/flow multiple

Various concepts of "flow" can be used for the price/flow multiple. The most traditional is "net profit" (*utilidad neta*). The flows generated by a company begin with its sales. Net profits are calculated by subtracting from sales direct costs, indirect costs, financing, depreciation, amortization and taxes. After calculating net profits, stockholders can decide whether to withdraw them as dividends, or reinvest them in the company.

However, net profits, owing to differing accounting treatment of key items such as financing, depreciation, amortization and taxes, are not always comparable between different companies, sectors, or countries. Therefore, many analysts use valuations based on other concepts of flow. The most common are: cash flow, and earnings before interest, taxes, depreciation and amortization (EBITDA).

Flows can be "trailing" (*históricos*), or "forecast" (*estimados*). Normally, trailing flows are calculated on the basis of results reported by the company during the previous four quarters, or twelve months ("trailing twelve months").[6] For example, in the month of August 1997, one would take the twelve months reported between June 1996 and June 1997. Flows are forecast for the current financial year, the following year, and, in some cases, the one after that. For example, in November 1997, flows would be forecast for 1997, 1998, and, possibly, 1999.

8.3.3.1 Net earnings

Net earnings per share (E), trailing or forecast, is calculated as the total net profit of the company, divided by the number of stocks in issue. The price of the stock is divided by the E to arrive at a price/earnings ratio (PER – *múltiplo precio/utilidad por acción*):

$$\frac{P}{E}$$

8.3.3.2 Cash flow

Cash flow per share (*CF - flujo de caja por acción*) is defined as the cash flow generated by the company, divided by the number of stocks in issue. It includes not only the net profit, but also the non-cash items (*partidas virtuales*) which are applied to the Profit and Loss Statement, but do not imply a cash outflow. These items normally include depreciation of fixed assets (*depreciación de activos fijos*) and amortization of prepaid expenses (*gastos prepagados*) or of goodwill (*crédito comercial*). The reason why this definition of flow may be more useful than net profit is that it represents the cash that is generated by the company, without taking account of the sometimes subjective forecasts of the non-cash items mentioned above. For example, a fixed asset can have a much longer useful life than that implied by its accounting depreciation.

The price/cash flow multiple (trailing and forecast) is calculated in the same way as the price/earnings multiple:

$$\frac{P}{CF}$$

---

[6]Companies listed on the MSE produce quarterly reports 20 working days after the end of each quarter, except for the fourth quarter (40 working days).

8.3.3.3 EBITDA

Earnings before Interest, Taxes, Depreciation and Amortization (EBITDA - *Utilidad antes de Financiamiento, Impuestos, Depreciación y Amortización,* or *UAFIDA*) represents an even broader concept of the flow that can be generated by a company. It is used to compare companies that may have differing financial and fiscal strategies, for example, between different sectors or countries. Eliminating financial and tax costs facilitates comparison of flows.

As financial cost is not being subtracted from the flow generated by the company, the debt corresponding to the financial cost is also taken into account to arrive at a concept of "enterprise value" or "firm value" (*valor de la empresa*). Enterprise value (*EV*) is the sum of a company's market value or market capitalization (*valor de mercado*), calculated as the number of stocks in issue multiplied by the market price, and its interest bearing debt. The *EV* is then compared to the *EBITDA* (trailing or forecast):

$$\frac{EV}{EBITDA}$$

8.3.4 Multiple expansion and contraction

When, in the case of a market, sector or stock, the multiple rises or falls owing to an increase or decrease in the numerator (price), and not the denominator (value or flows), this phenomenon is called multiple "expansion" (*expansión*) or "contraction" (*contracción*). Multiple expansion occurs when higher profits, or lower risk, are forecast for the future, or when there is more confidence in the future, implying that more years of profit can be discounted. Similarly, multiple contraction occurs when lower profits, or higher risk, are forecast, or when there is less confidence in the future.[7]

The relationship between multiple expansion and contraction and risk is clear from the relationship between the price/book value multiple and the sovereign spread on Brady bonds, a useful measurement of country risk (already discussed in 📖 3.4). The inverse correlation between the two variables is apparent in figure 8–1.

---

[7]This concept can also be understood by relating return with risk. The inverse of the multiple *P/E, E/P,* represents the "earnings yield" of each stock. When risk increases, the yield should increase, and the multiple *P/E* should contract. When risk falls, yield should fall, and the multiple *P/E* should expand.

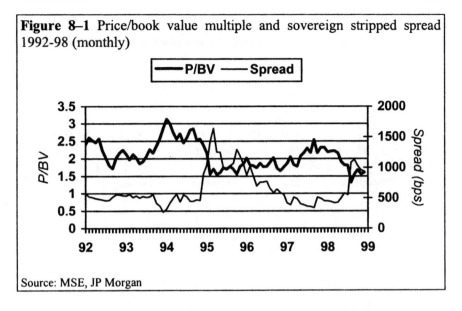

Figure 8–1 Price/book value multiple and sovereign stripped spread 1992-98 (monthly)

Source: MSE, JP Morgan

8.3.5 The problems with multiples

In figure 8–1 the multiple takes implicit account of term, because it rises and falls according to the number of future periods that are being discounted. However, it clearly does not take explicit account of term. The price/book value multiple only represents one moment in time, and the price/flow multiple includes just one flow, i.e., the most recent trailing flow, or the next forecast flow.

Nor does the multiple take explicit account of risk. Under normal circumstances, if one were looking for "anomalies", one would prefer a lower multiple to a higher multiple. But there is the paradox that a market, sector, or individual stock, can have a higher multiple because it has a lower risk.[8]

Modern financial theory (summarized in 📖 ch. 2) was developed to take more explicit account of term and risk, using the concepts of present value and modern portfolio theory.

8.3.6 The present value model

"Fair value" (*valor justo*) of the price (P_e) of a market, sector or stock (📖 2.4.1) can be calculated using the present value formula. Fair

---

[8]This reality will become apparent in the following sections, where these techniques are applied to markets, sectors and stocks.

value represents the present value of the flow of forecast net earnings (E) of the company, plus the estimated price (P_t) received from the sale of its stock, or

$$P_e = \sum_{n=1}^{t} \frac{E_n}{(1+R)^n} + \frac{P_t}{(1+R)^t} \qquad (8\text{-}1)$$

The concepts of term and risk are taken into account, because net earnings (E) and the sale price are discounted over t periods at a rate of return R that takes account of the riskiness of the investment.

For its practical application, the expression 8-1 becomes:

$$P_e = \sum_{n=1}^{t} \frac{E_0(1+g)^n}{(1+R)^n} + \frac{\left(\dfrac{E_{t+1}}{R-g_{t+1}}\right)}{(1+R)^t} \qquad (8\text{-}2)$$

which implies the need to forecast E (net earnings) based on a forecast of their growth rate (g) over t periods, and of a constant growth rate (g_{t+}) in the periods after t.[9]

To determine R, we remind the reader of the concepts of "reference currency" (📖 2.2) and "return ranking" (📖 2.3). R can be expressed in pesos or dollars, depending on the investor's reference currency (figure 8–2).

For the investor who wishes to compare the Mexican market to other markets, the dollar is the logical reference currency. For Mexico, the longest term risk-free rate in dollars is that offered by the sovereign bond UMS 2026. This rate can be expressed in absolute terms, or as a premium in basis points over the base rate in dollars, which is the yield on the long dated (30 year) US Treasury bond.

A premium should then be added to this risk-free rate in dollars that reflects equity risk - for market, sector or stock (the "equity risk premium" or *prima por riesgo accionario*). There is considerable theoretical discussion about the calculation of this premium (📖 D.2.3). The most logical calculation is the difference between the annual compound historical average return of the stock market (measured in dollars), and the risk-free rate for Mexico over the same term.

---

[9] 📖 D.1 for an explanation and derivation of the expression 8-2.

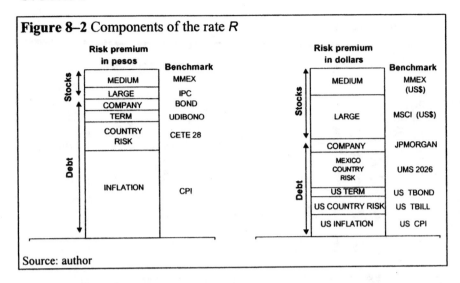

Figure 8–2 Components of the rate R

Source: author

8.4 RESEARCH APPROACHES - "TOP-DOWN" AND "BOTTOM-UP"

The investment styles referred to in 📖 2.6 can be applied to stock investment. "Top-down" (*de arriba para abajo*) implies the valuation of the overall market, followed by valuation of the different market sectors, and, subsequently, individual stocks. "Bottom-up" (*de abajo para arriba*) implies the analysis of a specific stock, followed by comparison with companies in the same sector, and then with the market as a whole.

Normally, a top-down approach is combined with a "passive" investment style (📖 2.6.1), where the asset allocation decision is considered more important than selection within an asset class (e.g. stocks). A bottom-up approach is normally combined with an "active" management style, where asset selection is considered more important than asset allocation (📖 2.6.2).

We prefer not to be wedded to a particular investment style, but to recognize that the analysis of stocks (and, in fact, all investments) is an iterative process, which moves from the general to the particular and from the particular to the general. The sequencing of the analysis does not matter so much as the different factors that it should cover.

In the following sections, for explanatory purposes, we present practical examples of the application of research techniques to market, sector and stock valuation, in that order. The fact that we have chosen this order does not imply that it is the only order, or that it reflects the way in which analysts and investors arrive at their investment decisions.

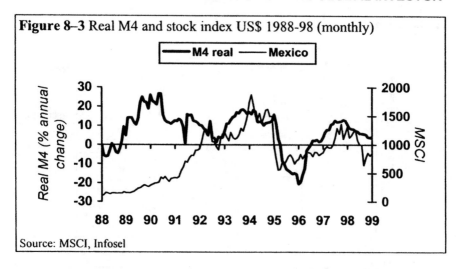

Figure 8–3 Real M4 and stock index US$ 1988-98 (monthly)

Source: MSCI, Infosel

8.5 MEXICAN MARKET VALUATION TECHNIQUES

We present five techniques for the valuation of the overall market:

- Liquidity cycle.
- Comparison of market valuation (as measured by market multiples) with previous levels (historical comparison), or with other markets (international comparison).
- Present value.
- Forecast of the level of the MSE index in one year.
- Comparison of the Mexican and US stock markets.

8.5.1 Liquidity cycle

In 📖 4.4 (figure 4-7), we showed the liquidity cycle and its relationship to different asset classes. At a global level, it can be observed that there is a positive correlation between liquidity and an upward trend in stock markets. Of the six stages of the liquidity cycle, two (III and IV in figure 4-7) are favorable for investment in emerging stock markets, and four (V, VI, I and II) are unfavorable.

For the specific case of the Mexican stock market, one can measure the percentage rises and falls in real M4 as the broadest indicator of liquidity in the Mexican monetary system (figure 8–3). As we saw in 📖 4.6.4, there is a correlation between the stock index and changes in the level of M4.

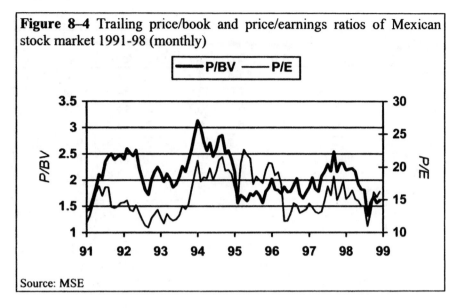

Figure 8–4 Trailing price/book and price/earnings ratios of Mexican stock market 1991-98 (monthly)

Source: MSE

8.5.2 Historical comparisons

Another technique for valuing the market is to compare it over time with market valuation multiples presented in 📖 8.3.

In figure 8–4 we present time series of price/earnings and price/book value multiples from 1991 to 1998. Until the 1994-95 crisis, they have a similar pattern. However, the price/book multiple serves as a better indicator of market highs and lows. The market reaches a high in February 1994 (which was also a high for the index in dollars), but only in the case of the price/book multiple: there is another high for the price/earnings multiple in September 1994. Subsequently, in the 1994-1995 crisis, the price/book multiple reflects the abrupt fall of the market, because prices fall, but book value does not fall to the same extent.

Meanwhile, the price/earnings multiple remains relatively high, because earnings fall (owing to the crisis), but prices do not fall to the same extent. At the end of 1998, the price/book multiple was at the same level as 1995 and 1991, a useful measure for gauging the Mexican stock market cycle.

In general, the price/book multiple is the best historical valuation indicator for the market. In times of crisis, companies' net profits can be distorted owing to inflation and devaluation accounting, but net worth reflects relatively accurately the revaluation of assets and the net effect of corporate performance on the retained earnings account in the balance sheet.

Figure 8–5 Comparison of Latin American stock markets (December 31, 1997)

	year	Arg	Brz	Chl	Col	**Mex**	Per	Ven
P/E	97E (x)	16.6	11.5	14.2	15.6	**17.4**	13.1	17.4
P/E	98E (x)	14.9	7.6	12.0	12.5	**14.2**	12.0	10.5
P/CF	97E (x)	8.1	6.0	10.7	7.6	**14.8**	8.9	6.6
P/CF	98E (x)	7.6	5.2	8.1	7.2	**10.7**	10.2	4.8
EV/EBITDA	97E (x)	7.4	6.1	12.5	11.5	**9.5**	9.5	5.5
EV/EBITDA	98E (x)	6.7	5.2	10.0	9.5	**7.6**	8.7	4.1
P/BV	(x)	2.0	0.9	1.8	1.3	**2.4**	2.5	1.3
Source: Deutsche Bank								

8.5.3 International comparisons

In a rapidly globalizing world, it is logical not only to make historical, but also international comparisons, i.e., with other stock markets. Comparisons can be made with markets in the same region (e.g. Latin America), or the universe of emerging markets.

In figure 8–5, we show comparisons between the principal Latin American stock markets at the end of 1997, from a brokerage recognized for its Latin American research. All the multiples mentioned in previous sections of this chapter are utilized in the figure. The Mexican market had a relatively attractive (low) *EV/EBITDA* multiple for 1998.

8.5.4 Problems with market valuation techniques

The problem with liquidity cycle analysis is that the level of liquidity in the financial system is only one of the variables that are important for stocks. Liquidity analysis takes no account of the future, i.e. the forecast of future earnings for the stock market.

One problem with historical and geographical comparisons is that a country can have a higher multiple (e.g. *EV/EBITDA*) because it is perceived as less risky than other countries. In figure 8–5, the *EV/EBITDA* multiple could be justified in the Chilean case because Chile is less risky than Mexico.

Another problem with historical and geographical comparisons is that they only help us to position ourselves under normal conditions. We can measure whether price/earnings and price/book multiples are relatively high or low in time and space. But these methods of comparative analysis, although useful and necessary, are not always sufficient, because comparative conditions may change, or may have changed.

Figure 8–6 Fair value calculations for the market index (US$)

rate R	5.0%	7.5%	10.0%	12.5%	15.0%
		rate of growth 5 years (g)			
14%	796	905	1,027	1,162	1,313
15%	641	726	821	927	1,045
16%	537	607	684	771	867
17%	462	521	587	659	740
18%	407	457	513	576	645

Assumptions:

Index in pesos (12/31/97)	5,229
Index in dollars (12/31/97)	650
Trailing multiple P/E	17.4
Trailing earnings (E_0) in pesos	301
Trailing earnings (E_0) in dollars	37.3
Constant rate of growth (g_{t+1})	10%
Exchange rate $/US$(12/31/97)	8.05

Source: author

For example, in the 1988-94 *sexenio* there were structural changes in the Mexican economy (including commercial and financial liberalization, privatization, fiscal restructuring and the development of financial markets) which could be used to justify higher valuation levels for Mexican capital markets than those prevailing in the 1980s, or in other emerging markets. [10]

8.5.5 Present value

The application of the present value formula (expression 8-2) to the market as a whole takes account of interest rate expectations, forecast earnings, and the equity risk premium.

To take an example, on December 31 1997, the level of the IPC was 5,229 in pesos, or US$650 in dollars, and the trailing price/earnings multiple for the market was 17.4. Long term earnings for the market were forecast to grow at 10% in US$. Over the next five years, earnings

---

[10]These arguments should be used with care. For example, during the 1987 Mexican stock market boom (□ 10.2.4), when it was clear that the stock market had passed all historical parameters, "historic changes" which were increasingly less credible were proposed (using the four magic words "this time it's different") to justify increasingly less justifiable price levels.

Figure 8–7 Estimates of the stock index with different scenarios

Scenarios	1	2	3
Forecast earnings (E) increase	5%	20%	35%
Forecast E	316	361	406
Trailing P/E multiple forecast for 31/12/98	15	18	20
Forecast Index ($)	4,733	6,311	8,114
Forecast exchange rate ($/US$)	9.50	8.70	8.40
Forecast index (US$)	498.2	725.4	965.9
Index change ($)	-9.5%	20.7%	55.2%
Index change (US$)	-23.3%	11.7%	48.7%
Assumptions:			
Stock index IPC $ (12/31/97)	5,229		
P/E multiple	17.4		
Historic earnings E_0	301		
Exchange rate $/US$ (12/31/97)	8.05		
IPC in US$ (12/31/97)	650		
Source: author			

were forecast to grow at 15% in US$, and the rate of return required from the Mexican stock market was 16% in US$.

We provide an explanation of the detailed calculations for the application of the expression 8-2 to market valuation in 📖 D.2. In figure 8–6 we provide different forecast levels of the stock market index in US$ (to facilitate comparison with other markets), under varying assumptions of *g*, the expected rate of earnings growth over five years, and of the rate *R* required from the Mexican stock market.

Fair value for the market index was US$867, i.e. under the assumptions of a rate of growth *g* of 15% and a rate of return *R* of 16%, the market was 33% undervalued (867 compared to its then level of 650). The closest rate of growth *g* that would have made the market fairly valued (at an index level of US$641) would have been 5%, with an *R* of 15%. Alternatively, a required *R* of 18%, with a *g* of 15%, would also have brought the market close to fair value (US$645).

8.5.6 Stock index forecasting

Simplifying concepts presented in previous sections, the stock index can be forecast over a one year horizon, on the basis of forecasts for earnings, the price/earnings multiple of the stock market, and of the exchange rate.

The trailing price/earnings multiple of the market is a known figure. On the basis of a forecast over one year of the increase in earnings of the market, and the assumption that there will be no change in the historic

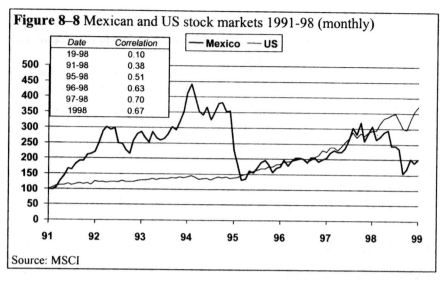

Figure 8–8 Mexican and US stock markets 1991-98 (monthly)

Date	Correlation
19-98	0.10
91-98	0.38
95-98	0.51
96-98	0.63
97-98	0.70
1998	0.67

Source: MSCI

price/earnings multiple of the market, we can apply the forecast earnings increase to the "price" (or index) of the market. We can perform sensitivity analysis on our forecast, by varying the increase in earnings, the historic price/earnings ratio in a year's time, and the exchange rate.

We provide arithmetic details of the calculation in 📖 D.3. There are three different scenarios for earnings growth, multiple expansion and contraction, and exchange rates (figure 8–7). Under the different scenarios for earnings increase (5-35%), price/earnings multiple (15-20x) and exchange rate at the end of the year ($8.4-9.5/US$), the forecast index change in dollars for 1998 varied between -23% and 49%[11].

8.5.7 Comparison with the US stock market

In recent years, there has been an increasing correlation between the Mexican and US stock market (see figure 8–8, which also includes correlation coefficients between 1919 and 1998). In 1997-8, there was a correlation of 0.7 between the Mexican and US stock markets.

---

[11]The index actually fell by 40% in US$ in 1998, because the worst case forecast for earnings increase (owing to the effect of the peso devaluation) was not pessimistic enough (see also 📖 4.8.4 for outturn of macroeconomic scenarios).

Taking data for just 1997-98, we might conclude that the best way to predict the trend of the Mexican stock market would be to predict the US market.

The problem with this approach is that there are only two years of history with such a close correlation. If we take an eight year period, the correlation is 0.38, and, for the period since 1919, the correlation falls to 0.10. Although we suspect that, with globalization and the increasing number of Mexican stocks traded as ADRs in the US, this correlation will remain high, it is still too early to speak of a proven relation between the two markets.

Evidently, if a more permanent correlation is established between the two markets, valuation of the US stock market will continue to be an important element in the valuation of the Mexican market.

8.6 MEXICAN SECTOR VALUATION

8.6.1 The concept of sector

The step following market valuation, as described in the previous sections, depends on the investment style of the investor. The passive investor (📖 2.6) allocates a specific percentage of his portfolio to the stock market, in the proportions represented by each sector and stock, on the basis that each sector reflects fair value, and that it is impossible to beat the market.

The active investor attempts to beat the market by selecting those stocks whose performance (*desempeño*) will be better than the overall market. A first filter for stock selection is the selection of a "sector" (*sector*), or sectors, of the stock market.

Listed stocks are grouped in sectors for two main reasons. The first is to determine those common factors at a macroeconomic level that can influence them. The second is to make comparisons between different companies: if they are in the same sector, they are competing in a similar environment, subject to similar factors. Recently, owing to the globalization of investment, comparing companies of the same sector in different countries can enrich analysis even further.

8.6.2 The role of brokerage research departments

An important part of the activity of stock research departments of brokerage houses (apart from the development of the analysis techniques described in previous sections of this chapter) is to select a sample from the universe of stocks open to investment, and to assign them to a stock market sector, in order to analyze their investment prospects.

The term used in the brokerage industry is to "cover" (*cubrir*) a company. A rigorous definition of coverage is that an analyst is assigned to write a research report (*estudio*) on a company, prepare detailed and reasoned forecasts of future flows, and reach a well argued investment conclusion and recommendation. The effect on stock prices of the publication of analysts' reports is evidence of the importance of this activity for the market. [12]

As there are relatively few listed companies in Mexico (156 on the main market and 39 on the MMEX at December 31, 1998) it is reasonable to ask why all listed companies are not covered by analysts.

The first answer is that given the volume of trading on the Mexican market, no financial institution has the human and financial resources to analyze all listed companies.

The second answer is that some companies are excluded from research coverage, for several reasons:

- Limited liquidity. Some companies, although attractive investments, are simply unavailable in the market.
- Disclosure. Some companies, for whatever reason, are not prepared to provide more information to the investor than the minimum required by market regulations.
- Unattractive investments. Some companies' corporate and financial circumstances are such that they do not, a priori, offer attractive investment prospects.
- Coverage programmed but not complete. Some companies are not covered by brokerages, because the brokerage has programmed coverage, but not yet "completed the research report". [13]

We would stress that only the investor can decide how much brokerage research departments (and other sources of information and recommendation) can help him in his investment decisions. The investor should arrive at his own decisions on the definition of each sector, on

---

[12]Their influence over the market (and their remuneration) depends to some extent on the recognition they receive from surveys among their main clients, institutional investors. These surveys, published by specialized magazines such as *Institutional Investor*, *Latinfinance* or *Globalfinance*, produce annual rankings of analysts by country, or sector, and frequently use sporting metaphors such as "Latin American Team" or "All-Star".

[13]Some foreign brokerages restrict their coverage to Mexican stocks with ADRs listed on a foreign exchange.

Figure 8–9 US stock market sectors (November 1997)

Capital goods	38 Server and enterprise hardware
1 Aerospace and defense electronics	39 Wireless equipment
2 Electrical equipment	40 Wireless services
3 Electronics/connectors and other components	41 Wireline equipment
4 Engineering and construction	42 Wireline services
5 Environmental services	*Energy*
6 Machinery	43 Electric utilities
7 Multi-industry	44 Natural gas/distributors
8 Packaging	45 Natural gas/pipelines
9 Semiconductor capital equipment	46 Oil/domestic
10 Semiconductors	47 Oil/international
Consumer	48 Oil and gas exploration and production
11 Autoparts	49 Oil services and equipment
12 Autos	*Basic materials*
13 Beverages	50 Chemicals/fertilizers
14 Building	51 Chemicals/major
15 Cosmetics and personal care products	52 Chemicals/specialty
16 Food	53 Nonferrous metals
17 Gaming	54 Paper and forest products
18 Household products	55 Steel
19 Lodging	*Health care*
20 Photography and electronic imaging	56 Biotechnology
21 Publishing and news media	57 Health care/facilities
22 Restaurants	58 Health care/information technology
23 Retailing/broadlines	59 Health care/managed care
24 Retailing/food and drug chains	60 Health care/medical supplies and technology
25 Retailing/hardlines	61 Pharmaceuticals
26 Retailing/softlines	*Financials*
27 Textiles, apparel and footwear	62 Banks/money center
28 Tobacco	63 Banks/regional
Computers and communications	64 Brokers and asset managers
29 Broadcasting	65 Insurance/life
30 Computer services	66 Insurance/nonlife
31 Cable	67 Real estate investment trusts
32 Data networking	68 S&Ls and GSEs
33 Entertainment	69 Specialty finance companies
34 The Internet	*Transportation*
35 PC hardware	70 Airlines
36 PC software	71 Railroads
37 Server and enterprise software	72 Trucking

Source: The 1997 All-America Research Team (Institutional Investor)

which stocks to include in each sector, the earnings forecast for each company, and his final stock selection.

8.6.3 Sectors of the Mexican stock market

To show the narrow definition of US stock market sectors, we provide as figure 8–9 the classification of US stock market sectors, provided by *Institutional Investor* magazine in its annual issue ranking the best sectoral analysts in the US brokerage industry. There are eight major sectors: capital goods, consumer goods, computers and communications, energy, basic materials, health, financial services, and

Figure 8–10 Mexican stock market sectors (December 31, 1997)

Sector	# Firms	Mkt. Cap (US$mn.)	% total	Sector	# Firms	Mkt. Cap (US$mn.)	% total
Capital goods				*Computers and Communications*			
1 Conglomerates	7	18,214	13.4	11 Media	3	6,711	4.9
2 Construction	5	2,747	2.0	12 Telecommunications	1	23,401	17.2
3 Building materials	1	93	0.1	*Energy NA*			
Consumer goods				*Basic Materials*			
4 Food	5	6,394	4.7	13 Steel	3	3,933	2.9
5 Beverage	8	17,133	12.6	14 Cement	4	9,585	7.0
6 Stores	6	19,584	14.4	15 Mining	1	2,182	1.6
7 Distribution	2	1,109	0.8	*Health NA*			
8 Paper	2	7,026	5.2	*Financial services*			
9 Tourism	1	314	0.2	16 Financial services	6	15,913	11.7
10 Housing	3	1,285	0.9	*Transportation*			
				17 Transportation	1	439	0.3
				Total	**59**	**136,063**	**100**

Source: Deutsche Bank

transportation. Within these major sectors, there are 72 more narrowly defined sectors.

In figure 8–10, we provide a sample of Mexican sectors and stocks at December 31, 1997, prepared by the same brokerage that produced figure 8–5. There are 17 sectors (grouped according to the *Institutional Investor* classification), consisting of 59 of the 155 listed companies, and accounting for 87% of total market capitalization (US$156 bn.) on December 31, 1997.

The largest sector in the table, in terms of capitalization, is Telecommunications, and it consists of just one company, TELMEX. It is followed by Stores, Conglomerates, Beverages, and Financial Services, all representing more than 10% of total capitalization of the sample.

According to the criteria used by the brokerage house, there are five "sectors" in the sample consisting of just one company. Only six of 20 listed financial groups are included in the sample.

These sectors do not have the same composition as the "official" sectoral classification of the MSE (📖 7.4.1). For example, within the category of Manufacturing of the MSE, there is one sector (Food and Beverages), which in this sample is divided into two. Similarly, within the Stores category of the MSE, both retail stores and wholesale distributors are included (which in this sample are presented separately).

Comparing Mexican and US stock market sectors, we note that two major sectors are not represented at all in Mexico (Energy and Health), and that three others are very limited (Computers and Communications,

Figure 8–11 Mexican stock market sectors, ranked by *P/BV* (December 31 1997)

Sector	# Firms	Mkt. cap. (US$mn.)	Growth % total	E. 98 %	P/E 97	P/E 98	P/CF 97	P/CF 98	EV/ EBITDA 97	EV/ EBITDA 98	P/BV 97
Tourism	1	314	0.2	NA	NA	NA	NA	NA	NA	NA	NA
Paper	2	7,026	5.2	-1	23.7	21.3	24.1	16.8	14.4	11.3	4.9
Commercial	6	19,584	14.4	12	32.4	25.5	30.5	24.5	27.2	18.5	3.7
Beverage	8	17,133	12.6	6	27.8	23.4	17.2	13.1	11.4	9.1	3.5
Media	3	6,711	4.9	NA	NA	30.8	29.8	28.1	20.3	16.0	3.2
Distribution	2	1,109	0.8	29	16.4	11.2	20.6	16.4	12.1	8.7	3.0
Housing	3	1,285	0.9	22	22.1	16.0	NA	17.1	14.0	9.2	2.8
Food	5	6,394	4.7	24	23.8	17.0	18.8	12.3	10.5	7.7	2.5
Holding	7	18,214	13.4	6	13.1	10.9	13.0	9.5	7.8	6.4	2.5
Total	**59**	**136,063**	**100.0**	**7**	**17.0**	**14.0**	**13.9**	**10.4**	**9.2**	**7.4**	**2.4**
Telecommunication	1	23,401	17.2	10	12.7	10.2	7.6	5.6	5.8	4.8	2.2
Cement	4	9,585	7.0	-19	12.1	13.1	13.0	9.5	9.3	7.5	2.0
Construction	5	2,747	2.0	NA	NA	NA	17.9	31.8	13.2	9.3	1.7
Financial services	6	15,913	11.7	11	12.8	10.2	NA	NA	NA	NA	1.7
Building materials	1	93	0.1	-18	8.5	9.2	13.2	3.0	6.5	5.0	1.4
Transportation	1	439	0.3	NA	NA	NA	58.7	5.8	10.3	6.7	1.4
Steel	3	3,933	2.9	-21	6.5	7.2	9.9	6.3	6.6	5.6	1.2
Mining	1	2,182	1.6	6	6.0	5.0	4.7	5.0	3.4	3.1	1.0

Source: Deutsche Bank

Financial Services, and Transport). Meanwhile, one sector (Cement) is strongly represented in Mexico, but not at all in the US. This is because the US cement industry is dominated by foreign companies (Holderbank of Switzerland, CEMEX of Mexico, and Ciments Lafarge of France).

Of the 59 companies in the sample, 40 obtained a listing during the 1990s. Six new sectors were formed (of 17 in total) which did not exist before the 1990s (Construction, Distribution, Financial Services, Housing, Media, and Tourism), and four were extended considerably during the decade (Beverages, Food, Stores, and Transport).

8.6.4 Sector analysis

8.6.4.1 Multiples

In figure 8–11 we show as an example the same 17 MSE sectors ranked by the *P/BV* multiple (price/book) at the end of 1997. In general there is a correlation between *P/BV* and *EV/EBITDA*. Consumer goods sectors on average have higher multiples than capital goods sectors.

In figure 8–12, we plot multiples over time, comparing the price/book multiple *P/BV* of four consumer goods sectors and four capital goods

Figure 8–12 Consumer and capital goods sectors: *P/BV* multiples relative to market multiple 1997 (monthly)

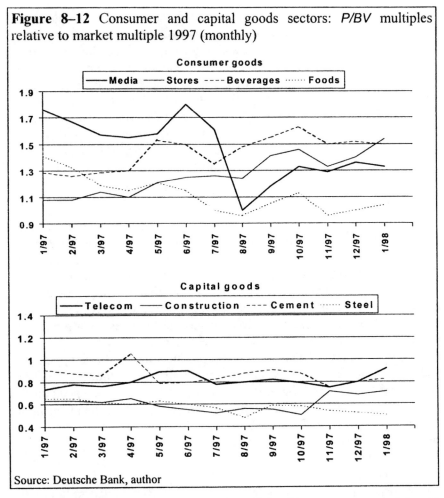

Source: Deutsche Bank, author

sectors (which include 38 companies of the 59 company sample) with the market average during the twelve months of 1997.[14]

In general, the relatively high multiples (Stores, Media, Beverages, and Food) stay above the average, and the relatively low multiples (Steel, Cement, Construction, and Telecom) stay below. However, there are interesting changes in relative position between the different sectors during the year. Among the consumer sectors, Stores is upgraded dramatically and Media is downgraded, although it later recovers in the

---

[14]The ratio was calculated by dividing the price/book (*P/BV*) multiple of the sector by the price/book (*P/BV*) multiple for the market.

second semester. Beverages is upgraded, and Food downgraded. Meanwhile, within the capital goods sectors, during the last quarter, Telecom and Construction sectors are upgraded, and Steel downgraded.

These movements reflect the change in sectoral prospects during the year 1997. Exporting companies (represented here by the Steel sector) had been market leaders since the 1995 crisis, as their sales were denominated in dollars. However, with the Asian crisis that began in mid-1997, and a less undervalued peso, the outlook was less positive for 1998. Meanwhile, the sectors that could benefit from a recovery in the domestic economy (Beverages, Stores, Construction, Media and Telecoms) recovered. [15]

8.6.4.2 Sector rotation

The phenomenon of multiple expansion and contraction in the different sectors of the stock market is called "sector rotation" (*rotación de sectores*). It reflects the reality that during the three upward stages of the stock market (Figure 4-7), not all sectors are equally attractive.

In general, whatever the country, the sectors that are most sensitive to movements in GDP (or "cyclical" - *cíclicos*) are Construction and Capital Goods. Cyclicality (*ciclicidad*), which implies volatility, and therefore risk, is the reason for their lower valuation.

The main cause of cyclicality is that products like real estate, houses, and steel, which are capital goods (or inputs for capital goods) are not of prime necessity and therefore their purchase can be postponed. Furthermore, as they are normally of high cost, they depend on high purchasing power, or the availability of credit – which are normally the first to suffer from a decline in economic activity.

Meanwhile, consumer products (e.g. Food and Beverages) are less volatile, because their purchase cannot be postponed and they are of lower cost. For these reasons, consumer sectors (or related sectors like Stores) are called "defensive" (*sectores defensivos*).

The problem is that the same sequence of sector rotation does not always recur in different market cycles. For example, in 1995, Mexican GDP declined by –6.2%, its worst performance since 1932. The effect of this decline on the most cyclical sector of the economy (Construction)

---

[15]For a complete analysis, sector-related factors should not be ignored. For example, the Media sector was affected by the death of the President of Televisa, the Construction sector by the resolution of the highway problem, and the Beverages sector by the increase of the beer tax. We present research techniques that take these factors into account in 📖 8.6.5.

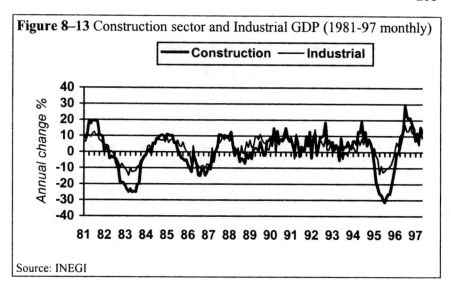

Figure 8–13 Construction sector and Industrial GDP (1981-97 monthly)

Source: INEGI

was predictable and can be observed dramatically in figure 8–13, which plots Construction and Industrial GDP between 1981 and 1997.

However, the boom for exporting companies was different from previous cycles, with its compensatory effect against the decline in the domestic economy on overall GDP. This boom was the result of three factors: greater efficiency in Mexican industry as a result of the liberalization of the economy that began with GATT entry in 1986, the drastic devaluation of the peso in 1994-95, and the boom in the economy of the US, Mexico's most important customer.

Although there is no "export sector" on the MSE, there are sectors (like Steel, or the chemical or automotive divisions of Conglomerates like DESC or ALFA), which have developed a major export capacity and which benefited to a greater or lesser degree (depending on the company) from the devaluation.

The rotation of export to domestic sectors only occurred in 1997, when internal consumption finally began to recover, and was reflected in the performance of the Consumer and Stores sectors. At the beginning of 1998, it was forecast that this recovery could expand during the year to the sectors most affected by the 1994-5 crisis (for example, Construction).

8.6.4.3 International multiples

Company multiples can also be compared for the same sector in different countries. We provide, as examples, comparisons of the Cement and Stores sectors in Latin America at the end of 1997.

Figure 8-14 Cement sector in Latin America (December 1997)

Company	Country	Rec	EV/t 98E (US$)	EV/sales 98E (US$)	real P/E 97E (%)	real P/E 98E (%)	P/BV 2Q97 (x)	EV/EBITDA 97E (x)	EV/EBITDA 98E (x)	P/CF 97E (x)	P/CF 98E (x)
Itaú	Brz	Buy	86	127	81	75	0.8	5.0	4.0	4.7	3.8
LCN	Ecu	Buy	138	138	122	108	2.4	5.2	4.2	7.6	6.2
Diamante	Col	Buy	186	192	88	51	1.0	5.0	3.7	4.4	3.8
Argos	Col	Buy	141	205	75	74	1.0	7.6	6.3	6.4	5.3
Corcemar	Arg	Hold	159	231	432	302	0.9	10.6	9.0	24.6	6.2
Apasco	Mex	Hold	215	242	102	84	1.7	11.7	7.9	16.1	10.5
JMinetti	Arg	Hold	154	247	105	109	1.2	8.8	6.9	14.6	8.5
GCC	Mex	Buy	200	250	86	63	1.4	8.2	6.3	12.8	7.4
Cemex	Mex	Hold	232	267	50	82	1.7	8.5	7.1	8.8	7.0
CNP	Per	Hold	188	268	78	85	2.6	5.8	5.4	8.0	7.7
Vencemos	Ven	Hold	241	272	60	81	1.4	6.3	6.1	6.8	5.4
Caribe	Col	Buy	152	273	88	91	1.0	15.0	10.5	8.1	6.6
Cmoctez	Mex	Buy	192	276	106	99	1.7	13.8	8.3	16.5	10.2
CPR	Col	Hold	179	278	180	140	0.8	7.3	6.6	9.9	9.3
Lima	Per	Hold	266	355	125	122	4.4	10.0	7.4	12.3	10.5
Valle	Col	Hold	253	371	81	84	1.3	15.1	11.0	10.2	8.5
Total/average			204	250	78	87	1.5	8.3	6.8	9.1	7.1

Source: Deutsche Bank

In the Cement sector (figure 8-14), key operating ratios (enterprise value (*EV*) to tonnage of capacity and sales) are compared, as well as the traditional multiples: price/earnings (*P/E* – in relation to the overall market), price/book (*P/BV*), *EV/EBITDA* and price/cashflow (*P/CF*).

None of the multiples are as important for the "Buy" recommendation as the operating ratio of enterprise value to tonnage (*EV*/t) - as all the companies with Buy recommendations have a *EV*/t ratio below the US$204 average. This demonstrates the power of international comparisons. As cement has a price that can be compared between countries, cost comparisons (per ton of capacity) can be made for each country, and this is a useful company valuation tool.

For the Stores sector (figure 8-15), comparative ratios are different from those of the Cement sector, owing to the different nature of the business (e. g. enterprise value/forecast sales and enterprise value/sales area in sq. mt.).

In contrast with the Cement sector, Mexican companies' ratios are systematically different from other countries. For example, in the case of the enterprise value/sales ratio, most Mexican companies have ratios above 2x (CIFRA, ELEKTRA, LIVEPOL), compared with a regional average of just 1x. This comparison does not necessarily imply

Figure 8–15 Stores sector in Latin America (December 1997)

Company	Country	Rec	Sales /m2 97E (US$)	Op. Prof/ m2 97E (US$)	Sales 98E (US$mn.)	Sales 97E (ch.%)	Sales area 97E (ch.%)	Op. Marg. 97E (%)	Op. Prof 97E (ch.%)	EV/ sales 97E (x)	EV/ m2 97E (US$)
Bevides	Mex	Sell	2,478	98	485	23.3	15.8	4.1	-15.7	0.8	2,085
Cadenalco	Col	Hold	4,881	80	913	1	3	1.6	8.7	0.3	1,646
Carulla	Col	Buy	6,384	56	390	5.7	2.8	0.9	22.5	0.2	1,475
Cifra*	Mex	Buy	2,712	136	5,833	18	13.8	5.0	25.7	2.6	6,952
Comerci*	Mex	Hold	2,433	64	2,600	13.7	8.4	2.5	-7	0.7	1,729
Disco	Arg	Hold	11,563	501	1,169	21.3	21.3	4.3	25	0.6	6,932
Elektra	Mex	Buy	2,618	425	1,211	43.9	11.9	16.2	24.5	2.5	6,667
Exito	Col	Buy	9,064	321	948	9.8	22.8	3.5	9.9	0.5	4,238
Globex**	Brz	Hold	11,278	-429	2,037	7.9	7.3	-3.8	6.8	0.2	2,673
Livepol	Mex	Hold	2,797	186	929	11.3	21.7	6.7	24.7	2.8	7,894
Lojas**	Brz	Sell	6,299	112	2,105	4.1	8.2	1.8	NM	0.2	1,038
P. Açucar**	Brz	Buy	9,464	273	3,612	6.8	13.1	2.9	82	0.4	3,928
S. Isabel	Chl	Hold	5,473	277	1,236	27.6	49.6	5.1	37.6	0.3	1,831
Soriana	Mex	Buy	2,678	204	1,763	16.2	15.5	7.6	27	1.8	4,751
Total/average			3,778	140	27,640	-	12.1	3.6	-	1.0	3,859

*Sales are calculated assuming consolidation of joint ventures
** % changes in sales and operating profits are in US$

Source: Deutsche Bank

overvaluation of Mexican companies, but, possibly, undervaluation of other Latin American companies.

These two examples show the benefits, and difficulties, of international comparisons. Much depends on the degree of globalization of the sector being analyzed. If there is a high degree of integration with the global economy (raw materials, technology, or markets), as in the case of Cement, it is more useful to make international comparisons than, for example, in the case of Stores, which is not so highly integrated. As the world economy becomes more global, international comparisons between different stock market sectors will become more relevant.

8.6.5 Structural analysis of sectors

Structural analysis of sectors serves as a "bridge" between sectoral and individual company analysis, for two reasons. First, it can offer an insight into the external and internal causes of sector rotation in the real economy, and, therefore, in the stock market. Second, it can explain the differing abilities of companies in a given sector to respond to the same macroeconomic factors. The analysis of the competitive situation within a sector is an important first step towards the estimation of earnings for its constituent companies.

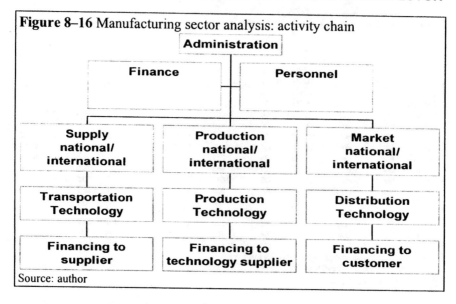

Figure 8–16 Manufacturing sector analysis: activity chain

Source: author

8.6.5.1 Market share

The first step in structural analysis of a sector is the identification of the products (or services) offered by each company, as a basis for estimating market share by product and by company.

Some sectors have an enormous variety of products, which, although from the same raw material, are sold into different markets (e.g. Steel, a raw material for the Construction, Automotive and Durable Goods sectors). Other sectors have a more limited number of products (e.g. Beverages, which would include beer, "cola" beverages, and "others"), but differing distribution channels. Other sectors have just one main product, with byproducts (e.g. Cement and concrete).

8.6.5.2 Activity chain

The second step is the analysis of the activity chain by sector, to identify the keys to success in the sector. Normally the competitive advantage that one company has over another in the same sector can be understood through analysis of the main functional areas: production, finance, and marketing.

For example, in a manufacturing sector, one can analyze a chain that includes: raw materials, production, marketing and distribution, and the financing implicit in each step of the chain. The concept can be adapted to companies in different manufacturing sectors, using the simplified structure in figure 8–16.

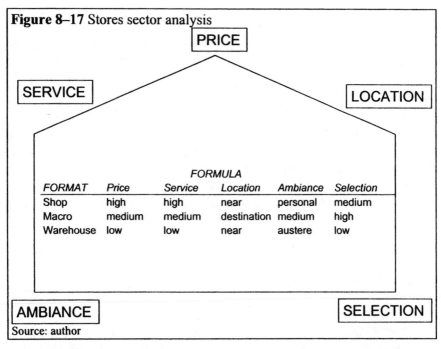

Figure 8–17 Stores sector analysis

PRICE

SERVICE

LOCATION

FORMULA

FORMAT	Price	Service	Location	Ambiance	Selection
Shop	high	high	near	personal	medium
Macro	medium	medium	destination	medium	high
Warehouse	low	low	near	austere	low

AMBIANCE

SELECTION

Source: author

This structure can be applied to capital and consumer goods manufacturing. In the case of capital goods (and raw materials), it becomes clear that the key lies in production technology, economies of scale, and access to international financing, which permit a company to compete at a global level, both in Mexico and internationally. These factors explain the success of companies like CEMEX (the third largest cement producer in the world), ALFA (as a world class producer of chemicals and steel) and DESC (autoparts and chemicals) on a national and international scale.

In the case of consumer goods, the key is not so much in production technology (as economies of scale are not so critical and technology is relatively easy to obtain) as in access to raw materials at competitive prices (normally agricultural in the case of Food and Beverages), and in mass distribution to the domestic market. An important competitive edge for companies like BIMBO, GMODELO and FEMSA are their huge fleets of distribution trucks, which reach all parts of the country.

8.6.5.3 Service companies

The structure for service companies (both retail and financial) is different from that for manufacturing companies. In figure 8–17, we provide a simplified structure of the five variables which determine the principal formats (*formatos*) of self-service stores for companies included in the listed Stores sector in Mexico.

There are five important variables: price, service, location, ambiance and selection. Different mixes of these variables determine the nature of the three main formats. The "shop" (*tienda*) format implies high prices, personalized service, location near the customer, personal ambiance, and a relatively broad selection. The "macro" (*macro*) format implies medium prices, limited service, less convenient location, neutral ambiance, and a broad selection. The warehouse (*bodega*) format implies low prices, reduced service, location near the customer, warehouse ambiance, and limited selection. These different formats, and the quality of execution of each of them, determine the competitive success of the principal self-service store companies listed on the MSE (CIFRA, COMERCI, GIGANTE, SORIANA).

Structural analysis similar to that used for the Manufacturing and Stores sectors can be applied to any sector. We invite the reader to apply it, for example, to the Financial Services or Telecommunications sectors.

8.6.6 Other definitions of sector

In developed markets, stocks are also classified in other ways which are not strictly "sectoral": by capitalization, growth, value, and yield. We analyze the relevance of these concepts to the Mexican stock market in this section.

8.6.6.1 *Capitalization*

Stocks are classified by their capitalization, or market value, between high capitalization, medium capitalization, and low capitalization stocks (*acciones de alta, mediana, y pequeña capitalización*). High capitalization stocks are normally components of the stock index of the relevant market. As the performance of many investment managers is compared to the market index as a benchmark (*estándar*), they are forced to invest in index stocks. In bull markets (*mercado alcista*) this normally occurs until the high cap stocks reach levels of overvaluation or "fair value". Subsequently, as investors search for undervalued stocks, there might be a rotation to medium or small cap companies.

A medium or small cap company normally does not have the market dominance or broad range of products of a large company, and therefore is exposed to higher business risk. This higher risk should be reflected in higher return for medium and small companies. However, as the MMEX is relatively new in Mexico (📖 7.5.3), it has not significantly outperformed the IPC of the MSE since its inception (figure 8–18).

Figure 8–18 IPC and MMEX index 1994-98 (monthly 100 = March 1994)

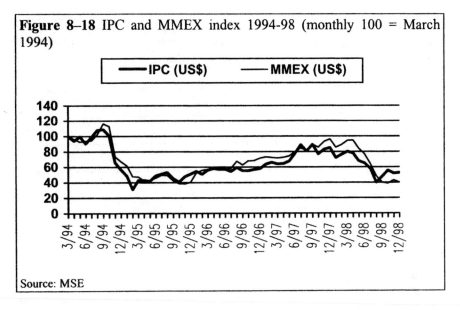

Source: MSE

8.6.6.2 Growth

Growth stocks (*acciones de crecimiento*) are most popular in bull markets. In the US, this term is normally applied to high technology sectors (e.g. computers, telecommunications, biotechnology) whose prospects are only limited by the limits of the technology itself and the ability of a company to gain market share against the competition. However, in the recent US stock market boom, the term has been extended to large companies that have been able to increase their operations enormously in the new emerging markets (e.g. Coca-Cola, GE).

In Mexico, owing to its status as an emerging market, all stocks are growth stocks. Indeed, in the US, emerging markets have been positioned as a "sector" with a similar risk-return profile to growth stocks in the US. It has been observed that periods of boom in emerging markets can coincide with booms in growth stocks in the US (📖 4.4.2). However, within the Mexican market, it is expected that the medium and small companies (e.g. those listed on MMEX) will grow faster than larger companies, and that this growth will eventually be reflected in higher returns.

8.6.6.3 Value

Value stocks (*acciones de valor*) are stocks whose multiples are low in relation to historic levels. In a bull market, there can be stocks which have not been understood by the market in general. In a bear market

Figure 8–19 CEMEX CPO price: October 28, 1997

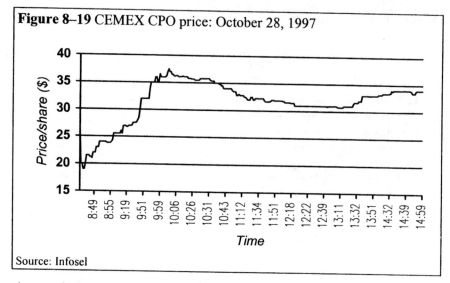

Source: Infosel

(*mercado bajista*), following important falls in growth stocks, there can be stocks that have fallen too far, or overshot (*exagerado*).

In Mexico, in a bull market, value stocks (*acciones de valor*) are normally those that, in spite of relatively favorable conditions, have suffered some specific problem. For example, despite a rise in the Mexican stock market since March 1995, there were stocks that were irreversibly affected by the crisis, such as SITUR and SYNKRO. Both companies underwent debt restructuring, with the result that creditor banks took majority control. There was the possibility of recovery, as a result of these restructurings. In the Mexican context, these stocks could perhaps be called "value stocks"

In a bear market, as in the US, any stock can become a value stock. This phenomenon occurred dramatically on October 28, 1997 when, as a result of the Asian crisis, the Mexican stock market showed extraordinary volatility. For example the price of CEMEX CPO stock lost 25% in the first ten minutes of trading, and then rose by 100% between 8.40 and 10.00 a.m. (figure 8–19).

8.6.6.4 Yield

Yield stocks (*acciones de rendimiento*) are stocks that are valued for the dividends that they pay. The ratio between dividend per share and share price is called the "dividend yield" (*rendimiento por dividendos*). A high dividend yield indicates that the company is in a mature industry that does not need major investment, and that it cannot find better use for its cash than to distribute it among stockholders. In the US, traditional yield stocks are public utilities (*empresas de servicios públicos*) such as electricity, gas and railway companies. ATT, the telephone company, used to be included in this category when it was a monopoly. However, when the telecommunications sector was deregulated, it became a growth sector rather than a yield sector.

In Mexico, TELMEX was also a yield stock, and paid high dividends. After the company was privatized in 1990, and listed on the NYSE and placed with international investors in 1991, it became a growth stock. In general, owing to its emerging market, and therefore, growth status, the Mexican market has few stocks that can be called "yield stocks".

8.7 MEXICAN STOCK VALUATION

8.7.1 Liquidity

A first filter for stock selection is their liquidity (*bursatilidad*). For most investors, there is no point in even analyzing a stock, if it cannot be traded relatively easily.

One liquidity criterion could be the "high" rating according to the MSE liquidity index (⬚ 7.7.3). But, in August 1997, only 21 stock series fulfilled this criterion. A less strict criterion would be inclusion in the MSE index (IPC), which (at the same date) contained 21 stock series of high liquidity and, 14 of medium liquidity.[16]

This criterion could be relaxed in two ways. The first would be the expectation of an increase in a stock's liquidity, for various reasons:

- The company's results could cause its price to rise, and therefore its market capitalization. Market capitalization is the most important determinant of liquidity.
- The company could grow through mergers and acquisitions, increasing its capitalization, and therefore liquidity.
- The majority stockholders of a company could decide to sell an important percentage of their stock, increasing the number of stocks freely available in the market (the "free float" or *flotante libre*).
- The company could undertake a publicity campaign[17] about its financial performance or future plans among brokers and investors

---

[16]The same company can have different stock series, some with high and others with low liquidity.

[17]There are companies that specialize in financial public relations (PR), which sell a company's financial image in the same way as advertising agencies sell its products' image.

Figure 8-20 Stock market analysis (December 31, 1997)

Sector / MSE	DB Rec	Price 12/31/97 (P)	Rel. ch. (%) 3m	12m	yr	Av. Day Vol. (US$mn.)	Mkt cap. (US$mn.)	Net. Div Equity (%)	EPS growth 97E (%)	EPS growth 98E (%)	EPS 97E (P)	EPS 98E (P)	P/E 97E (x)	P/E 98E (x)	P/CF 97E (x)	P/CF 98E (x)	EV/EBITDA 97E (x)	EV/EBITDA 98E (x)	P/BV 3Q97 (x)
MSE		5,229.25																	
BEVERAGES																			
Argos	Hold	14.50	0	22	22	0.4	461	54	-15	0	1.05	1.18	13.8	12.2	17.9	12.8	9.2	7.2	2.9
Contal	Buy	28.70	27	17	17	0.7	1,337	20	23	18	1.27	1.69	22.6	17.0	20.3	15.1	11.0	8.6	4.5
Emvasa	Hold	8.80	-1	32	32	0.2	137	16	-13	33	0.35	0.52	25.3	16.9	10.3	6.8	8.2	6.6	1.3
Femsa	Buy	64.50	-2	54	54	10.1	4,337	48	-19	4	2.69	3.15	24.0	20.5	11.9	9.0	8.8	6.9	3.3
Geupec	Buy	18.00	-13	-10	-10	0.1	125	3	-11	1	1.52	1.73	11.8	10.4	8.5	11.2	7.3	5.7	1.2
KOF	Hold	47.00	6	32	32	0.3	2,773	78	9	4	1.33	1.56	35.4	30.1	24.7	22.9	17.0	14.5	6.4
Modelo	Hold	67.80	-6	-5	-5	3.5	6,845	-17	6	7	1.85	2.25	36.6	30.1	20.7	15.6	12.8	10.2	3.4
Pepsi	Hold	19.20	-13	7	7	0.9	1,120	40	10	-8	1.05	1.09	18.4	17.6	15.7	10.5	12.0	9.5	2.5
Total/average						**16.0**	**17,133**	**18**	**-3**	**5**			**27.8**	**23.4**	**17.2**	**13.1**	**11.4**	**9.1**	**3.5**
BUILDING MATERIALS																			
Ceramic	Buy	13.79	-13	5	5	0.1	93	143	-32	-18	1.62	1.49	8.5	9.2	13.2	3.0	6.5	5.0	1.4
Total/average						**0.1**	**93**	**143**	**-32**	**-18**			**8.5**	**9.2**	**13.2**	**3.0**	**6.5**	**5.0**	**1.4**
CEMENT																			
Cmoctezb2	Buy	10.06	1	NA	NA	1.4	276	2	44	14	0.63	0.80	16.1	12.5	13.1	8.6	10.4	6.9	1.6
Apasco	Hold	56.00	-4	-33	-33	3.6	1,936	13	-60	73	1.95	3.79	28.8	14.8	20.3	11.7	12.7	8.8	1.8
Cemex	Hold	43.10	-6	-11	-11	7.9	6,960	104	-37	-31	4.23	3.31	10.2	13.0	14.0	8.5	8.9	7.3	2.0
GCC	Buy	9.86	-5	-31	-31	0.8	413	28	-13	69	0.51	0.98	19.2	10.0	13.4	7.7	8.4	6.5	1.4
Total/average						**13.7**	**9,585**	**81**	**-38**	**-19**			**12.1**	**13.1**	**14.8**	**8.9**	**9.3**	**7.5**	**2.0**
CONGLOMERATES																			
Alfa	Buy	54.70	-24	-4	4	10.7	4,076	61	5	-6	6.21	6.62	8.8	8.3	7.0	6.5	6.6	5.6	1.8
Cydsa	Hold	22.50	-14	1	1	0.4	335	99	194	80	2.23	4.52	10.1	5.0	4.0	4.0	4.4	3.8	0.7
Desc	Buy	77.10	-5	15	15	3.3	2,913	49	-30	7	6.15	7.40	12.5	10.4	11.9	9.3	9.0	6.5	2.8
Gcarso	Buy	54.00	-12	-17	-17	9.5	6,136	78	-7	0	3.86	4.37	14.0	12.4	19.8	15.2	9.1	7.1	3.7
Moderna	Hold	43.90	4	-28	-28	3.8	2,509	40	-68	99	0.73	1.64	60.0	26.7	39.4	21.3	15.5	13.0	3.2
Sanluis	Hold	66.30	-1	-15	-15	1.3	655	135	-27	20	4.53	6.11	14.6	10.8	15.0	17.0	13.5	9.1	3.5
Vitro	Buy	35.55	-9	60	60	3.9	1,589	114	NA	14	3.14	4.03	11.3	8.8	20.3	4.7	5.1	4.5	1.7
Total/average						**32.8**	**18,214**	**72**	**5**	**6**			**13.1**	**10.9**	**13.0**	**9.5**	**7.8**	**6.4**	**2.5**
CONSTRUCTION																			
Bufete	Hold	26.00	-46	-70	-70	0.2	212	146	NA	-73	2.54	0.78	10.2	33.3	12.6	10.9	13.1	8.8	1.5
GMD	Sell	4.53	-53	-77	-77	0.1	25	-141	NA	NA	-46.83	-27.32	24.3	NA	3.4	NA	NA	NA	-0.1
ICA	Buy	21.75	-2	-28	-28	3.5	1,875	-19	0	19	0.90	1.21	15.7	18.0	11.7	9.8	11.0	8.2	1.5
PYP	Buy	31.35	-11	-41	-41	1.9	34	-76	24	16	1.99	2.61	NA	12.0	NA	7.7	18.3	7.9	2.1
Tribasa	Hold	23.75	18	-21	-21	1.6	601	38	NA	NA	-1.24	1.14	NA	20.8	17.9	NA	11.0	7.9	1.3
Total/average						**7.3**	**2,747**	**24**	**NA**	**NA**			**NA**	**NA**	**17.9**	**31.8**	**13.2**	**9.3**	**1.7**
DISTRIBUTION																			
Aty	Hold	17.20	-1	-28	-28	0.4	598	25	-10	57	0.73	1.30	23.5	13.2	35.6	11.9	15.2	9.8	2.9
Nadro	Buy	6.98	-16	-43	-43	0.2	511	-11	-11	12	0.58	0.73	12.1	9.6	13.8	23.5	9.6	7.6	3.3
Total/average						**0.5**	**1,109**	**9**	**-10**	**29**			**16.4**	**11.2**	**20.6**	**15.4**	**12.1**	**8.7**	**3.0**
FINANCIAL SERVICES																			
Banacci	Hold	24.15	0	-7	-7	6.4	5,030	NA	38	6	1.65	1.97	14.6	12.3	NA	NA	NA	NA	1.8
GFB	Hold	5.20	6	6	6	5.0	3,912	NA	266	30	0.29	0.43	17.7	12.0	NA	NA	NA	NA	1.6
GFBital	Hold	8.00	2	-15	-15	0.1	512	NA	-7	48	0.99	1.66	8.1	4.8	NA	NA	NA	NA	0.7
GFinbur	Hold	33.00	-1	-21	-21	1.3	4,283	NA	-4	-2	3.89	4.30	8.5	7.7	NA	NA	NA	NA	2.5
GFNorte	Hold	14.06	-4	16	16	0.9	800	NA	31	14	1.41	1.81	10.0	7.8	NA	NA	NA	NA	1.9
Gserin	Sell	5.28	-29	-58	-58	0.2	1,376	NA	NA	77	0.11	0.21	50.0	25.0	NA	NA	NA	NA	1.3
Total/average						**17.5**	**15,913**	**NA**	**NA**	**11**			**12.8**	**10.2**	**NA**	**NA**	**NA**	**NA**	**1.7**

Sector	DB Rec	Price 12/31/97 (P)	Rel. ch. (%) 3m	12m	yr	Av. Day Vol (US$mn.)	Mkt cap. (US$mn.)	Net. DV Equity (%)	EPS growth 97E (%)	EPS growth 98E (%)	EPS 97E (P)	EPS 98E (P)	P/E 97E (x)	P/E 98E (x)	PCF 97E (x)	PCF 98E (x)	EV/EBITDA 97E (x)	EV/EBITDA 98E (x)	P/BV 3Q97 (x)
FOOD																			
Bimbo	Buy	78.00	12	7	7	0.8	3,245	20	-6	35	2.63	4.03	29.6	19.4	19.9	13.5	11.3	8.2	3.0
Gruma	Hold	32.00	-12	-57	-57	1.2	1,392	23	-69	64	1.01	1.88	31.5	17.0	30.7	10.7	10.2	7.3	1.8
Maseca	Hold	8.34	-10	-46	-46	2.0	951	-2	-29	-9	0.59	0.61	14.0	13.7	11.9	13.2	8.9	7.6	2.2
Sigma	Buy	122.5	-2	13	13	0.1	638	65	11	13	6.40	8.15	19.2	15.0	20.2	11.6	11.8	8.5	3.9
Tablex	Hold	18.50	-18	-47	-47	0.1	167	4	-36	-7	1.55	1.63	11.9	11.4	8.3	7.4	5.8	4.4	1.0
Total/average						4.3	6,394	19	-34	24			23.8	17.0	18.8	12.3	10.5	7.7	2.5
HOUSING																			
ARA	Hold	39.20	24	40	40	1.1	533	-7	34	34	1.54	2.34	25.4	16.8	NA	45.4	17.8	11.4	2.7
GEO	Buy	49.50	3	-18	-18	1.5	605	27	34	-2	2.60	2.88	19.0	17.2	37.2	16.5	12.5	8.4	2.8
Hogar	Buy	19.20	40	NA	NA	1.0	147	-9	40	24	1.24	1.73	15.5	11.1	NA	5.5	11.5	7.6	3.1
Total/average						3.6	1,285	9	56	22			22.1	16.0	NA	17.1	14.0	9.2	2.8
MEDIA																			
CIE	Buy	62.80	36	89	89	1.9	414	-7	7	18	1.59	2.13	39.5	29.5	61.2	21.1	17.7	12.8	5.6
Rcentro	Buy	12.75	-13	36	36	0.6	268	-9	283	-7	0.80	0.84	15.9	15.2	9.9	9.8	6.9	6.9	1.9
Televisa	Hold	157.1	16	0	0	2.5	6,029	39	234	NA	0.04	4.74	NA	NA	32.3	32.5	22.1	17.1	3.2
Total/average						5.0	6,711	34	NA	NA			NA	30.8	29.8	28.1	20.3	16.0	3.2
MINING																			
Gmexico	Buy	25.50	-5	-8	-8	2.3	2,182	-1	-2	6	4.24	5.10	6.0	5.0	4.7	5.0	3.4	3.1	1.0
Total/average						2.3	2,182	-1	-2	6			6.0	5.0	4.7	5.0	3.4	3.1	1.0
PULP & PAPER																			
Empaq	Buy	6.96	1	-8	-8	0.8	428	26	-64	33	0.58	0.88	11.9	7.9	14.7	6.5	10.4	6.7	2.2
Kimber	Buy	39.5	-1	-18	-18	6.4	6,598	-2	-15	-6	1.56	1.65	23.7	23.9	25.1	18.8	14.8	11.9	5.3
Total/average						7.3	7,026	2	-14	-1			NA	21.3	24.1	16.8	14.4	11.3	4.9
STORES																			
Bevides	Sell	20.00	2	2	2	0.3	301	63	-34	12	0.88	1.11	22.8	18.1	NA	74.0	15.2	12.5	3.2
Cifra	Buy	18.08	8	21	21	5.1	10,798	-25	-11	-5	0.52	0.56	35.1	32.6	21.5	25.4	40.4	24.7	4.2
Comerci	Hold	10.52	8	-7	-7	2.0	1,419	24	-35	0	0.60	0.67	17.7	15.6	51.9	27.7	22.4	14.7	1.7
Elektra	Buy	14.00	15	45	45	2.5	2,121	42	28	17	0.62	0.82	22.7	17.2	37.8	20.6	14.7	9.8	4.8
Livepol	Hold	13.80	17	26	26	0.1	2,300	0	9	-5	0.39	0.41	35.8	33.4	33.0	20.0	32.2	25.0	3.3
Soriana	Buy	35.50	17	51	51	1.9	2,645	-8	0	6	1.52	1.82	23.3	19.5	26.1	20.0	19.3	15.2	4.0
Total/average						12.0	19,584	-5	9	12			32.4	25.5	30.5	24.5	27.2	18.5	3.7
SHIPPING																			
TMM	Hold	62.00	11	-4	-4	0.0	439	139	NA	NA	-2.64	1.06	NA	58.7	NA	5.8	10.3	6.7	1.4
Total/average						0.0	439	139	NA	NA			NA	58.7	NA	5.8	10.3	6.7	1.4
STEEL																			
Ahmsa	Hold	20.00	-11	-22	-22	2.2	965	120	-56	-26	4.78	3.97	4.2	5.0	25.6	8.1	6.6	5.5	0.7
Hylsamex	Buy	47.50	-28	-2	-2	2.1	1,439	64	-25	-40	7.42	5.04	6.4	9.4	6.6	5.5	6.3	5.5	1.2
Tamsa	Buy	173.9	-2	-10	-10	4.3	1,529	14	-27	21	15.28	20.84	11.4	8.3	10.9	6.3	6.6	5.9	1.9
Total/average						8.6	3,933	75	-35	-21			6.5	7.2	9.9	6.3	6.6	5.6	1.2
TELECOMMUNICATIONS																			
Telmex	Buy	22.75	14	13	13	27.1	23,401	12	-7	10	1.80	2.23	12.7	10.2	7.6	5.6	5.8	4.8	2.2
Total/average						27.1	23,401	12	-7	10			12.7	10.2	7.6	5.6	5.8	4.8	2.2
TOURISM																			
Posadas		5.60	-5	-16	-16	0.1	314												
Total/average						0.1	314												
TOTAL/AVERAGE							136,065	35	-3	7			17.0	14.0	13.9	10.4	9.2	7.4	2.4

Source: Deutsche Bank

through investor meetings, visits to its facilities, or written or electronic material.[18]

- A broker could publish a favorable research report on the company.

An investor could buy an illiquid stock, because he thought that its liquidity would increase for any of the above mentioned reasons. The increase in liquidity could, in turn, have a positive effect on the stock price.

Another way to relax the strict liquidity criterion would be that the investor were fully conscious of a stock's lack of liquidity. His investment horizon could be so long term, or the investment quality of the stock so outstanding, that liquidity considerations might be of lesser importance. This is the viewpoint of so-called "strategic investors" (*inversionistas estratégicos*), that is, investors who see investment in a listed stock as if it were an unlisted stock.

8.7.2 Allocation of stocks to sectors

In figure 8–20, we provide the complete sample of 59 companies, each with seven multiples, and divided into 17 sectors at the end of 1997. The breakdown by company shows how the sectoral and overall market averages were calculated.

Of the 17 sectors and 59 companies, we analyze for explanatory purposes one sector, Stores (figure 8–21), which includes 6 companies, or approximately 10% of the overall sample. There are three "Buy" recommendations in the sector: CIFRA, ELEKTRA and SORIANA.

As investors, our specific interest is in a subsector of the Stores sector, Self-service Stores, which we analyzed structurally in ▢ 8.6.5.3. We must therefore adjust the definition already made by the analyst of the "Stores sector". The sector is composed of three subsectors. There is a subsector of "Self-service Stores", which includes CIFRA, COMERCI and SORIANA[19]: a subsector of "Department Stores", which includes LIVEPOL; and a subsector of "Specialty Stores", which includes

---

[18]See Porvenir Online (www.porvenir.com) for a directory of websites of all listed Mexican companies (and of companies in 6 other Latin American countries).

[19]GIGANTE, another company in the sector, is not included in the sample, because the broker was completing the research report when this chapter was being written.

Figure 8–21 Stores sector (December 1997)

Sector	Rec	Price 12/31/97 (P)	Mkt. cap. (US$mn.)	Net debt/ Equity (%)	E real growth 97E (%)	EPS 98E (%)	97E (P)	98E (P)	P/E 97E (x)	98E (x)	P/CF 97E (x)	98E (x)	EV/EBITDA 97E (x)	98E (x)	P/BV 3Q97 (x)
Bevides	Sell	20.00	301	63	-34	12	0.88	1.11	22.8	18.1	NM	74.0	15.2	12.5	3.2
Cifra	Buy	18.08	10,798	-25	-11	-5	0.52	0.56	35.1	32.6	21.5	25.4	40.4	24.7	4.2
Comerci	Hold	10.52	1,419	24	-35	0	0.60	0.67	17.7	15.6	51.9	27.7	22.4	14.7	1.7
Elektra	Buy	14.00	2,121	42	28	17	0.62	0.82	22.7	17.2	37.8	20.6	14.7	9.8	4.8
Livepol	Hold	13.80	2,300	0	9	-5	0.39	0.41	35.8	33.4	33.0	27.9	32.2	25.0	3.3
Soriana	Buy	35.50	2,645	-8	9	6	1.52	1.82	23.3	19.5	26.1	20.0	19.3	15.2	4.0
Total/average			19,584	-5	0	12			32.4	25.5	30.5	24.5	27.2	18.5	3.7

Source: Deutsche Bank

BEVIDES, a chain of drugstores, and ELEKTRA, a chain of consumer durable stores.

8.7.3 Multiples

Two techniques can be combined to select stocks within the sector. One is to compare current and historic multiples. The other is to forecast company earnings to arrive at a medium term valuation of the company through the present value formula, and, for the short term, to calculate a price target.

In figure 8–21, we show price/book multiples (*P/BV*) of the three stocks in the sector. The highest multiple is that of CIFRA, reflecting its size, its long history on the MSE, its excellent management, its good and consistent financial performance, its growth prospects, its lack of indebtedness, and the controlling interest held by Wal-Mart, the largest company in the sector in the US. SORIANA is in second place, with a similar *P/BV* multiple, but lower levels in the other multiples. COMERCI is in third place.

In figure 8–22, we show the *P/BV* multiple of each stock in relation to the average *P/BV* multiple for the sector, during the year 1997. During the first nine months of the year CIFRA was being rerated against the other stocks. Subsequently, the relative position of CIFRA deteriorated in relation to SORIANA, i.e. SORIANA was undervalued in relation to CIFRA. Any analyst who recognized this situation would have retained his exposure to the Stores sector, but would have switched between two stocks in the same sector, from SORIANA to CIFRA, to take maximum advantage of the upward move in the sector as a whole (figure 8–12). In the second half of the year, the investor in COMERCI would have also had interesting returns, as its relative position remained the same, but the whole sector was rerated.

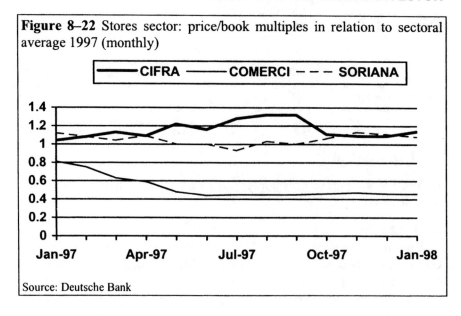

Figure 8–22 Stores sector: price/book multiples in relation to sectoral average 1997 (monthly)

Source: Deutsche Bank

8.7.4 Earnings forecasts

8.7.4.1 Company information

The forecast of earnings is a stock investor's most important activity. It is an essential prerequisite for the application of any of the valuation techniques described in previous sections to the market, sectors, or individual stocks.

It might seem that the easiest way to produce an earnings forecast would be to ask for one from a company executive. However, there are two problems with this approach. The first is that there are strict regulations about the disclosure of "inside information" (*información privilegiada*) for listed companies. In this context, "inside" means any information not publicly available that can affect the price of a stock. Therefore, in a private interview with executives of a listed company, one cannot expect to obtain more information about earnings forecasts than any other investor – although one can obtain information about the company's operations and about the assumptions that need to be used for the preparation of one's own forecasts.

The second problem is that, frequently, the company has no more information about its future earnings than the analyst or investor himself. To take an extreme example, it can be as difficult for the Finance VP of GMEXICO, the largest Mexican copper producer, as for the investor, or analyst, to forecast the price of copper (which is a key input for earnings estimation). In other cases, for example, the Stores sector, the forecast can depend on economic assumptions about GDP growth, inflation, or the exchange rate, where the company can make as many mistakes as the analyst. To understand the problem of earnings forecasting, we suggest that the reader think for a moment about the accuracy of his forecasts for his own company's earnings over the last year.

8.7.4.2 Sales

Earnings are forecast on the basis of the main items in a company's Profit and Loss Statement, beginning with Sales.

To forecast Sales, it is necessary to forecast increases (or decreases) in volumes and prices for the company's products.

Volume increase can depend on an increase in demand for the product in general, owing to macroeconomic factors (e.g. an increase in consumer disposable income) that affect the whole sector. It can also depend on company-specific factors: a new or improved product, market expansion geographically, or capacity expansion (new equipment, an expansion of existing plant, or construction of a new plant). Similarly, product prices can increase more than, less than, or in line with, inflation, depending on the market, domestic and international competition, and the presence or absence of price controls.

8.7.4.3 Operating costs

Operating costs are the direct costs of raw material and labor in the finished product, and indirect costs attributable to the different products. The deduction of these costs from sales produces an operating profit, which, as a percentage of sales, is called "operating margin" (*margen operativo*).

Frequently the determining factor in the operating margin is percentage capacity utilization. If this percentage is low, it normally implies high operating costs, as high fixed costs are often the same at different levels of operation. As more spare capacity is utilized, operations are more productive, and the operating margin increases.

8.7.4.4 Financial cost

After operating profit, the next major item is financial cost. Estimation of this cost depends largely on assumptions about the trend of peso interest rates, and, increasingly (owing to the financing of Mexican companies in dollars), of the peso/dollar exchange rate and of US$ interest rates.

Knowing the amount of short and long term debt, one can apply different interest and exchange rates (where relevant) to examine the sensitivity of operating profit to financial cost. Similarly, with the application of Mexican Accounting Bulletin B10 (on inflation accounting), it is important (above all in inflationary periods) to forecast the "monetary result" (*resultado monetario* - profit or loss from inflation accounting) which can be applied to the financial cost, to arrive at a net financial cost for the company.

8.7.4.5 Net earnings (profit)

After deducting financial cost from operating profit, one arrives at net earnings before taxes and worker participation (*utilidad neta antes de impuestos y participación de los trabajadores en la utilidad - PTU*). After applying a rate for taxes and PTU, taking account of all applicable tax deductions, the result is a forecast for the earnings per share (*utilidad por acción – UPA*) available for distribution to stockholders.

Only with this number, and after a detailed analysis of all aspects of the company (production, finance, marketing, labor, technology) is it worth approaching the company to confirm the earnings forecast and its underlying assumptions.

8.7.4.6 Consensus forecasts

Consensus earnings forecasts (*consenso de estimaciones de utilidades*) represent the average forecasts of stocks covered by brokerages. They are useful for placing the investor's forecasts within a range, but they should not substitute them. The investor can conduct his own survey of earnings forecasts published by the different brokerages. Alternatively, professional services in the US (e.g. First Call, I/B/E/S) collect forecasts and publish them through print or electronic media.

In figure 8–23 we show examples of consensus forecasts of the three companies in the self-service store sector. They include EPS (*UPA*) forecasts for 1997-9 and a forecast for the long term EPS growth rate. There are more than 20 forecasts for the year 1997-8 for CIFRA and SORIANA, but only one forecast for 1999 and for the long term growth rate of EPS. CIFRA has the highest forecast long term growth rate, and COMERCI the lowest.

8.7.5 Stock valuation

Once company earnings have been forecast, one can arrive at a medium term valuation of its stock price, and a one year price target, using techniques already applied in previous sections to the overall market.

8.7.5.1 Present value model

The expression for the calculation of fair value for stocks was:

Figure 8–23 Consensus forecasts for EPS of stocks in Stores sector (December 1997)

	year	average	maximum	minimum	# estimates
($/share)					
CIFRA	1997	0.648	0.950	0.450	22
	1998	0.612	0.938	0.500	20
	1999	0.725	0.725	0.725	1
LT growth (%)		27.5	27.5	27.5	1
COMERCI	1997	0.607	0.930	0.470	16
	1998	0.640	0.890	0.360	18
	1999	0.710	0.710	0.710	1
LT growth (%)		7.0	7.0	7.0	1
SORIANA	1997	1.497	1.800	1.240	21
	1998	1.752	2.073	1.422	20
	1999	1.935	2.200	1.570	2
LT growth (%)		13.6	13.6	13.6	1

Source: I/B/E/S, author

$$P_e = \sum_{n=1}^{t} \frac{E_0(1+g)^n}{(1+R)^n} + \frac{\left(\dfrac{E_{t+1}}{R-g_{t+1}}\right)}{(1+R)^t} \tag{8-2}$$

where:

E_0: trailing earnings per share

g: forecast earnings growth rate for t years

g_{t+}: forecast earnings growth rate in perpetuity, after the year t

R: discount rate of forecast flows.

One can use the valuation formula in two ways. One can make assumptions about the rates g, g_{t+1} and R, calculate the value of P_e, and compare it to the market price of the stock. Alternatively, one can forecast prices with different reasonable assumptions about the rates g, g_{t+1} and R, and see which rates are implied by the current price of the stock.

Owing to the sensitivity of the calculations to the different rates, we prefer the second method. We provide price forecasts for three stocks (CIFRA, COMERCI and SORIANA) in figure 8–24 under differing assumptions of the rates R and g (maintaining the rate g_{t+1} constant at 10% for all three stocks).[20] The price of CIFRA ($18.08) reflects a rate g

---

[20] D.4 for a fuller explanation of the application of the expression to stock valuation.

Figure 8–24 Stores sector: stock prices varying assumptions for *g* and *R*

Company ($)	Price (12/31/97)	EPS 97	P/E	rate R	10.0%	12.5%	15.0%	17.5%	20.0%
CIFRA	18.08	0.52	35.1	14%	14.17	16.03	18.11	20.42	22.98
				15%	11.33	12.80	14.42	16.23	18.23
				16%	9.44	10.64	11.96	13.43	15.06
				17%	8.09	9.10	10.21	11.44	12.80
				18%	7.08	7.94	8.90	9.95	11.11
COMERCI	10.52	0.59	17.7	14%	16.34	18.50	20.90	23.57	26.52
				15%	13.08	14.76	16.64	18.72	21.03
				16%	10.90	12.27	13.80	15.50	17.38
				17%	9.34	10.50	11.78	13.20	14.77
				18%	8.17	9.16	10.26	11.48	12.82
SORIANA	35.50	1.52	23.3	14%	41.90	47.43	53.58	60.41	67.98
				15%	33.52	37.85	42.66	48.00	53.91
				16%	27.93	31.47	35.39	39.74	44.54
				17%	23.94	26.91	30.20	33.84	37.87
				18%	20.95	23.49	26.31	29.43	32.87

The header "rate of growth 5 years (*g*)" spans the columns 10.0%, 12.5%, 15.0%, 17.5%, 20.0%.

Source: author

of 15% and *R* of 14%, COMERCI ($10.52) *g* of 12.5% and *R* of 17%, and SORIANA ($35.50) *g* of 15% and *R* of 16%. The investor has to decide, comparing these forecasts with consensus forecasts and his own, whether these assumptions are realistic, and whether the stock price is under or overvalued in relation to fair value.

8.7.6 One year price targets

Individual stock prices can be forecast over a one year term using the same technique we presented in 🕮 8.5.6 for the overall market.

We know the trailing price/earnings multiple of each stock. If we forecast for the next year the rate of earnings increase for each stock, and assume no change in the trailing price/earnings multiple for each stock at the end of the year, we can apply the same growth rate to the stock price. We provide detailed calculations for the three stocks in CIFRA, COMERCI and SORIANA in figure 8–25.[21] The price of each stock rises with the increase in earnings, if there is no multiple expansion or contraction. We can conduct sensitivity analysis on our price forecast, by varying the rate of earnings increase, and the trailing price/earnings

---

[21] 🕮 D.5 for a fuller explanation of the application of the technique to individual stocks.

Figure 8–25 One year price targets under varying assumptions

Forecast earnings (E) increase	5%	20%	35%
CIFRA			
Forecast E	0.54	0.62	0.70
Trailing P/E forecast for 31/12/98	32.50	35.00	37.50
Forecast price ($)	17.58	21.63	26.08
Forecast exchange rate ($/US$)	9.50	8.70	8.40
Forecast price (US$)	1.85	2.49	3.10
Increase in price ($)	-2.8%	19.7%	44.2%
Increase in price (US$)	-17.6%	10.7%	38.2%
Price (31/12/97)	18.08		
Trailing P/E multiple	35.10		
Trailing earnings E0	0.52		
Exchange rate $/US$ (31/12/97)	8.05		
Price in US$	2.25		
COMERCI			
Forecast E	0.62	0.71	0.80
Trailing P/E forecast for 31/12/98	15.00	17.70	20.00
Forecast price ($)	9.36	12.62	16.05
Forecast exchange rate ($/US$)	9.50	8.70	8.40
Forecast price (US$)	0.99	1.45	1.91
Increase in price ($)	-11.0%	20.0%	52.5%
Increase in price (US$)	-24.6%	11.0%	46.2%
Price (31/12/97)	10.52		
Trailing P/E multiple	17.70		
Trailing earnings E0	0.59		
Exchange rate $/US$ (31/12/97)	8.05		
Price in US$	1.31		
SORIANA			
Forecast E	1.60	1.83	2.06
Trailing P/E forecast for 31/12/98	20.00	23.30	27.00
Forecast price ($)	32.00	42.60	55.54
Forecast exchange rate ($/US$)	9.50	8.70	8.40
Forecast price (US$)	3.37	4.90	6.61
Increase in price ($)	-9.9%	20.0%	56.4%
Increase in price (US$)	-23.6%	11.0%	49.9%
Price (31/12/97)	35.50		
Trailing P/E multiple	23.30		
Trailing earnings E0	1.52		
Exchange rate $/US$ (31/12/97)	8.05		
Price in US$	4.41		

Source: author

multiple in a year's time. If we wish to compare Mexican stocks with similar stocks in other countries, we can also vary our one year exchange rate assumptions.

Chapter 9
Derivatives

"Mathematicians are like Frenchmen: whatever you say to them they translate into their own language and forthwith it is something entirely different."
Johann Wolfgang von Goethe (1749-1832)

9.1 INTRODUCTION

A derivative (*derivado*) is any instrument whose value depends (or "is derived from") an underlying asset (*subyacente*).[1] The most important derivatives are futures (*futuros*), options (*opciones*), forwards (*contratos adelantados*) and swaps (*swaps*). The underlying assets for derivatives include: financial instruments (debt securities, stocks, currencies, and financial indices), hard and soft commodities, and agricultural products. "Financial derivatives" (*derivados financieros*) are derivatives whose underlying assets are financial instruments.

In recent years, financial derivatives have grown explosively, for three main reasons:

- The collapse between 1971 and 1973 of the Bretton Woods system of fixed exchange rates introduced greater volatility into two key financial market prices, exchange rates and interest rates. There was a consequent necessity to measure this volatility and hedge against it.
- Advances in financial and economic theory have provided technical and practical tools for valuing increasingly complex derivatives.[2]
- The globalization process (described in 📖 1.2) and the technological and financial integration of markets have made derivatives trading possible in any market, at any time.

---

[1] Rodríguez de Castro, James, *Introducción al Análisis de Productos Financieros Derivados* (Bolsa Mexicana de Valores, Limusa, Noriega Editores, 1996), p. 27.

[2] In 1997, Professors Myron Scholes and Robert Merton were awarded the Nobel Economics Prize for their work in derivatives valuation.

Figure 9–1 Main derivatives exchanges

AEX	Amsterdam Exchanges
BMF	Bolsa de Mercadorías y Futuros de Brasil
CBOE	Chicago Board Options Exchange
CBOT	Chicago Board of Trade
CME	Chicago Mercantile Exchange
DTB	Deutsche Terminbörse (Frankfurt)
FES	Sydney Futures Exchange
FINEX	Financial Instruments Exchange (Dublin)
KCBT	Kansas City Board of Trade
LCH	London Clearing House
LIFFE	London International Financial Futures and Options Exchange
MATIF	Marché a Terme International de France
MEFF RF	Mercado Español de Futuros Financieros de Renta Fija (Barcelona)
MidAm	The MidAmerica Commodity Exchange
MIF	Mercato Italiano dei Futures
MME	Malaysia Monetary Exchange
MSE	Midwest Stock Exchange
NYCE	New York Cotton Exchange
NYSE	New York Stock Exchange
OM	Optionsmarket Stockholm AB
OMLX	The London Securities and Derivatives Exchange
OSE	Osaka Securities Exchange
ÖTOB	Austrian Futures and Options Exchange (Vienna)
PHLX	Philadelphia Stock Exchange
PSE	Pacific Stock Exchange
SAFEX	South African Futures Exchange
SIMEX	Singapore International Monetary Exchange
SOFFE	Swiss Options and Financial Futures Exchange
SOM	Finnish Securities and Derivatives Exchange Clearing House
TIFFE	Tokyo International Financial Futures Exchange
TSE	Tokyo Stock Exchange

Source: BIS, author

Derivatives markets are new, complex, expanding, and offer opportunities for huge profits (and losses). They have therefore become a popular, almost mystical, subject with the media. Furthermore, derivatives trading by speculators (*especuladores*) and arbitrageurs (*arbitrajistas*) - who are indispensable for market liquidity - has produced the popular impression that they are only speculative, and therefore very risky.

However, the investor can also use derivatives for investment (and hedging (*cobertura*)) in all Mexican financial instruments described in previous chapters: debt, currencies, and stocks.

In 📖 9.2-9.5, we provide a historical outline of the development of derivatives in the world and in Mexico, and a description of the markets for Mexican derivatives, both in Mexico and offshore. In 📖 9.6-9.9, we explain techniques for using derivatives to maximize return and minimize risk in Mexican investments.

9.2 HISTORY OF GLOBAL DERIVATIVES

9.2.1 Origins

It is believed that forward contracts were used as instruments of exchange in India in the year 2,000 BC, and subsequently in Greco-Roman times.

Derivatives had reached a high level of sophistication in the Dutch financial markets of the XVII century, which were the most advanced in the world at that time (📖 5.2 and 📖 7.2). One of the reasons for the spectacular rise in the price of tulip bulbs in the years 1636-37 was the availability of futures contracts (📖 10.2.2). In his description of the Amsterdam Stock Exchange, written in 1688, Joseph de la Vega describes a vigorous market for options in Dutch East India Company stock:

"The price of the shares is now 580: it seems to me they will climb to a much higher price because of the extensive cargoes that are expected from India, because of the good business of the Company, of the reputation of its goods, of the prospective dividends, and of the peace in Europe. Nevertheless, I decide not to buy shares through fear that I might encounter a loss and might meet with embarrassment if my calculations should prove erroneous. I therefore turn to those persons who are willing to take options and ask them how much [premium] they demand for the obligation to deliver shares at a price of 600 each at a certain later date. I come to an agreement about the premium, have it transferred [to the taker of the options] immediately at the Bank, and I am sure that it is impossible to lose more than the price of the premium. And I shall gain the entire amount by which the price [of the stock] shall surpass the figure of 600."[3]

---

[3]De la Vega, Joseph, *Confusión de Confusiones*, ed. Martin S. Fridson (John Wiley & Sons, Inc., 1996), p. 156.

Figure 9–2 Global history of derivatives: important dates

AC 2000	Forward contracts in India
400	Forward contracts in Greece
AD 50	Forward contracts in Rome
1636	Tulip futures in Holland
1680	Options on Dutch East India Company shares in Holland
1720	South Sea Bubble caused by issue of futures on South Sea Company
1730	Rice futures in Osaka
1790	Put and call options in US
1848	Chicago Board of Trade (CBOT) founded by 82 traders in Chicago
1851	First corn forwards traded on CBOT
1854	Standardization of wheat and oats contracts in bushels on CBOT
1865	Standardization of forward contracts (as futures) and introduction of margin as guarantee for buyer and seller on CBOT
1870	New York Cotton Exchange
1874	Chicago Produce Exchange
1882	MidAm establishes clearing house and margin system
1898	Chicago Produce Exchange forms Chicago Butter and Egg Board
1919	Chicago Butter and Egg Board becomes Chicago Mercantile Exchange (CME)
1922	Grain Futures Law establishes regulatory framework for US futures markets
1934	US Securities Law authorizes SEC to regulate options trading Put and Call Brokers and Dealers Association
1936	Commodities Exchange Act extends regulation to futures brokers and traders
1961	Frozen pork futures on CME
1964	Cattle futures on CME
1968	CBOT studies stock futures.
1971-73	Collapse of Bretton Woods agreements
1972	International Money Market (CME): trading in currency futures
1973	Chicago Board Options Exchange (CBOE) Publication of option valuation model by Fischer Black and Myron Scholes
1974	Commodities Futures Trading Commission (CFTC)
1975	Futures on certificates backed by GNMA mortgages on CBOT Call options on stocks on AMEX and PHLX.
1976	Call options on stocks on PSE and MSE US Tbill futures traded on CME
1977	US Tbond futures traded on CBOT Put options on stocks traded on CBOE, AMEX, PHLX, PSE, MSE SEC calls moratorium on expansion of options, which expires in 1980
1978	Standardization of options trading in Amsterdam and London
1981	Eurodollar futures on CME
1982	Stock index futures on KCBT Currency options on PHLX Options on Tbond futures on CBOT S&P 500 index futures on CME Financial futures market (LIFFE) in London
1983	S&P100 and S&P500 index options on CBOE
1984	SIMEX begins operation in Singapore Options on currency futures on CME
1985	Futures on Japanese government bonds on TSE MATIF begins operations in Paris
1988	SOFFE begins operations in Switzerland
1989	TIFFE begins operations in Tokyo Interest rate options on CBOE
1990	DTB begins operations in Germany
1991-98	Expansion of US derivatives markets to emerging markets products

Source: author

Futures trading in stocks of the South Sea Company is also thought to have been an important contributing cause to the 1720 crash in England (South Sea Bubble - *Burbuja del Mar del Sur* - 📖 10.2.2).

Derivatives were also traded outside Europe. Rice futures were traded in Osaka (Japan) in 1730, and put and call options on stocks in the US in 1790 - before the foundation of the NYSE in 1792.

9.2.2 The Chicago futures markets

Modern futures markets developed in Chicago in the XIX century (figure 9-2). During the second half of the century, as railways opened up the enormous cornfields of the Mid-West United States, Chicago became the center of the grain trade.[4] Faced with a frequent mismatch between grain supply and demand, 82 Chicago traders decided in 1848 to establish an organized market to trade grain contracts (mainly corn and wheat), both spot (*mercado inmediato*) and forward (*a plazos*). It was called the Chicago Board of Trade (CBOT).

During the following decades, the main features of an efficient futures market evolved: standardized contracts, margin, and a clearing house.[5] In 1865, general rules were introduced for the standardization of forward contracts, and the new contracts were called "futures contracts" (*contratos futuros*). In the same year, market participants were required to provide as guarantee a deposit called "margin" (*margen*), to cover price deviations from the original contract and ensure contract fulfillment at maturity. In 1874, the Chicago Produce Exchange was formed in competition to the CBOT. In 1882, the "clearing house" (*cámara de compensación*) was established as counterparty for all contracts, and assurance of contract fulfillment.

In 1919, the Chicago Butter and Egg Board, a division of the Chicago Produce Exchange, was consolidated, and changed its name to the Chicago Mercantile Exchange (CME). The CBOT and CME became the principal derivatives markets in Chicago. In 1922, when the first regulatory framework for futures markets was introduced in the US, the underlying assets were still agricultural and mining products. However, when the new Securities and Exchange Commission (SEC) was formed in 1934 it included regulation of options trading, implicitly recognizing an incipient activity in stock options. That same year, the Put and Call

---

[4]See Mansell Carstens, Catherine, *Las Nuevas Finanzas en Mexico* (Editorial Milenio, S. A. de C. V., 1992), pp. 276-281.

[5]See www.cbot.com.

Brokers and Dealers Association (*Asociación de Corredores e Intermediarios de Opciones de Compra y Venta*) was formed.

In 1936, the Commodities Exchange Act (*Ley de Bolsas de Commodities*) was passed to regulate futures trading and brokers. In the same year, soybean contracts began trading on the CBOT. However, in the two decades following World War II, market development was slowed, owing to the US government's policy of keeping grain prices stable. In the 1960s, as trade expanded, the CME and CBOT renewed their expansion, with an increase in the range of underlying assets for futures contracts: frozen pork, live pigs, and live cattle on the CME, and wood and silver on the CBOT.

9.2.3 The introduction of financial derivatives

The CME and CBOT had now developed the model for an organized market for any commodity where there was a demand for hedging and speculation: contract standardization, clearing house, margin, and a trading floor. It was logical to seek new products, and, during the stock market boom of the 1960s, financial instruments such as stocks and bonds offered interesting opportunities.

In 1968, the CBOT had commissioned a study on the possibility of trading futures contracts on listed stocks. Surprisingly, the study recommended options on stocks, rather than futures, within the framework of an organized market. The result was the birth of the Chicago Board Options Exchange (CBOE), which, in April 1973 began to trade options on listed stocks, with calls (*opciones de compra*) on 16 stocks that formed part of the NYSE index.[6] In 1973, Fischer Black and Myron Scholes published their option valuation model, which is the foundation of modern derivatives theory: this provided a major impetus to the understanding and trading of the instrument.[7]

In 1975 and 1976, other US exchanges (AMEX, PHLX, PSE and MidAm 📖 figure 9–1) began to trade call options, and, in 1977, put options (*opciones de venta*). In 1978, the London and Amsterdam stock exchanges began options trading.

The fixed exchange rate system established at Bretton Woods broke down between 1971 and 1973. During this period, participants in the two main Chicago markets, CME and CBOT, realized that demand for hedging instruments against changes in interest and exchange rates could

---

[6]See www.cboe.com.

[7]Black, Fischer and Myron Scholes, "The Pricing of Options and Corporate Liabilities", (*Journal of Political Economy*, May-June, 1973).

be met by their markets. In 1972, trading began in futures on seven currencies on the International Monetary Market, a new division of the CME.[8] In 1975, the futures contract on interest rates (on government guaranteed mortgage bonds – GNMAs) was introduced on the CBOT. Immediately, in 1976, a competitive product, futures on Tbills, was introduced on the CME. In 1977, the CBOT responded with the introduction of Tbond futures, which are currently the most liquid futures contract in the world.

9.2.4 Expansion and consolidation of derivatives markets

During the 1980s, instruments, underlying assets and markets for financial derivatives expanded and consolidated. In 1981 eurodollar futures were introduced on the CME, and, in 1982, stock index futures on the KCBT.[9] During the same decade, options on financial futures were introduced in various US markets (interest rate futures CBOT 1982, stock index futures CME 1983, currency futures CME 1984); so too were options on financial instruments (currencies PHLX 1982, indices CBOT 1983, interest rates CBOE 1989).

Meanwhile, faced with a similar demand for hedging and speculation in their own financial markets, other important financial centers outside the US established markets for financial derivatives: London (LIFFE - 1982), Singapore (SIMEX - 1984), Paris (MATIF - 1985), Switzerland (SOFFE - 1988), Tokyo (TIFFE - 1989), and Germany (DTB - 1990).

In the 1990s, there was a logical expansion of underlying assets to emerging markets. Derivatives of emerging market Brady bonds, stocks and currencies were introduced to the established derivatives markets in the US.

9.3 STRUCTURE OF GLOBAL DERIVATIVES MARKETS

9.3.1 Introduction

Derivatives are traded globally in two ways: over-the-counter (OTC - *extrabursátil*), and on the organized markets whose development we described in the previous section. Owing to the nature of OTC markets, it is difficult to obtain statistics on them. Similarly, it is difficult to consolidate data on organized markets by instrument, underlying asset, term and counterparty, owing to differences in methods of data collection and presentation, according to country and market.

---

[8]See www.cme.com.
[9]See www.kcbt.com.

Figure 9–3 OTC and organized markets, outstanding value (June 1998)

OTC MARKETS

Underlying asset	Total (US$bn.)	Total (%)	Forwards	% total Swaps	Options
Exchange rate	22,022	30.8	20.5	3.3	7.1
Interest rate	48,072	67.3	9.2	46.1	11.9
Stocks and indices	1,341	1.9	0.3	-	1.6
Total OTC	**71,435**	**100.00**	**30.0**	**49.4**	**20.6**

ORGANIZED MARKETS

Underlying asset			Futures	Options	
Exchange rate	103	0.72	0.5	0.2	
Interest rate	13,107	91.93	61.7	30.2	
Stocks and indices	1,047	7.35	2.7	4.6	
Total organized	**14,257**	**100.00**	**64.9**	**35.1**	

Source: BIS

The most complete statistics of derivatives in OTC and organized markets are those collected every three years by the Bank for International Settlements (BIS - *Banco Internacional de Pagos*): the most recent available statistics reflect data until June 1998.[10] At the time of writing, these had been updated to September 1998 for organized markets, but as the update does not cover OTC markets, it cannot be used for comparative purposes, and we do not use it in the following sections.

9.3.2 Market, underlying asset, instrument and counterparty

At the end of June 1998 (figure 9–3), the total value outstanding of organized markets (US$14.3 trn.) was one fifth of the value of OTC markets (US$71.4 trn.).

In the two markets, the most important underlying assets were interest rate derivatives (67% in OTC and 92% in organized markets). In OTC markets, currency derivatives were in second place (31%), followed by stocks and stock indices. In organized markets, stock index derivatives (7%) were in second place, followed by currencies.

---

[10]See "Central Bank Survey of Foreign Exchange and Derivatives Market Activity 1998" (www.bis.org).

Figure 9–4 Instruments, underlying assets and counterparties in OTC markets June 1998 (% of outstanding value)

	Market makers	Investors	Governments and corporates	Total
Instruments				
Forwards	13.4	12.0	4.6	30.0
Swaps	22.7	20.0	6.7	49.4
Options	10.2	7.0	3.5	20.6
Total	46.2	38.9	14.8	100.0
Underlying asset				
Exchange rates	13.6	10.9	6.3	30.8
Interest rates	32.0	27.2	8.1	67.3
Stocks and indices	0.7	0.9	0.3	1.9
Total	46.2	38.9	14.8	100.0
Total value (US$bn.)				71,435

Source: BIS, CrossBorder Capital, author

In OTC markets, the most important instruments were swaps, followed by forwards, and options. In organized markets, the most important instruments were futures, followed by options.

The reason for the relative importance of interest rates can be better understood from figure 9–4 where data is presented on instruments, underlying assets and counterparties for OTC markets, as at June 1998. The largest users of derivatives are market-makers (*formadores de mercado*), i.e. financial institutions, with 46% of the total, while investors represent 39% of the total. This implies that the main users of derivatives are those that make markets in the underlying assets, in order to cover their own risks of investment and intermediation.

In figure 9–5 there is further evidence for the conclusions of the previous paragraph. While interest rate and currency derivatives represent an important percentage of the value of their underlying markets (106.6% and 28% respectively), stocks and stock indices only

Figure 9–5 Relation between derivatives and underlying assets 1998

	(US$bn.) Derivatives	Underlying Asset*	Derivatives/ underlying asset (%)	Concept
Exchange rates (<7 days)	328	1,172	28.0	daily trading value
Interest rates	61,178	57,397	106.6	outstanding value
Indexes and stocks	2,388	25,721	9.3	outstanding value

* The underlying assets for interest rates are the financial assets at June 1998 of the countries participating in the BIS study. The underlying assets for stocks are the market capitalizations at June 1998 of participating countries. For currencies, the underlying asset is the daily traded value at April 1998.

Source: BIS, author

represent 9.3%, divided between 5.2% OTC and 4.1% organized markets.

9.4 HISTORY OF MEXICAN DERIVATIVES

For Mexico, it is suspected that, as in other cultures, there was probably some activity in forward contracts in pre-Columbian and Colonial times. However, the recorded history of derivatives (figure 9–6) only begins in 1977, with the first issue of so-called "petrobonds" (*petrobonos*). The petrobond was a derivative, because its value depended on the price of oil and the peso/dollar exchange rate.[11]

In the period 1978-82, futures of the Mexican peso were traded outside Mexico, on the CME. In 1983, a system for stock futures trading was introduced to the MSE, and in 1985 it reached 5% of the volume of stocks traded. In 1986, petrobond futures also began trading on the MSE. However, by 1987, low volume in both stock and petrobond futures led to their suspension.[12]

In 1987, "Currency Hedging Contracts" (*Contratos de Coberturas*

Figure 9–6 History of Mexican derivatives: important dates

1977	Petrobonds (*petrobonos*) first issued
1978-82	Peso futures on CME
1983	Stock futures on MSE
1985	Project for options exchange presented to Bolsa board
1986	Petrobond futures on MSE
1987	Suspension of stock and petrobond futures trading on MSE owing to lack of volume
1987	Exchange rate hedging instruments (*coberturas cambiarias*)
1990	Brady bonds issued with Value Recovery Rights (*derechos de valor de recuperación*)
1991	Options on Mexican stocks in US
1991	Feasibility study for stock options by MSE, AMIB and CNV
1992	Issue of warrants on MSE authorized by CNV (circular 10-157)
1992	First warrant issue for Telmex by Acciones y Valores
1993	First IPC warrant issued by Serfin
	First bull and bear spread warrants
	Derivatives on CPI issued by Invex
1994	Budget authorized by MSE to develop derivatives market
1995	Peso futures (and options on peso futures) renewed on CME
1996	Publication of rules for MSE listed derivatives
	Futures (and options on futures) for Bradys and IPC on CME
1997	Futures on Cetes and TIIE on CME
	Framework for prudential regulation of derivatives markets published by CNBV
1998	MexDer (Mexican derivatives market) begins operations

Source: author

---

[11]For a complete analysis of this instrument, now extinct, see Timothy Heyman, *Inversión contra Inflación* (Editorial Milenio S. A. de C. V., 1988), pp. 223-30.

Cambiarias) instruments were introduced as hedging instruments for peso/dollar exposure. They were traded OTC (not on the MSE) and regulated by the Bank of Mexico.

In 1990, following renegotiations of Mexico's external debt, Brady bonds were issued with Value Recovery Rights (VRR - *Derechos de Recuperación de Valor*) on oil exports. These VRRs envisage quarterly payments between June 1996 and December 2019, and can be understood as options.[13] In 1991, the first options on ADRs of Mexican stocks were issued on the US OTC markets.

In 1992, the National Securities Commission (*Comisión Nacional de Valores*) authorized listed companies and financial intermediaries to issue and trade "warrants", also called "títulos opcionales" [14], on the MSE. In the same year, Acciones y Valores de Mexico (Accival), the broker, issued the first put and call warrants, with 20 TELMEX L stocks as the underlying asset.

In 1993, warrants on the IPC (MSE index) were issued by the brokerage Operadora de Bolsa Serfin; and "bull and bear spreads" (*títulos opcionales topados*) by Accival. By December 1993, there were 50 warrants in the market, and there were 4,570 trades during the year

Figure 9–7 Warrants traded on MSE 1993 (number issued)

| | Underlying Asset | | | Form of settlement | | Type | | Total |
	Stocks	IPC	INPC	Cash	Underlying asset	American	European	
Call Warrants	38	7	1	40	6	24	22	46
Put Warrants	1	3		4		2	2	4
Total	39	10	1	44	6	26	24	50

Source: MSE

[12]"El Mercado Mexicano de los Derivados (MexDer)" (Boletín 20, Instituto Mexicano de Ejecutivos de Finanzas, 1997), pp. 9-10.

[13]Díaz de León Carrillo Alejandro, "Descripción y Valuación de los "Value Recovery Rights" de los Bonos Brady a la par y a descuento" (Banco de Mexico, documento de investigación No. 9703, agosto de 1997).

[14]Mexican warrants are not the same as options, as the counterparty risk for options on organized markets is the clearing house (implying little credit risk), whereas, in the case of Mexican warrants, the risk is the issuer. Furthermore, Mexican warrants can only be issued by companies or financial institutions, whereas options can be issued by any investor. In Mexico, brokers are the main issuers of warrants.

(figure 9–7).

In 1995, for the first time since 1982, peso futures and options on peso futures were issued on the CME. In the two subsequent years, futures (and options on futures) of more Mexican underlying assets were introduced on the CME: in 1996, of the IPC (MSE index) and Bradys and, in 1997, on 91 day Cetes and the 28 day interbank rate (TIIE). In December, 1998, the Mexican Derivatives Market (*Mercado Mexicano de Derivados - MexDer*) was inaugurated with trading in peso futures.

9.5 STRUCTURE OF MEXICAN DERIVATIVES MARKETS

The markets for Mexican derivatives can be classified as OTC and organized, and offshore and domestic. There are OTC markets in Mexico and offshore, operated by Mexican and international intermediaries, and they trade mainly peso and TIIE forward contracts, peso options, and structured products[15] based on stock options.[16]

The main organized offshore markets are the CME and the CBOE. In Mexico, they are the MSE and the Mexican Derivatives Market.

9.5.1 International organized markets

On the CME in 1998, futures (and options on futures) were available in the peso, the IPC, 91 day Cetes, 28 day interbank rate (TIIE) and Brady bonds.

On the CBOE, options were available on the IPC[17] and on the MEX index of the CBOE. The MEX index is an index of 10 equally weighted

Figure 9–8 Traded value of Mexican derivatives in Chicago (December 1998) (US$m.)

		CME		CBOE		
Underlying asset	*Total*	*Future*	*Options on futures*	*Options on MEX index*	*Options LEAPS MEX index*	*Options on IPC*
Exchange rates	1,093,209	1,016,449	76,761			
Interest rates	201	201	-			
Stocks and indices	8,980	-	-	8,980	-	-
For options, traded value is contract value, not premium value						
Source: MSE						

---

[15]A structured product is a derivative structured to order which may, or may not, be the result of a combination of other derivatives.

[16]In March 1998 Mexican financial institutions were authorized to trade futures and options OTC and in recognized markets in the following underlying assets: precious metals, currencies, government securities, real and nominal interest rates, stocks and stock indices, UDIs, and swaps.

Figure 9–9 Warrants traded on the MSE 1998 (number issued)

	Underlying asset		Form of settlement		Type		Total
				Underlying			
	Stocks	IPC	Cash	asset	American	European	
Call Warrants	26	17	41	2	27	16	43
Put Warrants	2	1	3		1	2	3
Total	28	18	44	2	28	18	46

Source: MSE

Mexican stocks with ADRs listed in the US. In addition, options on the MEX were available with long maturities, called LEAPS (Long-term Equity AnticiPation Securities) as well as options on Mexican ADRs.

In December 1998, peso futures contracts on the CME were by far the most important Mexican derivative, followed by options on peso futures. On the CBOE, the issued value of derivatives linked to indices was insignificant (figure 9–8).

9.5.2 Mexican organized markets

9.5.2.1 Mexican Stock Exchange

Put and call warrants on stocks and the IPC are traded on the MSE. At December 1998, the market capitalization of warrants outstanding was US$150.9mn., and the value of underlying assets was US$620.6mn. Details of warrants traded during 1998 are provided in figure 9–9.

Figure 9–10 Instruments traded on or planned for MexDer

	Futures on dollars	Futures on Cetes	Futures on TIIE	Futures on UDIs	Futures on IPC	Futures on stocks
Underlying asset	US dollar	91 day Cetes	28 day TIIE	UDI	IPC	1*
Contract size	US$10,000	$100,000	$100,000	UDI$50000	$10 X IPC	1,000 shares
Contract period	M,J,S,D	M,J,S,D	2*	M,J,S,D	M,J,S,D	3*
Regular trading hours	7:20-14:00	7:20-14:00	7:20-14:00	7:20-14:00	8:30-15:00	8:20-15:00
Settlement	Underlying asset	Cash	Cash	Cash	Cash	Underlying asset

1* TELMEXL, MASECAB, AHMSA*, ICA*, CEMEXCPO, GCARSOA1, ALFAA, VITRO*, KIMBERA, SAVIAA, CIFRAB, TLEVISACPO, FEMSAB, DESCB and TAMSA*
2* Monthly cycle to three months and semiannual to two years
3* Quarterly cycle (the cycle depends on the share)

Source: MexDer

[17]Contracts on the IPC trade on both the CME and the CBOE under license from the MSE.

Figure 9–11 Relation of Mexican derivatives to underlying assets 1998

	Derivatives	Underlying asset	Derivatives/ underlying asset (%)	concept
Exchange rates (<7 days)	US$383mn.	US$8,239mn.	4.64	daily trading value
Interest rates	US$201m.	US$253.2 bn.	0.0001	issued value
Stocks and indices	US$629.6mn.	US$118.0bn.	0.53	issued value

The underlying asset for interest rates are financial assets at June 1998. The underlying asset for stocks is Mexican stock market capitalization at June 1998.

Source: MSE, author

9.5.2.2 MexDer

The MexDer began trading in December 1998, with futures on the peso. Other instruments planned are futures on the IPC, 28 day TIIE, UDIs, stocks and 91 day Cetes, as well as options on futures. We provide details of the instruments on this new market in figure 9–10.

9.5.3 Importance in relation to underlying market

In figure 9–11 statistics on Mexican derivatives in both domestic and offshore markets on currencies, interest rates, stocks, and stock indices, compared with their related underlying assets, indicate the level of underdevelopment of Mexican derivatives markets. For currencies, the proportion is 4.6% (compared to 28% in global markets). For interest rates, the proportion is minimal (0.0001%, compared with 22.8% in global organized markets), and for stocks and indices it is 0.5% (compared to 4.1% in global organized markets).

9.6 USE OF DERIVATIVES

In 📖 9.6 to 9.8, we present the basic elements for understanding futures and options, the two main Mexican derivatives, related to three types of underlying asset, debt securities, currencies, and stocks and stock indices. Subsequently, in 📖 9.9, we explain the application of these instruments to the management of Mexican investments, using the example of a stock portfolio.

The return and risk of derivatives is no different from their underlying assets. However, derivatives permit the investment manager to modify a portfolio's expected return and risk profile, without changing its basic structure. The main advantages of derivatives, and the reason for their increasing use as a tool for investment management, are lower transaction costs and greater flexibility than can be offered by the underlying investments.

There are four main uses for derivatives in investment management:

- Hedging (*cobertura*) of existing investments

If an investor wishes to reduce the weighting of stocks in his portfolio, he can sell a future of the relevant stock index without incurring the cost of selling stocks in the portfolio. Similarly, if he wishes to hedge a specific stock, he can buy a put option (*opción de venta*), without selling the underlying stock.

- Investment strategy (*estrategia de inversión*)

If an investor wishes to increase his exposure to stocks as an asset class, or to a specific stock, he can buy a call option on the stock index, or on a specific stock, instead of buying the underlying stocks. In contrast with an investment in the underlying stock, this strategy limits the possibility of loss should the stock fall, but offers the opportunity of profit, should it rise (the case described by de la Vega in 🕮 9.2.1).

- Leverage (*apalancamiento*)

Financial derivatives facilitate investment in an underlying value several times greater than the investor's resources. In the case of options, this value is limited by the option premium. In the case of futures, it is limited by the value of the margin. This feature of derivatives offers the possibility of higher returns than investment in the underlying asset, but with commensurate risks.[18]

- Price discovery (*descubrimiento de precios*)

Derivatives (both futures and options) provide a useful indication of market expectations about price trends.[19]

9.7 FORWARDS AND FUTURES

9.7.1 Definition

Futures (*futuros*) and forwards (*contratos adelantados*) are contracts between two parties to buy or sell an underlying asset (*subyacente*) at a future time at a price set today. Futures have standardized amounts and maturities, can be settled in cash or kind, are traded on organized markets with a clearing house (*cámara de compensación*) which minimizes counterparty risk (*riesgo de contraparte*), and are traded in

---

[18]This use of derivatives, which can also be called "speculative" (🕮 Glossary), was the cause of several losses in recent years (e.g. Metallgesellschaft, Sumitomo, Barings, Orange County). The publicity surrounding these losses has tended to obscure in the public mind the fact that derivatives are much more widely used for hedging and investment strategy.

[19]🕮 6.7.2.2 for the use of futures for exchange rate forecasting.

Figure 9–12 Theoretical and market prices of peso futures on the CME

	Formula	Exchange Rate
Spot Price 12/19/97	$P_s =$	8.12
91 day Cetes (annual)	$R_{Dom} =$	19.75%
90 day Tbills (annual)	$R_{For} =$	5.36%
Equation (9-3)	$R = [(1+R^*_{Dom})/(1+R^*_{For})]-1 =$	3.59%
	$(1+R) =$	1.0359
Theoretical price of futures (March 20, 1998) Eq.(9-2)	$P_f = P_s(1+R) =$	8.41
Market price of futures (March 20, 1998)		8.41

*The rate should be divided by 360 and multiplied by 91

Source: author, CME

the secondary market.[20] Forwards are contracts normally made between a financial institution and its client with amounts and maturities which are not standardized, but tailored to the needs of the client: as they are not registered on an organized market, they are called over-the-counter (OTC) operations.

The party who contracts to buy the underlying asset takes on a "long position" (*posición larga*) or has "bought" the instrument. The party who contracts to sell the underlying asset takes on a "short position"[21] (*posición corta*) or has "sold" the instrument.

9.7.2 Valuation

The spot (*spot*) price of the underlying asset (P_s) can be related to the price of the future (P_f) at a discount rate R through the present value formula:

$$P_s = \frac{P_f}{1+R} \qquad (9\text{-}1)$$

In the same way, rearranging expression 9-1, the future price can be related to the spot price:

$$P_f = P_s(1+R) \qquad (9\text{-}2)$$

The rate R varies according to the underlying asset:

---

[20]For a complete analysis of futures trading, clearing house, margin, and price quotations, see Mansell Carstens, Catherine, *Las Nuevas Finanzas en Mexico* (Editorial Milenio, S. A. de C. V., 1992), pp. 281-303.

[21]It represents an extension of the concept of "short sale" (*venta en corto*) - sale of an investment the investor does not own - 📖 Glossary.

Figure 9–13 Theoretical and market prices of 91 day Cete futures on the CME

	Formula	Cetes price
Cete face value at June 19, 1998	$P_f=$	100.00
Yield on 182 day Cete	$R_{f+p}=$	19.83%
Yield on 91 day Cete	$R_f=$	19.75%
Equation (9-5)	$R=[(1+R^*{}_{f+p})/(1+R^{**}{}_f)]-1=$	4.79%
	$(1+R)=$	1.0479
Theoretical price of futures (March 20, 1998) Eq.(9-4)	$P_s=P_f/(1+R)=$	95.43
Market price of futures (March 20, 1998)		95.40

*The rate should be divided by 360 and multiplied by 182
**The rate should be divided by 360 and multiplied by 91
Source: author, CME

- For stock futures or stock indices (without dividend payments) it is the risk-free rate for the same term as the future.
- For currency futures (e.g. $/US$), it is the relationship between the domestic and foreign interest rate (📖 6.7.2):

$$R = \left(\frac{1+R_{Dom}}{1+R_{For}}\right) - 1 \qquad (9\text{-}3)$$

- Interest rate futures are purchased as zero coupon bonds at a discount to face value. Their present value (P_s) represents a price discounted at R, and the future value (P_f) is always the face value of the instrument.

The Cete is an example of a zero coupon bond (📖 6.2.1). The discounted price of a Cete bought as a future is represented by the following formula:

$$P_s = \frac{P_f}{1+R} \qquad (9\text{-}4)$$

where

$$R = \frac{1+R_{f+p}}{1+R_f} - 1 \qquad (9\text{-}5)$$

i.e. the rate R represents the relation between the rate at maturity of the underlying asset ($R_{f\,+p}$) (consisting of two periods, the period of the future, f, and the period of the underlying asset, p) and the rate at maturity of the future (R_i).

Confirmation of the expressions 9-2 and 9-4 can be observed in the prices of peso futures and 91 day Cetes futures quoted on the CME (figure 9–12 and figure 9–13).

9.7.3 Cost

The important difference between spot and futures trading is that, in futures trading, there is very little immediate cash outflow. If there is a favorable movement in the price of the underlying asset, the buyer of the futures contract can sell it before maturity, and realize a profit with minimal expenditure. Conversely, in the case of an adverse movement in the price of the underlying asset, the buyer can also lose money that he does not have.

To minimize the risk of non-fulfillment implicit in these contracts, the markets have developed institutions and systems which require from the investor (on both sides of the contract) initial and maintenance payments, known as "initial margin" (*margen inicial*) and "margin calls" (*llamados de margen*), respectively. These requirements could be considered a cost of futures trading, as they represent an allocation of investor resources. However, margin accounts receive interest and the amount deposited depends on the volatility of the underlying asset: therefore the real cost of a futures trade is difficult to estimate a priori.

9.7.4 Payoff functions

"Payoff functions" (*funciones de pagos*), also known as "risk profiles" (*perfiles de riesgo*), are used to present graphically profit and loss on a derivative due to price variations in the underlying asset. Graphic representation can be useful for understanding the more complex strategies analyzed at the end of this chapter.

We take as an example the purchase of a futures contract on the dollar with a contract size of US$20,000 and maturity on December 24, 1997, at a price of 8 pesos to the dollar ($/US$). Three scenarios at maturity are presented in figure 9–14:

1. *Breakeven – exchange rate $8/US$ on December 24.* Payment in pesos was $160,000 for the receipt of US$20,000 dollars. As the exchange rate was the same as for the futures contract, there was no profit or loss.

2. *Profit – exchange rate $8.5/US$ on December 24.* The future produced a profit of $0.5 per US$ (8.5-8.0), or, for the US$20,000

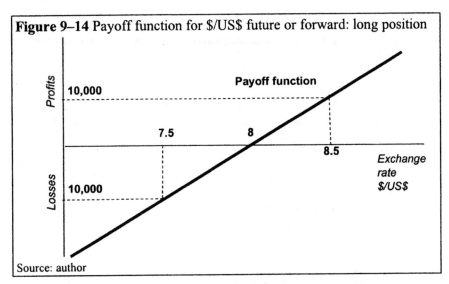

Figure 9–14 Payoff function for $/US$ future or forward: long position

Source: author

dollars, a total of $10,000 pesos. Without the future, the payment would have been $170,000.

3. *Loss – exchange rate $7.5/US$ on December 24.* The loss is $10,000 pesos ((7.5-8.5)*20,000). Without the future, payment would have been $150,000.

It is easy to show with similar examples that the payoff function for the sale of a future with similar features is the obverse of the function for the long position described above. Similar functions can be developed for futures of other underlying assets such as: stock indices, individual stocks, and bonds (or interest rates).

9.8 OPTIONS

9.8.1 Definitions

Options are contracts that give the buyer, in exchange for a premium (*prima*), the right (but not the obligation) to buy (in the case of a call) and to sell (in the case of a put) an agreed amount of the underlying asset at an agreed strike price (*precio de ejercicio*) during an agreed period or on an agreed date.

Similarly, the seller of the contract receives the premium, in exchange for the obligation to sell (in the case of a call option) or to buy (in the case of a put option) the underlying asset at the agreed price during the agreed period or on the agreed date.

As in the case of futures, there are two sides to the contract: the seller, who takes a short position (*posición corta*), and the buyer, who takes a long position (*posición larga*) in the option. There are two kinds of option, depending on the rights they offer. From the point of view of the buyer, the right to buy the underlying asset is known as a "call option" (*opción de compra*) and the right to sell the underlying asset is known as a "put option" (*opción de venta*).

In relation to the time at which the option can be exercised, i.e. the moment at which the trade in the underlying asset can be made, there are two kinds of option:

- American-style options (*opciones del tipo americano*), which can be exercised at any time, from the beginning of the contract until the expiration of the instrument, and
- European-style options (*opciones del tipo europeo*) which can only be exercised on the expiration date.

9.8.2 Valuation

9.8.2.1 Intrinsic value and time value

The price of an option has two components:

- Intrinsic value (*valor intrínseco*), measured as the differential between the price of the underlying asset and the exercise price of the option. As the exercise price of the option is fixed from the beginning, this value can only change during the life of the option owing to changes in the price of the underlying asset.
- Time value (*valor por tiempo* or *valor temporal*). This value is the difference between the market value of the option and its intrinsic value, and reflects changes in its market price caused by changes in three factors: time to expiration, the volatility of the underlying asset, and the risk-free rate.

For a call option:

- when the exercise price is below the price of the underlying asset, an option is "in the money" (*dentro del dinero*),
- when it is above, it is "out of the money" (*fuera del dinero*), and
- when it is at the same level, it is "at the money" (*en el dinero*).

Intrinsic value is only "positive" when the option is in the money, and is determined as the difference between the price of the underlying asset and the strike price.

Conversely, for a put option:

- when the exercise price is below the price of the underlying, it is "out of the money" (*fuera del dinero*),
- when it is above, it is "in the money" (*dentro del dinero*), and
- when it is at the same level, it is "at the money" (*en el dinero*).

Figure 9–15 Intrinsic value and time value
a. American and European call option.

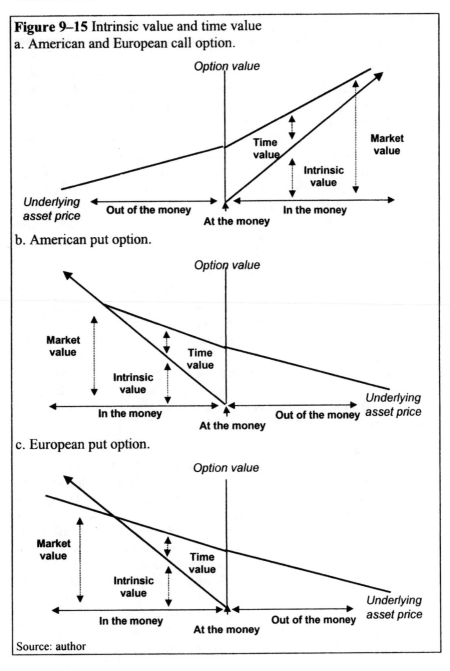

b. American put option.

c. European put option.

Source: author

Intrinsic value is only "positive" when the option is in the money, and is determined by the difference between the exercise price and the price of the underlying asset.

For European and American-style call options and American-style put options, time value can be either zero or positive. In the case of European-style put options, time value can be negative when the option is very "in the money".

The relation between intrinsic value and time value of a call option is shown in figure 9–15a. When the option is out of the money, there is no intrinsic value: however, there is some time value, owing to the possibility of a rise in the price of the underlying asset before expiration.

In the case of an American-style put option (figure 9–15b), the time value component falls to zero when the option is very in the money. This occurs if it is expected that the price of the underlying asset will reach its minimum, zero: the underlying asset cannot fall more, and the maximum profit from a put option can only be received if the option is exercised. Time value becomes valueless, as the only thing that can happen during the period remaining to expiration is a rise in the price of the underlying.

The previous paragraph helps us to understand why the time value of a European-style put option is negative when the option is very in the money (figure 9–15c). As a European-style option cannot be exercised at that moment, it loses the opportunity of obtaining the maximum profit from the put option. When it is very in the money, a European-style option is worth less than an American-style option, and has a negative time value.

9.8.2.2 Theoretical value

Until 1973, option prices were calculated on the basis of intrinsic value. However, beginning in the 1960s, as new financial theories were developed (📖 2.4.2) people began to look for ways of taking into account the three variables mentioned above (time to expiration, volatility of the underlying asset, and the risk-free rate) which clearly affected option valuation. In 1973, the "Black-Scholes" model was published (named after the professors who developed it).

The Black-Scholes model is a formula that calculates the price of European-style options on stocks that do not pay dividends. Subsequently, the model has been adapted to the valuation of European-style options on stocks which pay dividends, currencies, indices and bonds, and procedures have been developed to approximate the value of

Figure 9–16 Movement necessary in key variables to generate an increase in option premium

| | | Intrinsic value | | Time Value | | |
	Premium	Underlying asset price	Strike price	Time to Maturity	Underlying asset volatility	Risk-free rate
Call option Short/long position	Increase	Increase	Decrease	Increase (American) uncertain	Increase	Increase
Put option Short/long position	Increase	Decrease	Increase	(European)	Increase	Decrease

Source: author

American-style options.[22] Other models have also been developed, of which the most popular is the Binomial model, which involves the use of numerical procedures for the valuation of American and European-style options.[23]

Five key variables determine the two main components (intrinsic value and time value) of the option premium, and the relationship between them. In figure 9–16 we show the change necessary in each variable to generate a positive increase in the two components of the option premium.

9.8.3 Cost

The cost of buying options (both calls and puts) is the premium paid for the option. This is always a known quantity, and less than the price of the underlying asset, at the moment that the option is purchased. The sale of options (both puts and calls) implies that the seller receives a premium, but, in exchange, takes on a risk that cannot be precisely quantified. There is therefore a system of initial and maintenance margin similar to futures[24], which usually consists in depositing the premium received for sale of the option plus a percentage of contract value.

A simple way to understand options is as an insurance policy. One pays a premium against the possibility that an event occurs. In the case of a call option, the event that is being insured against is the possibility of not benefiting from a price rise in the underlying asset above the exercise price before, or on, the expiration date. In the case of a put

---

[22] E.1 for Black-Scholes formulas for different underlying assets.

[23] See Cox, J. C., S. A. Ross, M. Rubinstein, "Option Pricing: A Simplified Approach" (*Journal of Financial Economics*, October 1979), pp. 229-63.

[24] For a complete analysis of options trading in organized markets (clearing house, margins, price quotations and information), see Hull, John C., *Options, Futures, and Other Derivative Securities* (Prentice Hall, 1993), pp. 136-148.

Figure 9–17 Payoff function for call option on peso future, long position.

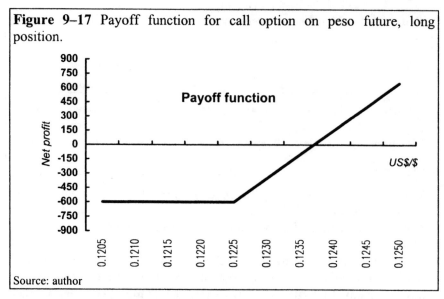

Source: author

option, the event that is being insured against is the possibility of being negatively affected by the downward movement of the price of the underlying asset below the exercise price before, or on, the expiration date. If the event does not occur during the period of insurance, the premium is lost: if it does occur, the insurance is collected.

9.8.4 Option payoff functions

Payoff functions for options (as for futures) are graphical representations of profit and loss (taking premiums received or paid into account), due to changes in the price of the underlying asset.

9.8.4.1 Call and put options

The investor who takes on a long position (buy) in a call option benefits from a rise in price of the underlying asset and his loss is limited when the price of the underlying asset falls.

For example, on December 4 1997, a call option on peso futures was traded on the CME. The size of the futures contract was $500,000 maturing on December 19, 1997, the exercise price of the option was US$0.1225/$, and the premium was US$600. At expiration date, if the

Figure 9–18 Payoff functions

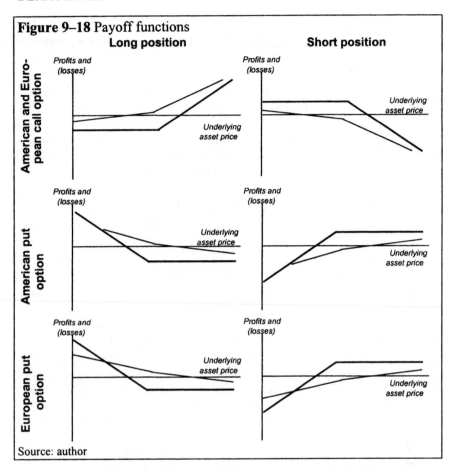

Source: author

option had not yet been exercised, there were three possible scenarios (figure 9–17)[25]:

1. Exchange rate less than US$0.1225/$. There is no point in exercising the option, because it is cheaper to buy pesos in the spot market. Therefore the option implies a cost (loss) equal to the premium paid of US$600.

2. Exchange rate between US$0.1225 and 0.1237/$, for example US$0.1230/$. It is cheaper to buy pesos by exercising the option than in the spot market, with a savings per peso of US$0.0005 (0.1230-0.1225), multiplied by the $500,000 value of the futures contract, i.e., a total savings of US$250. However, the cost of the premium was

---

[25]In valuing the various scenarios at expiration date, time value is zero. There is only intrinsic value.

US$600, which implies that only a portion has been covered. The value of the uncovered portion of the premium is US$350, which is the net loss to the investor.

3. Exchange rate above US$0.1237/$, for example US$0.1240. There is a net profit of (US$0.1240-US$0.1225)*500,000, i.e. US$750 less the cost of the premium of US$600, or US$150.

Figure 9–18 shows profit and loss from different types of option taking into account intrinsic value (the thick line) and time value (thin line). The conclusions can be summarized as follows:

• Short positions in options (sale of call or put options) limit profits. Losses can be unlimited for call options with increases in the price of the underlying asset and limited for put options with decreases in the price of the underlying asset.

• Long positions in options (purchase of call or put options) limit losses. Profits can be unlimited for call options with increases in the price of the underlying asset, and limited for put options with decreases in the price of the underlying asset.

9.9 BASIC ELEMENTS IN THE USE OF DERIVATIVES

Derivatives can be used in an infinite variety of ways for portfolio hedging and investment. The aim of this section is to use the example of an investor in a Mexican stock portfolio to illustrate some basic features of the use of futures and options.

9.9.1 Futures

To plan a strategy with futures, the investor with a stock portfolio must make assumptions in relation to certain key variables:

9.9.1.1 Price trend of underlying asset

On the assumption of rising prices, a purchase strategy can increase exposure. On the assumption of falling prices or an uncertain trend, a sale strategy can lower exposure, in differing degrees.

9.9.1.2 Potential profit and loss

Potential profit and loss depends on the position taken in futures and stocks. For example, for a total hedge (reduction in exposure) in:

• A specific stock. With the sale of a future on the stock, profit and loss are recognized.[26]

---

[26]Stock futures are traded on the new MexDer.

Figure 9–19 Strategies with futures and stocks

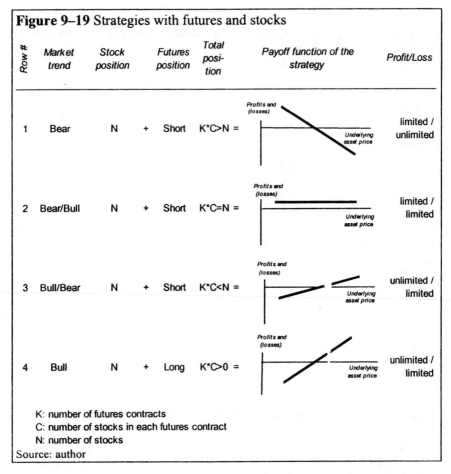

Row #	Market trend	Stock position		Futures position	Total position	Payoff function of the strategy	Profit/Loss
1	Bear	N	+	Short	K*C>N =		limited / unlimited
2	Bear/Bull	N	+	Short	K*C=N =		limited / limited
3	Bull/Bear	N	+	Short	K*C<N =		unlimited / limited
4	Bull	N	+	Long	K*C>0 =		unlimited / limited

K: number of futures contracts
C: number of stocks in each futures contract
N: number of stocks

Source: author

- A stock portfolio. With the sale of a future on the stock index, profit and loss depend on the level of correlation between the portfolio and the stock index, measured by beta (📖 E.2).

9.9.1.3 Term

Term is important because it adjusts assumptions to a specific time period. If a price trend is assumed, and not fulfilled during the term of the future, it forces the investor to recognize profit or loss on the instrument. The situation is different for the underlying asset: as it has no term, profit or loss is only recognized when it is sold.

9.9.1.4 Cost

Although the theoretical price of a future is zero (there is no cost to the investor) in reality the investor is limited by the initial margin and the margin calls implicit in futures contracts.

9.9.2 Futures strategies

Figure 9–19 shows payoff functions of some strategies with futures that the investor with a stock portfolio could execute depending on his assumptions about market trends.

Let us take the example of an expected rising price trend during the investor's time horizon. In row 4 ("bull") N is the number of stocks that the investor holds, in this case, of a single issuer. He should take a long position in futures (long – column 3). The amount depends on the investor's objectives, where K is the number of futures and C is the number of stocks in each futures contract. The fifth column shows the payoff function expected from the strategy.

9.9.3 Options

To plan strategies with options, the investor should make assumptions about the following key variables:

9.9.3.1 Trend and volatility of price of underlying asset

In contrast to futures, option positions are not only determined by assumptions of price trends, but also by assumptions about changes in expected volatility. For example, an investor who expects a rising price trend but a fall in volatility could decide on a present cash inflow through the sale of a put option instead of increasing his exposure to the stock market. He benefits from the premium collected today, which implies a higher volatility than that expected in the future, on the assumption that the premium will fall in the future.[27]

9.9.3.2 Potential profit and loss

The potential profit and loss from options, as in the case of futures, can be limited, unlimited or mixed depending on the strategies adopted by the investor and his stock position. However, options offer the opportunity to develop a more flexible payoff function than futures.

9.9.3.3 Term

Term has the same effect as in the case of futures for the assumptions about trend and volatility. However, as the cost is limited to the option premium, option buyers can recognize their maximum loss, and option

---

[27]See figure 9–16 for the sensitivity of the premium to a change in volatility.

sellers can recognize their maximum profit, at the beginning of the option contract.

9.9.3.4 Cost

The cost to option buyers is simply the premium paid for the option, plus its opportunity cost (*prima actualizada*). For sellers of options, the premium collected does not represent disposable income, as markets require that the premium plus a certain amount be deposited as margin against possible future price movements.

9.9.4 A hedging strategy with put options

An investor can use an infinite number of strategies with options, depending on his assumptions about market trends and volatility. In this section, we present one of the simplest strategies, a stock position combined with the purchase of a put option. Adoption of this strategy implies assumptions about market trends and volatility:

1. In relation to trend, there is the possibility of a market fall, and the investor wishes to buy "insurance", without reducing his stock position.

2. In relation to volatility, there is the possibility of greater volatility, which would imply an increase in the option premium.

Let us take the example of an investor whose portfolio has a long position in stock X at a price of $100 and a put option on stock X. Assuming that the premium (including opportunity cost) is $17 and the exercise price (A) is $100, we can plot the payoff function for the stock, the option, and the portfolio in figure 9–20.

Conclusions can be summarized as follows:

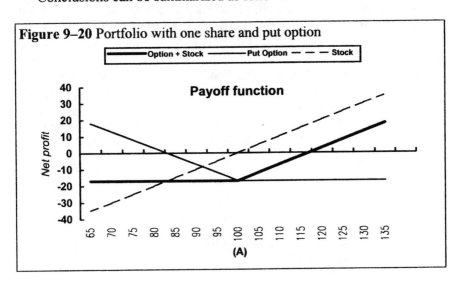

Figure 9–20 Portfolio with one share and put option

- Stock price of X above exercise price A ($100). The put option is not exercised, the option premium is not recovered, and it is recognized as a loss. The stock, however, benefits from its rise above A. The portfolio value is the sum of the profit from the stock less the cost of the premium (including opportunity cost).
- Stock price of X below A. A fall in the price of the stock produces a loss. However, the loss is compensated by the profit produced from exercising the put option. The portfolio value is the sum of the profit from the option and the loss on the stock less the premium (including opportunity cost) paid.

In the case of a rise in the price of the stock, the best strategy is to be invested in the stock, followed by the strategy with the put option. For any price above A, the difference between the two strategies is the original option premium ($17), updated to include opportunity cost. However, in the case of a negative movement in the stock price (below $83), the strategy with the put option is best. For prices below $83, the difference between strategies increases as the stock price falls.

The reader will have realized that the payoff function of the strategy presented is the same as that in figure 9–17, which shows a call option on a peso future.

This is no accident, as the strategy described is also called "Long Call" (*posición larga en opción de compra*). The strategy generates a payoff function similar to that generated by a long position in a call option, because a call option has similar implications: unlimited profit when the price of the underlying asset rises above the sum of the value of the premium (including opportunity cost) and the exercise price, and a limited loss, when the price of the underlying asset falls below the exercise price.

This is only one example of the flexible investment strategies that can be developed with options. The combination of an investment portfolio with put and call options can be used to create "synthetic instruments" (*instrumentos sintéticos*) that allow the investor an infinity of permutations and combinations in relation to the portfolio he holds – or wishes to hold.[28]

---

[28]For advanced option strategies, see Mansell Carstens, *op. cit.*, pp. 378-389, and Hull, *op. cit.*, pp. 173-189.

Chapter 10
Irrationality

"Bull markets are born in pessimism, rise on skepticism, mature with optimism, and die in euphoria. The stage of maximum pessimism is the best time to buy, and the stage of maximum optimism is the best time to sell."

Sir John Templeton

10.1 RATIONALITY AND IRRATIONALITY

10.1.1 The Wall Street tribe

"Wall Street was a tribe that occupied the southern tip of a small island and wielded enormous influence throughout the globe. The tribe worshipped a superior life form called "The Market", and their lives were completely consumed by contemplation about The Market's moods, what it thought, and how it reacted to global events. They fretted about whether The Market was depressed, overexcited, acting irrationally, or correcting its past mistakes. The tribe derived its power from its professed ability to answer a single question - 'What's The Market going to do?' – posed constantly by people from all over the world, who paid the Wall Street tribe billions and billions of dollars to answer this question. One way or another, every member of the tribe was involved in predicting The Market."

"Judging from paintings, sculptures and names of Wall Street eating places, it seemed that the tribe also worshipped two important idols, the Bull and the Bear, symbolizing The Market's good and bad moods. The tribe formed two rival cults, consisting of Bull and Bear worshipers. The Bulls believed that The Market would shower them with untold material wealth; the Bears believed The Market would steal back their material riches..."[1]

10.1.2 Beyond technique

The activity of investment can be compared to religion because it has a rational and irrational element. But there is an important difference. In religion, the irrational element is called "faith" and is positive and

---

[1]Sherden, William A., *The Fortune Sellers* (John Wiley & Sons Inc, 1998), pp. 86-87.

irreducible. In investment, the irrational element is negative, and one tries to reduce it to a minimum.[2]

Irrationality can occur in any market, at any time. There is a mysterious process whereby, apparently, investors wish to lose money. This can occur daily, when investors tend to buy in a rising market and sell in a falling market, when the reverse should be the case. It can also occur at certain major turning points, when for longer periods a group of investors, or the market itself, almost literally goes mad for an investment or an asset class, causing prices to rise far beyond any rational level (a boom[3]).

Rationality has been the foundation of the analysis techniques presented in previous chapters: investment theory, the analysis of country risk and cycles, and the explanation of debt securities, stocks and derivatives. But in times of boom, or crash, and also in daily trading, investors can move beyond rationality, i.e. become irrational. One form of describing this irrationality is that:

"the tendency to look beyond the simple fact of increasing value to the reasons on which it depends greatly diminishes."[4]

In terms of this book, to be irrational would imply discarding its analytical structure (which is a form of making explicit what every investor does - or should do - implicitly). In definitional terms, to be "irrational" is equivalent to being "stupid", in the sense of acting against one's own interest. Finally, in everyday language, there have been many ways of describing these periods of irrationality: "frantic speculation", "financial orgy", "investors intoxicated with the urge to become rich", "fools' paradise", "bubbles", "speculative manias", etc.

In this chapter, beginning with booms, we identify the nature of irrationality in portfolio investment, with examples from different centuries, countries and markets, and special reference to Mexico. Subsequently, we present techniques for the analysis of irrationality in financial markets, with applications to the Mexican case.

---

[2]This chapter, owing to the timeless nature of its subject matter, bears a resemblance, in form and content, to chapter 7 ("Análisis de la Irracionalidad") of a previous book by the author, *Inversión contra Inflación* (Editorial Milenio, S. A. de C. V., 1988), pp. 251-279.

[3]There is no Spanish translation.

[4]See Galbraith, John K., *The Great Crash 1929* (Houghton Mifflin, 1954), p. 9.

10.2 BOOMS AND CRASHES

10.2.1 Financial crises and booms

Between 1637 and 1998, there have been 40 important financial crises in capitalist countries, an average of approximately one every nine years.[5] A financial crisis in this context can be understood as a disruption in the financial system that affects, or could affect, the real economy.

Financial crises are normally analyzed in the context of a broader discussion about capitalism as an economic system. According to classical economics, the capitalist system always "self-adjusts" (*se autoajusta*) to external events. However, financial crises, which occur so frequently, appear to be an important exception to this theory. Defenders of capitalism must find explanations for financial crises, while proponents of other economic systems use them as examples of the structural flaws (or "internal contradictions") of the capitalist system.

In a world where most economic systems are "mixed" (i.e. there is some state involvement), the analysis of financial crises has important practical implications. If markets do not automatically self-adjust in all cases, there are arguments in favor of official intervention by the "authorities" (central banks, governments, or supranational organizations like the International Monetary Fund – IMF). If they do self-adjust, intervention is unnecessary.

In most capitalist systems there is currently a practical consensus. Markets should act as if they were free, but, in cases of emergency, authorities should intervene. We can cite three examples. In the two recent Mexican crises, the IMF intervened in 1982, and the US government in 1994. In the Asian, Russian and Brazilian crises of 1997-99, the IMF intervened, along with the US Fed (which lowered rates).

Booms and crashes are linked to financial crises (figure 10–1). A boom can be defined as an exaggerated (i.e. abnormal) increase in the price of a good: the proof of this exaggeration is the crash that follows the boom.[6] A boom can be the result of a financial crisis, or its cause. The boom of the Mexican stock market in 1987 was caused by the oil and financial crisis of 1986. The famous 1929 boom and crash in the US was the cause of the financial crisis in the US and, subsequently, of the depression of the 1930s.

---

[5] Kindleberger, Charles, *Manias, Panics and Crashes, a History of Financial Crises - revised edition* (Basic Books Inc., 1989).

[6] A boom without a crash would be an "expansion".

Figure 10–1 Important financial crises 1637-1998

Year	Country	Asset	Displacement	Source of liquidity	Peak	Crash
1637	Holland	Tulips	Development of tulip	Futures	Feb 1637	Feb 1637
1719	France	Compagnie des Indes	Development of Mississippi	Paper money	Dec 1719	May 1720
1720	England	South Sea Company	Development of Latin America	Futures	Apr 1720	Sep 1720
1763	Holland	Commodities	End of 7 year War	Wisselruitij (commercial paper)	Jan 1763	Sep 1763
1772	England	Canals, highways	End of 7 year War	Regional banks	Jun 1772	Jan 1773
1772	Holland	East India Company (VOC)	End of 7 year War	Bank of Amsterdam	Jun 1772	Jan 1773
1793	England	Canals	Reign of Terror (France)	Capital flows from France	Nov 1792	Feb 1793
1797	England	Stocks, Canals	Collapse of French assignats	Regional banks	1796	Jun 1799
1799	Hamburg	Commodities	European blockade	Commercial paper	1799	Nov 1799
1810	England	Exports to Brazil	Wellington's campaign in Spain	Regional banks	1810	Jan 1811
1815-16	England	Commodities	End of Napoleonic War	Banks	1815	1816
1825	England	Bonds, shares in Latin America	Success of Baring loan	Partial payment of bonds	Jan 1825	Dec 1825
1827	France	Canals, cotton	Fall in interest rates	Paris banks	1827	Dec 1827
1837	USA	Land, cotton	Jackson presidency	Pirate banks	Nov 1836	Sep 1837
1837	France	Cotton, land	Restoration of monarchy 1830	Regional banks	Nov 1836	Jun 1837
1847	England	Railways, corn	Potato and corn drought 1846	Partial payment of shares	Jan 1847	Sep 1847
1847	Continental Europe	Railways, corn	Potato and corn drought 1846	Regional banks	1847	Mar 1848
1857	USA	Railways, land	End of Crimean War	Gold discovered	1856	Aug 1857
1857	England	Railways, corn	End of Crimean War	Bank mergers	1856	Oct 1857
1857	Continental Europe	Railways, heavy industry	End of Crimean War	Crédit Mobilier, new German banks	Mar 1857	Nov 1857
1864	France	Cotton, shipping companies	End of Civil War (USA)	Crédit Mobilier	1863	Jan 1864
1866	England, Italy	Cotton, shipping companies	Introduction of limited companies	Formation of joint stock banks	Jul 1865	May 1866
1873	Germany, Austria	Railways, stocks, commodities, land	French indemnification after Franco-Prussian War	New investment and commercial banks	Sep 1872	Sep 1873
1873	USA	Railways, Chicago real estate	Electoral fraud 1872	Capital flows from Europe	Mar 1873	Sep 1873
1882	France	Bank stocks	Expansion to Southern Europe	Securities bought on margin	Dec 1881	Jan 1882
1890	England	Latin American and South Africa securities	Opening up of Latin America, Africa	Conversion to gold standard	Aug 1890	Nov 1890
1893	USA	Gold, silver	Sherman Silver Act (1890)	Sherman Silver Act (1890)	Dec 1892	May 1893
1893	Austria	Land	Urban growth	Capital flows	1891	Apr 1893
1907	USA	Coffee, shares in Union Pacific	Russo-Japanese War San Francisco earthquake	Banks	Jan 1907	Oct 1907
1907	France, Italy	Credit	Russo-Japanese War San Francisco earthquake	Banks	Mar 1906	Aug 1907

Figure 10–1 Important financial crises 1637-1997 (cont.)

Year	Country	Asset	Displacement	Source of liquidity	Peak	Crash
1921	England, USA	Stocks, ships, commodities	End of World War I	Banks	Jun 1920	Mar 1921
1929	USA	Land 1925 stocks 1926-1929	Boom after World War I	Stocks bought on Margin	Sep 1929	Oct 1929
1970s	World	Currencies (e.g. England 1964, USA 1973)	Convertibility without macroeconomic coordination	Eurocurrency markets	NA	NA
1973	World	Gold, silver, oil	Collapse of Bretton Woods system, Yom Kippur War	Increase of "petrodollars"	Dec 1973	Jun 1974
1980	World	Gold, silver, oil	Iran revolution (Feb 1979) Invasion of Afghanistan (Dec 1979)	Increase of "petrodollars"	Jan 1980	Mar 1980
1987	USA	Stocks	Republican boom (1980-88)	Development of derivatives	Sep 1987	Oct 1987
1990	Japan	Stocks	Global free trade, technological development	Derivatives (warrants)	1990	1991
1994	Emerging markets	Stocks, bonds	Collapse of communism (1989), technology	Capital flows	Feb 1994	Dec 1994
1997	Asia	Stocks, bonds	Return of Hong Kong to China (June 1997)	Capital flows	Mar 1997	Oct 1997
1998	World	Stocks, bonds	Russian default on domestic debt	Capital flows	Jan 1998	Aug 1998

Source: Kindleberger, author

But booms do not only occur in stock markets. There have been booms in many kinds of portfolio investments: canal stocks (England 1772; France 1827), commodities (Germany, 1799; France 1827 and 1864), foreign bonds (England 1825 and 1890), foreign mining stocks (England 1825 – Latin American mines), railway stocks (England 1847 and 1857; France 1847 and 1857; US 1857 and 1873), currencies (German mark 1973; Swiss franc 1973), gold and silver (1973, 1980), emerging markets currencies (Mexican peso 1982 and 1994, Asian currencies 1997-8).

Although occurring in different centuries, countries, and markets, booms show surprising similarities. Before analyzing patterns of irrationality in financial markets, we describe some outstanding examples in the following section: historical booms in four of the main industrialized countries (Holland, France, England and the US); more recent booms in gold and silver; and, finally, booms of the Mexican stock market in 1979, 1984 and 1987, and of the Mexican peso in 1982 and 1994.

10.2.2 Historical booms

10.2.2.1 Tulipomania (Holland)

The tulip, whose etymology derives from a Turkish word meaning "turban" (*turbante*), was introduced to Western Europe in the middle of the XVI century. The unique feature of this flower is that it can be

Figure 10–2 Viceroy tulip in Holland: equivalent value (in florins) 1636

Two lasts of wheat	448
Four lasts of rye	558
Four fat oxen	480
Eight fat swine	240
Twelve fat sheep	120
Two hogheads of wine	70
Four tuns of beer	32
Two tuns of butter	192
One thousand pounds of cheese	120
A complete bed	100
A suit of clothes	80
A silver drinking-cup	60
Total	2500

Source: Mackay, *op. cit.*, p. 115

cultivated either from seeds, or the buds that grow on the tulip bulb. Tulips flower (in Europe) in April or May and last for approximately one week. In June, bulbs must be extracted from the earth, to be planted in September, so that they can flower again the following May. Tulips are exposed to infection from a "mosaic" virus whose effect is called a "breakout", and produces extraordinary patterns on the flower. These patterns can be reproduced in new bulbs only through cultivation of the tulip's buds (as opposed to its seeds).[7]

Owing to their beauty, difficulty of cultivation, scarcity, and the development of new varieties of bulbs with different patterns, tulips became increasingly popular during the second half of the XVI century and the beginning of the XVII century among the rich of Northern Europe. Gradually, tulip cultivation became so widespread that a huge variety of bulbs was developed, from the most scarce (or "aristocratic") to the most popular. The result was that tulips became affordable not just for the rich, but also the middle and lower classes. In addition, with a predictable growing cycle, tulips lent themselves to the development of a spot and a futures market.

Three important facts about Holland in the XVII century made tulipomania possible:

---

[7]See Garber, Peter M., "Who put the Mania in the Tulipomania?" *Crashes and Panics: the Lessons of History*, ed. Eugene N. White (Business One Irwin, 1990), pp. 3-32, Charles Mackay, *Extraordinary Popular Delusions and the Madness of Crowds*, ed. Martin S. Fridson (John Wiley & Sons, Inc., 1996), pp. 113-121, and Simon Schama, *The Embarrassment of Riches* (Fontana Press, 1991), pp. 350-366.

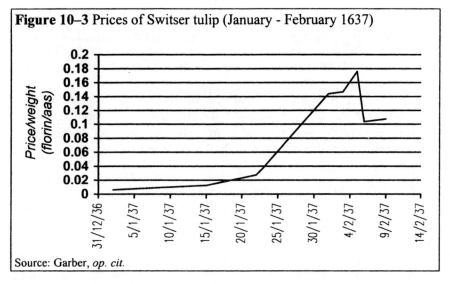

Figure 10–3 Prices of Switser tulip (January - February 1637)

Source: Garber, *op. cit.*

- A very suitable climate for tulip growing (which continues to this day),
- Commercial leadership of the Western world, owing to a combination of circumstances - economic, political and maritime, and
- The existence of the most sophisticated financial market in the world, both for debt and stocks (📖 5.2.2 and 📖 7.2.4).

By 1634, tulip fever was so strong that the Dutch began to neglect ordinary economic activity. As the fever increased, prices rose. In 1636, a price of 2,500 florins was paid for a tulip variety called *Viceroy* (figure 10–2). In the same year, formal spot and futures markets were established for tulip trading. Futures trading bore similarities to the present day, with delivery at an agreed future date at an agreed price (📖 9.7). However, as there was no margin or clearing house, transaction risk (that the counterparty would not fulfill his side of the trade) was high.

By the beginning of 1637, the classic symptoms of a true mania began to appear. Prices rose, not only of the rarer bulb varieties, but also of the more common ones. Brokers on the Amsterdam Stock Exchange now traded only in tulips. Everyone believed that the passion for tulips would never end: nobles, citizens, farmers, mechanics, sailors, maids, even washerwomen, everyone was speculating in tulip bulbs. So common did trading become that notaries and lawyers were appointed to deal only in the tulip business. In some towns the profession of notary public was so little known that the only kind of notary that was recognized was the "tulip notary".

Tulipomania ended during the first week of February 1637, with prices reaching their peak on February 5, 1637 (figure 10–3). The main reason was that the major producers began to worry about high prices, and, to protect their own good name, to advise clients to sell, or at least to stop buying.[8]

Many cities followed the example of Haarlem, a center for tulip growers. In the month of May 1638, the Haarlem City Council approved a rule permitting any buyer of a tulip futures contract to settle his obligations under the contract with the payment of just 3.5% of the agreed price.

10.2.2.2 The Mississippi boom (France)

In 1716 John Law, son of a Scottish banker, who had been exiled from Scotland for having killed a rival suitor in a duel, arrived in France to offer his financial talents to the government. Soon after his arrival, he persuaded the authorities to issue for the first time paper money worth twice the national reserves of gold and silver. It was a rather advanced monetary idea for its time, and the result was a major increase in economic activity. Having been awarded the monopoly concession to develop the enormous Mississippi valley in the US, Law then organized a company around the concession (called Compagnie d'Occident), and began to sell its stock to the public.

Law offered two incentives to investors. They could subscribe three quarters of the value of their stocks using the paper money he himself had promoted. At the time, it was trading at an 80% discount to face value - such was the lack of confidence in non-metal money. The second incentive was the promise of a 40% dividend on the amount invested after just one year.

With these incentives, plus the magic of the Occident, there were 300,000 subscriptions for the first 50,000 stocks, and the company was forced to make further issues. In addition, Law increased the attractiveness of the company by buying the commercial monopolies of China, India and Africa and changing its name to an even more exotic one, Compagnie des Indes.

The increase in the company's price drove the printing of more paper money, which in its turn increased the price of the stock even further. The result was that the price rose from 300 livres (*libras francesas*) in

---

[8]An interesting, and little known, explanation (see Garber, *op. cit.*), is that tulipomania coincided in Holland with the bubonic plague of 1635-36, when 17,193 people died just in Amsterdam. When the effects of the plague diminished, speculators began to think of the future.

1719 to 20,000 livres in 1720. In that year the value of the company reached the equivalent of 80 times all the gold and silver in France.

The rue de Quincampoix in Paris, the street where the company's stocks were traded, began to look like a fairground. A cobbler rented his shop to some brokers at ten times his monthly wage, and rentals for the houses on the street rose between twelve and sixteen times. More than 30,000 people came from the provinces to Paris to participate in trading in the stock.

Until the bubble burst. Investors began to lose confidence both in paper money and in stocks of the Compagnie des Indes. Panic prevailed and the stock price fell from 20,000, its high at the beginning of 1720, to a level of 200 livres in December of the same year. Law fled Paris, and died in Venice, in poverty and obscurity, in 1729.

10.2.2.3 South Sea Bubble (England)

Sir Isaac Newton, the famous English physicist, said: "I can calculate the movement of heavenly bodies, but not the madness of people". He therefore sold his stock in the South Sea Company in April 1720.

The South Sea Company had been formed in London in 1711 with the monopoly concession to exploit South America. However, there was little interest in the stock until 1719. An important reason was the speculation in France in stock of the Compagnie d'Occident (📖 10.2.2.2). Seeing what was happening in Paris, investors in London

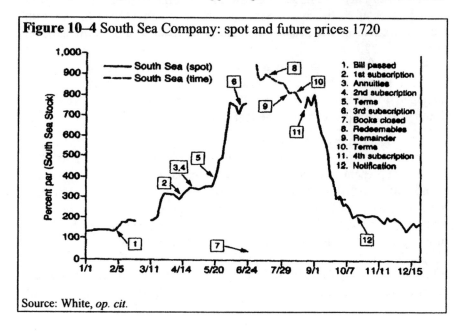

Figure 10–4 South Sea Company: spot and future prices 1720

Legend:
— South Sea (spot)
-- South Sea (time)

1. Bill passed
2. 1st subscription
3. Annuities
4. 2nd subscription
5. Terms
6. 3rd subscription
7. Books closed
8. Redeemables
9. Remainder
10. Terms
11. 4th subscription
12. Notification

Y-axis: Percent par (South Sea Stock)
X-axis: 1/1 2/5 3/11 4/14 5/20 6/24 7/29 9/1 10/7 11/11 12/15

Source: White, *op. cit.*

Figure 10–5 Dow Jones index 1926-30

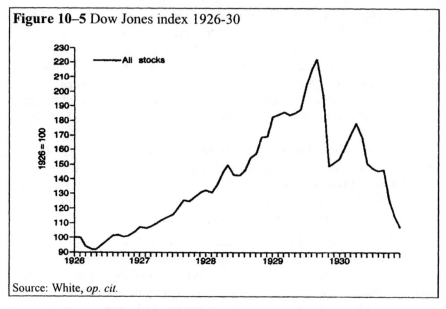

Source: White, *op. cit.*

began to buy an increasing number of stocks in their own version of the French company. There were nine stock issues in the months of April, July and August of 1720 (figure 10–4).

The stock price rose from £100 pounds sterling in 1719 to £1,000 in the month of July 1720. But the collapse of some fraudulent companies in England caused the South Sea stock price to fall as well (along with the government of the period) and the price reached a level of £160 in December 1720.

Meanwhile, Newton, who had sold in April with a profit of 100%, returned to the market when prices were at their highest level and managed to lose, in total, £20,000. He prohibited all mention of the South Sea in his presence for the rest of his life.

10.2.2.4 The crash of 1929 (US)

Owing to its importance in US economic history, the 1929 crash has come to represent the prototype of all financial crashes. After almost a decade of expansion in the New York stock market, investors had become accustomed to a market that only moved in one direction - up. They were encouraged to act based on their feelings, with the possibility of margin credit at more than nine times their investment.

But when the market began to totter, there was nothing to block its fall. On Tuesday, October 29 (the famous Black Tuesday - *martes negro*), the Dow Jones index fell 30 points (10%), with a record level of

Figure 10–6 Gold and silver prices 1979-82 (monthly)

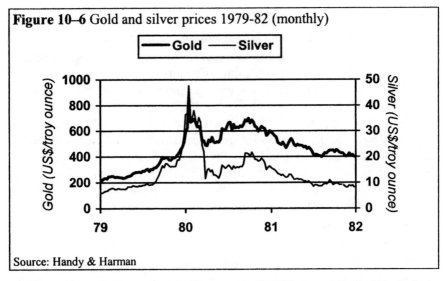

trading at 16 million stocks (figure 10–5). When stocks reached their lowest point, in 1932, they had fallen 83% from their peak in September 1929. The Dow Jones index did not return to its 1929 level until 1954.

10.2.3 Gold and silver

In October 1979, on the fiftieth anniversary of the 1929 crash, there was a wave of news articles and TV programs on "Could it happen again?" Obviously, everyone arrived at the conclusion that, with modern and sophisticated financial systems, a repeat was impossible.

Just three months later, in January 1980, the question was answered differently, this time correctly, but in other markets. Gold reached US$850 per troy ounce and silver US$50 per troy ounce: the prices of the two metals had risen by 100% in December 1979 (figure 10–6). Silver fell to US$11, i.e. by 80%, in the month of March 1980, just two months after reaching its historic high.

The main causes of the boom in gold and silver, both in 1979-80 and in 1973-4, were the increase in the oil price, causing an important increase in the US inflation rate, accompanied by a high degree of global instability (the Yom Kippur War in October 1973, and the Russian invasion of Afghanistan in December 1979).[9] For the purposes of this chapter, suffice it to say that these booms show the classic boom pattern described in 📖 10.2.2.

---

[9]See Heyman, *op. cit.,* pp. 204-210.

10.2.4   Mexican stock market booms

10.2.4.1   1979

The Mexican stock market boom of 1979 was a direct result of the 1976 devaluation. The devaluation affected companies in two ways. Companies with dollar debt had an exchange loss, and the economic crisis of 1976 caused a recession in 1977, which affected company profits during that year. The economic recovery of 1978, along with certain special factors (tax advantages for stock market investment, and a publicity campaign launched by the MSE) culminated in the euphoria of 1979, and the subsequent crash. The stock index reached an all-time high on May 7 1979, but its fall was practically continuous during the last two years of the López Portillo *sexenio*. It reached its low for the *sexenio* in August 1982, when Mexico's financial crisis erupted (figure 10–7).

10.2.4.2   1984

The financial crisis of 1982, with its multiple devaluations, was the cause of the stock market boom of 1984. As in 1977, companies were affected by the 1983 recession. Similarly, exchange losses from dollar debt would have been even more negative, had it not been for the introduction in May 1983 of FICORCA (Fideicomiso para la Cobertura de Riesgos Cambiarios). The economic recovery expected for 1984, and certain special factors (the introduction of Bulletin B10 for inflation accounting and the sale of non-bank assets of the nationalized banking system) caused a spectacular rise in the market in the first two months of 1984. The index reached its peak at the end of February 1984, 50% in US$ above its level at the end of 1983, but only returned to this level in October 1986.

10.2.4.3   1987

In September 1985, there was the tragic earthquake and, in January 1986, a collapse in the world oil price. By July 1986, it seemed as if a major external problem of the Mexican economy had been solved with a credit agreement with the IMF, which implied a gross flow of resources to Mexico of a minimum of $2 bn. At the same time, the price of oil began to rise.[10]

Four more factors had a positive effect on the Mexican stock market:

---

[10]See Heyman, Timothy, *Investing in Mexico* (Editorial Milenio, S. A. de C. V., 1989), pp. 58-79 for a detailed description of the 1987 Mexican market boom.

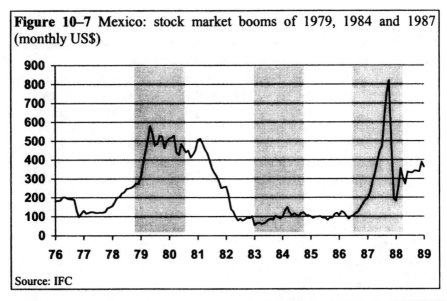

Figure 10–7 Mexico: stock market booms of 1979, 1984 and 1987 (monthly US$)

Source: IFC

- Low interest rates at a world level encouraged an important repatriation of capital to Mexico from mid-1986.
- In September 1986, measures to restructure the foreign debt of Mexican companies were formalized through "swap" operations, and other methods of debt capitalization or prepayment. The effect of these operations on corporate balance sheets was a major cause of the revaluation of Mexican companies during the boom.
- The partial privatization of an important group of issuers (the nationalized banks) through the issue of CAPs (*Certificados de Aportación Patrimonial*) beginning in February 1987 had a major effect on the stock market.
- Finally, the rise in international stock markets, above all in the US, had an effect on Mexico.

But international markets also affected the Mexican stock market on the downside. On October 19 (Black Monday - *lunes negro*), the Dow fell 508 points, or 23%, its largest percentage fall in history. As a consequence, just as the Mexican stock market had been the best performing in the world until October 16, 1987, it was the worst performing in the subsequent period. In fact, we suspect that the index fall of 74% in US$ in the 28 trading days from October 6 to November

18, 1987, might be a world record for crashes, in terms of distance and velocity.[11]

10.2.5 Mexican peso booms 1982 and 1994

Both in 1982 and in 1994, the peso became seriously overvalued. In 1982, the cause was the excessive flow of capital to Mexico as a result of the oil boom and bank credit to both the public and private sector, which in turn caused unsustainable imbalances in the public sector deficit and the current account. In 1994, the cause was again excessive capital inflows, this time the result of the global expansion of emerging markets, and Mexico's entry to NAFTA and the OECD. This time, the inflows' main effect was on the current account balance. However, the need to cover the current account deficit also distorted the government's external debt profile (the *tesobono* problem).

In both cases, the result was an overvalued currency (a peso boom) with the consequent abrupt devaluation from $0.0275/US$ to $0.150/US$ between January 1982 and December 1982 and from $3.47/US$ in December 1994 to $7.65/US$ in December 1995 (figure 10–8). These devaluations in turn affected the principal financial variables in the Mexican economy: interest rates and the stock market index.

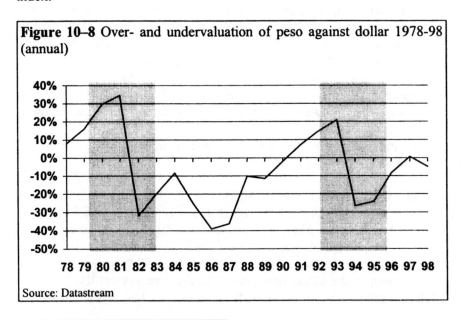

Figure 10–8 Over- and undervaluation of peso against dollar 1978-98 (annual)

Source: Datastream

---

[11]The collapse of the *Soukh-Al-Manakh* (stock exchange) of Kuwait in 1981

10.3 THE ANALYSIS OF IRRATIONALITY

The economist J. K. Galbraith, referring to the 1929 crash, wrote:

"And one can relish the varied idiocy of human action in a financial panic to the full, for, while it is a time of great tragedy, nothing is being lost but money."[12]

But, apart from being intrinsically interesting, the analysis of booms and crashes, crises and panics can be of practical use. If we can find a pattern in booms, this will permit us to understand their different stages, benefit from the irrational part, but still sell in time. Furthermore, quite apart from the relatively abnormal periods of boom, if, through an analysis of investor behavior during booms, we can deduce psychological patterns, we can benefit from recognizing them in our daily activity in investment markets. We will examine these two subjects in the rest of this chapter.

10.4 THE CLASSIC BOOM CYCLE

10.4.1 The Minsky model

Based on the pioneering work of the US economist Hyman Minsky[13] stages have been identified that are common to most booms. These stages (some of which may be simultaneous) are called: displacement, gradual growth, increase in liquidity, entry of novices, euphoria, insider selling, crash, panic and rejection.

10.4.1.1 Displacement

Each boom occurs as the result of a drastic change (displacement – *desplazamiento*) in the investment environment. This change can be a war – the 1929 crash was a result of the prosperity of the years following the I World War. It can also be a discovery (the Mississippi and Latin America in the case of the booms of the Compagnie des Indes and The South Sea Company, respectively), or an invention (canals, railways, the obsession for high technology companies in the US in the 1990s). It can be an important change in political relationships (e.g. the new power of OPEC which caused increases in the price of oil, with a consequent increase in metals prices, in 1973-4 and 1979-80). It can also be a combination of technological and political factors. The emerging markets boom was a product of technological change in computing and

---

was probably steeper, but as there was no formal index, no exact record exists.

[12]Galbraith, *ibid.*, p. 26.

[13]Cited in Kindleberger, *op. cit.*, pp. 16-27.

telecommunications, and the opening of new markets as the result of the collapse of the Berlin Wall in 1989 (📖 1.2 and 📖 4.2).

In Mexico, the devaluations of 1976 and 1982 were direct causes of the booms of 1979 and 1984. The devaluation of 1985, the earthquake of the same year and the oil price collapse in 1986 were causes of the stock market boom of 1987. The peso boom of 1994 was a result of the general emerging markets boom mentioned above, along with the specific factor of the approval of NAFTA by US Congress on November 17, 1993.

10.4.1.2 Gradual growth

After the drastic change in the investment environment caused by the "displacement event", there is normally a gradual adjustment to these new circumstances. This can be observed most clearly in the gradual rise in the US stock market in the 1920s, and the smooth increase in metals prices in 1979 and in Mexican stock prices in 1977 and 1978, as well as in the appreciation of the real peso/dollar exchange rate between 1991-93 prior to the approval of NAFTA.

10.4.1.3 Increase in liquidity

An increase in liquidity normally occurs at the same time as the gradual growth described in the previous section. In fact, the availability of money to invest in the relevant asset (or object of speculation) is a necessary condition for a subsequent boom (📖 4.4 on the liquidity cycle and also figure 10-1). It can be observed clearly in the cases of Mississippi (which was the result of paper money) and Wall Street in 1929 (margin credits). Similarly, the gold and silver booms of 1973-4 and 1979-80 were directly caused by the increased liquidity (petrodollars) generated by the rise in oil prices.

In the Mexican market, the withdrawal from circulation of bank bonds, which occurred in 1977-78, had a direct effect on funds available for the stock market in the 1979 boom. In the 1984 boom, the existence of an enormous money market since 1982 facilitated the transference of resources from this large market to a relatively small stock market. An important factor in the 1987 boom was the availability of funds to invest in stocks created by the repatriation of capital, estimated at US$5 bn. between July 1986 and October 1987. In the peso boom of 1993-4, capital had been repatriated owing to the bank privatization and fiscal amnesty of 1991-2, and there was the opening to foreign portfolio investment (through the Nafin Trust) implemented in November 1989, and the flow of capital to emerging markets which began with the collapse of Communism in 1989.

10.4.1.4 Entry of novices

The entry of novices is a stage which results from the conditions described in previous sections. Owing to the great profits that have been generated, the novice begins to become aware of them, and enters the market without experience or knowledge. Signs of this stage are comments in non-specialized media (which are normally not interested in such technical subjects), conversations at dinners or cocktail parties (which are not the usual place for this kind of conversation), and interest shown in the market by people who are not usually considered to be highly qualified investors (housewives, taxi-drivers, dentists, etc.). Another useful indicator of this stage are official speeches made by professional executives of the relevant market about the advantages of investment in it.

10.4.1.5 Euphoria

Market entry by novices produces euphoria. This euphoria is reflected in spectacular and indiscriminate price moves in the object of speculation (metals, stocks, commodities). It becomes very easy to make money, and practically impossible to lose it. As a result, investors (and the intermediaries who advise them) begin to feel omnipotent.

10.4.1.6 Insider selling

With the entry of novices and spectacular price rises, insiders see the signs of a classic boom and begin to exit the market. This in turn can have a stabilizing effect on prices, which begin to level off from their previous dizzying increases.

10.4.1.7 Crash

The crash comes when for the first time there is an important fall in the price of the object of speculation. The crash can be precipitated by some outside event (as, in the case of the Mexican boom in 1987, the Wall Street crash of the same year). Or it can occur, quite simply, because the object was overvalued (tulips, Mississippi, South Sea, 1929 in New York).

10.4.1.8 Panic

After the first crash, there can be a light rebound, as there are still investors who refuse to believe that the boom is over. The panic comes next, when everyone attempts to sell his investment in any way he can. A recent panic was that of the Indonesian rupiah, which devalued by 79% between November 3, 1997 and January 23, 1998 (figure 10–9).

Each language has its own terminology for this stage. "Every man for himself" (English), which in French becomes "sauve qui peut" (*sálvese*

Figure 10–9 Indonesian rupiah/US$ October 1997- March 1998 (daily)

Source: Datastream

quien pueda); "den letzten beissen die Hünde" (German – "let the dogs bite the hindmost", or *que los perros muerdan a los últimos*); "Torschlüsspanik" (German – "the urge to reach the door before it shuts" or *las ansias de llegar a la puerta antes de que se cierre*).

10.4.1.9 Rejection

After suffering so much financial loss (not to mention emotional distress), many investors wish to have absolutely nothing to do with the object of speculation. This is the stage of rejection, which we already saw in the case of Sir Isaac Newton. It can last a long time – as in the case of the New York stock market which only reached 1929 levels in 1954. It can also be shorter: there were metals booms in 1973-4 and 1979-80, and in the Mexican stock market in 1979, 1984 and 1987. However, at the end of 1998, the Japanese stock market had still not recovered from the 1990 crash (figure 10–10).

10.4.2 Application of the Minsky model to Mexico

There is a practical application of the model. Let us take the three Mexican stock booms. A good orthodox analyst using the valuation techniques described in 📖 8.5 would have realized that the market had begun to be overvalued in January 1979, January 1984, and April 1987, respectively. He would therefore have sold his entire stock position in those months. This is exactly what Newton did, realizing a good profit, before re-entering the market and losing everything.

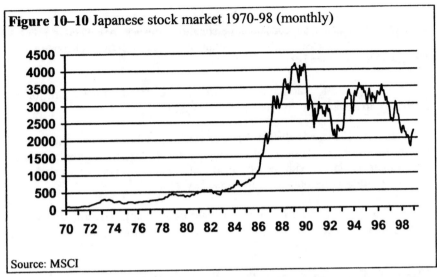

Figure 10–10 Japanese stock market 1970-98 (monthly)

Source: MSCI

But although it would have solid reasoning behind it, this market exit would have implied giving up significant potential profits. The market rose 48% (in US$) between January and May 1979, 50% between January and February 1984, and 149% between the beginning of April and October 1987. With some understanding of the boom phenomenon, the investor can benefit by maintaining a position until the last stage before the crash (euphoria and insider selling). Depending on his risk tolerance, this strategy would imply, for example, selling a quarter of the position when the market begins to look overvalued, another quarter during the stage of novice entry, another quarter during the euphoria stage, and the final quarter just before the crash.

10.5 THE CAUSE OF BOOMS – GROUP PSYCHOLOGY

10.5.1 Investors as a group

The psychological foundation of the phenomenon of booms and crashes is that human beings act differently as members of groups than as individuals. As the activity in financial markets is necessarily social (because there must be a buyer and a seller), psychological analysis of markets necessarily implies the analysis of groups.

The pioneer in the analysis of large groups, i.e., "the crowd" (*la muchedumbre*), was Gustave Lebon, a French psychologist, who published his book "The Crowd" in 1895. About the crowd, Lebon said:

"The sentiments and ideas of all persons in a gathering take one and the same direction, and their conscious personality vanishes. A collective mind is formed, doubtless transitory, but presenting very clearly defined characteristics. The gathering has then become...a psychological crowd."[14]

One important feature of the crowd, according to Lebon, is its difficulty in separating the real from the imaginary:

".....a crowd scarcely distinguishes between the subjective and objective. It accepts as real the images evoked in its mind, though they most often only have a very distant relation with the observed facts...Crowds being only capable of thinking in images are only to be impressed by images."[15]

The basic elements of Lebon's crowd can be applied in their totality to financial markets: a lot of people, a lot of movement, and a very simple image. The simple image is of easy, ready, money.

10.5.2 The consequences of the collective mind

There are various consequences for the investor's perception as member of a group:

• The investor lets himself be influenced by other members of the group, but
• The group, in a situation of high uncertainty, prefers to be guided by an expert: however,
• In problems as complex as those of investment, experts can also make mistakes. This is because
• Experts also form part of a group.

Let us examine each of these points in more detail.

10.5.2.1 The influence of the group

Dreman[16] describes a series of experiments, which show the influence a group of people can have on the perceptions of an individual. In one experiment, a person is injected with a light dose of epinephrine, a drug that causes heart palpitations and involuntary hand movements. This person is placed unknowingly in a waiting room with another person (employed by the psychologist conducting the experiment) who begins to act strangely, with brow and arm movements, etc. In very little time,

---

[14]Quoted in Dreman, David, *The New Contrarian Investment Strategy* (Random House, 1982), pp. 65-66.
[15]*ibid.*, p. 66.
[16]*ibid.*, pp. 72-73

the other person begins to act in the same way, without it being a result of the injection.

In another experiment, a group of people is shown a small point of light in a dark room. The point seems to move, without actually moving. Members of the group are asked how much the point has moved. When they answer individually, there is a very wide variation of response. When they answer openly, in front of the other members of the group, the variation in response is reduced to practically zero.[17]

These physical and measurable phenomena reflect a psychological reality which we all recognize: that we have the tendency to let ourselves be influenced by the group to which we belong.

10.5.2.2 The influence of the expert

When a group confronts a situation of high uncertainty – like investment – it tends to have recourse to an expert to help in its decision making process. The greater the uncertainty, the greater the need for an expert, or several experts. The greater the agreement among experts, and the larger the group, the more right they seem to be. This means that however difficult and subjective investment might seem to be, the reality perceived by the group can become almost objective, owing to the number of opinions expressed in its favor.

10.5.2.3 The fallibility of the expert

But the expert, above all in the investment industry, has a tendency to make mistakes. In the US stock market, a study found that of investments chosen by professional investment advisers between 1929 and 1980, 77% had a worse performance than the corresponding benchmark.

10.5.2.4 Experts are also members of a group

The reason for the mistakes of many experts is that they are also members of a group and let themselves be influenced by it. In any market, it is very difficult to isolate oneself from other professionals. They might have established a relationship on the trading floor. In the case of stock analysts, it is difficult for them to avoid contact when they meet in corporate analysts' meetings (*encuentros de análisis*). They can hardly avoid meeting at the professional associations and conventions whose purpose is to improve the operational efficiency of the markets.

---

[17] *ibid.*, pp. 77-78

10.5.3 Rules of contrary opinion

An understanding of the psychological reality of markets in relation to the investment problem can be summarized in one single phrase: "contrary opinion" (*opinión contraria*). If the crowd (investors or experts) tends to be wrong, it is necessary to have a contrary opinion.

We saw a classic application of contrary opinion when we proposed a technique to analyze and benefit from booms. But contrary opinion can also be applied to the daily activity of investment in the different areas described in this book.

10.5.3.1 Investment objectives

Normally, the establishment of investment objectives, in relation to the key parameters of return, risk, term and liquidity should depend on the individual – and has nothing to do with the group. However, the investor can also be influenced by the group in his establishment of investment objectives.

A classic example occurs during bull markets. The investor has allocated a certain percentage of his portfolio to stocks, depending on his risk tolerance. But who has not received advice in a bull market to increase the stock percentage, as "everyone is doing it"? And this occurs at a time when the stock weighting in the portfolio has already increased as a result of stock price increases: to maintain his original weighting, the investor should be lowering his stock position.

10.5.3.2 Economic assumptions

We have explained in previous chapters that asset allocation in a portfolio depends, on the one hand, on investor objectives, and, on the other, on assumptions about Mexico country risk, and future economic scenarios. These imply assumptions about inflation, interest rates, GDP and the peso/dollar exchange rate.

There is usually a consensus on these indicators – and investment valuation reflects it. But the investor who acts against consensus can derive important benefits. After an almost 50% devaluation between December 1994 and December 1995, there was a consensus that the rate of devaluation would continue the following year. But the peso/dollar parity remained practically static between December 1995 ($7.65/US$) and December 1996 ($7.85/US$). During this period, an investment in peso debt would have yielded 26% in US$, more than the return from the stock market in US$ over the same period (20%), and with lower volatility.

10.5.3.3 Specific investments

Contrary opinion can also be applied at the level of specific investments. Within the stock market there are stocks that are "hot", and stocks that are not. Most people, by definition, look for hot stocks, when what they should be doing (contrary opinion) is looking for stocks that are not yet hot.

10.5.3.4 Trading

Contrary opinion can be applied, finally, at the trading level in a given market. If there are more buyers than sellers, one should be a seller, and viceversa. If prices are rising, this means that there are buyers who have already bought. This, in turn, reduces the number of future buyers, and implies that it is more probable that they will be sellers than before.

10.6 INVESTMENT AS A LONELY ACTIVITY

Contrary opinion is an attitude of mind, which we have attempted to apply to most phenomena that occur in investment markets - from the major and infrequent movements of booms, to the daily activity of analysis and trading.

Humans are social animals. But the application of contrary opinion is an individual activity. That is why it is difficult, and why there are few "active" investors with a better performance than their benchmarks, either in Mexico or in other countries (📖 2.6.2).

Chapter 11
Investors

"Man made the money. Money never made the man."

ll cool j

11.1 INDIVIDUAL AND INSTITUTIONAL INVESTORS

"Investment advisors are frequently asked at cocktail parties which stocks, bonds or commodities they recommend. Just as frequently, the advisors answer with detailed investment recommendations."

"Both the question, and the answer, are fundamentally wrong. Nobody goes to the doctor to ask which pills he is recommending today. Nor do they go to the tennis pro to ask him for his list of recommended strokes for the weekend."

"The questions asked of any professional should be related to the needs and objectives of the questioner. The reason why the questions about investments at a cocktail party do not seem as absurd as the medical or tennis questions is that, apparently, the only goal of investment is 'to make money'."

"But we have already seen...that it is not so simple. The return required from an investment should be set in relation to the liquidity, risk and term requirements of the investor."[1]

In other words, *There is no investment without an investor.* There are two main types of investor, individual and institutional. The difference between the individual and institutional investor is that the individual investor sets his investment objectives according to his personal goals and risk tolerance, and is absolutely free to change them whenever he wishes. The objectives of the institutional investor are determined by the nature of the institution, and are frequently defined through its company statutes.

In this chapter we describe the different types of individual and institutional investor, and trends in individual and institutional investment in global and Mexican investment markets. In 📖 ch. 12, we analyze the practical process of investment management (*administración de inversiones*), taking into account the different kinds of investor.

---

[1]Heyman, Timothy, *Inversión contra Inflación* (Editorial Milenio, S. A. de C. V, 1988), pp. 283-284.

11.2 THE INDIVIDUAL INVESTOR

The individual investor fixes his own objectives and takes his own investment decisions, with or without outside advice (📖 12.5). He can also formalize his investment objectives through the establishment of trusts (*fideicomisos*) for his family and other dependents.

Trusts are set up for individuals when a person (or settlor - *fideicomitente*) wishes to transfer property (in the form of investments) to another person or persons (the beneficiary - *beneficiario*), but wants the property to be managed through a trustee (*fiduciario*) for a fixed period, or irrevocably. The beneficiary can receive from the trust income, the principal amount, or both. The trustee can be a financial institution, lawyer, investment manager, or some combination. In this case, investment through a trust can become institutional investment (or not) depending on the level of independence (from the settlor) of the trustee.

The individual investor can be characterized in relation to his objectives of return and risk through two main techniques. One technique defines an investor's risk tolerance (*tolerancia hacia el riesgo*) according to his psychological characteristics, the other according to his stage in the life cycle (*ciclo de vida*). Normally, there is a correlation between the results of the two techniques.

11.2.1 Return and risk

11.2.1.1 Risk tolerance

Psychographics describes people's psychological characteristics. A psychographic study of risk tolerance distinguishes five kinds of investor (figure 11-1).[2] The model classifies investors by two personality traits: their confidence level (vertical axis: "confident-anxious") and their behavior (horizontal axis: "careful-impulsive"). The confidence level is related not only to the attitude to investments but also to life in general - career, health, and marriage. Behavior can be methodical, careful, and analytical, or emotional, intuitive and impulsive.[3]

---

[2]Bailard, Thomas E., David L. Biehl, Ronald W. Kaiser, *Personal Money Management, 5th edition*, (Science Research Associates Inc., 1986), cited en John L. Maginn, Donald L. Tuttle, ed., *Managing Investment Portfolios*, (Warren, Gorham & Lamont, 1990), cap. 3, pp. 7-12.

[3]The fact that an investor is classified in one way according to one decision - for example, in relation to his career – is not necessarily related to his investment decisions, although they tend to be correlated.

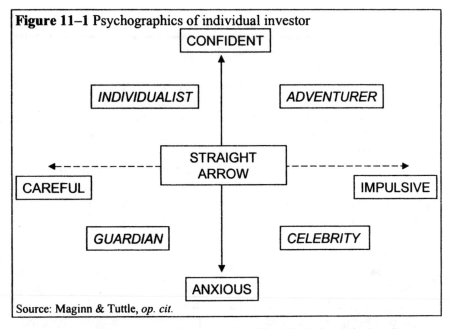

Figure 11–1 Psychographics of individual investor

Source: Maginn & Tuttle, *op. cit.*

Five investment personalities can be identified through the diagram. Top right is the "adventurer". He is confident and impulsive. Highly motivated entrepreneurs often belong to this category.

Bottom right, is the "celebrity". This person likes being "where the action is", and does not like to be "out of the game". This category might include sports and movie stars.

Top left is the "individualist". This person normally finds his own way, and could be an entrepreneur, independent professional (lawyer, accountant, engineer, or doctor). He makes his own decisions and behaves methodically and analytically.

Bottom left is the "guardian". This character type recognizes that his capacity for generation of resources is limited and wishes to conserve what he has. Normally as people grow older, they tend towards this category.

Finally, there are people who are so balanced that they belong in the absolute center of the diagram. This kind of investor is called "straight arrow".

11.2.1.2 Life cycle

The investment objectives of individual investors are not only influenced by their risk tolerance, but also by the different ages, or stages, of their life (figure 11–2):[4]

- *Accumulation.* At the beginning of his career, the investor's priorities are normally for immediate expenditure or investment (e.g. house, car, children's education). Owing to the long term, and the possibility of recovery from investment mistakes, the investor can afford greater risk, to earn a greater return (point A in figure 11–2).

- *Consolidation.* At this stage (point B), income normally begins to exceed expenditure, and savings begin to increase. Therefore, the investor begins to form an investment portfolio. However, the investor can also foresee a period when he will retire (in ten or twenty years), and therefore his risk tolerance diminishes as there is less time to recover from investment mistakes.

- *Spending.* This stage (point C) is defined as that of financial independence, i.e. when daily expenditure is covered not by wage or salary income, but by assets accumulated as investments or pension plans. Owing to the need to live off investment income, there is a greater emphasis on investment security, and therefore the level of portfolio risk is reduced. It is worth pointing out that the investment horizon can be longer than 10 years, and even at this stage investments with prospects for growth (and therefore risk) should not be excluded.

- *Gifting.* At this stage (point C) the investor realizes that he has more assets than required for his own expenditure, and therefore begins to think in terms of future generations. These future generations can include his own children (or other relations or friends) or causes or ideas that he wishes to promote (charitable foundations - *fondos de beneficencia*).

Clearly, an investor can combine different stages at the same time. For example, even in the accumulation stage he can be thinking of retirement, and of the possibility of making donations. However, normally one stage tends to predominate. Similarly, the borders between the different stages can vary considerably depending on individual cases. Finally, the determining factor of an investor's objectives can be much more related to his risk tolerance (📖 11.2.1.1) than his stage in the life cycle.

---

[4]Maginn & Tuttle, *op. cit.* cap. 3, pp. 17-19.

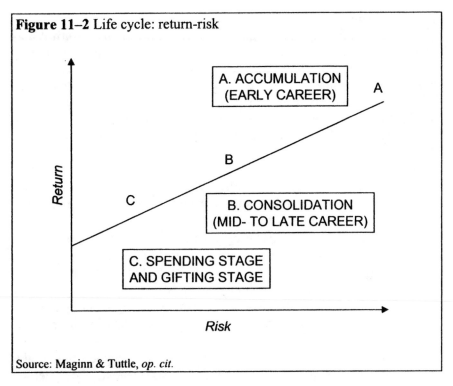

Figure 11–2 Life cycle: return-risk

A. ACCUMULATION (EARLY CAREER)

A

B

B. CONSOLIDATION (MID- TO LATE CAREER)

C

C. SPENDING STAGE AND GIFTING STAGE

Return

Risk

Source: Maginn & Tuttle, *op. cit.*

11.2.2 Term and liquidity

The previous sections help classify investors according to their return and risk objectives. Investors also have objectives of term and liquidity (📖 2.2).

11.2.2.1 Term

In the short term, there can be one to five year objectives like a new house, children's education, or a new business. Longer term, a frequent objective might be financial independence. Normally, this concept should be taken into account in conjunction with an investor's corporate pension plan. While these plans might be sufficient to cover daily living expenses, as they are normally fixed as a reasonable percentage (50-70%) of final salary, a personal investment plan provides the investor with a margin of "comfort" (*comodidad*) so that his standard of living does not fall once he stops working.

For investors with greater resources, there is always the possibility of allocating a certain amount to riskier investments, sharing the investment process with his investment advisor.

11.2.2.2 Liquidity

We defined the liquidity of an investment as the ability to turn it into cash. For debt securities, liquidity can be same day: for stocks, from one day to one week; for blocks of stock in listed companies, several weeks. For unlisted companies, real estate or other illiquid investments (📖 2.1.2), the time it takes to turn them into cash can vary considerably, depending on the market and the cash needs of the investor. The greater the hurry in selling, the worse the price obtained on an illiquid investment.

There are four main reasons for having liquidity:

• *Emergency cash*. Normally one calculates 2-3 months' expenditure, but it can be higher if the main source of income of the investor is considered to be at risk.

• *Expenditure with a five year horizon*. As mentioned above, five year objectives could include a car, house, or children's education. Normally, when a specific expense has been programmed, the investor should seek high liquidity, and low risk.

• *Taxes*. Normally, the investor knows the timing of tax payments (e.g. April for income taxes in Mexico) and plans his investment liquidity to cover them.

• *Flexibility*. The investor maintains some liquidity to take advantage of market opportunities. In this context, the level of liquidity depends on the investor's risk tolerance.

11.2.3 Taxes and inheritances

11.2.3.1 Taxes

Taxes and inheritances are relevant to investment planning. In all countries, taxes change constantly. In Mexico, individuals are currently exempt from taxes on practically all Mexican portfolio investments. However, there are taxes on non-portfolio investments (e.g. real estate and unlisted companies), and on offshore investments. There are ways of reducing the effect of these taxes on investments, but the investor needs a competent fiscal advisor to provide him with appropriate tax planning advice.

11.2.3.2 Inheritances

In relation to inheritance planning, several items should be covered:

• Method of transference. This depends on whether the investor wishes to transfer the asset to the beneficiary now, over a reasonable timeframe, or after his death.

• Taxes. Taxes can arise from the transference itself, but if the transference is for family or charitable reasons, there may be ways of avoiding or reducing taxes.

• Remaining property. It is important that, even if an efficient transfer of assets has been organized with effective tax planning, the investor makes sure that he is left with sufficient resources to maintain his lifestyle.

11.3 TRENDS IN INDIVIDUAL INVESTMENT

11.3.1 United States

The availability of statistics on trends in individual investment, even in a country with highly developed databases such as the US, is complicated by the definition of the term. An "individual investor" can be defined as someone with a bank savings account, a brokerage account, or a mutual fund account.

One indicator of the level of individual investment in stocks in the US is a survey conducted in 1992 on the percentage of households involved in the stock market through direct investment, mutual funds, or pension

Household income	% households with income	% households with savings	% stock investors	% stock investment
1992				
<$15,000	27.9	10.0	7.5	3.8
$15,000-$25,000	18.0	23.6	11.3	3.3
$25,000-$50,000	28.1	44.9	33.8	18.4
$50,000-$75,000	13.4	64.6	23.1	16.7
$75,000-$100,000	5.5	67.1	9.9	12.1
$100,000-$250,000	5.9	75.3	11.9	23.0
>$250,000	1.2	79.3	2.5	22.7
Total	100.0	NA	100.0	100.0
1983				
<$15,000	26.0	7.4	5.8	0.8
$15,000-$25,000	19.8	22.8	13.6	2.3
$25,000-$50,000	32.2	40.0	38.7	9.1
$50,000-$75,000	13.9	57.3	23.9	12.6
$75,000-$100,000	3.8	69.1	7.9	7.3
$100,000-$250,000	3.7	75.2	8.3	24.9
>$250,000	0.7	91.5	1.8	43.1
Total	100.0	NA	100.0	100.0

Figure 11–3 US households with stock investments 1983 and 1992

Source: Hale, *op. cit.*

plans (figure 11–3).[5]

The most important conclusion from the table is that stock investment, and therefore risk tolerance, has become "democratized". In 1983, 0.7% of households with an annual income above US$250,000 represented 43.1% of stock investment. In 1992, even though the percentage of total households with income above US$250,000 rose to 1.2%, they only represented 22.7% of total stock investment. Meanwhile, households with annual incomes lower than US$15,000 raised their participation of total stock investment from 0.8% in 1983, to 3.8% in 1992. The strata between US$25,000 and US$100,000 also raised their percentage of stock investment significantly. For example, households with annual income between US$25,000 and US$50,000 rose from 9.1% in 1983 to 18.4% in 1992.

11.3.2 Mexico

Measurement of individual investment is as difficult in Mexico as in the US. One indicator is the number of accounts in brokerages and mutual funds. At December 31 1997, there were 143,790 brokerage accounts[6] (i.e. 0.15% of the estimated population of 95 mn.), but the breakdown between debt and equity securities is unknown. Of these accounts, 50,000 (i.e. 0.05% of the population) were estimated to have direct stock investments. At the same date, there were 289,182 individual mutual fund accounts, of which 92% were in debt funds and 8% (i.e. 22,223 accounts) in stock funds.[7]

However, the picture is different if we include accounts in the SAR (*Sistema de Ahorro para el Retiro* – System of Savings for Retirement). On December 31 1997, there were 11,091,283 accounts of workers affiliated to the *Administradoras de Fondos para el Retiro* (*Afores* – Managers of Retirement Funds), representing 12% of the population, and 64% of total households. These accounts imply the possibility of an enormous increase in the number of individual investors in non-bank investments (11.5.3).

---

[5]Cited in Hale, David, "Economic Implications of the Mutual Fund Boom", (Zurich Kemper Investments Inc., March 1996).

[6]Asociación Mexicana de Intermediarios Bursátiles A. C. (December, 1997).

[7]Análisis Sociedades de Inversión (*El Financiero*, January 8, 1998).

11.4 INSTITUTIONAL INVESTMENT

11.4.1 Types of institutional investment

There are six main types of institutional investment: mutual funds, pension funds, charitable foundations, insurance companies, financial institutions, and companies.

11.4.1.1 Mutual funds

Mutual funds invest in a diversified investment portfolio and are managed by investment managers *(empresas administradoras de inversión)*. Investors pay management fees to the investment managers, and have the right to the net income and net worth of the fund in proportion to their shareholding. The investment portfolio of the fund is managed according to investment policies and objectives defined in its offering prospectus *(prospecto de colocación)*.

The investor bases his selection of a mutual fund on three main criteria:

- The matching of his own investment objectives with those of the fund,
- The extent to which the historical performance *(desempeño)* of the fund has matched its investment objectives,
- The cost of managing the fund – fund managers normally charge a one time entry fee (as well as, sometimes, an exit fee), and an annual commission for managing the fund.

There are two kinds of mutual fund: closed-end and open-end. A closed-end fund *(sociedad de inversión cerrada)* raises funds for investment according to the objectives of the fund, through an offering of a fixed number of shares, which are listed on an exchange. After the initial listing, the price of the stock is determined by the market and it therefore can trade at a premium *(prima)* or discount *(descuento)* to the net asset value per share of the fund, which is based on the value of its investments.[8]

On open-end fund *(sociedad de inversión abierta)* can sell or redeem shares according to the demand and supply that exists for it among the public. The purchase or sale price is based on the net asset value per share of the fund. Therefore, there is no discount or premium, as in the case of a closed-end fund. Currently, in Mexico, both debt and stock funds are open-end funds.

---

[8] The Mexico Fund *(Fondo Mexico)* and most so-called "country funds" *(fondos país)*, which specialize in investment in an individual country, are closed-end funds.

11.4.1.2 Pension funds

Pension funds (*fondos de pensiones*) are funds allocated by an organization (public or private) according to a pension plan (*plan de pensiones*) to cover its employees' needs following retirement. There are two main types of pension plan: defined benefit (*beneficio definido*) and defined contribution (*contribución definida*).

A defined benefit pension plan implies that the organization is obliged to provide an employee with a determined benefit level following retirement – normally calculated as a percentage of his last salary prior to retirement and, possibly, indexed to the annual inflation rate. The level of funding by the organization of the pension fund depends on actuarial calculations that take into account the agreed level of payments and the life expectancy of beneficiaries, compared with estimates of return for the fund's investments.

A defined contribution pension plan implies that the organization is required to provide regular contributions to savings accounts opened in the name of employees registered with the plan. A defined contribution pension plan has two main differences from a defined benefit plan:

- A defined contribution plan is portable (*portátil*). This implies that when an employee changes job, he takes his pension account with him, without losing his rights. In a defined benefit plan, the retirement rights of an employee remain with the plan. Depending on his time in the organization, when he changes employment the employee might retain the right to a certain level of pension in the future from his prior employment. However, he must register with the pension plan of his new employer, and effectively start accumulating pension plan benefits in the new plan all over again.

- A defined contribution plan transfers responsibility of the management of the pension account from the organization to the employee. In some cases, the organization itself helps the employee choose its investment manager: in other cases, the employee makes the selection. The selection can be made from mutual funds managed by investment managers, as in the US, or from funds managed by specialized pension fund managers, with their own system of regulation and supervision, as in Chile (the system of *Administradoras de Fondos de Pensiones - AFPs*), and Mexico (the *Afores*).

11.4.1.3 Charitable funds

Charitable funds are funds established for non-profit purposes. They are financed through donations of their sponsors and are managed by charitable organizations whose tax status as charitable institutions (or, in Mexico, as organizations of "private assistance" - *asistencia privada*) can offer tax deductibility on donations. Normally, the objectives of this kind of institution are to produce an income flow that permits it to fulfill the charitable objectives for which it was established.

11.4.1.4 Insurance companies

Insurance companies insure risks for which their clients pay premiums. The two main categories of risk assured are life, and property and casualty. The level of premiums charged is calculated according to the actuarial incidence of the risks being insured, and the estimated return on the funds provided by premiums. Over time, insurance companies have become one of the most important types of institutional investor in global markets.

11.4.1.5 Other financial institutions

Other financial institutions (e.g. banks) are investors, because they invest on their own account. This is frequently because they are market makers (*formadores de mercado*) in the markets where they operate – in debt securities, stocks and derivatives.

11.4.1.6 Companies

Funds invested by companies fall into two main categories. First, defined benefit pension plans are their responsibility (📖 11.4.1.2). Second, treasury funds are excess funds that they may not need immediately but can invest by the day, or week. In general, these funds require almost instant liquidity.

11.5 TRENDS IN INSTITUTIONAL INVESTMENT

11.5.1 Global institutional investment

There are no readily available comparative statistics on four of the six types of institutional investment described above: charitable funds, insurance companies, financial institutions and companies. However, two types of investment (pension funds and mutual funds) are managed by one kind of institution, the investment manager. There are statistics about investment managers in various countries, which are helpful in understanding the historical development, current situation, and future prospects of institutional investment (defined as investment in pension funds and mutual funds) in the world, and in Mexico.

In figure 11–4 we present basic statistics for institutional investment, compared to population, GNP, and the total market for bonds and stocks, in 27 developed and emerging countries.

Figure 11–4 Global institutional investment (US$)

column		A	B	C	D=B+C	E	F	G=E+F	H=D/A	I=G/A	J=G/D
						Pension	Mutual		Total	Inst.	Inst.
	Popula-	GNP	Bonds	Stocks	Total	funds	funds	Inst.	mkt. /	inv./	inv./
	tion 95	95	96*	96	mkt.	94	94	inv.	GNP	GNP	Tot. mkt.
	(mn.)	(bn.)	(bn.)	(bn.)	(bn.)	(bn.)	(bn.)	(bn.)	(%)	(%)	(%)
Australia	18	347	124	300	424	82	44	126	122.2	36.3	29.7
Canada	30	563	467	514	982	238	98	336	174.4	59.6	34.2
Germany	82	2414	2,598	666	3,264	124	253	377	135.2	15.6	11.6
Holland	16	396	327	378	705	264	50	314	178.1	79.3	44.5
Japan	125	5111	4,533	2,675	7,208	1,118	467	1,585	141.0	31.0	22.0
Switzerland	7	304	217	413	629	191	90	281	207.1	92.4	44.6
UK	58	1102	523	1,684	2,206	775	135	910	200.2	82.6	41.3
US	263	6952	8,592	8,864	17,456	3,760	2,161	5,921	251.1	85.2	33.9
Others (19)	203	4,480	2,965	1,808	4,774	501	1184	1,685	106.6	37.6	35.3
Total	801	21,668	20,345	17,302	37,647	7,053	4,482	11,535	173.7	53.2	30.6
Mexico 97	**95**	**400**	**100**	**156**	**256**	**13.6**	**14.5**	**28**	**64.0**	**7.0**	**11.0**

* including Mexican external debt in US$

Source: CrossBorder Capital, Intersec, Investment Company Institute, author

The relationship between the different variables can be observed more clearly in figure 11–5 and figure 11–6 where the relationship is plotted between the total investment market, defined as the sum of the stock and bond markets (column D in figure 11–4) and GNP (A), and between institutional investment (G) and the total investment market.

From the three charts, the main conclusions are:

- There is a general correlation between the size of the total investment market and the size of GNP. However investment in relation to GNP is relatively more developed in the US than in Germany and Japan. Other developed countries (e.g. Switzerland, Canada) have an investment market commensurate with their GNP.

- There is an apparent correlation between the development of

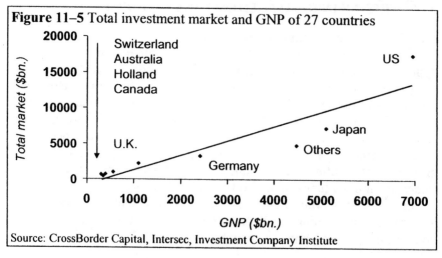

Figure 11–5 Total investment market and GNP of 27 countries

Source: CrossBorder Capital, Intersec, Investment Company Institute

Figure 11–6 Institutional investment and total investment market in 27 countries

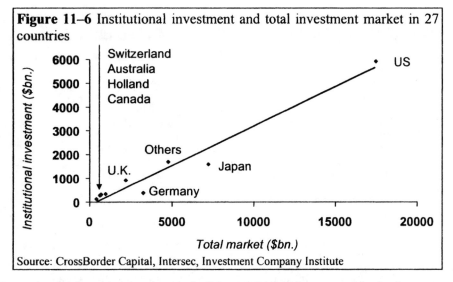

Source: CrossBorder Capital, Intersec, Investment Company Institute

institutional investment and of the total investment market. In the case of Germany and Japan, their underdevelopment in relation to the overall market is probably due to the relative strength of two kinds of institutional investment not included in these statistics, - insurance companies and financial institutions.

• Institutional investment in Mexico is underdeveloped, with a ratio of institutional investment to the total investment market of just 11% compared to an average of 30.6% (figure 11–4).

• The US is clearly the most advanced country in terms of development of its investment markets and of institutional investment.

It is for this last reason that we analyze trends in institutional investment in the US in the next section, before analyzing the situation in Mexico.

11.5.2 Institutional investment in the US

11.5.2.1 History

The history of institutional investment in the US is relatively recent. Although the first closed-end funds were established in Belgium in the 1820s, and in Scotland (by Robert Fleming) in the 1860s, it was only in the 1920s that an investment fund culture began to develop in the US. However the 1929 crash slowed their development, and it was only after World War II that the investing public began to accept them.

There were two main reasons for this:

Figure 11-7 History of institutional investment in US: important dates

1860	Development of closed-end investment trusts by Robert Fleming in Scotland
1920s	Boom of investment trusts in USA
1962	*Self-Employed Individuals Tax Retirement Act* authorizes "Keogh plans" in US for self-employed individuals
1974	*Employment Retirement Income Security Act* (ERISA) in US permits *Individual Retirement Accounts* - IRAs
1978	*Revenue Act* permits tax exemptions under clause 401(k)
1981	*Economic Recovery Tax Act* permits tax deductibility for IRAs
1982	Banks permitted to offer IRA accounts
1986	*Tax Reform Act* permits two new categories of contribution to IRAs: non-deductible and partially deductible
1996	*Small Business Job Protection Act* (increases amounts that can be contributed by spouses)
1997	*Taxpayer Relief Act* increases limits for deductible income in IRAs

Source: Goldman Sachs, author

- In the case of stock mutual funds, a series of fiscal incentives encouraged the creation of defined contribution pension plans. In contrast to the Mexican system (which implies the creation of specialized pension funds), these plans permitted investment in already existing mutual funds (figure 11-7).
- In the case of debt mutual funds, regulations limiting interest paid by bank deposits accelerated the movement of funds away from banks to funds managed by money managers, i.e. institutional investment.

11.5.2.2 Recent growth

Investment managers in the US have three main business lines:

- Defined benefit pension plans, charitable funds, and funds for states and municipalities (the so-called "traditional institutional business"),
- Defined contribution pension plans, and
- Mutual funds.

Total business grew explosively, from US$427bn. in 1975 to US$6,045bn. in 1995, or 14 times (figure 11-8).[9] Mutual funds grew more than other business lines, averaging 22% annually over 19 years, compared with defined contribution (15%) and traditional business (11.6%). The growth rate was lower, although still substantial, in the last ten and five years of the period (figure 11-9).

---

[9]See Hurley, Mark, Sharon Meers, Ben Bornstein, Neil Strumingher, "The Coming Evolution of the Investment Management Industry: Opportunities and Strategies", (Goldman Sachs, 1995).

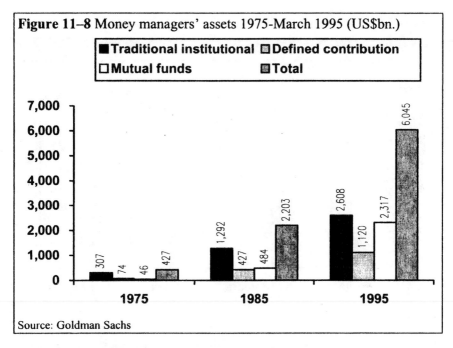

Figure 11–8 Money managers' assets 1975-March 1995 (US$bn.)

Legend: ■ Traditional institutional ▨ Defined contribution □ Mutual funds ▨ Total

Source: Goldman Sachs

11.5.2.3 Traditional institutional business

The traditional institutional business, although still the largest in absolute terms, had the lowest growth in the last five years of the period (figure 11–9). The reason for this is that many companies have changed from a defined benefit pension plan to a defined contribution plan, with a consequent reduction in the proportion of the total represented by defined benefit plans. Between 1989 and 1994 there was an average annual decrease in flows to this segment of -4.4%, with the increase in assets accounted for entirely by price increases in the markets. Meanwhile, the flow to the most popular defined contribution plans (called "401(k)" plans)[10] and to mutual funds, increased at average annual rates of 4.2% and 6.1% respectively between 1989 and 1994.

Defined contribution plans are more attractive to companies than defined benefit plans for an important reason: investment risk. In a defined benefit plan, the company has to assume the risk that funds are well invested. If returns are less than expected, the company may have to allocate funds out of profits to the pension plan – and this can affect its stock price. By contrast, in the case of a defined contribution plan, it is

---

[10]They are called 401(k) plans because this is the number of the income tax exemption clause in the US 1978 Revenue Act.

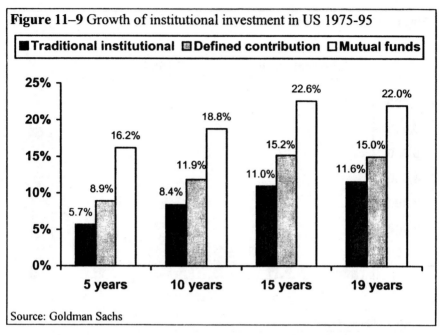

Figure 11–9 Growth of institutional investment in US 1975-95

■ Traditional institutional ▨ Defined contribution ☐ Mutual funds

Source: Goldman Sachs

the employee who is responsible for the investment policy of his pension plan (📖 11.4.1.2).

The risk of this type of plan is that the employee makes a bad choice of investment manager, as there is no specific control over investment managers for pension plans in the US, as there is in Chile or Mexico. In the US, it is assumed that regulation and supervision of all kinds of mutual funds are sufficient to cover this risk.

11.5.2.4 Defined contribution pension plans

Owing to factors mentioned in the previous paragraph, the assets of defined contribution pension plans increased from US$74 bn. to US$1120 bn. between 1975 and 1995, an average annual compound rate of 15% (figure 11–9). Clearly part of this growth was due to price appreciation. However, the average annual compound growth of flows from 401(k) plans to mutual funds was 12%.

401(k) plans are similar to the SAR that was introduced to Mexico in 1992. However, their introduction is not obligatory for companies, as in Mexico, and there is a correlation between the size of companies, and their tendency to set up 401(k) plans. In 1994, 96% of companies with more than 5,000 employees had these plans, but just 11% of companies with less than 50 employees.

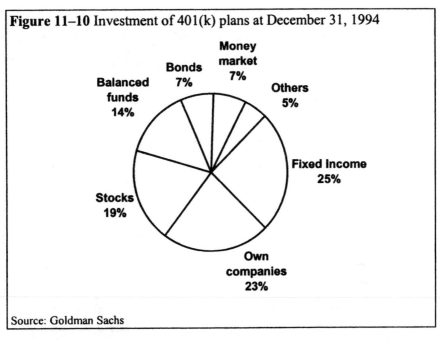

Figure 11–10 Investment of 401(k) plans at December 31, 1994

Source: Goldman Sachs

At the end of 1994, the most important feature of the investment mix of 401(k) plans in the aggregate (figure 11–10) was that the highest proportion was invested in stocks of the employees' own companies. This implied a dual risk for employees in case of bankruptcy of their own company: loss of employment, and loss of a relevant part of their pension fund.

11.5.2.5 Mutual funds

Mutual funds were the most dynamic business line for investment managers, with assets under management increasing from US$46 bn. in 1975 to US$2,317 bn. in 1995. This growth was not only due to investment price appreciation, but also to significant cash inflows, with an average annual compound increase of 9.3% between 1979 and 1994. The business grew both in terms of the number of investment managers, and the number of funds (figure 11–11).

Figure 11–11 Growth of managers and mutual funds 1985-94

	1985	*1990*	*1994*
# Investment managers	252	423	512
# Funds	1528	2917	5357

Source: Goldman Sachs

Figure 11–12 Investments of US mutual funds 1975–95

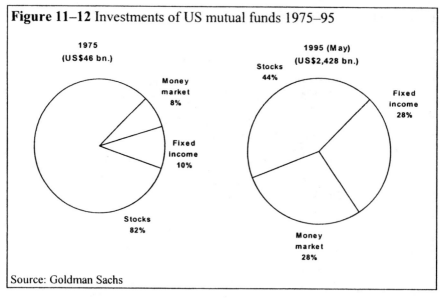

Source: Goldman Sachs

In March 1998, the assets of US mutual funds were valued at US$4.5 trn., compared to US$4.7 trn. in the banking system, and it was estimated that mutual fund assets would overtake banking system assets by mid-1998.[11]

Within the segment, stock funds accounted for the highest proportion (44%) of total assets. However, since 1975, this proportion has been

Figure 11–13 History of institutional investment in Mexico: important dates

1956	FIRME established by Banco Mexicano Somex
1957	FONBNM established by Banco Nacional de México
1964	MULTIFONDO (now FINLAT5) established by Banco Comercial Mexicano
1964	FIMSA (now IXECON) established by Banco del Atlántico
1960s	Tax legislation for establishment of defined benefit pension funds
1980	Establishment of first stock funds by brokerage firms:
	ACCIVAL (Accival), FOBUR (Probursa), FONMEX (Operadora)
1981	Mexico Fund (*Fondo México*) established and listed on NYSE
1983	Establishment of first debt funds by brokerage firms:
	ACCIMEX (Accival), CBILIQ (CBI), DINBUR (Inbursa),
1992	System of Savings for Retirement (SAR)
1997	Retirement Fund Managers (Afores)
	Specialized Mutual Funds for Retirement Funds (Siefores)

Source: author:

---

[11]Hale, David D., "How The Rise Of Pension Funds Will Change The Global Economy In The 21st Century" (Zurich Kemper Investments, March 1998).

decreasing owing to the deregulation of interest rates, which has caused outflows from banks to debt and money market funds (figure 11–12).

There is no separation between mutual funds for pension plans, and ordinary mutual funds. However, it is estimated that a significant percentage of mutual fund assets (up to 50%) is accounted for by defined contribution pension plans.

11.5.3 Institutional investment in Mexico

11.5.3.1 History

Institutional investment in Mexico is relatively recent (figure 11–13). The first stock mutual funds (called *sociedades de inversión comunes*), administered by banks, were established in the 1950s. In the 1960s, legislation was introduced giving tax benefits to defined benefit pension plans set up by companies.

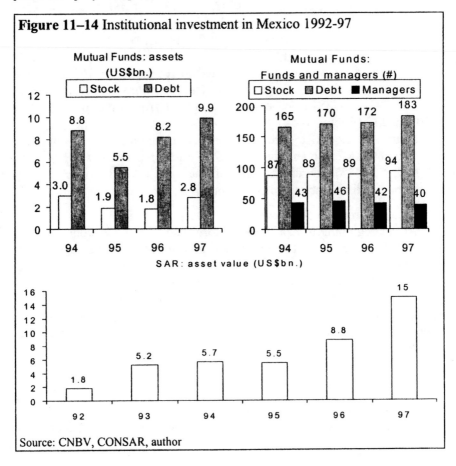

Figure 11–14 Institutional investment in Mexico 1992-97

Source: CNBV, CONSAR, author

Figure 11–15 Institutional investment: Mexico and US

(US$bn.)	Mexico	US
Stock funds	2.8	2,228
Debt funds	9.9	1,992
SAR/Pension system	15.0	6,658
Total	27.7	10,878
Value per capita (US$)	292	41,361
Population (mn.)	95	263
GDP-GNP (est. 97 US$bn.)	400	8,000
GDP-GNP per capita (US$)	**4,211**	**30,418**
Source: CNBV, CONSAR, ICI		

In 1980, brokers were authorized to set up their own stock funds and, in 1983, money market funds (*sociedades de inversión de mercado de dinero*, now called debt funds - *sociedades de inversión de deuda*). The SAR system was established in 1992, and the first *Afores* and *Siefores* (*Sociedades de Inversión Especializadas para Fondos de Retiro* – specialized mutual funds for retirement funds) in 1997.

After their initial surge, investment in mutual funds, and their institutional development, has stagnated in recent years. However, the growth of SAR funds has been rapid, with assets growing from US$1.8 bn. in 1992, to US$15 bn. in 1997, an annual growth rate of more than 50% in US$ (figure 11–14).

Even so, the difference between the penetration of institutional investment in Mexico and the US (US$292 per capita against US$41,361 – figure 11–15) represents one of the greatest disparities of any economic statistic between the two countries.

11.5.3.2 Afores and Siefores

At the beginning of April 1998, Afores had 11.9 mn. accounts, which represented a significant incorporation into the Mexican savings system of people who had never previously saved. To manage these accounts, there were 17 Afores, each with its own Siefore (figure 11–16).[12] The funds were invested in debt instruments, almost all issued by the government (figure 11–17). It was expected that investment of a small percentage of portfolios in the stock market would be permitted in either 1999 or 2000.

---

[12]At the end of March 1998, SAR funds allocated to Afores had not all been transferred to them.

Figure 11–16 Afores and Siefores (April, 1998)

Afore	Siefore	Assets ($mn.)	Share (%)	Affiliated workers (#)	Share (%)	Assets / workers
Atlántico-Promex	APINDEX	269	1.1	182,557	1.5	1,475
Banamex	SIEBNM1	6,834	27.5	1,405,937	11.8	4,860
Bancomer	AFOMER1	7,348	29.6	1,917,214	16.1	3,833
Bancrecer-Dresdner	CREDBI1	597	2.4	557,632	4.7	1,071
Sólida Banorte	SOLBAN1	741	3.0	960,874	8.1	772
Bital	BITALS1	1,169	4.7	1,091,268	9.2	1,071
Capitaliza	GECAP1	82	0.3	38,533	0.3	2,131
Confia	ACPATRI	138	0.6	79,182	0.7	1,745
Garante	GARANT1	1,921	7.7	1,304,748	11.0	1,472
Génesis Metropolitan	GENESI1	117	0.5	131,842	1.1	884
Inbursa	INBURSI	2,502	10.1	302,582	2.5	8,270
Previnter	PREVIN1	340	1.4	287,668	2.4	1,181
Profuturo- GNP	PROFUT1	1,016	4.1	1,479,556	12.4	687
Santander-Mexicano	AHORRO1	945	3.8	1,717,388	14.4	550
Tepeyac	TEPEYAC	105	0.4	98,383	0.8	1,066
XXI	XXIREAL	593	2.4	333,291	2.8	1,780
Zurich	ZURICH-AFO	102	0.4	22,418	0.2	4,553
TOTAL/AVERAGE		24,820		11,911,073		2,084

Source: Infosel, CONSAR, author

11.5.3.3 *The Chilean pension system*

One of the stimuli for the reform of the Mexican pension system was the reform of the Chilean system, which was implemented in 1981. At the end of 1997, total assets managed by Chilean pension fund managers

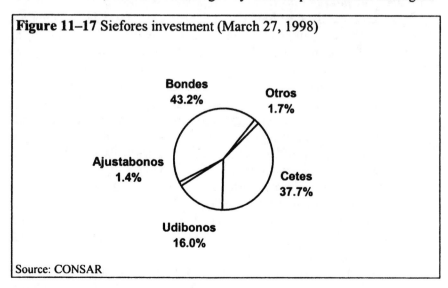

Figure 11–17 Siefores investment (March 27, 1998)

Bondes 43.2%

Otros 1.7%

Ajustabonos 1.4%

Cetes 37.7%

Udibonos 16.0%

Source: CONSAR

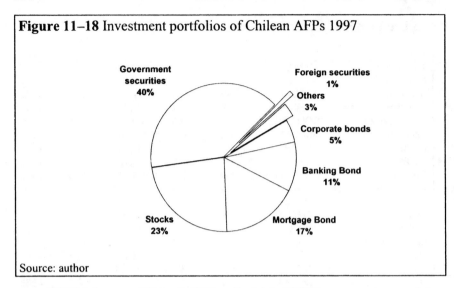

Figure 11–18 Investment portfolios of Chilean AFPs 1997

Government securities 40%

Foreign securities 1%

Others 3%

Corporate bonds 5%

Banking Bond 11%

Mortgage Bond 17%

Stocks 23%

Source: author

were US$31 bn., or 37% of GDP, of which US$7bn. were invested in Chilean stocks, accounting for 10% of Chilean stock market capitalization. There were 13 AFPs (_Administradoras de Fondos de Pensiones_), of which 7 were listed. The investment portfolios of the Chilean AFPs could provide an idea of the future portfolio composition of the Mexican Afores, when the system matures (figure 11–18).

11.5.3.4 The future of institutional investment in Mexico

It is likely that the development of the SAR will provide an important impetus to the development of institutional investment in Mexico, as occurred in the US following the passage of the Employment Retirement Income Security Act (ERISA) in 1974 (figure 11-7), for two reasons:

*   First, the SAR system will form an increasingly important part of the Mexican financial system, through a combination of obligatory monthly contributions, and the rise in value of funds invested. Forecasting the value of SAR funds over time is difficult, because it depends on GDP growth (which determines the level of annual contributions) and the price appreciation of the investments themselves. However, taking the the Chilean system as a basis for comparison, the equivalent figure for Mexico would be US$148bn. This is calculated as 37% of estimated GDP for 1997 of US$400bn., and would be ten times the level of the SAR at the end of 1997 of US$15 bn.
*   Second, as a result of the SAR, voluntary savings mechanisms, such as mutual funds, are also likely to expand. Once the saver

becomes accustomed to see his "obligatory" savings grow through Siefores, he will probably wish to increase his voluntary savings through mutual funds that operate in a similar way to Siefores.

The synergy of these two phenomena, the growth of the SAR and of mutual funds, will be very positive not only for savers, but also for financial intermediaries, the financial system, and, ultimately, the growth of the Mexican economy.

Chapter 12
Management

"In fact, the more we look around, the more we shall come to acknowledge that there is no test of a man's character more generally adopted than the way in which his money is managed."

Edward Bulwer-Lytton (1803-1873)

12.1 INVESTMENT MANAGEMENT

If business management consists of the planning and control of direct investment (2.1), "investment management" (*administración de inversiones*) consists of the planning and control of portfolio investment. In the first part of this last chapter, we analyze the process of planning and control of portfolio investment, and suggest systems and organizational structures for institutional and individual investors in Mexico. In the second part, we summarize the principal lessons of the book in five rules for portfolio investment.

12.2 PLANNING

The planning part of the investment management process consists of the steps implicit in chs. 2 through 10 (figure 12–1).

12.2.1 Formulation of objectives

In ch. 2 (Investment) we identified investment objectives in terms of return, risk, term and liquidity. These objectives depend on the type of investor, individual (11.2) or institutional (11.4).

12.2.2 Formulation of analysis techniques

Also in ch. 2, we provided a conceptual and theoretical framework for investment: present value, portfolio theory, the CAPM model, and the concepts of active and passive investment management. In ch. 3 (Country risk), we provided analysis techniques for investment in "space", comparing Mexico to other countries, and, in ch. 4 (Cycles), in "time", selecting the right moment for each asset class. In ch. 5 through 9, we described the principal financial instruments (Debt, Stocks, and Derivatives) in their global and Mexican context, along with techniques for analyzing them. In ch. 10 (Irrationality),

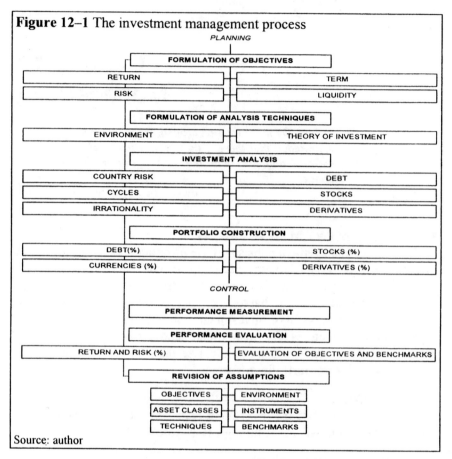

Figure 12-1 The investment management process

Source: author

we explained irrationality in financial markets, and provided techniques for analyzing it.

Analysis techniques change in, and with, time, owing to developments in theory and technology and changes in investment instruments themselves. Therefore, the development of analysis techniques is not a static, one time, process, but dynamic like the other steps described in figure 12-1.

12.2.3 Investment analysis

Investment analysis is the application of analysis techniques to the investment environment and to different asset classes and investments.

Figure 12–2 Model portfolio in US$ (January 1998)			
Asset classes	*Expected return (US$)*	*Weighting*	*Weighted return (US$)*
Cetes	12.0%	15.0%	1.8%
Eurobonds	8.0%	30.0%	2.4%
Bradys	10.0%	20.0%	2.0%
Stocks	20.0%	35.0%	7.0%
Total expected return		**100.0%**	**13.2%**
Source: author			

12.2.4 Portfolio construction

The construction of an investment portfolio is the logical result of the previous steps. It is the adaptation to the investor's objectives of a combination of investments through the application of analysis techniques developed for the purpose.

12.2.4.1 Asset allocation

The first step in portfolio construction is the percentage allocation of total assets among different asset classes. The second is the percentage allocation within each asset class among different specific investments. For control purposes, it is prudent to assign to each investment an expected return, in relation to its estimated risk. We provide a simple model portfolio (with asset classes and expected returns) in figure 12–2.

12.2.4.2 Optimization of return-risk

The problem with asset allocation as described in the previous section is that it takes no explicit account of risk. There are computer programs[1] that use the tools of Modern Portfolio Theory to optimize combinations of investments according to differing assumptions of estimated return, estimated risk (measured by standard deviation), and expected correlations between asset classes, or between different investments within an asset class.

Normally, on the basis of historical data, an estimate is made of return, risk and the correlation between different asset classes. The program finds a series of investment combinations (or portfolios) with varying asset allocations that provide the highest level of return, for each level of risk.

---

[1] For example, Elton, Edwin & Martin Gruber, *Portfolio* (John Wiley & Sons Inc., 1995).

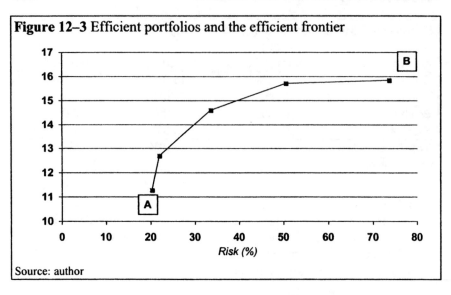

Figure 12–3 Efficient portfolios and the efficient frontier

Source: author

We show the graph of the "efficient frontier" (*frontera eficiente*) which was generated with one of these programs (and originally presented in 📖 2.4.2) as figure 12-3. Usually, the least risky portfolio (A) has 100% of the least risky investment and the riskiest portfolio (B) has 100% of the riskiest investment. The other portfolios are combinations of more and less risky investments, and therefore lie between A and B.

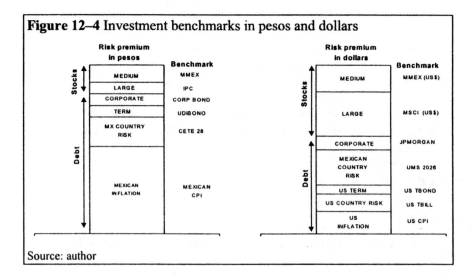

Figure 12–4 Investment benchmarks in pesos and dollars

Source: author

12.2.4.3 Benchmark selection

In investment planning, it is important to select a benchmark (*estándar*) for each asset class to evaluate the subsequent performance of the portfolio (📖 2.6.1). As in any management activity, this helps us to compare actual return (the result) to expected return (budget), and to the benchmark for the asset class. The selection of a benchmark depends on the investor's return and risk objectives. Depending on his reference currency, the investor uses as his benchmark the index for each asset class contained in his portfolio. Using the return ranking concept introduced in 📖 2.3, we present relevant benchmarks for each asset class in figure 12–4.

12.3 CONTROL

12.3.1 Performance measurement

The first step in investment control is regular measurement (daily, weekly, monthly, quarterly, semiannual, or annual) of portfolio performance (*desempeño*).

In its simplest form, the value of funds invested at the beginning and end of the relevant period can be measured. If there were no outflows or inflows of funds, the difference between portfolio value at the beginning and end of the period expressed as a percentage of the beginning value, is the return for the period. This return consists of a combination of capital gains and income through dividends and interest during the control period.

The problem is that very few investment funds are static. Even during relatively short periods, there are almost always outflows and/or inflows. To give an example, the investor contributes $50,000 on January 1, which at June 30 is worth $65,000. On June 30 the investor withdraws

Figure 12–5 Performance measurement with inflows and outflows

Day	Fund value	Outflows (-) and inflows (+)	Number of shares	Share value	Apparent return	Real return
12/31/97	50,000		1,000	50.0		
6/30/98	65,000		1,000	65.0		
6/30/98		(15,000)	(231)	65.0		
6/30/98	50,000		769	65.0	0	30
12/31/98	65,000		769	84.5		
12/31/98		15,000	178	84.5		
12/31/98	80,000		947	84.5	60	69

With the withdrawal in the sixth month and the contribution in the twelfth, the apparent return is 60%, but the real return should be 69%

Source: author

$15,000 from his account. On June 30, the investment is valued at $50,000, and the apparent "return" was zero (figure 12–5).

There is a way to solve the problem. We divide the original amount into 1,000 "shares" each worth $50. On June 30, each share was worth $65. When $15,000 was withdrawn, this implied withdrawal of 231 shares, leaving 769 shares in the fund, each valued at $65. When we measure the return on investment, we measure the capital gain according to the increase in the share price, which in this case was not zero, but 30% (figure 12–5).

12.3.2 Measurement of one asset class

In the case of a portfolio with only one asset class (for example, a stock or debt mutual fund) there appears to be no problem in the application of benchmarks to performance. In the case of a stock portfolio, it can be compared to the IPC of the MSE and in the case of a debt portfolio, it can be compared to the return on Cetes or Udibonos (depending on the term of the portfolio). This is the way in which stock fund performance is presented, not only in Mexico, but also, for example, in the US. In figure 12–6 we show a ranking for the returns of the first ten stock funds compared to the stock index (IPC) for 1997.

The problem with this measurement method is that it takes no account of the level of risk taken by the investment managers. Even though a

Figure 12–6 Stock mutual funds: annual return (in pesos) of top ten Mexican funds 1997

Symbol	Annual return 1997 (%)
BITALV3	66.16
GBMATV6	66.07
ACTICRE	63.68
ACCIAR	63.25
GBMATV5	59.40
IPC	**55.59**
GBMATV4	53.52
BITALV2	53.39
FINLAT8	50.35
ZCAP1	49.72
GFBVIND	48.79
Average of 94 stock mutual funds	33.92

Source: Infosel, author

Figure 12–7 Stock mutual funds: top ten Mexican funds ranked by Sharpe ratio 1997

	Annual return (%)	Annualized standard deviation (%)	Sharpe ratio
GBMATV6	66.07	17.592	2.629
ACTICRE	63.68	18.444	2.377
BITALV3	66.16	20.822	2.225
GBMATV4	53.52	15.388	2.189
GBMATV5	59.40	19.592	2.020
ACCIAR	63.25	21.545	2.015
FINLAT8	50.35	17.704	1.724
BITALV2	53.39	20.117	1.668
ZCAP1	49.72	20.501	1.458
IPC	55.59	27.376	1.306
GFBVIND	48.79	25.806	1.122
Cetes 28 day annualized return	19.83		

Source: Infosel, author

mutual fund only invests in stocks, it may invest in stocks that are riskier than those that make up the market index.

One technique for comparing return with risk is the Sharpe ratio introduced in 📖 2.4.2.3. This ratio compares the level of additional return (above the risk-free rate) provided by a portfolio, with its level of risk measured by its standard deviation, and is defined by the formula:

$$P = \frac{I - C}{\sigma}$$

where:
I = portfolio return
C = risk-free rate
σ = standard deviation of historic returns of portfolio

In figure 12–7 we provide the same returns as in figure 12-6, each with its related standard deviation (calculated as the annualized standard deviation of daily returns) as a measure of risk. The Sharpe ratio is calculated using the annualized yield on 28 day Cetes for 1997 of 19.83% as the risk-free rate.

Owing to the inclusion of risk, the ranking of funds changes from figure 12–6. GBMATV6 rises from second to first place and BITALV3 falls from first to third place. The MSE index (IPC) falls from sixth to penultimate place.

These results can be seen even more clearly in figure 12–8. Funds with the best Sharpe ratio are above the line (which reflects the level of

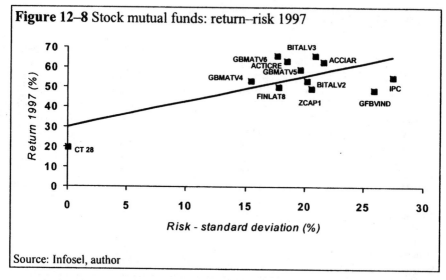

Figure 12–8 Stock mutual funds: return–risk 1997

Source: Infosel, author

correlation between return and risk for the funds analyzed) and funds with the worst Sharpe ratio are below the line.

Nine of the ten funds have a better Sharpe ratio than the IPC which implies that the investment managers are "adding value" (*agregando valor*), or making better investment combinations than the market itself. However, these were the 10 best returns of 94 mutual funds. The average return of these 94 funds during 1997 was 33.92%, or 22% below their benchmark, the IPC, which produced a return of 55.59%.[2]

12.3.3 Performance measurement of a portfolio with several asset classes

Performance measurement using the Sharpe ratio is even more effective, when the portfolio contains several different asset classes. First, within an asset class, it is important to evaluate whether the manager is taking risks commensurate with the returns in the relevant asset class (e.g. stocks, or debt). Second, there can be many changes in the portfolio within and between asset classes during the measurement period. The best form of judging the effect of these changes on the portfolio is with the Sharpe ratio. As we saw in the previous section,

---

[2]The choice of a stock fund should not be based on the performance of just one year, and the potential investor should also analyze the compatibility of the fund's investment objectives with his own, as well as the management costs of the fund (📖 11.4.1.1).

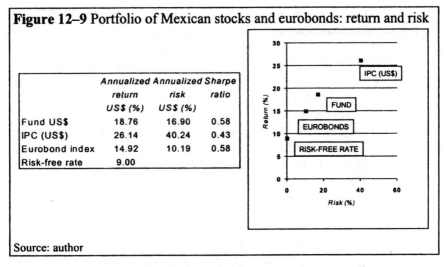

Figure 12–9 Portfolio of Mexican stocks and eurobonds: return and risk

	Annualized return US$ (%)	Annualized risk US$ (%)	Sharpe ratio
Fund US$	18.76	16.90	0.58
IPC (US$)	26.14	40.24	0.43
Eurobond index	14.92	10.19	0.58
Risk-free rate	9.00		

Source: author

these results can also be plotted and located on the risk-return line (or curve) for each asset class used in the portfolio.

We take as another example a real portfolio, whose main components are Mexican stocks and government and corporate US$ eurobonds. The benchmarks used are the IPC of the MSE (in US$), and the government and corporate eurobond indices provided by JP Morgan. The results are provided in figure 12–9. The risk-free rate used was 9% in US$, which was the three year Mexican sovereign bond yield in US$ when the yield objective of the portfolio was established.

While the stock market has had a higher return, it has been achieved with a disproportionate risk, reflected in a worse Sharpe ratio. Eurobonds have had a lower return, with lower risk, but with the same Sharpe ratio as the portfolio. This implies that the investment manager has tailored the return of the fund to the return/risk requirements of the investor who wants a higher return than eurobonds, with proportionately higher risk. In this sense, the investment manager has "added value" for the investor.

12.3.4 Revision of assumptions

After measuring and evaluating portfolio performance, it is important to analyze why results were achieved (or not), based on assumptions about the investment environment, asset classes, or the individual investments selected.

Usually, in any period, events occur, or information is received, that implies a change in these basic assumptions. In terms of 📖 4.7, either the future scenarios themselves might have changed, or their probability of occurrence. These changes should be incorporated in possible changes in portfolio composition.[3]

Similarly, as part of the process of regular revision (we suggest, minimally, monthly meetings) there might be changes in investment objectives, as a result of changes in the investor's circumstances, or the investment environment. These changes should also be taken into account in the revised portfolio.

Less frequently (but not as infrequently as the investment manager might like), there might be changes in techniques for investment analysis, and in the benchmarks used for performance measurement. These changes should also be included in the revision of the investment process included in figure 12–1.

12.4 SYSTEMS AND ORGANIZATION

One way to institutionalize investment management is to introduce organizational (or, where relevant, individual) systems for the ongoing activity of investment planning and control.

12.4.1 Institutional investment

On an institutional basis, we consider the financial investment activity so important that we recommend the formation of an investment committee (*comité de inversión*) as a subcommittee of the board (or its equivalent) of the organization. The function of this committee is the formulation of investment objectives and the monitoring of their fulfillment. The committee should include the Finance VP and other executives with an understanding of financial investments or whose activity provides them with access to the information about external factors on which a good appreciation of investment problems depends. Where relevant, the external investment advisor of the organization can also be a member of this committee.

The Finance VP should, in turn, form an "investment department", which reports directly to him. The function of this department is to carry out operationally the objectives of the investment committee. The

[3]George Soros, one of the most successful investors of the XX century (📖 2.6.2.3), included in his book *The Alchemy of Finance* (Touchstone, 1987) a diary of his investments between August 1985 and November 1986, which shows dramatically and dynamically the process of daily planning and control of a portfolio (The Real-Time Experiment, pp. 139-196). It is interesting that performance over the period was outstanding, which supports the conclusion that a process of explicit control contributes to success in investment management.

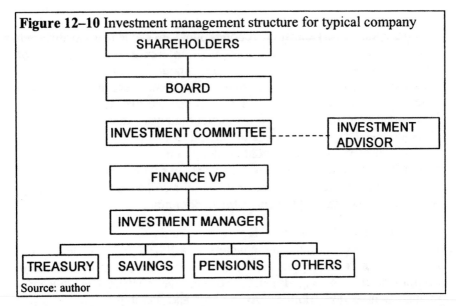

Figure 12–10 Investment management structure for typical company

Source: author

number of people involved in this activity depends on the value and variety of investments in the portfolio (figure 12–10).

A relatively complex form of this structure must exist in the organizations of institutional investors (e.g. Afores or insurance companies). In the case of industrial, commercial or service companies, the "investment department" should not only manage the company's treasury investment, but also, where relevant, all the investment funds of the organization (pension funds, savings funds, etc.). Even in the case of defined contribution pension plans (e.g. Afores) where the weight of the decision on investment manager selection falls on the company's employees, and not its executives, company management should also be aware of its employees' decisions in terms of investment manager selection.

With this structure, we recommend that the investment committee meet at least monthly to review the fulfillment of investment objectives. This review covers the control activities described above: monthly measurement and evaluation of investment returns against risks and benchmarks, and revision of assumptions about investment objectives, the investment environment and factors that could affect each asset class. As these assumptions change, changes should be considered in asset classes, individual investments, and their weighting in the portfolio.

12.4.2 Individual investment

Conceptually, organization for individual investment is no different from institutional investment. The only difference is the number of people involved, and, possibly, the amount of resources under management. In this case, the "investment committee" consists of the investor and his investment advisor. Between the two of them, they fix investment objectives, perform investment analysis, develop investment strategy, and design the investment portfolio.

They also execute investment strategy, and control it. Usually, it is the investment advisor who executes the investment plan once it has been formulated. Investment control should also be performed monthly, with regular meetings of the "investment committee".[4]

12.5 INVESTMENT ADVICE

From previous sections and chapters, it will have become clear to the reader that investment management implies a unique combination of disciplines: economics, finance, accounting, mathematics, business management, history, politics, psychology, and sociology.

The portfolio investor can act as his own advisor, with concepts, techniques and information like that provided in this book, and with magazines, newspapers and specialized publications. He can also seek help from investment advisors who specialize in this activity.

There is no precise definition of "investment advisor" (*asesor de inversión*), in the same way that there is no precise definition of "management consultant" (*asesor, o consultor, de administración*). There are management consultants who specialize in strategy, operations (e.g. production, finance, marketing, human resources) or technology (e.g. systems and information).

In the US, where the role of investment advisor is most developed, the concept is frequently used to describe what we have called "investment manager", i.e. the person or organization who manages the investment process described in ⊞ 12.2 and 12.3. However, portfolio investment has become so highly developed that the term "investment advisor" has been extended to include almost any of the activities described in figure 12-1. Consequently, there are investment advisors who specialize in the "big picture" (*entorno*) (country risk, cycles or

---

[4]The importance of this activity should not be minimized, with the excuse that the "amount invested does not justify it". The only way to make a modest initial investment become interesting is through conscientious and disciplined investment management.

economics in general), in specific asset classes (stocks, debt, derivatives, currencies), in portfolio construction, or in any combination of these. The industry has become so sophisticated in the US that there are now "pension fund consultants" (*asesores de fondos de pensiones*), whose job is to select investment advisors (or managers) for pension funds.

12.6 FIVE INVESTMENT RULES

In previous sections, we have shown that investment analysis and management is a logical process, which consists in the formulation of premises about investment objectives, the investment environment and investments. The conclusion of these premises is an investment portfolio, which can be modified according to changing circumstances through the control process, which is implicit in the investment management activity.

However, it is obvious that, in real life, however many books, studies and reports are produced, the steps described in previous sections are not always followed. There is the example of a group of New York investors in 1929:

"A group of economists and market analysts used to meet regularly for lunch at a bar on Wall Street. In July 1929, we arrived at the conclusion that the market was extremely overvalued. Therefore, we all agreed to take advantage of this expert prediction to sell all the stocks and bonds in our portfolios. We were all going to sell our securities, both speculative and conservative, and turn them into cash. Those who wished to speculate, and could afford to take some risk, could short US Steel above US$200 and General Electric at US$350, and there were other opportunities among the Blue Chips. There had never been so much unanimity, or so much enthusiasm for immediate action."

"Did we do it? Did we become rich? No! When the crash eventually happened at the end of October 1929, followed by the slight recovery in 1930, I discovered that no one in the group had sold his securities as promised. Some had sold half, or less, but many who sold in August or September decided that our forecasts were wrong and that the other experts were right. Therefore they bought back again at high prices, and...their technical knowledge was useless."[5]

Although investment seems to be a very logical and disciplined process, investors make mistakes like the one described above, because they forget certain basic rules, all of which are contained in chapters of this book. It might therefore be useful, after the presentation of theory, techniques and practical examples in the book, to end it by summarizing

---

[5]Cited in Kiril Sokoloff, *The Thinking Investor's Guide to the Stock Market* (McGraw-Hill Inc., 1978), p. 68.

its principal lessons in five investment rules, all of which have specific relevance to investing in Mexico.

12.6.1   Term

Over the long term, in general, the riskiest investments (e.g. stocks) have offered higher returns than less risky investments (e.g. debt) and the risky countries (e.g. emerging markets) have offered higher returns than less risky countries (e.g. developed markets).

However, there are moments when it is easy to forget these realities, above all in the periods of high volatility which inevitably go with high returns. In these moments, it is important to remember the long term.

12.6.2   Diversification

One way of reducing investment volatility is diversification: of asset classes (stocks – debt), term (short – long) and currency (peso – dollar).

Modern tools of risk analysis help us to identify which investments can reduce the volatility inherent in financial investment. Similarly, modern investment tools such as derivatives can help us to reduce our risk at a lower cost than traditional instruments.

12.6.3   Discipline

Any human activity, to achieve sustained success, needs the discipline of planning and control. Investment is no exception.

Planning implies a very clear definition of return, risk, term and liquidity objectives in relation to investor needs. Control implies the regular and precise measurement of the degree to which these objectives are being achieved, the understanding of the reasons why they are being achieved, or not, and the execution of the necessary corrective measures.

12.6.4   Knowledge and understanding

There is possibly no subject that generates more information, through electronic media, radio, television, newspapers, and books, than portfolio investment. The result is often an oversupply of information, and an undersupply of understanding.

The investor should be conscious of what he does not know, or understand. If he does not know, he should find out where to look for information. If he does not understand, he should not be afraid of seeking help and advice.

12.6.5   Contrary opinion

Owing to its unique combination of volatility, immediacy, and information overload, portfolio investment generates emotion, both positive and negative. However, it would be a mistake for the investor to try to suppress his emotions, because they offer important information about his own and the market's psychology.

Almost always, when the investor feels that he wants to buy, he should sell, and viceversa. More importantly, when he has the sensation that he should "do something", i.e. "invest", it is quite probable that he should do absolutely nothing.

It might seem inappropriate to end an investment book praising the virtues of *not* investing. But perhaps, like the silence of the good actor or the good musician, the *summum artis* of the good investor is precisely knowing when *not* to invest.

Appendices

Notes to appendices

Main variables used in appendices A-E:

FV_t future value at period t

PV present value

$NV_{security}$ face value of security (*título*)

$P_{security.t}$ price at period t

$DC_{security}$ discount

F_t flow t

U_t profit t

D_t dividend t

$R_{security}$ annualized rate of return for specified term

$RD_{security}$ discount rate for a specified term

$RE_{security}$ equivalent rate of return for equivalent term

$RC_{security}$ annualized rate of return of coupon for specified term

$RR_{security}$ annualized real rate of return for specified term

$E(R_{security})$ expected value of returns

$\sigma_{security}$ variance of returns

$\sigma_{security}$ standard deviation of returns

t period

n number of periods

TM term in days

TME equivalent term in days

$q_{security}$ proportion invested in security

β_i beta, increase in risk contributed by security i to market portfolio

$\Delta\%$ percentage change in variable

Δ absolute change in variable

e 2.718282 (approximate value of e) is inverse function of ln

ln natural logarithm

$N(x)$ cumulative probability function for standardized normal variable

Appendix A
Investment

A.1 GEOMETRIC AND ARITHMETIC MEAN

There are two ways to calculate the historical return on an investment. The "geometric mean return" (*rendimiento promedio geométrico*) is a compound rate of return, and implies reinvestment of returns during the period of measurement. It is defined by the formula:

$$R_g = 100 * \left[\left(\frac{TV}{IV} \right)^{\left(\frac{1}{n} \right)} - 1 \right]$$

where:

R_g: geometric mean return
IV: initial value of investment
TV: terminal value of investment after n periods

The "arithmetic mean return" (*rendimiento promedio aritmético*) is the average return over a series of periods, and is defined by the formula:

$$R_a = \frac{\sum_{t=1}^{n} R_t}{n}$$

where:

R_a: arithmetic mean return
R_t: return for period

To illustrate the difference between the two concepts, we take an extreme case. The initial investment (IV) is $100. After one year, it has grown to $200 ($R_1 = 100\%$): after two years, it has decreased to a terminal value (TV) of $100 ($R_2 = -50\%$).

The geometric mean return was:

$$R_g = 100 * \left[\left(\frac{100}{100} \right)^{\left(\frac{1}{2} \right)} - 1 \right] = 0$$

The arithmetic mean return was:

$$R_a = \frac{(100-50)}{2} = 25\%$$

To avoid these distortions, the geometric mean return is used for the measurement and evaluation of the average growth of investments over time. All the calculations of historical return in this book are made in this way, except where otherwise indicated.

A.2 PRESENT VALUE

If the rate of return in the market is 20% annual, this implies that $100 today will be worth $120 in one year. In two years, it will be worth $144.

In more formal terms, the future value (FV_t) at the end of the year will be:

$$FV_1 = \$100\left(1+\frac{20}{100}\right) = 120 \qquad \text{(A- 1)}$$

If this amount is invested at the end of the first year, at the end of the second year, the investment will be worth:

$$FV_2 = \$120\left(1+\frac{20}{100}\right) = 144 \qquad \text{(A- 2)}$$

The problem can also be expressed in reverse. Suppose that one wants $120 in a year's time. A rate of return of 20% implies that $120 has a present value (PV) of $100, or:

$$PV = \frac{\$120}{\left(1+\frac{20}{100}\right)} = 100 \qquad \text{(A- 3)}$$

Similarly, if one wants $144 in two years at a rate of return of 20%, this implies that $144 also have a present value of $100, or:

$$PV = \frac{\$144}{\left(1+\frac{20}{100}\right)^2} = 100 \qquad \text{(A- 4)}$$

Generalizing, the present value formula can be expressed as:

$$PV = \frac{FV_t}{(1+R)^t} \qquad \text{(A- 5)}$$

where R is the return and t is the number of future periods.

A.3 MODERN PORTFOLIO THEORY (MPT)

A.3.1 Measurement of return and risk of a single investment

The expected return of a single investment (X) is expressed as $E(R_x)$, and as a percentage of the amount invested (e.g. 10%).

The risk of the investment is expressed as the variance (σ^2_x) or the standard deviation (σ_x) of expected returns.

Variance is defined as the average of the squared differences between the returns $R_{x,t}$ of an investment, and its expected return $E(R_x)$, or:

$$\sigma^2_x = \frac{1}{n}\sum_{t=1}^{n}\left(R_{x,t} - E(R_x)\right)^2 \tag{A-6}$$

The standard deviation is defined as the square root of the variance, or:

$$\sigma_x = \sqrt{\sigma^2_x} \tag{A-7}$$

A.3.2 Measurement of return of a portfolio

The return of an investment portfolio is measured as the weighted average of the expected returns of its components. Let us assume a portfolio which consists in equal parts of a Cete, and a mutual fund which invests in the MSE index.

Let us assume a return on the Cete (Ct) of 10%, and on the index fund (I) of 20%. The estimated portfolio return (R_c) $(q$ is the percentage allocated to $Ct)$ is:

$$E(R_C) = qR_{Ct} + (1-q)E(R_I) \tag{A-8}$$

or:

$$E(R_C) = q(10) + (1-q)(20) \tag{A-9}$$

With $q = 50\%$, the portfolio return is:

$$E(R_C) = 5 + 10 = 15 \tag{A-10}$$

Another way to understand the return of this combination is that it consists in the risk-free rate (10%) plus the risk premium (the difference between the return on the risky investment and the risk-free rate), multiplied by the proportion of the portfolio invested in the risky investment, or:

$$E(R_C) = 10 + 0.5(20 - 10) = 15 \tag{A-11}$$

or, generalizing:

$$E(R_C) = R_{Ct} + (1-q)\left[E(R_I) - R_{Ct}\right] \tag{A-12}$$

A.3.3 Measurement of risk for a portfolio of one risky and one risk-free investment

While calculating combinations of return is simple, calculating combinations of risk is more complicated. In the case of a portfolio with one risk-free and one risky investment, the risk of the portfolio is the standard deviation of the risky investment *(I)* multiplied by its percentage in the portfolio. Taking the example of the portfolio in the previous section, assuming a standard deviation for the risky investment of 40%, the standard deviation for the combined portfolio *(C)* would be:

$$\sigma_C = 0.5(40) = 20 \qquad\qquad\qquad\text{(A- 13)}$$

or, generalizing:

$$\sigma_C = (1 - q)\sigma_I \qquad\qquad\qquad\text{(A- 14)}$$

These combinations can be plotted with the expected return on the vertical axis and the risk on the horizontal axis (figure A–1). In the figure, the Cete return has no risk, and is located on the vertical axis. The expected return of the index fund (20%) is plotted against its corresponding risk level of 40%. A balanced portfolio (50/50) would produce a return of 15% with a standard deviation of 20%.

The line is expressed by the linear equation:

$$E(R_C) = R_{Ct} + 0.25\sigma_C \qquad\qquad\qquad\text{(A- 15)}$$

Where $E(R_C)$ is the expected return of the portfolio, R_{Ct}, is the risk-free rate (Cete) and σ_c is the risk of the portfolio.

The line *Ct-I* is called the "capital allocation line" *(línea de asignación de*

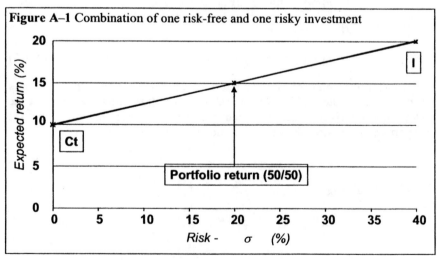

Figure A–1 Combination of one risk-free and one risky investment

recursos), and shows all the combinations of return and risk (of the universe of investments comprised by *Ct* and *I*) open to the investor. The slope *(B)* of the line *Ct-I* represents the increase in return for the increase in risk of each portfolio:

$$B = \frac{E(R_I) - R_{Ct}}{\sigma_I} \qquad \text{(A- 16)}$$

$$= \frac{10}{40} = 0.25 \qquad \text{(A- 17)}$$

This slope is called the slope of return/variability, and its ratio (the increase in return per increase in risk) in this case is *0.25*.

A.3.4 Measurement of risk for a portfolio of two risky investments

The variance of a portfolio *(C)* with two risky investments *(X* and *Y)* is defined by the following equation:

$$\sigma_C^2 = q_X^2 \sigma_X^2 + (1 - q_X)^2 \sigma_Y^2 + 2q_X(1 - q_X)Cov(R_X, R_Y) \qquad \text{(A- 18)}$$

The standard deviation is the square root of the variance.

$$\sigma_C = \sqrt{\sigma_C^2} \qquad \text{(A- 19)}$$

The covariance between the returns on the two investments is the product derived from multiplying the difference between the observed return and the expected return of each investment, or:

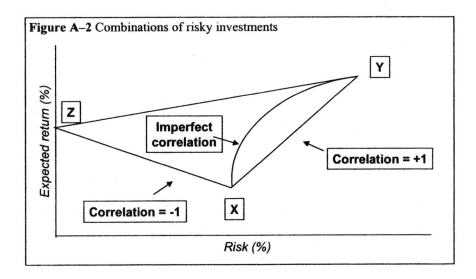

Figure A–2 Combinations of risky investments

$$Cov(R_X, R_Y) = \frac{1}{n}\sum_{t=1}^{n}(R_{X,t} - E(R_X))(R_{Y,t} - E(R_Y)) \qquad \text{(A-20)}$$

The most important implication of the combination of risky investments is that one can diminish the risk of a portfolio by adding risky investments, provided that there is not a perfect positive correlation between the risk of the two investments (figure A–2).

When X and Y are perfectly positively correlated, risk increases in linear fashion (line XY). When they are perfectly negatively correlated they can be combined so that return increases, but risk diminishes (line XZY). When they are imperfectly correlated, return can be increased with a lower proportionate increase in risk (arc XY).

A.4 CAPITAL ASSET PRICING MODEL (CAPM)

The line between the risk-free rate (TC) and the expected market return (M) is called the "securities market line" (*línea del mercado de valores*) (figure A–3). This line is expressed by the equation:

$$E(R_i) = R_{TC} + (E(R_M) - R_{TC})\beta_i \qquad \text{(A-21)}$$

$E(R_i)$ is the expected return on investment i, R_{TC} is the risk-free rate, $E(R_M)$ is the expected market return and β_i is the level of risk of investment i compared to the market.

β_i is calculated with the formula:

$$\beta_i = \frac{cov(R_i, R_M)}{var(R_M)} \qquad \text{(A-22)}$$

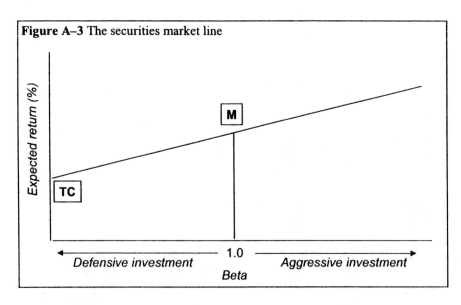

Figure A–3 The securities market line

The market has a risk of 1.0. Therefore, a beta higher than 1.0 reflects an aggressive investment, and a beta lower than 1.0 reflects a defensive investment.

A.5 ARBITRAGE PRICING THEORY

The difference between Arbitrage Pricing Theory (APT) and CAPM is that, whereas CAPM explains the return of an investment through one factor (the market), APT uses several.

According to APT, the expected return of an investment $E(R_i)$ can be explained by a combination of factors. To the risk-free rate (R_{TC}) is added a series of risk premia, which reflect the sensitivity of the investment to each of the factors that can affect return (e.g. industrial production, inflation). In general terms:

$$E(R_i) = R_{TC} + \gamma_1\lambda_1 + \gamma_2\lambda_2 + \ldots\ldots + \gamma_n\lambda_n \tag{A-23}$$

Where:

$\gamma_{1\ldots n}$ = sensitivity of the investment to factors 1 through n
$\lambda_{1\ldots n}$ = risk premium for factors 1 through n.

Appendix B
Debt II

B.1 BASIC MEXICAN MONEY MARKET CALCULATIONS

B.1.1 Discount rate and price

The discount rate (*tasa de descuento*) is another way of expressing the price of a money market security. The price is calculated from the discount rate as follows:

$$P_{security} = NV_{security} - \left(NV_{security} * \frac{RD_{security}}{100} * \frac{TM}{360} \right) \qquad (\text{B- }1)$$

where:

$P_{security}$ = purchase price
$NV_{security}$ = face value
$RD_{security}$ = discount rate
TM = days to maturity (term)

With the practical example of a Cete (*Ct*) with 28 day maturity and an annual discount rate of 20%, the calculation is made as follows:

$$P_{Ct} = 10 - \left(10 * \frac{20}{100} * \frac{28}{360} \right) = 9.8444 \qquad (\text{B- }2)$$

With the same formula, the discount rate can be derived from the price.

B.1.2 Rate of return

The capital gain on the investment is equivalent to the difference between the buy price and face value, i.e. the discount ($DC_{security}$).

$$DC_{security} = NV_{security} - P_{security} \qquad (\text{B- }3)$$

This capital gain is converted into an annual rate of return ($R_{security}$) as follows:

$$R_{security} = \frac{DC_{security}}{P_{security}} * \frac{360}{TM} * 100 \qquad (\text{B- }4)$$

Applied to the previous example:

$$R_{Ct} = \frac{0.1555}{9.844} * \frac{360}{28} * 100 = 20.32\% \qquad (\text{B- }5)$$

B.1.3 Rate of return with sale prior to maturity

Money market securities are frequently sold before maturity. When this occurs, the same calculation is made for the sell price as the buy price. To calculate the return received during the holding period of the Cete, face value is substituted in the return calculation formula by the sell price.

Taking the same Cete as an example, after holding it for 14 days (with a maturity now of 14 days, or 28 less 14), it is sold at the same discount rate:

$$P_{Ct} = 10 - \left(10 * \frac{20}{100} * \frac{14}{360}\right) = 9.922 \tag{B- 6}$$

The capital gain is the difference between buy price and sell price, or:

$$DC_{Ct} = 9.922 - 9.844 = 0.0778 \tag{B- 7}$$

The annual rate of return is the capital gain, divided by the buy price, and annualized, or:

$$R_{Ct} = \frac{0.0778}{9.844} * \frac{360}{14} * 100 = 20.32\% \tag{B- 8}$$

As the buy discount rate was the same as the sell discount rate, it is not surprising that the return was the same as in the previous example.

However, if the sell discount rate is lower than the buy discount rate (i.e. if the general level of interest rates has fallen), the investor receives a higher return than originally contracted.

With a lower discount rate (e.g. 18%), the sell price is:

$$P_{Ct} = 10 - \left(10 * \frac{18}{100} * \frac{14}{360}\right) = 9.93 \tag{B- 9}$$

This produces a capital gain of:

$$DC_{Ct} = 9.93 - 9.844 = 0.086 \tag{B- 10}$$

Which represents a return of:

$$R_{Ct} = \frac{0.086}{9.844} * \frac{360}{14} * 100 = 22.46\% \tag{B- 11}$$

With a higher discount rate (e.g. 22%), the sell price is:

$$P_{Ct} = 10 - \left(10 * \frac{22}{100} * \frac{14}{360}\right) = 9.9144 \tag{B- 12}$$

This produces a capital gain of:

$$DC_{Ct} = 9.9144 - 9.844 = 0.0704 \tag{B- 13}$$

Which represents a return of:

$$R_{Ct} = \frac{0.0704}{9.844} * \frac{360}{14} * 100 = 18.39\% \qquad \text{(B-14)}$$

These calculations show yet again the importance in debt investment of an accurate forecast of interest rate trends.

B.2 REPOS AND EQUIVALENT RATES

The money market is a market for debt securities where all the features of portfolio investment (return, risk, term and liquidity) are present, although short term. A series of techniques has been developed to optimize these features for market participants, taking into account maturities available in the market.

One of these techniques is the repo (*reporto*). A repo is a money market operation, where a financial institution agrees with the investor to sell him a specified amount of a money market security and at the same time agrees to buy it back after an agreed period at an agreed price, guaranteeing the investor a return over the period.

For the investor the advantage of repo operations is that they extend the range of available maturities, if there are no securities available in the market with the required return to maturity. For the financial institution, repo operations imply the possibility of profit if the rate of return agreed with the investor is lower than the rate at which it purchased the security.

To calculate what rate to offer the client, the financial institution calculates the equivalence between the annualized rate of return at which it bought the security, and the rate at which it offers the security to the client for a shorter period. The equivalence formula is:

$$RE_{security} = \left(\left(1 + \left(R_{security} * \frac{TM}{360} \right) \right)^{\left(\frac{TME}{TM} \right)} - 1 \right) * \frac{360}{TME} \qquad \text{(B-15)}$$

where:

TM = original term to maturity (agreed by the financial institution)
TME = equivalent term to be calculated (term agreed by client)
$R_{security}$ = original annualized return
$RE_{security}$ = annualized return at equivalent term

Based on this formula, which is a simple extension of the concepts of financial mathematics explained in 📖 2.4.1 and 📖 B.1, one can calculate equivalent rates for any rate and any term.

In figure B–1, equivalent rates for 20% are shown for different maturities (7 to 364 days) and different periods of equivalence. For example, to calculate the equivalent rate of 20% agreed at 28 days by the financial institution to 7 days agreed by the client, the formula is applied as follows:

Figure B–1 Equivalent rates for different maturities (20% return)

Equivalent days	Term						
	7	14	21	28	91	182	364
7	20.00	19.96	19.92	19.88	19.55	19.09	18.25
14	20.04	20.00	19.96	19.92	19.59	19.12	18.28
21	20.08	20.04	20.00	19.96	19.62	19.16	18.31
28	20.12	20.08	20.04	20.00	19.66	19.19	18.34
91	20.47	20.43	20.39	20.35	20.00	19.52	18.64
182	21.00	20.96	20.92	20.88	20.51	20.00	19.08
364	22.12	22.07	22.02	21.98	21.57	21.01	20.00

Source: author

$$RE = \left[\left(1 + \left(.20 * \frac{28}{360} \right) \right)^{\left(\frac{7}{28} \right)} - 1 \right] * \frac{360}{7} = 19.88\% \qquad \text{(B- 16)}$$

If the financial institution, having agreed a security at a rate of 20% for 28 days sells to the client at a rate higher than 19.88% for 7 days, it makes a loss, and if it sells at a lower rate, it makes a profit.

B.3 BASIC UDIBONO CALCULATIONS

There are two ways to value Udibonos (U):

a) Real rate of return to maturity

The real rate of return to maturity of a bond is the return which the investor would obtain if he decided to keep the bond to maturity. To calculate the price of the bond, once the real rate to maturity is determined, all the flows to maturity (coupons and principal) are discounted at this rate. The formula is:

$$P_U = NV_U * \left(\frac{\left(C + C \left(\frac{1}{r} - \frac{1}{r(1+r)^{n-1}} \right) + \frac{1}{(1+r)^{n-1}} \right)}{(1+r)^{\frac{DVC}{TM_{coupon}}}} - C * \frac{DTC}{TM_{coupon}} \right) \qquad \text{(B- 17)}$$

where:

$$C = RC_U * \frac{TM_{coupon}}{360}$$

$$r = RR_U * \frac{TM_{coupon}}{360}$$

P_U = price of udibono in UDIs
NV_U = face value of udibono
RR_U: real annualized rate of return to maturity
RC_U: real annualized rate of return of coupon

DVC = days to maturity of current coupon

TM_{coupon} = term of coupon

DTC = days lapsed of current coupon

n = number of coupons remaining, including current coupon

b) Methodology with different real rates for each flow

There is also a more general methodology, which takes account of the possibility of different real rates of return for each flow. For this methodology, the formula is:

$$P_U = NV_U * \left(\sum_{i=1}^{n} \frac{C}{\left(1 + r_i\right)^{\frac{DVC_i}{TM_{RR,i}}}} + \frac{1}{\left(1 + r_n\right)^{\frac{DVC_n}{TM_{RR,n}}}} - C * \frac{DTC_1}{TM_{coupon}} \right) \quad \text{(B-18)}$$

where:

$$C = RC_U * \frac{TM_{coupon}}{360}$$

$$r_i = RR_i * \frac{TM_{RR,i}}{360}$$

RR_i: real annualized rate of return of security for the term i, with a different rate for each flow

DTC_1 = days lapsed of current coupon

DVC_i = days to maturity of ith coupon

DVC_n = days to maturity of security

$TM_{RR,i}$ = term of ith real rate

TM_{coupon} = term of coupons

The problem with the second technique is the need to project RR for each flow. Therefore, in practice, the first technique is used more for Udibono valuation.

B.4 DURATION

To explain the concept of duration in more detail, we take the example of three securities, each with a three year maturity (figure B–2). Security 1 is a zero coupon security, with payment of principal at maturity: security 2 is a security with coupons, with amortization in equal installments during the life of the security; and security 3 is a security with coupons, with amortization in one (bullet) payment at maturity. All three securities have a nominal rate of 10%. When the general level of interest rates is 10%, the three securities have the same price of 1,000. However, when there is a change in the general level of interest rates from 10 to 11%, each security reacts differently.

The security which falls the most is security 1 (-2.7%), because interest and amortization accumulate in the third year, i.e. cash flow is deferred for the maximum term. The security which falls least is security 2 (-1.7%) because it has the most rapid amortization. The fall in security 3 lies between securities 1 and 2, because its amortization is quicker than 1, but slower than 3.

Figure B–2 Sensitivity of debt securities to changes in interest rates

Year	Flows 1	2	3	Price	Amortization	Coupon	Return
Case 1: nominal rate (10%) equal to rate of return (10%)							
Security 1	0	0	1331	1000	final	0%	10%
Security 2	402	402	402	1000	equal	10%	10%
Security 3	100	100	1100	1000	final	10%	10%
Case 2: nominal rate (10%) less than rate of return (11%)							
Security 1	0	0	1331	973	final	0%	11%
Security 2	402	402	402	982	equal	10%	11%
Security 3	100	100	1100	976	final	10%	11%

Price change

	Case 1	Case 2	Change %
Security 1	1000	973	-2.7%
Security 2	1000	983	-1.7%
Security 3	1000	976	-2.4%

Source: author

Different levels of sensitivity to changes in the general level of interest rates can be captured by the measure of duration for different securities. Duration is expressed by the following formula, which represents the weighting by the number of periods *(t)* of *n* discounted flows of the security during periods *1* to *t*, where $D_{security}$ is the duration and flows $F_{security}$ include both coupons and amortizations of the security

$$D_{security} = \frac{1}{P_{secuity}}\left(1^* \frac{F_1}{(1+R)^t} + 2^* \frac{F_2}{(1+R)^2} + .. + (t-1)^* \frac{F_{n-1}}{(1+R)^{t-1}} + t^* \frac{F_n}{(1+R)^t}\right) \quad \text{(B-19)}$$

In figure B–3, duration is calculated for each one of the securities presented

Figure B–3 Calculation of duration

		Flows (Fn) 1	2	3	Total	Price (P)	Duration (years)
Security 1	Flows (Fn)	0	0	1331			
	Discount (1/(1+R)^t)	1.1	1.21	1.331			
	t*Fn*1/(1+R)^t	0	0	3000	3000	1000	3.0
Security 2	Flows (Fn)	402	402	402			
	Discount (1/(1+R)^t)	1.1	1.21	1.331			
	t*Fn*1/(1+R)^t	366	665	906	1937	1000	1.9
Security 3	Flows (Fn)	100	100	1100			
	Discount (1/(1+R)^t)	1.1	1.21	1.331			
	t*Fn*1/(1+R)^t	91	165	2479	2736	1000	2.7

Source: author

in figure B–2, assuming an interest rate of 10%. Security 2 has the shortest duration and security 1 the longest: calculation of duration permits us to forecast the change in price when rates change from 10% to 11% (figure B–2).

From the previous formulae, we can derive a formula to forecast the price of debt securities as a result of changes in the level of interest rates:

$$\Delta\% P_{security} = \frac{-D_{security} * \Delta R}{1+R} \qquad \text{(B- 20)}$$

The formula can be illustrated with security 3 of figure B–2. Its duration was calculated at 2.7 years. Assuming a rise in rates from 10% to 11%, we can calculate the expected change in price:

$$\Delta\% P_{security} = \frac{-2.7 * (.11 - .10)}{1.10} = -2.5\% \qquad \text{(B- 21)}$$

This estimate of price change is very close to the number calculated in figure B–2: -2.4%.[1]

B.5 BRADY BONDS: CALCULATION OF STRIPPED YIELD AND STRIPPED SPREAD

The yield on Brady bonds (Bdy) consists of a mix of US risk (owing to the guarantee of principal and three coupons with zero coupon Treasury bonds) and Mexican risk (owing to the remaining coupons). The classic bond valuation formula

$$P = \frac{F_1}{(1+R)^1} + \frac{F_2}{(1+R)^2} + ... + \frac{F_n}{(1+R)^t} \qquad \text{(B- 22)}$$

can be reexpressed to distinguish explicitly coupons (C) and face value (NV), i.e, the principal amount of the security

$$P_{Bdy} = \sum_{i=1}^{n} \frac{C_i}{(1+R)^i} + \frac{NV_{Bdy}}{(1+R)^n} \qquad \text{(B- 23)}$$

The principal amount is totally guaranteed by US Treasury bonds (Tb) and, therefore, the rate of return used to discount it is the rate of return of US Tbonds (R_{Tb}) of the equivalent term. If we subtract the collateral (discounted at R_{Tb}) from the price of the bond, the formula can be reexpressed:

$$P_{Bdy} - \frac{NV_{Bdy}}{(1+R_{Tb})^n} = \sum_{i=1}^{n} \frac{C_i}{(1+R)^i} \qquad \text{(B- 24)}$$

---

[1]The formula works better for smaller changes in interest rates, and becomes less precise as changes increase.

But the R of the coupons consists in one part which is guaranteed by US Tbonds (i.e. R_{Tb}) and another part which is the "stripped yield" (*rendimiento sin colateral*) (R_{sc}), which in turn consists of R_{Tb} and the relationship between R_{sc} and R_{Tb}, or S (the "stripped spread" – *diferencial sin colateral*):

$$(1 + R_{SC}) = (1 + S) * (1 + R_{Tb}) \tag{B-25}$$

Taking into account this mix of rates, the flow of guaranteed and non-guaranteed coupons is reexpressed:

$$\sum_{i=1}^{n} \frac{C_i}{(1+R)^i} = \sum_{i=1}^{n} \frac{S * C_i}{(1+S)^i * (1+R_{Tb})^i} + \sum_{i=1}^{n} \frac{C_i}{(1+S)^i * (1+R_{Tb})^i} \tag{B-26}$$

Subtracting also the collateral of the guaranteed coupons, the complete formula for the calculation of stripped yield is:

$$P_{Bdy} - \frac{NV_{Bdy}}{(1+R_{Tb})^n} - \sum_{i=1}^{n} \frac{S * C_i}{(1+S)^i * (1+R_{Tb})^i} = \sum_{i=1}^{n} \frac{C_i}{(1+S)^i * (1+R_{Tb})^i} \tag{B-27}$$

Knowing P, NV, R_{Tb}, and C_i, the equation can be resolved to calculate S, the stripped spread and, consequently, the stripped yield.

C.1 INDICES OF THE MEXICAN STOCK MARKET

Stock market behavior is normally described in terms of an index composed of the principal stocks, or stock series, of the relevant market. There are six main indices of the Mexican stock market, two national, and four international (figure C–1).

C.1.1 National indices

The first indices were developed to reflect the general trend of the stock market. The Dow Jones Industrial Average, which began in January 1897 with 12 stocks, currently consists of 30 stocks, and is calculated as the sum of the prices of the stocks of the 30 largest industrial companies of the NYSE, divided by the number of companies in the index (i.e. 30).

Since this first index, the most important advance in subsequent indices was to weight the components of the index according to their relative importance, normally measured by their market capitalization and, in some cases, the level of trading (liquidity) of each share. In the US, the Standard & Poor's index (of 500 stocks) is a market capitalization weighted index. The price index of the MSE (*Indice de Precios y Cotizaciones (IPC) de la BMV*) is a capitalization weighted index, but also takes into account liquidity, changing its composition every two months (bimester), according to the liquidity of its component stock series.[1]

Figure C–1 Main Mexican stock market indices 1999

Mexican Index	Produced by	# stocks	Begins (date)		
IPC	MSE	35-50	1978		
INMEX	Banamex	20-25	1993		
				# countries	
International				emer-ging	deve-loped
FT/S&P	Financial Times/ S & P Actuaries	28	1981	8	20
IFC Global	International Finance Corporation	74	1975	45	0
ING Barings	ING Barings	17	1992	24	0
MSCI	Morgan Stanley Capital International	40	1987	23	22

Source: author

---

[1] The different stock series (A, B, C, L, etc.) reflect different rights (e.g. to vote), inherited from the period when foreign investment in Mexico was restricted.

Figure C–2 Stock series used for IPC of MSE (bimester XI-XII 1998)

Issuer		%	Issuer		%	Issuer		%	Issuer		%
TELMEX	L	26.71	ALFA	A	3.37	VITRO	A	1.00	COMERCI	UBC	0.45
CIFRA	V	9.75	GMODELO	C	2.79	DESC	B	0.95	ELEKTRA	CPO	0.40
TELECOM	A1	6.30	CEMEX	B	2.15	ICA		0.93	GFNORTE	B	0.39
GCARSO	A1	6.23	CEMEX	CPO	1.99	TAMSA		0.90	BBVPRO	B	0.29
TLEVISA	CPO	5.80	BANACCI	B	1.92	GFB	A	0.85	HERDEZ	B	0.18
MODERNA	A	5.47	APASCO		1.88	CIE	B	0.73	GCC	B	0.15
KIMBER	A	4.59	CIFRA	C	1.71	MASECA	B	0.66	SANLUIS	CPO	0.12
SORIANA	B	3.92	TVAZTCA	CPO	1.48	HYLSAMX	BCP	0.62	GCORVI	UBL	0.03
FEMSA	UBD	3.58	GFB	B	1.13	GEO	B	0.56			

Figure C–3 Stock series used for INMEX (semester VII-XII 1998)

Issuer		%	Issuer		%	Issuer		%	Issuer		%
TELMEX	L	12.33	SORIANA	B	7.04	BANACCI	B	3.46	DESC	B	1.70
TELECOM	A1	11.30	FEMSA	UBD	6.43	APASCO		3.38	ICA		1.68
GCARSO	A1	9.97	ALFA	A	6.05	TVAZTCA	CF	2.66	TAMSA		1.62
CIFRA	V	9.92	GMODELO	C	5.02	GFB	B	2.02	COMERCI	UBC	0.81
KIMBER	A	8.24	CEMEX	B	3.85	VITRO	A	1.80	ELEKTRA	CPO	0.71

Figure C–4 IPC and INMEX 1993-98 (monthly US$)

Source: MSE

There are two problems with weighted indices such as the IPC:

- one stock can have a major weight in the index: in December 1998, TELMEX (L series) represented 27% of the IPC (figure C–2), and
- the IPC includes stock series of relatively low liquidity.

For these reasons, the INMEX index was introduced in 1992 with between 20-25 of the most marketable and highest capitalization stocks.[2] The INMEX differs in three ways from the IPC:

- it changes each semester,
- no stock series represents more than 10% of it, and

---

[2]Another important reason for the introduction of the INMEX was that, by including only liquid stocks, it could be used as an underlying asset for derivatives (📖 9.5.2).

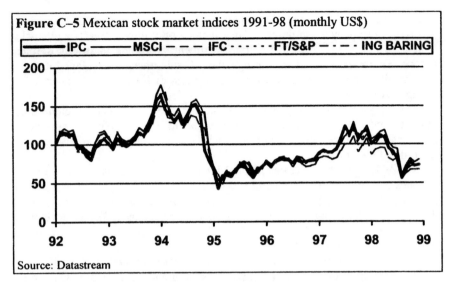

Figure C–5 Mexican stock market indices 1991-98 (monthly US$)

IPC ——— MSCI — — — IFC · · · · · · FT/S&P — · — · ING BARING

Source: Datastream

- only one stock series per company can be part of it (figure C–3).

Despite differences of composition and weighting, the two indices show quite similar behavior (figure C–4).

C.1.2 International indices

The problem with national stock market indices is that they are normally produced with differing methodologies. International indices were developed to respond to the need by investors to compare stock markets with indices prepared according to a common methodology.

International indices show similar behavior to the IPC of the MSE, and to each other (figure C–5). There are two relevant criteria for selecting international indices for a specific market: the degree to which they faithfully reflect market performance from the point of view of the foreign investor, and the level of comparability with other stock markets, both emerging and developed.

The global indices (*indices globales*) of emerging markets published by the International Finance Corporation (IFC) are the oldest international indices, with a series for Mexico that begins in 1975. They have the broadest coverage of emerging markets, with indices for 45 markets. However, from the beginning, the IFC indices included stocks in the indices for each emerging market without taking liquidity into account, and without distinguishing between stocks open to purchase by foreign investors and stocks limited to domestic investors.[3]

---

[3]The IFC, with the development of these indices for emerging markets, along with the launch of the Emerging Markets Growth Fund in 1986 (📖 1.3.1), had a determining influence on emerging markets development. It is a relevant example of the government (through a development bank) acting as a motor for the private sector.

The ING Barings indices, also for emerging markets, were launched in 1992, precisely to remedy these defects. They include only those markets and stocks which are liquid and open to foreign investment, according to strictly defined criteria. To compete with ING Barings, the IFC subsequently developed its own "investables" index, according to its own criteria of liquidity and openness to foreign investment.

The FT/S&P Actuaries indices, like the ING Barings indices, include only markets and stocks open to foreign investment. They have the additional advantage of comparing Mexico not only to 7 other emerging markets but also to 20 developed markets.

The MSCI (Morgan Stanley Capital International) indices have two indices for Mexico: one (*free*) which includes stocks unrestricted to foreign investment and the other (*global*), which includes both restricted and unrestricted stocks. The MSCI indices cover a wider range of both emerging (23) and developed (22) markets than the FT/S&P indices, but a smaller number of emerging markets than IFC or ING Baring.

There is competition between international indices, which is healthy for their development and refinement. The investor should choose the index which best reflects his investment, or research, objectives. For example, if the investor limits his investment to emerging markets, the IFC indices might provide the broadest, and ING Barings the most accurate coverage. If he wishes to cover both developed and emerging markets, the MSCI indices might be the most useful.

In this book, for domestic purposes, we use the IPC of the MSE[4], because it is the best known and understood index in Mexico. For international purposes, with certain exceptions[5], we have chosen the MSCI indices because they offer the broadest comparison of the Mexican stock market with other emerging and developed stock markets, and with other instruments (e.g. 📖 3.5).

---

[4]Expressed in dollars, owing to the book's global focus.

[5]For example, the comparison of the Mexican and US stock markets between 1918 and 1998 (figure 3-16), because the MSCI does not cover that period.

C.2 STOCK SYMBOLS OF ISSUERS ON MSE MAIN MARKET CLASSIFIED BY SECTOR 1998

Mining	*III.* *Construction*	101 BANACCI
1 Mining	12 Construction	102 BBVPRO
1 AUTLAN	51 BUFETE	103 GBMATLA
2 GMEXICO	52 GMD	104 GFB
3 PE&OLES	53 ICA	105 GFBITAL
4 YPF	54 IRSA	106 GFCRECE
II. *Manufacturing*	55 TRIBASA	107 GFCREMI
2 Chemical	13 Cement	108 GFFINA
5 MEXCHEM	56 APASCO	109 GFINBUR
6 TEKCHEM	57 CEMEX	110 GFINLAT
3 Pulp and paper	58 GCC	111 GFINTER
7 EMPAQ	59 TTOLMEX	112 GFMEXI
8 GIDUSA	14 Building materials	113 GFMULTI
9 KIMBER	60 CERAMIC	114 GFNORTE
4 Printing and publishing	61 CMOCTEZ	115 GPROFIN
10 GFESA	15 Housing	116 GSERFIN
5 Steel	62 ARA	117 INVEX
11 ACEYAC	63 GEO	118 IXEGF
12 AHMSA	64 HOGAR	119 SANMEX
13 HYLSAMX	*IV.* *Retail*	120 SURESTE
14 SIMEC	16 Retail stores	21 Commercial Banks
15 TAMSA	65 ACERLA	121 BAINLAT
6 Metals	66 ATY	122 BANCEN
16 METAVER	67 BEVIDES	123 BANORIE
17 ICH	68 CIFRA	124 BANPAIS
18 TFMEX	69 COFAR	125 BQ
19 TUACERO	70 COLLADO	126 CONFIA
7 Machinery and transportation equipment	71 COMERCI	127 CREMI
20 DANA	72 ECE	128 INTENAL
21 DINA	73 EDOARDO	129 PROMEX
22 IASASA	74 ELEKTRA	22 Brokers
23 PERKINS	75 FRAGUA	130 CBESTRA
8 Food, beverages and tobacco	76 GCORVI	131 CBI
24 ARGOS	77 GIGANTE	23 Other credit institutions
25 ARSA	78 GMARTI	132 ALSA
26 BACHOCO	79 GPH	24 Other services
27 BAFAR	80 GSANBOR	133 GCALIND
28 BIMBO	81 GSYR	134 GVIDEO
29 CONTAL	82 LIVEPOL	135 POSADAS
30 EMVASA	83 NADRO	136 REALTUR
31 FEMSA	84 SEARS	137 SITUR
32 GAM	85 SORIANA	138 VIDEO
33 GEUPEC	*V.* *Communications and transport*	139 WINGS
34 GMODELO	17 Transport	*VII.* *Miscellaneous*
35 GRUMA	86 CINTRA	25 Holding companies
36 HERDEZ	87 TMM	140 ACCELSA
37 KOF	18 Communications	141 ALFA
38 MAIZORO	88 BIPER	142 CAMESA
39 MASECA	89 IUSACEL	143 CIE
40 MINSA	90 RCENTRO	144 CYDSASA
41 MODERNA	91 TEAR2	145 DESC
42 PEPSIGX	92 TECO2	146 FIASA
43 SIGMA	93 TELECOM	147 GCARSO
44 TABLEX	94 TELMEX	148 GEPM
45 VALLE	95 TLEVISA	149 GISSA
9 Textiles, apparel and leather	96 TVAZTCA	150 IMSA
46 COVARRA	*VI.* *Services*	151 OPCAP
47 HILASAL	19 Insurance	152 PROCORP
48 PARRAS	97 GENSEG	153 SANLUIS
10 Non-metallic mineral products	98 GNP	154 SIDEK
49 VITRO	99 SEGCOAM	155 SYNKRO
11 Other manufacturing industries	20 Financial Groups	26 Others
50 EKCO	100 ABACOGF	156 GACCION

Source: MSE

Appendix D
Stocks II

D.1 THE FORMULA OF PRESENT VALUE AND CONSTANT GROWTH

D.1.1 The dividend discount model (DDM)

The dividend discount model (DDM - *modelo de descuento de dividendos*) is an adaptation of the net present value formula to stock valuation. The return from a stock consists of a combination of dividends and capital gains from the increase in the price of the stock ($\square$ 2.2.1). Therefore, the price (P_0) of the stock today represents a combination of the dividend (D_1) and the price (P_1) which is received at the end of period 1, discounted to the present at a rate of return (R), or:

$$P_0 = \frac{D_1}{(1+R)^1} + \frac{P_1}{(1+R)^1}$$

(D- 1)

For a longer horizon, the formula is reexpressed in general terms, for periods *1* to *t*:

$$P_0 = \sum_{i=1}^{t} \frac{D_i}{(1+R)^i} + \frac{P_t}{(1+R)^t}$$

(D- 2)

The greater the number of periods, the less significant the price at *t* (owing to the present value phenomenon), and therefore the price of the stock depends only on the dividend flow and the rate of return, or:

$$P_0 = \sum_{i=1}^{t} \frac{D_i}{(1+R)^i}$$

(D- 3)

D.1.2 The constant growth model

There are two problems with the DDM. The first is that there are many companies (above all in emerging markets like Mexico) which do not pay dividends. The second is that it implies a forecast of dividends and the rate R for an infinite number of periods in the future.

There has been some controversy in academic and professional circles about the use of dividends in the DDM. We consider that this controversy was resolved in a famous article written in 1961 by Miller and Modigliani, who received the Nobel Economics Prize for their research on financial valuation of companies.[1] In the article, they demonstrate that the value of a company is not affected by its dividend policy, i.e. the percentage of earnings that shareholders decide to withdraw from the company. Taking these arguments into account to broaden the application of the model to companies that do not pay dividends, we prefer to substitute earnings (*utilidades netas* - *E*) for dividends (*D*) in the expression (D-3), or:

$$P_0 = \sum_{i=1}^{t} \frac{E_i}{(1+R)^i} \qquad \text{(D-4)}$$

To resolve the second problem, that of the estimation of *E* for an infinite number of periods, the DDM has been simplified. The assumption is made that the trailing E_0 (of period 0) grows at a constant annual rate, *g*. This rate implies a compound growth rate of E_0 in the periods *1* to *t*, which in turn is discounted at a constant rate *R*:

$$P_0 = \frac{E_0(1+g)}{(1+R)^1} + \frac{E_0(1+g)^2}{(1+R)^2} + \dots + \frac{E_0(1+g)^t}{(1+R)^t} = \sum_{i=1}^{t} \frac{E_0(1+g)^i}{(1+R)^i} \qquad \text{(D-5)}$$

The expression can be simplified even further, on the important assumption that the annual growth rate of earnings is constant in perpetuity. With this assumption, the previous expression can be reduced mathematically to:

$$P_0 = \frac{E_0(1+g)}{R-g} \qquad \text{(D-6)}$$

D.1.3 Combination of DDM and constant growth

There are two problems with the use of the constant growth formula. The first is the assumption that the return rate *R* is greater than the growth rate *g* - if not, the expression D-6 becomes negative.[2] But there can be periods (for example, in the US between 1995 and 97) when this situation does not occur (i.e. when *g* is greater than *R*).

The second problem is the need to forecast a constant growth rate for profits in perpetuity. The reality is that analysts (and businessmen) are better positioned to make an accurate forecast for earlier, than for later, more remote, time

---

[1] Miller, Merton H. and Franco Modigliani, "Dividend Policy, Growth and the Valuation of Shares" (*Journal of Business*, vol. 34, no. 4, October 1961), pp. 411-33. See also James H. Lorie, Mary T. Hamilton, *The Stock Market, Theories and Evidence* (Richard D. Irwin, 1973), pp.119-122.

[2] See David Durand, "Growth Stocks and the Petersburg Paradox" (*Journal of Finance 12*, September, 1957), pp. 348-363, and Javier Gavito, "El múltiplo y la valuación del mercado de valores" (*Inversionista, diciembre, 1987*).

periods. But this possibility is not taken into account with the constant growth formula.

These two problems can be resolved with a combination of the DDM and the constant growth model. We wish to compare P (the price of a stock, or market index, or sector) with an estimated value P_e through the formulae presented in previous sections. This value consists of a flow of forecast earnings (E) which grows at a rate g (which can be greater than R) during t periods, plus the price P_t which is realized when the stock is sold in the market in period t:

$$P_e = \sum_{i=1}^{t} \frac{E_0(1+g)^i}{(1+R)^i} + \frac{P_t}{(1+R)^t} \qquad \text{(D-7)}$$

The problem is how to calculate P_t. This price can be expressed through the constant growth formula, i.e. the profit forecast for period $t+1$:

$$E_{t+1} = E_0(1+g)^{t+1} \qquad \text{(D-8)}$$

discounted by the required rate of return (R) less the rate of growth forecast for $t+1$ and succeeding periods (the constant rate of growth), g_{t+1} (which cannot be greater than R), or:

$$P_t = \left(\frac{E_{t+1}}{R - g_{t+1}} \right) \qquad \text{(D-9)}$$

The equation D-7 is reexpressed:

$$P_e = \sum_{n=1}^{t} \frac{E_0(1+g)^n}{(1+R)^n} + \frac{\left(\dfrac{E_{t+1}}{R - g_{t+1}} \right)}{(1+R)^t} \qquad \text{(D-10)}$$

D.2 APPLICATION OF THE PRESENT VALUE FORMULA TO MEXICAN MARKET VALUATION

For the application of the expression D-10, values are needed for the variables E_0, g, g_{t+1}, and R.

D.2.1 Trailing earnings

In December 1997, the level of the stock market index (IPC) was 5,229, and the trailing multiple (P/E) was 17.4 times trailing earnings. Taking the index as if it were a price P, one can calculate the trailing earnings implicit in the multiple, by dividing the index by the multiple, or:

$$E_0 = \frac{P}{\dfrac{P}{E_0}} = \frac{5,229}{17.4} = 301 \qquad\qquad \text{(D- 11)}$$

To make international comparisons, this number is converted to dollars, taking the exchange rate at the same date (31/12/97), \$8.05/US\$1:

$$E_0 = \frac{301}{8.05} = 37.3 \qquad\qquad \text{(D- 12)}$$

D.2.2 Growth rates

The forecast of g, the average growth rate of market earnings for the next five years (t) 1998-2002 was 15% in US\$, the average of three international brokerages.

The forecast of the constant growth rate (g_{t+1}) of 10% in US\$ for the period after the year 2002 was made in the following way. It was forecast that the rate of earnings growth of the best Mexican companies (because they are listed) can at least double the rate of 5%, which is considered as a sustainable long term growth rate for Mexican GDP.[3]

D.2.3 The rate of return

The rate R represents the minimum rate in US\$ required from the Mexican stock market to justify the risk, reflected by two elements, the country risk

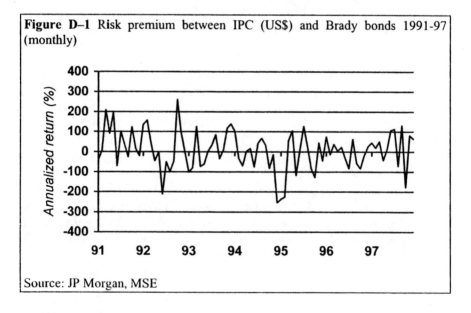

Figure D–1 Risk premium between IPC (US\$) and Brady bonds 1991-97 (monthly)

Source: JP Morgan, MSE

---

[3]See the National Program for Financing Development (*Programa Nacional para el Financiamiento del Desarrollo - PRONAFIDE*) (www.shcp.gob.mx).

premium, and the equity risk premium.

In December 1997, the yield to maturity offered by the UMS 2026 bond was 9.9%, i.e. the country risk premium was 400 basis points above the rate for the US Tbond for the same term of 5.9%.

For the period 1991-1997, the equity risk premium, measured as the difference between the annualized average monthly return on the IPC and Brady bonds, was 6.1% (figure D–1).

Adding together the Mexico risk-free rate (9.9%), and the equity risk premium (6.1%), we arrive at an *R* of 16%.

D.2.4 Fair value estimates for the index

Applying values for E_0, g, g_{t+1}, and R to the expression D-10, we estimate fair value (*valor justo*) for the index in figure D–2. Fair value for the index (in US$), on the assumption of growth in earnings (g) of 15% over 5 years and 10% thereafter, and a required rate of return (R) of 16% is 867, or 33% above its level on 12/31/97 of US$649.6, implying a level of undervaluation of 33%.

There are other ways to interpret the table, by varying the rates g and R. For example, the index level is near US$649.6, with a g of 5% and an R of 15%, or a g of 15% and an R of 18%.

D.2.5 Weighting of the sale price in the fair value calculation

The expression D-9 (the sale price) has a greater impact on the level of the index than the annual flows. The reason for this is shown in figure D–3, where calculations for the index are shown for rates R at 14% and 15%, with rates g between 5 and 15%. The annual flows of the first five years show relatively small variations for changes in g and R. The main variation is in the sale price, which accounts for between 77.6% and 85.4% of the total calculation.

The relative importance of the sale price comes from the constant growth

Figure D–2 Fair value calculations for stock index (US$)

rate R	rate of growth 5 years (g)				
	5.0%	7.5%	10.0%	12.5%	15.0%
14%	796	905	1,027	1,162	1,313
15%	641	726	821	927	1,045
16%	537	607	684	771	867
17%	462	521	587	659	740
18%	407	457	513	576	645

Assumptions:

Index in $ (12/31/97)	5,229
Index in US$ (12/31/97)	650
Trailing P/E multiple	17.4
Trailing earnings (E_0) in $	301
Trailing earnings (E_0) in US$	37.3
Constant rate of growth	10%
Exchange rate $/US$ (12/31/97)	8.05

Source: author

Figure D–3 Fair value calculations for index: annual flows and sale price

rate R: 14%		rate of growth 5 years (g)				
years		5.0%	7.5%	10.0%	12.5%	15.0%
	1	34.4	35.2	36.0	36.8	37.7
	2	31.7	33.2	34.8	36.4	38.0
	3	29.2	31.3	33.5	35.9	38.3
	4	26.9	29.5	32.4	35.4	38.7
	5	24.7	27.8	31.2	34.9	39.0
total flows		146.8	157.1	167.9	179.4	191.6
sale price		649.6	748.1	858.7	982.7	1121.2
total		796.4	905.1	1026.6	1162.1	1312.8
% price/total		81.6%	82.6%	83.6%	84.6%	85.4%
rate R: 15%						
years						
	1	34.1	34.9	35.7	36.5	37.3
	2	31.1	32.6	34.2	35.7	37.3
	3	28.4	30.5	32.7	34.9	37.3
	4	25.9	28.5	31.3	34.2	37.3
	5	23.7	26.6	29.9	33.4	37.3
total flows		143.3	153.2	163.7	174.8	186.7
sale price		497.5	572.9	657.6	752.5	858.6
total		640.7	726.0	821.3	927.4	1045.3
% price/total		77.6%	78.9%	80.1%	81.1%	82.1%

Source: author

formula:

$$P_t = \frac{\left(\dfrac{E_{t+1}}{R - g_{t+1}}\right)}{(1 + R)^t} \qquad \text{(D-13)}$$

In the numerator of the expression if we assume a rate g_{t+1} of 10%, any change in the rate R has an important effect on total value.

At a rate of 14%:

$$\left(\frac{E_{t+1}}{R - g_{t+1}}\right) = \frac{50.03}{.14 - .1} = \frac{50.03}{.04} = 1250.68 \qquad \text{(D-14)}$$

If we change the rate to 15%:

$$\left(\frac{E_{t+1}}{R - g_{t+1}}\right) = \frac{50.03}{.15 - .1} = \frac{50.03}{.05} = 1000.54 \qquad \text{(D-15)}$$

Even discounted to the present through the factor $(1+R)^t$, the forecast for the index diminishes significantly between the rate R (14%):

$$\frac{\left(\frac{E_{t+1}}{R-g_{t+1}}\right)}{(1+R)^t} = \frac{1250.68}{1925} = 649.6 \tag{D-16}$$

and the rate (15%):

$$\frac{\left(\frac{E_{t+1}}{R-g_{t+1}}\right)}{(1+R)^t} = \frac{1000.54}{2.011} = 497.5 \tag{D-17}$$

Clearly, the same would occur with a change in the rate of constant growth g_{t+1}.

D.3 A TECHNIQUE FOR FORECASTING THE MEXICAN STOCK INDEX

For the forecast of the stock index over a one year term (P_1), a forecast is made of the level of the trailing price/earnings multiple at the end of 1998 $(P/E)_1$, and of the rate of growth g of E_0 (which has already been calculated as 301 in 📖 D.2.1):

$$P_1 = \left(\frac{P}{E}\right)_1 * E_0(1+g) = 17.5 * 301 * 1.20 = 6{,}311 \tag{D-18}$$

Figure D–4 Index forecasts for one year term			
Scenarios	1	2	3
Forecast earnings (E) increase	5%	20%	35%
Forecast E	315.5	360.6	405.7
Trailing P/E multiple forecast for 31/12/98	15	18	20
Forecast Index ($)	4,733	6,311	8,114
Forecast exchange rate ($/US$)	9.50	8.70	8.40
Forecast index (US$)	498.2	725.4	965.9
Index change ($)	-9.5%	20.7%	55.2%
Index change (US$)	-23.3%	11.7%	48.7%
Assumptions:			
Stock index IPC $ (12/31/97)	5,229		
P/E multiple	17.4		
Trailing earnings E_0	301		
Exchange rate $/US$ (12/31/97)	8.05		
IPC in US$ (12/31/97)	650		
Source: author			

One can calculate different levels of the index with different scenarios of price/earnings multiple at the end of 1998, rates of growth g and rates of exchange (figure D–4).

D.4 PRESENT VALUE FORMULA FOR INDIVIDUAL STOCK VALUATION

The expression:

$$P_e = \sum_{n=1}^{t} \frac{E_0(1+g)^n}{(1+R)^n} + \frac{\left(\dfrac{E_{t+1}}{R-g_{t+1}}\right)}{(1+R)^t} \qquad \text{(D- 19)}$$

can be applied in the same way to individual stocks as to the market. Values for E_0, g, g_{t+1}, and R are needed for individual stocks.

In the case of the three companies CIFRA, COMERCI and SORIANA, E_0 varies by company, g_{t+1} remains constant at 10%, g varies between 10 and 20% and R between 14 and 18% (figure D–5).

D.5 PRICE FORECASTS FOR INDIVIDUAL MEXICAN STOCKS

As in the case of the stock index, for the forecast of an individual stock price (P_t) over a one year term, one makes a forecast of the trailing price/earnings multiple at the end of 1998 $(P/E)_t$, and of the growth rate g of E_0.

Figure D–5 Fair value estimates for individual stock prices

Company	Price	EPS 97	P/E		rate of growth 5 years (g)				
($)	(12/31/97)			rate R	10.0%	12.5%	15.0%	17.5%	20.0%
CIFRA	18.08	0.52	35.1	14%	14.17	16.03	18.11	20.42	22.98
				15%	11.33	12.80	14.42	16.23	18.23
				16%	9.44	10.64	11.96	13.43	15.06
				17%	8.09	9.10	10.21	11.44	12.80
				18%	7.08	7.94	8.90	9.95	11.11
COMERCI	10.52	0.59	17.7	14%	16.34	18.50	20.90	23.57	26.52
				15%	13.08	14.76	16.64	18.72	21.03
				16%	10.90	12.27	13.80	15.50	17.38
				17%	9.34	10.50	11.78	13.20	14.77
				18%	8.17	9.16	10.26	11.48	12.82
SORIANA	35.50	1.52	23.3	14%	41.90	47.43	53.58	60.41	67.98
				15%	33.52	37.85	42.66	48.00	53.91
				16%	27.93	31.47	35.39	39.74	44.54
				17%	23.94	26.91	30.20	33.84	37.87
				18%	20.95	23.49	26.31	29.43	32.87

Source: author

Figure D–6 Price forecasts for individual stocks for one year term

Forecast earnings (E) increase	5%	20%	35%
CIFRA			
Forecast E	0.54	0.62	0.70
Trailing P/E forecast for 31/12/98	32.50	35.00	37.50
Forecast price ($)	17.58	21.63	26.08
Forecast exchange rate ($/US$)	9.50	8.70	8.40
Forecast price (US$)	1.85	2.49	3.10
Increase in price ($)	-2.8%	19.7%	44.2%
Increase in price (US$)	-17.6%	10.7%	38.2%
Price (31/12/97)	18.08		
Trailing P/E multiple	35.10		
Trailing earnings E_0	0.52		
Exchange rate peso/US$ (31/12/97)	8.05		
Price in US$	2.25		
COMERCI			
Forecast E	0.62	0.71	0.80
Trailing P/E forecast for 31/12/98	15.00	17.70	20.00
Forecast price ($)	9.36	12.62	16.05
Forecast exchange rate ($/US$)	9.50	8.70	8.40
Forecast price (US$)	0.99	1.45	1.91
Increase in price ($)	-11.0%	20.0%	52.5%
Increase in price (US$)	-24.6%	11.0%	46.2%
Price (31/12/97)	10.52		
Trailing P/E multiple	17.70		
Trailing earnings E_0	0.59		
Exchange rate peso/US$ (31/12/97)	8.05		
Price in US$	1.31		
SORIANA			
Forecast E	1.60	1.83	2.06
Trailing P/E forecast for 31/12/98	20.00	23.30	27.00
Forecast price ($)	32.00	42.60	55.54
Forecast exchange rate ($/US$)	9.50	8.70	8.40
Forecast price (US$)	3.37	4.90	6.61
Increase in price ($)	-9.9%	20.0%	56.4%
Increase in price (US$)	-23.6%	11.0%	49.9%
Price (31/12/97)	35.50		
Trailing P/E multiple	23.30		
Trailing earnings E_0	1.52		
Exchange rate peso/US$ (31/12/97)	8.05		
Price in US$	4.41		

Source: author

$$P_1 = \left(\frac{P}{E}\right)_1 * E_0(1+g) \qquad\qquad (D\text{-}20)$$

We show specific calculations, with variations in the forecast for earnings increase, trailing price/earnings multiple, and exchange rate, for the three stocks CIFRA, COMERCI and SORIANA in figure D–6.

Appendix E
Derivatives

E.1 THEORETICAL OPTION VALUE: BLACK-SCHOLES MODEL

Based on the original formula for option valuation published by Fischer Black and Myron Scholes in 1973, a series of adaptations have been developed to value options on shares which pay dividends, currencies, indices and bonds. The equations are shown in figure E–1, where:

c: premium on European-style call option
p: premium on European-style put option
X: exercise price of option

Figure E–1 Black-Scholes formulae for different underlying assets

European call options	European put options

On stocks with no dividends

$$c = SN(d_1) - Xe^{-R(T-t)}N(d_2) \qquad\qquad p = Xe^{-R(T-t)}N(-d_2) - SN(-d_1)$$

where

$$d_1 = \frac{\ln\left(S/X\right) + \left(R + \sigma^2/2\right)(T-t)}{\sigma\sqrt{T-t}} \qquad and \qquad d_2 = \frac{\ln\left(S/X\right) + \left(R - \sigma^2/2\right)(T-t)}{\sigma\sqrt{T-t}}$$

On stocks and indices with dividends

$$c = Se^{-q(T-t)}N(d_1) - Xe^{-R(T-t)}N(d_2) \qquad p = Xe^{-R(T-t)}N(-d_2) - Se^{-q(T-t)}N(-d_1)$$

where

$$d_1 = \frac{\ln\left(S/X\right) + \left(R - q + \sigma^2/2\right)(T-t)}{\sigma\sqrt{T-t}} \qquad and \qquad d_2 = \frac{\ln\left(S/X\right) + \left(R - q - \sigma^2/2\right)(T-t)}{\sigma\sqrt{T-t}}$$

On exchange rates

$$c = Se^{-R_f(T-t)}N(d_1) - Xe^{-R(T-t)}N(d_2) \qquad p = Xe^{-R(T-t)}N(-d_2) - Se^{-R_f(T-t)}N(-d_1)$$

where

$$d_1 = \frac{\ln\left(S/X\right) + \left(R - R_f + \sigma^2/2\right)(T-t)}{\sigma\sqrt{T-t}} \qquad and \qquad d_2 = \frac{\ln\left(S/X\right) + \left(R - R_f - \sigma^2/2\right)(T-t)}{\sigma\sqrt{T-t}}$$

On bonds

$$c = BN(d_1) - Xe^{-R(T-t)}N(d_2) \qquad\qquad p = Xe^{-R(T-t)}N(-d_2) - BN(-d_1)$$

where

$$d_1 = \frac{\ln\left(B/X\right) + \left(R + \sigma^2/2\right)(T-t)}{\sigma\sqrt{T-t}} \qquad and \qquad d_2 = \frac{\ln\left(B/X\right) + \left(R - \sigma^2/2\right)(T-t)}{\sigma\sqrt{T-t}}$$

T-t: period to expiration of option, expressed in years

R: annual risk-free interest rate continuously capitalized of an investment to expiration of the option in the same currency

N(x): accumulated probability function for a normal standardized variable

S: current price of underlying asset (index, stock price, exchange rate)

B: current price of bond[1]

σ: annual standard deviation of instantaneous changes in price of underlying asset

q: constant annual rate of continuously capitalizable dividends

R_i: annual risk-free interest rate continuously capitalized of an investment to expiration of the option in a foreign currency

E.2 OPTIMAL COVERAGE RATIO WITH FUTURES AND THE CHANGE OF BETA IN A STOCK PORTFOLIO

The optimal coverage ratio refers to the size of the position taken in futures to minimize risk. It is expressed in the formula:

$$h = \left(\frac{S}{F}\right)\beta \qquad\qquad (\text{E-1})$$

where:

h: optimal coverage ratio,

S: instrument or portfolio to be covered,

F: future used to make the coverage, and

β: beta

Beta is the concept introduced in 📖 A.4 and represents the level of risk of the security or portfolio in relation to the market, in this case in relation to the future:

$$\beta = \frac{cov(\Delta\%S, \Delta\%F)}{var(\Delta\%F)} \qquad\qquad (\text{E-2})$$

where:

$\Delta\%S$: percentage change in stock or portfolio, and

$\Delta\%F$: percentage change in future.

If one wants to reduce the beta from β to β^* ($\beta > \beta^*$), one sells a proportion less than *h* contracts. This proportion is calculated by the formula:

---

[1]The model overvalues options on bonds, because it assumes that the price volatility of the underlying asset increases with time. This assumption is not correct for bonds, because the final value is always known. The premium for options on bonds with coupons can be calculated using the same formula as that for stocks with dividend payments.

$$\frac{\beta - \beta^*}{\beta}$$

(E-3)

Multiplied by h contracts this becomes:

$$(\beta - \beta^*)\frac{S}{F}$$

(E-4)

If one wants to increase the beta from β to β^* ($\beta^* > \beta$), one buys a proportion larger than h contracts. This proportion is calculated by the formula:

$$(\beta^* - \beta)\frac{S}{F}$$

(E-5)

Glossary

A

ADR (ADR - American Depositary Receipt)

A receipt issued by an authorized depositary in the US and backed by stocks purchased on a foreign exchange and held in the depositary, that facilitates the registration and trading of foreign stocks in the US capital markets (📖 7.6.2).

Annual rate (*tasa anual*)

Rate of return expressed annually without specifying reinvestment of flows received during the year (📖 2.2.1).

Annualized rate (*tasa anualizada*)

Return on an investment for a period of less than one year converted to an annual rate. This conversion is performed through the multiplication of the return by the number of days in the year, divided by the period of the investment expressed in days. Formally:

$$R = R_{TM} * \frac{365}{TM}$$

where: R is the annualized rate of return, R_{TM} is the return on the investment for the period and TM is the period of the investment in days (📖 2.2.1)[1].

Arbitrage Pricing Theory (*Arbitrage Pricing Theory - APT*)

Development of the CAPM (q.v.)[2] which considers that a stock's return can be explained not only by the index of the relevant stock market, but macroeconomic factors such as unexpected changes in industrial production or in the inflation rate (📖 2.4.2.4).

Asset class (*categoría de inversión*)

Classification of investments (usually portfolio investments - q.v.) with similar characteristics for the purpose of asset allocation in investment portfolios (📖 2.6.1).

---

[1] See "Notes to appendices " p. 320.

[2] "q.v." refers to word included in Glossary.

B

Bank acceptance (*aceptación bancaria*)
Debt security issued by banking institutions in the money market at a discount to its face value (📖 5.7.1).

Benchmark (*estándar*)
Indicator of the behavior of an asset class (q.v.), normally measured by an index (q.v), for the purposes of planning and performance evaluation of an investment portfolio (📖 2.6.1 and 12.2.4.3).

Beta (*beta*)
According to the CAPM (q.v.), indicator of sensitivity of the value of an investment (or investment portfolio) to the index (q.v.) of its relevant asset class (📖 2.4.2.2).

Bond (*bono or obligación*)
Long term debt security in the capital market. Synonym of "debenture" (📖 5.7.4).

Boom (*boom*)
Exaggerated increase in the price of an asset, followed by a crash (📖 10.2).

Brady bond (*bono Brady*)
Bond issued in substitution of bank debt by sovereign government of an emerging market as a consequence of a renegotiation between debtor and creditors (📖 5.8.1).

C

Capital market (*mercado de capitales*)
Investment market where long term securities are traded (in Mexico, mainly stocks and bonds) (📖 5.4).

CAPM (*CAPM - Capital Asset Pricing Model*)
Extension of Modern Portfolio Theory (q.v.) which simplifies the calculation of the return correlations between the different components of an investment portfolio, using "beta" (q.v.) as the measure of sensitivity of an investment or an investment portfolio to the index of an asset class (📖 2.4.2.2).

Certificado de Tesorería - Cete (*Cete*)
Debt instrument issued by the Mexican government in the money market at terms between 7 and 728 days at a discount to its face value (📖 5.6.1).

Clearing house (*cámara de compensación*)
Institution in a derivatives market which is the counterparty of all transactions and ensures their fulfillment (📖 9.2.2).

Commercial paper (*papel comercial*)
Corporate debt security issued in the money market at a discount to its face value (5.7.2).

Common stock (*acción común*)
Part of the equity capital of a company which confers on its holder a "property right" (to participate in the profits and net worth of the company), and a "corporate right" (to participate in the decisions of the shareholders' meeting) (8.2).

Compound rate (*tasa compuesta*)
Return on an investment taking into account reinvestment of flows received during the period of the investment, normally expressed as an annual rate. Formally:

$$R = \left(\left((1 + R_{TM})^{\frac{365}{TM}} \right) - 1 \right)$$

where R is the annual compound rate of return, R_{TM} is the return on the investment for the period and TM is the period of the investment expressed in days (2.2.1).

Contrary opinion (*opinión contraria*)
Process of determining the opinion of "the crowd" and reaching the opposite conclusion (10.5.3 and 12.6.5).

Convertible bond (*obligación convertible*)
Bond (q.v.) which confers on its holder the right to convert into an agreed number of shares of the issuer at an agreed price and date(s) (5.7.4).

Corporate bond (*obligación corporativa*)
Bond (q.v.) issued by a company (5.7.4).

Country risk (*riesgo país*)
Concept of risk (q.v.) applied to investments in a specific country (3.1.1).

Crash (*crac*)
Fall in the price of an asset that confirms the overvaluation of the boom preceding it (q.v.) (10.2).

Cyclicality (*ciclicidad*)
The sensitivity of sectoral GDP (q.v.) to total GDP of an economy (8.6.4.2).

D

Debt rating (*calificación de deuda*)
Expression of opinion about the probability and relative risk of the capacity and intention of the issuer of a debt security to effect payment in full and at the agreed date(s) (📖 6.5.5.1).

Deflation (*deflación*)
Decrease in the general price level, normally measured by the consumer price index – see "inflation" (📖 4.8.6).

Depreciation (*depreciación*)
The process of gradual decrease in the exchange rate of one currency against another (📖 6.7).

Derivative (*derivado*)
Security whose value depends on another underlying asset (q.v.) (📖 9.1).

Devaluation (*devaluación*)
Sudden change in the exchange rate of one currency against another (📖 6.7).

Development bond (*bono de desarrollo - Bonde*)
Debt instrument issued by the Mexican government in the money market with a minimum term of 364 days and rate of return that is reset and payable every 28 days (📖 5.6.2).

Direct investment (*inversión real*)
Application of non-liquid resources to obtain a future benefit (📖 2.1.2).

Discount rate (*tasa de descuento*)
- Rate used to calculate the price of money market instruments (📖 B.1).
- Synonym of rate of return (R) used to discount expected futures flows of an investment to calculate its present value (q.v.) (📖 A. 2).

Disinflation (*desinflación*)
Decrease in the rate of increase of inflation (q.v.) (📖 4.8.6).

Displacement (*desplazamiento*)
Drastic change in the investment environment (📖 10.4.1.1).

Duration (*duración*)
Measure using the concept of present value (q.v.) of the average maturity of debt securities, that indicates their sensitivity to changes in the general level of interest rates (📖 6.4).

E

Economic cycle (*ciclo económico*)
The process of increase and decrease over time of economic activity of a country or group of countries, normally measured by percentage changes in the level of GNP or GDP (q.v.) (📖 4.3).

Efficient market (*mercado eficiente*)
Financial market where the level of expected return reflects accurately the level of expected risk (📖 2.5).

Emerging market (*mercado emergente*)
Term applied to capital market of developing country where financial investments can be made, also applied to developing economies without capital markets (📖 1.3.1).

Euro (*euro*)
New currency of 11 countries of the European Union introduced in 1999 (📖 2.2.1.2).

Eurobond (*eurobono*)
Bond denominated in a Eurocurrency (q.v.) issued on the international capital market by a public or corporate issuer (📖 5.8.3).

Eurocurrency (*eurodivisa*)
Currency traded or deposited outside its country of issue (e.g. the "eurodollar") (📖 5.8.3).

Exchange rate (*tipo de cambio*)
See "parity" (📖 6.7).

F

Financial crisis (*crisis financiera*)
Disruption of financial system of a country or group of countries that affects, or could affect, the real economy (📖 10.2.1).

Financial derivative (*derivado financiero*)
Derivative (q.v) whose underlying asset is a financial security (📖 9.1).

Forward (*contrato adelantado*)
Contract between two parties to buy or sell an underlying asset at an agreed future time and price with non-standardized amounts and maturities, i.e. not in an organized market (over-the-counter (q.v.) – see also "Future") (📖 9.7).

Future (*futuro*)
Contract between two parties to buy or sell an underlying good at an agreed future time and price with standardized amounts and terms in an organized market (📖 9.7).

G

GATT (GATT - General Agreement on Trade and Tariffs)
  Organization established in Geneva in 1948 to encourage free trade: its name was changed in 1995 to World Trade Organization (WTO - *Organización Mundial de Comercio – OMC*) (📖 1.4.1).

Globalization (*globalización*)
  The process of increasing international interaction of ideas, information, capital, goods and services, and people (📖 1.2.1).

Gross Domestic Product (*Producto Interno Bruto*)
  The sum of all goods and services consumed by government, industry and individual consumers in a country or group of countries (📖 4.6.1).

Gross rate (*tasa bruta*)
  Pre-tax rate of return (📖 2.2.1).

I

Index (*índice*)
  Average of price sample of an asset class, used for measurement of asset class performance and the planning and performance measurement of investment portfolios (see also "benchmark") (📖 2.6.1 and C.1).

Index bond (*bono indexado*)
  Bond with face value linked to an index. The Udibono (q.v.), with face value denominated in UDIs (q.v.) that derive their value from the National Consumer Price Index, is an example of an indexed bond (📖 2.3.2.3 and 6.2.4).

Individual investment (*inversión individual*)
  Investment by individuals (📖 11.2).

Inflation (*inflación*)
  Sustained increase in the general price level, normally measured by the percentage increase in the national consumer price index (CPI – *Indice Nacional de Precios al Consumidor (INPC)* in Mexico) (📖 2.3.1)

Inside information (*información privilegiada*)
  Information not yet publicly available to investors, of which knowledge could affect the price of portfolio investments (📖 8.7.4.1).

Institutional investment (*inversión institucional*)
  Investment by institutions, such as insurance companies, companies, trusts, charities, pension funds, financial institutions and mutual funds (📖 11.4).

Internal rate of return (IRR - *tasa interna de rendimiento (TIR)*)
  Rate of return used to discount expected future flows of an investment so that the sum of the discounted flows, or present value (q.v.), is equal to the original investment (📖 2.4.1).

Intrinsic value (*valor intrínseco*)
Difference between the exercise price of an option (q.v.) and the price of the underlying asset (q.v.) (📖 9.8.2).

Investment (*inversión*)
Application of resources to obtain a future benefit (📖 2.1.1).

Investment advice (*asesoría de inversión*)
Assistance in any of the activities that form part of the investment management process (📖 12.5).

Investment management (*administración de inversiones*)
Planning, implementation, and control of an investment strategy (📖 12.1-4).

Issuer (*emisor(a)*)
Entity which raises funds through the issue of securities (📖 5.5).

L

LIBOR (*LIBOR*)
London Interbank Offered Rate. Interest rate offered in London Eurocurrency (q.v.) market for deposits for a specified term and currency (📖 5.8.3.3).

Liquidity (*liquidez*)
- The ability to buy or sell an investment (📖 2.2.2 and 7.7.3).
- The level of money supply in an economy (see "liquidity cycle") (📖 4.4).
- The level of liquid assets held by a company to meet its debt obligations (📖 6.5.5.2).

Liquidity cycle (*ciclo de liquidez*)
The process of expansion and contraction over time of the supply of money in a country or group of countries, normally represented by the percentage change in an indicator of money supply such as M1 or M4 (📖 4.4).

Listing (*inscripción*)
Registration of a security on an organized market (normally an exchange), after satisfying the market and its regulators' requirements for information, issue size, and number of investors (📖 7.5.1).

Long cycle (*ciclo largo*)
The process of increase and decrease over the very long term of the economic activity of a country or group of countries, normally measured as the percentage change in GDP (q.v.), and focussed on changes in this process caused by major historical events, such as wars, geographic expansion, or technological invention (📖 4.2).

M

Margin (*margen*)
Deposit required in derivatives markets to cover any change in agreed prices during the term of the derivatives contract, and to assure contract fulfillment at maturity (📖 9.2.2 and 9.7.3).

Market capitalization (*capitalización de mercado*)
The size of a company measured by the number of shares in issue multiplied by the market price of the shares (📖 8.6.6.1).

Mexico Fund (*Fondo México*)
Closed-end mutual fund established in 1981 and listed on the New York Stock Exchange, which invests in Mexican stocks (📖 11.4.1.1).

Modern Portfolio Theory (MPT - *Teoría Moderna de Portafolios – TMP*)
Branch of financial theory that analyzes and measures risk and return of investment portfolios (📖 2.4.2.1).

Money market (*mercado de dinero*)
Investment market where short term or liquid debt securities are traded (in Mexico, mainly Cetes, Bondes, bank acceptances, commercial paper and Udibonos) (📖 5.4).

Mortgage bond (*obligación hipotecaria*)
Corporate bond with repayment guaranteed by a mortgage on the assets of the issuing company (📖 5.5.2).

Multiple (*múltiplo*)
Division of one number (the numerator) by another (the denominator), with emphasis on the numerator. Used to value stocks, it normally compares the price of the share as numerator, with, as denominator, its historic and estimated flows (earnings per share, cash flow per share, earnings before interest, taxes depreciation and amortization), or its net worth per share (📖 8.3.1).

Mutual fund (*sociedad de inversión*)
Fund established for investment in a variety of investments that offers the investor the advantages of diversification and professional investment management (📖 11.4.1.1 and 12.3.2).

N

Negative real rate (*tasa real negativa*)
Real rate of return (q.v.) on an investment which is less than zero (📖 2.3.2).

Net present value (*valor presente neto*)
Difference between the present value (q.v.) of an investment and the original investment (📖 2.4.1).

Net rate (*tasa neta*)
After-tax rate of return ($\square$ 2.2.1).

Neutral Fund (*Fondo Neutro o Fondo Nafin*)
Trust established in Mexico in 1989 by Nacional Financiera to facilitate, by separating property rights from voting rights, foreign investment in stocks restricted to Mexican investors ($\square$ 7.6.1).

Nominal rate (*tasa nominal)*
Contractual rate of return on nominal value of debt instruments ($\square$ 5.5).

North American Free Trade Agreement (NAFTA - *Tratado de Libre Comercio - TLC*)
Treaty implemented in 1994 between Canada, Mexico and the USA to increase the trade of goods and services between the three countries ($\square$ 1.4.1).

O

OECD (*OCDE*)
Organization for Economic Cooperation and Development (*Organización para la Cooperación y el Desarrollo Económico*) established in 1961 in Paris as a consequence of the Marshall Plan to encourage further economic development among developed countries ($\square$ 1.4.1).

Option (*opción*)
Contract which grants the right to buy (call option) or sell (put option) an agreed quantity of an underlying asset (*subyacente*) at an agreed strike price (*precio de ejercicio*) during an agreed period or at an agreed date ($\square$ 9.8).

Organized market (*mercado organizado*)
Market which complies with the requirements of marketplace, intermediaries, authorities and rules for listing, trading and information, which assure liquidity (q.v.) for portfolio investments (q.v.) ($\square$ 2.2.2).

Over-the-counter (OTC - *extrabursátil*)
Term applied to the trading of a financial instrument outside an organized market, or to the instrument itself ($\square$ 9.3.1).

P

Par value (*valor nominal*)
Principal amount of a security ($\square$ 5.5.4).

Parity (*paridad*)
Exchange rate of one currency against another ($\square$ 6.7).

Payoff function (*función de pago*)
Graphic representation of the variation in profit and loss of a derivative due to variations in the price of the underlying asset ($\square$ 9.7.4 and 9.8.4)

Portfolio (*cartera*)
Combination of financial investments (📖 2.4.2).

Portfolio investment (*inversión financiera*)
Application of resources in an organized market to obtain a future benefit (📖 2.1.2).

Positive real rate (*tasa real positiva*)
Real rate of return (q.v.) on an investment which is greater than zero (📖 2.3.2).

Present value (*valor presente*)
Sum of expected future flows of an investment discounted at a rate of return (or discount rate) (📖 2.4.1 and A2).

Primary market (*mercado primario*)
Market where new securities issues are placed through an initial public offering (IPO), primary offering, secondary offering or mixed offering (📖 7.5.1).

Purchasing power parity (*paridad de poder de compra*)
Technique for evaluating the parity of one country against another by comparing their respective inflation rates (📖 6.7.2).

R

Rating agency (*calificadora de valores*)
Organization which issues a debt rating (q.v.) for debt securities issued by the public and private sector according to consistent and comparable criteria, to facilitate their issue and subsequent trading in financial markets (📖 3.2.1 and 6.5.5.1).

Real rate (*tasa real*)
Return on an investment deflated by the inflation rate for the same term (📖 2.3.2).

Reference currency (*moneda de referencia*)
Currency in which the investor denominates the expected return from portfolio investments (📖 2.2.1.2).

Repo (*reporto*)
Money market operation whereby a financial institution guarantees a return to its counterparty through sale of a security with the simultaneous obligation to repurchase the security at an agreed future date and price (📖 5.6.1 and B.2)

Return (*rendimiento*)
Benefit obtained from an investment through capital gains, interest or dividends, normally expressed as a percentage of the amount invested (📖 2.2.1).

Return ranking (*jerarquía de rendimientos*)

Ranking of estimated returns in a reference currency (q.v.) of different asset classes or securities in accordance with their estimated risk (📖 2.3)

Risk (*riesgo*)

- Possibility of not receiving return expected from an investment (📖 2.2.4).
- The variation (*variación*) or volatility (*volatilidad*) of historical returns, measured as their standard deviation (📖 2.2.4).
- Expected variation of an expected return (📖 2.2.4).
- Factor which can affect the possibility of obtaining the return expected on an investment (e.g. "political risk" or "legal risk).

Risk premium (*prima por riesgo*)

The additional expected return required by an investor in compensation for incurring an additional expected risk (📖 2.3).

Risk-free rate (*tasa carente de riesgo*)

Return in a country that can be obtained from a liquid debt security denominated in the country's currency with no risk of not obtaining the expected return (📖 2.3.2).

S

Savings (*ahorro*)

What remains after consumption. The act of not consuming (📖 2.1.1).

Scenario (*escenario*)

Tool to order perceptions about alternative future environments that will affect the consequences of decisions taken today, utilized for the planning of direct and portfolio investments (📖 4.7.2).

Secondary market (*mercado secundario*)

Market where securities are traded after their initial issue in the primary market (q.v.) (📖 7.5.1 and 7.7)

Sector rotation (*rotación de sectores*)

Expansion or contraction (corresponding to the stages of the economic cycle) of multiples (q.v.) of different sectors (q.v.) of the stock market (📖 8.6.4.2).

Securities Deposit Institute (*INDEVAL - Instituto para el Depósito de Valores*)

Organization established in Mexico in 1978 for the custody, settlement, transference, and administration of securities (📖 2.2.2).

Securities market (*mercado de valores*)

Market organized for trading portfolio investments. It normally consists of several subsidiary markets: a capital market (for long term investments) a money market (for short term investments), a primary market (for new issues of securities) and a secondary market (for the trading of securities once issued) (📖 2.2 and 📖 7.5-7).

Selection (*selección*)
The choice of a specific investment within an asset class (📖 2.6.2.2).

Sharpe ratio (*razón Sharpe*)
Technique for comparing investments or investment portfolios, by measuring the additional return (over the risk-free rate) in proportion to the risk (measured as the standard deviation of returns) of an investment or portfolio (📖 2.4.2.3 and 12.3.2).

Short sale (*venta en corto*)
Financial market operation which implies the sale of an investment not owned by the investor, which is covered by the purchase of the investment at a subsequent date, with the expectation of buying it at a lower price than the sale price (📖 9.7.1).

Sovereign ceiling (*techo soberano*)
Minimum return offered by a corporate issuer in a country, defined as the return on a sovereign debt security for the same maturity (📖 6.6.6.1).

Speculation (*especulación*)
Investment for the short term, with high risk and the expectation of high return (📖 2.6.2 and 9.6).

Stock exchange (*bolsa de valores*)
Organization for trading in securities which usually fulfills the requirements of an organized market: marketplace, intermediaries, authorities and rules for registration, trading and information (📖 2.2.2).

Stock market sector (*sector accionario*)
Grouping of companies for two main purposes: 1) analysis of common factors which can affect their prices, and 2) comparative valuation (📖 8.6).

Stripped spread (*diferencial sin colateral*)
Difference between the stripped yield (q.v.) of a Brady bond and the yield of the US Treasury bond of the same maturity (📖 B.5).

Stripped yield (*tasa de rendimiento sin colateral*)
Return on Brady bond flows not guaranteed by US Treasury bonds (see "stripped spread") (📖 B.5).

Swap (*swap*)
Derivative that consists of the exchange of one flow of payments for another (📖 9.1).

T

Tequila effect (*efecto "tequila"*)
Effect caused by the Mexican financial crisis of December 1994 on other emerging markets (📖 1.4.1).

Term (*plazo*)
Period between the purchase of an investment and its sale, or maturity (📖 2.2.3).

Time value (*valor por tiempo*)
Difference between the market value of an option and its intrinsic value (q.v.) (📖 9.8.2)

Timing (*timing*)
Selection of the right moment to buy or sell an asset class or investment (📖 2.6.2.1).

U

UDI (*UDI - Unidad de Inversión*)
Unit of investment whose value increases daily with the Mexican inflation rate, measured by the increase in the Consumer Price Index: used as the basis for valuation of debt securities (e.g the Udibono - q.v.) (📖 5.6.3).

Udibono (*Udibono*)
Debt security with maturities between 3 and 5 years, whose return is indexed to inflation through the mechanism of a face value denominated in UDIs, and a guaranteed real rate of return, applied to its face value (📖 2.3.2.3, 5.6.3 and 6.2.4).

Underlying asset (*subyacente*)
Asset or security on which the value of a derivative depends (q.v.) (📖 9.1).

Unsecured bond (*obligación quirografaria*)
Corporate bond issued without a specific guarantee from the issuing company (📖 5.5.2).

Y

Yield curve (*curva de rendimiento*)
Graphical representation of the yields of debt instruments against their corresponding maturities, utilized for the forecasting of interest rates (📖 6.3.2).

Z

Zero coupon bond (*bono cupón cero*)
Bond whose yield is obtained through a discount on its face value (📖 6.2.1).

Bibliography

Books

Bernstein, Peter, *Capital Ideas* (The Free Press, 1992)

_____, *Against the Gods, The Remarkable Story of Risk* (John Wiley & Sons, 1996)

Bootle, Roger, *The Death of Inflation* (Nicholas Brealey, 1996)

Brealey, Richard, *An Introduction to Risk and Return on Common Stocks* (MIT Press, 1983)

Burr Williams, John, *The Theory of Investment Value* (Harvard University Press, 1938)

Carande, Ramón, *Carlos V y Sus Banqueros* (Sociedad de Estudios y Publicaciones, 1965)

Cerda, Luis C., *Historia Financiera del Banco Nacional de México* (Fomento Cultural Banamex A. C., 1994)

Cohen, Edward E., *Athenian Economy & Society: a Banking Perspective* (Princeton University Press, 1992)

Davies, Norman, *Europe, a History* (Oxford University Press, 1996)

De la Vega, Joseph, *Confusión de Confusiones* ed. Martin S. Fridson (John Wiley & Sons, 1996)

Dreman, David, *The New Contrarian Investment Strategy* (Random House, 1982)

Edwards, Sebastian, Moisés Naím ed., *Mexico 1994 - Anatomy of an Emerging-Market Crash* (Carnegie Endowment for International Peace, 1997)

Ellis, Charles D., James R. Vertin ed., *Classics, an Investor's Anthology* (Dow Jones-Irwin, 1989)

Farrell, Jr., James L., *Portfolio Management: Theory and Applications, 2nd edition* (McGraw-Hill, 1997)

Galbraith, John K., *The Great Crash 1929* (Houghton Mifflin, 1955)

Graham, Benjamin, David Dodd, Sidney Cottle, Charles Tatham, *Security Analysis, Principles and Techniques, 4th edition* (McGraw-Hill Book Company, 1962)

Greider, William, *One World, Ready or Not* (Touchstone, 1998)

Haber, Stephen ed., *How Latin America Fell Behind* (Stanford University Press, 1997)

Hackett Fischer, David, *The Great Wave: Price Revolutions and the Rhythms of History* (Oxford University Press, 1996)

Heyman, Timothy, Arturo León y Ponce de León, *La Inversión en México* (Universidad del Valle de México, 1981)

Heyman, Timothy, *Inversión contra Inflación* (Editorial Milenio, 1988)

_____, *Investing in Mexico* (Editorial Milenio, 1989)

_____, *Inversión en la Globalización* (Bolsa Mexicana de Valores, Editorial Milenio, Instituto Mexicano de Ejecutivos de Finanzas, Instituto Tecnológico Autónomo de México, 1998)

Homer, Sidney, *A History of Interest Rates* (Rutgers University Press, 1963)

Hull, John C., *Options, Futures, and Other Derivative Securities* (Prentice-Hall, 1993)

Ibbotson Associates, *Stocks Bonds Bills and Inflation 1996 Yearbook* (Ibbotson Associates, 1996)

Ibbotson, Roger G., Gary P. Brinson, *Global Investing* (McGraw-Hill, 1993)

Keay, John, *The Honourable Company, A History of the East India Company* (HarperCollins, 1993)

Kindleberger, Charles, *Manias, Panics and Crashes, a History of Financial Crises - revised edition* (Basic Books, 1989)

_____, *A Financial History of Western Europe* (George Allen & Unwin, 1984)

Krayer & Asociados, Jorge Fernández Font, Gabriela Breña Valle, *Historia de la BMV* (Bolsa Mexicana de Valores, 1996)

Lagunilla Iñarritu, Alfredo, *La Bolsa en el Mercado de Valores de México y su Ambiente Empresarial, 1895-1933* (Bolsa de Valores de México, 1976)

_____, *Historia de la Banca y Moneda en México* (Editorial Jus, 1981)

Lorie, James H., Mary T. Hamilton, *The Stock Market, Theories and Evidence* (Richard D. Irwin, 1973)

Lowenstein, Roger, *Buffett, The Making of an American Capitalist* (Random House, 1995)

Mackay, Charles, *Extraordinary Popular Delusions and the Madness of Crowds*, ed. Martin S. Fridson (John Wiley & Sons, 1996)

Maginn, John L, Donald L. Tuttle, ed., *Managing Investment Portfolios*, (Warren, Gorham & Lamont, 1990)

Mansell Carstens, Catherine, *Las Nuevas Finanzas en México* (Editorial Milenio, Instituto Mexicano de Ejecutivos de Finanzas, Instituto Tecnológico Autónomo de México, 1992)

_____, *Las Finanzas Populares en México* (Centro de Estudios Monetarios para América Latina, Editorial Milenio, Instituto Tecnológico Autónomo de México, 1995)

Newman, Peter, Murray Milgate, John Eatwell eds., *The New Palgrave Dictionary of Money and Finance* (The Macmillan Press, 1992)

O'Brien, Richard, *Global Financial Integration, The End of Geography* (New York: Council on Foreign Relations, 1992)

Rodríguez de Castro, James, *Introducción al Análisis de Productos Financieros Derivados* (Bolsa Mexicana de Valores, Limusa, Noriega Editores, 1996)

Schama, Simon, *The Embarrassment of Riches* (Fontana Press, 1991)

Secretaría de Hacienda y Crédito Público, *Deuda Externa Pública Mexicana* (Fondo de Cultura Económica, 1988)

Sharpe, William F., *Investments* (Prentice-Hall, 1981)

Sherden, William A, *The Fortune Sellers* (John Wiley & Sons, 1998)

Sokoloff, Kiril, *The Thinking Investor's Guide to the Stock Market* (McGraw-Hill, 1978)

Solnik, Bruno, *International Investments* (Addison Wesley Publishing Company, 1996)

Soros, George, *The Alchemy of Finance* (Touchstone, 1997)

_____, *Soros on Soros* (John Wiley & Sons, 1995)

Train, John, *The Money Masters* (Harper & Row, 1980)

_____, *The New Money Masters* (Harper Perennial, 1989)

Waters, Malcolm, *Globalization* (Routledge, 1995)

White, Eugene N. ed., *Crashes and Panics: the Lessons of History* (Business One Irwin, 1990)

Williams III, Arthur, *Managing Your Investment Manager* (Business One Irwin, 1992)

Articles

Black, Fischer, Myron Scholes, "The Pricing of Options and Corporate Liabilities", (*Journal of Political Economy*, May-June, 1973)

Brinson, Gary P., Brian D. Singer, Gilbert L. Beebower, "Determinants of Portfolio Performance II: an Update" (*Financial Analysts' Journal*, May/June 1991)

Cantor, Richard, and Frank Packer, "Determinants and Impacts of Sovereign Credit Ratings", (Federal Reserve Bank of New York, Research Paper #9608, April 1996)

Cohen, Benjamin J., "Phoenix Arisen: The Resurrection of Global Finance" (*World Politics 48*, January 1996)

Cox, J. C., S. A. Ross, M. Rubinstein, "Option Pricing: A Simplified Approach" (*Journal of Financial Economics*, October 1979)

Díaz de León Carrillo, Alejandro, "Descripción y Valuación de los 'Value Recovery Rights' de los Bonos Brady a la par y a descuento" (Banco de México, documento de investigación No. 9703, agosto de 1997)

Durand, David, "Growth Stocks and the Petersburg Paradox" (*Journal of Finance 12*, September 1957)

Fukuyama, Francis, "The End of History?" (*The National Interest*, 1989)

Gavito, Javier, "El múltiplo y la valuación del mercado de valores" (*Inversionista*, diciembre de 1987)

Hale, David D., "The World Economy After the Russian Revolution, or Why the 1990s Could Be the Second Great Age of Global Capitalism Since the 19th Century" (Kemper Financial Companies, September 1991)

_____, "Economic Implications of the Mutual Fund Boom" (Zurich Kemper Investments Inc., March 1996)

_____, "How The Rise Of Pension Funds Will Change The Global Economy In The 21st Century" (Zurich Kemper Investments, March 1998)

Heyman Timothy, "¿Es México aún un Mercado Emergente?" (*Revista IMEF*, octubre de 1993)

Heyman Timothy, "Is Mexico Still an Emerging Market?" (Baring Securities, May 1993)

Hurley, Mark, Sharon Meers, Ben Bornstein, Neil Strumingher, "The Coming Evolution of the Investment Management Industry: Opportunities and Strategies" (Goldman Sachs, 1995)

Instituto Mexicano de Ejecutivos de Finanzas, "El Mercado Mexicano de los Derivados (MexDer)" (Boletín 20, Instituto Mexicano de Ejecutivos de Finanzas, 1997)

Kondratieff, Nikolai, "Major Economic Cycles" (*Voprosy kon'iunktury I*, 28-79, 1925)

Mariscal, Jorge O., Rafaelina M. Lee, "The Valuation of Mexican Stocks: An Extension of the Capital Asset Pricing Model to Emerging Markets" (Goldman Sachs, 1993)

_____, "The Valuation of Latin American Stocks: Part II" (Goldman Sachs, 1994)

Markowitz, Harry M., "Portfolio Selection" (*Journal of Finance*, 1952)

Miller, Merton H., Franco Modigliani, "Dividend Policy, Growth and the Valuation of Shares" (*Journal of Business*, vol. 34, no. 4, October 1961)

Nai-fu Chen, Richard Roll, Stephen A. Ross, "Economic Forces and the Stock Market (*Journal of Business*, July 1986)

Rodrick, Dani, "Has Globalization Gone Too Far?" (Institute for International Economics, 1996)

Ross, Stephen A., "The Arbitrage Theory of Capital Asset Pricing" (*Journal of Economic Theory*, 1976)

Sharpe, William F., "A Simplified Model for Portfolio Analysis" *(Management Science* Vol. 9, 1963)

Standard & Poor's, "Calificaciones y Comentarios" (julio de 1997)

Wien, Byron, "The Ten Surprises of 1998" (Morgan Stanley, January 1998)

Internet

Banco de México (www.banxico.org.mx)

Bank for International Settlements, "Central Bank Survey of Foreign Exchange and Derivatives Market Activity 1995" (www.bis.org)

Bolsa Mexicana de Valores, S. A. de C. V. (www.bmv.com.mx)

Chicago Board of Trade (www.cbot.com)

Chicago Board Options Exchange (www.cboe.com)

Chicago Mercantile Exchange (www.cme.com)

CrossBorder Capital (www.liquidity.com)

Erb, Claude B., Campbell R. Harvey, Tadas E. Viskanta, "Political Risk, Economic Risk and Financial Risk" (www.duke.edu)

Porvenir Online (www.porvenir.com)

Programa Nacional para el Financiamiento del Desarrollo (PRONAFIDE) (www.shcp.gob.mx)

Schwartz, Peter, "The Art of the Long View, User's Guide" (www.gbn.org)

Secretaría de Hacienda y Crédito Público (www.shcp.gob.mex)

Index of figures

1 Globalization   1
1–1 Mexican and US stocks 1976-98 (base 100: annual - US$)   1
1–2 91 day Cetes and Mexican inflation 1978-98 (monthly annualized rates - %)   2
1-3 Mexico and globalization   6
1–4 Steps towards globalization: 1944-98   8
1–5 Principal emerging markets: 1986 and 1998   10
1–6 Flows to emerging markets 1991-99 (US$bn.)   11
1–7 World stock market indices 1988-98 (monthly - US$)   12
1–8 The stages of economic growth 1995 (GNP/GDP per capita US$)   13
1–9 Emerging and developed countries 1999   14
1–10 The world economy in 1994 and 2010   14
1–11 World stock markets in 1994 and 2010   15
1–12 Mexico: steps towards globalization 1984-98   17
1–13 Mexico: development of capital and money markets 1990-98   18
1–14 Net balance of foreign debt Mexico 1990-98 (US$bn.)   19
1–15 Emerging markets: comparative figures (February 1999)   20
1–16 National and international markets 1998   21
1–17 Principal foreign financial institutions in Mexico 1998   22

2 Investment   25
2–1 Global investment   26
2–2 Return from Mexican investments   27
2–3 Rates of return   29
2-4 The securities markets and the Mexican financial system 1998   31
2–5 Real rate in Mexico 1983-98 (difference between Cete 28 days and monthly CPI - % annualized)   33
2–6 Real rate in US 1983-98 (difference between 3 month Tbill and monthly CPI - % annualized)   34
2–7 Real rate of Udibono 1092 days and Cete 28 days 1996-98 (% - annualized)   35
2–8 Return and risk   36
2–9 Return ranking in pesos and dollars   37
2–10 Historical risk and return 1945-95   38
2–11 Correlation between return of investments A and B   40
2–12 Efficient portfolios and the efficient frontier   41
2–13 Graphical representation of Sharpe ratio for portfolios with one risk-free and one risky asset   43
2–14 Explanation of pension fund returns in US 1977-87   47
2–15 Principal stock and bond indices used in this book   48

3 Country risk   51
3–1 Country risk: the risk-return line   52
3–2 Rating scales (above C - high default risk) of principal rating agencies   53
3–3 Brady bonds: spread over Treasuries vs. S&P rating (December 1996)   54
3–4 Ratings of 49 developed and emerging countries 1995   56
3–5 Country risk analysis services   57
3–6 Real rate of 25 countries against country risk (ICRG) 1996   58
3–7 Risk and return of 30 stock markets   59
3–8 Stock risk and debt risk   60
3–9 Debt (D) and stocks (S): risk and return 1991-98 (monthly US$, annualized)   61

3–10 Mexican debt in a global context 1991-8 (monthly)   62
3–11 Mexican stocks in a global context 1991-8 (monthly)   63
3–12 Sovereign stripped spread of Mexican Brady bonds (bps) 1992-98 (monthly)   65
3–13 Mexico: sovereign stripped spread and price/book value 1992-98 (monthly annualized)   65
3–14 Mexican asset classes 1991-98 (100 = January, 1991)   66
3–15 Mexican investments: risk and return 1991-98 (monthly)   67
3–16 Mexico and the US: stock markets 1918-98 (annual US$ - logarithmic scale)   68
3–17 Mexican and US stocks: risk and return for different terms   69

4 Cycles   71

4–1 Original Kondratieff cycles   72
4-2 Updated long cycles   73
4–3 Economic cycles in the US 1956-98 (annual)   75
4–4 US: stocks and interest rates 1988-98 (monthly US$)   77
4–5 M4 (advanced 12 months) and GNP of OECD countries 1985-2000 (% annual change)   78
4–6 World liquidity cycle 1969-99   79
4–7 Investment for each stage of liquidity cycle   80
4–8 The liquidity cycle and emerging markets flows 1991-99   81
4–9 Tbill, emerging markets and US 1988-98 (monthly US$)   82
4–10 Mexico: sexennial cycles 1958-98 (annual)   83
4–11 Mexico: stocks and interest rates 1988-98 (monthly)   86
4–12 Mexico: GDP and increase in real M4 1982-98 (quarterly)   87
4–13 Mexico: real M4 and stock market index 1988-98 (monthly)   87
4–14 International calendar for 1998   91
4–15 The ten surprises of 1998   92
4–16 Consensus forecast: average of five economic forecasts   93
4–17 Scenarios for 1998   93

5 Debt I   97

5–1 Interest rates in antiquity (%)   98
5–2 History of global debt: important dates   100
5–3 History of debt in Mexico: important dates   105
5–4 Growth of foreign debt 1946-82   110
5–5 Mexican foreign debt: net value 1990-98 (US$bn.)   110
5–6 Main Mexican debt securities 1998   111
5–7 Mexican securities market trading 1991-98   112
5–8 Main Mexican debt securities: value traded 1991-98   113
5–9 Traded debt: value outstanding 1998 (US$bn.)   114
5–10 Main government debt securities   117
5–11 Main corporate debt securities   120
5–12 Emerging markets and US debt 1989-96 (US$bn.)   122
5–13 J. P. Morgan Brady bond index (December 1998)   123
5–14 Main Mexican US$ government debt securities 1998   124

6 Debt II   129

6–1 Price calculation for bond with semiannual coupon (%)   131
6–2 Inflation and 91 day Cetes in Mexico 1978-98 (monthly annualized - %)   133
6–3 Inflation and 91 day Tbills in the US 1983-98 (monthly annualized - %)   134
6–4 Yield curves: upward and downward sloping   135
6–5 Yield curves: horizontal and humped   136
6–6 Yield curve: US Treasury securities   137
6–7 Yield curve: Cetes in Mexico   138
6–8 Calculation of duration for different levels of F, R and n (annual payments)   139
6–9 Yield and duration of 4 Mexican eurobonds (weekly)   139
6–10 Return ranking: peso debt securities   140
6-11 Yield on Cetes and commercial paper 1991-98 (monthly)   141

6-12 Standard & Poor's: rating scale — 142
6-13 Standard & Poor's: selected long and short term ratings (July 1997) — 143
6-14 Application of credit quality indicators — 144
6-15 Return ranking: dollar debt securities — 145
6-16 Mexican sovereign eurobonds: spread vs. duration — 147
6-17 Sovereign and corporate eurobonds: 1991-98 (monthly) — 148
6-18 Corporate eurobonds: spreads over Treasuries, ratings, and financial ratios 1997 — 149
6-19 Nominal parity and purchasing power parity of the peso vs. the dollar 1979-98 (annual) — 150
6-20 Peso futures and interest rates 1997-98 — 151
6-21 Risk and return of Mexican investments 1991-98 — 152

7 Stocks I — 153

7-1 Global stock market history: important dates — 154
7-2 Dow Jones industrials 1910-98 (annual – log scale) — 158
7-3 Mexican stock market history: important dates — 160
7-4 MSE index in US$ 1917-98 (annual – log scale) — 164
7-5 Emerging stock markets: basic statistics (February 1999) — 165
7-6 Main market and GDP: sectoral breakdown (1998) — 166
7-7 Main market sectors (December 1998) — 167
7-8 IPC (US$) and Dow Jones index 1976-98 (annual) — 168
7-9 Stock markets: main listing requirements — 169
7-10 Main market and MMEX: new issue value 1991-98 — 170
7-11 Mexican and foreign investment in stocks (December 1998) — 173
7-12 Main Mexican stocks traded abroad (December 1998) — 174
7-13 Daily average trading value (US$mn.) and IPC (US$) 1978-98 (annual) — 176
7-14 Trading value of 10 top stock series 1997-8 — 177
7-15 Percentage of total capitalization (%) represented by top 10 companies: Latin American markets 1993-6 — 177
7-16 Liquidity index: stock series with "high" liquidity (August 1997) — 178
7-17 MMEX: traded value of new and reclassified stocks and the MMEX index 1995-98 (monthly) — 179
7-18 Traded value of stocks offshore and on the MSE 1998 — 180

8 Stocks — 183

8-1 Price/book value multiple and sovereign stripped spread 1992-98 (monthly) — 189
8-2 Components of the rate R — 191
8-3 Real M4 and stock index US$ 1988-98 (monthly) — 192
8-4 Trailing price/book and price/earnings ratios of Mexican stock market 1991-98 (monthly) — 193
8-5 Comparison of Latin American stock markets (December 31, 1997) — 194
8-6 Fair value calculations for the market index (US$) — 195
8-7 Estimates of the stock index with different scenarios — 196
8-8 Mexican and US stock markets 1991-98 (monthly) — 197
8-9 US stock market sectors (November 1997) — 200
8-10 Mexican stock market sectors (December 31, 1997) — 201
8-11 Mexican stock market sectors, ranked by P/BV (December 31 1997) — 202
8-12 Consumer and capital goods sectors: P/BV multiples relative to market multiple 1997 (monthly) — 203
8-13 Construction sector and Industrial GDP (1981-97 monthly) — 205
8-14 Cement sector in Latin America (December 1997) — 206
8-15 Stores sector in Latin America (December 1997) — 207
8-16 Manufacturing sector analysis: activity chain — 208
8-17 Stores sector analysis — 209
8-18 IPC and MMEX index 1994-98 (monthly 100 = March 1994) — 211
8-19 CEMEX CPO price: October 28, 1997 — 212
8-20 Stocks market analysis (December 31, 1997) — 214
8-21 Stores sector (December 1997) — 217

8–22 Stores sector: price/book multiples in relation to sectoral average 1997 (monthly)   218
8–23 Consensus forecasts for EPS of stocks in Stores sector (December 1997)   221
8–24 Stores sector: stock prices varying assumptions for *g* and *R*   222
8–25 One year price targets under varying assumptions   223

9 Derivatives   225

9–1 Main derivatives exchanges   226
9–2 Global history of derivatives: important dates   228
9–3 OTC and organized markets, outstanding value (June 1998)   232
9–4 Relation between derivatives and underlying assets 1998   233
9–5 Instruments, underlying assets and counterparties in OTC markets June 1998 (% of outstanding value)   233
9–6 History of Mexican derivatives: important dates   234
9–7 Warrants traded on MSE 1993 (number issued)   235
9–8 Traded value of Mexican derivatives in Chicago (December 1998) (US$m.)   236
9–9 Warrants traded on the MSE 1998 (number issued)   237
9–10 Description of instruments to be traded on MexDer   237
9–11 Relation of Mexican derivatives to underlying assets 1998   238
9–12 Theoretical and market prices of peso futures on the CME   240
9–13 Theoretical and market prices of 91 day Cete futures on the CME   241
9–14 Payoff function for $/US$ future or forward: long position   243
9–15 Intrinsic value and time value   245
9–16 Movement necessary in key variables to generate an increase in option premium   247
9–17 Payoff function for call option on peso future, long position.   248
9–18 Payoff functions   249
9–19 Strategies with futures and stocks   251
9–20 Portfolio with one share and put option   253

10 Irrationality   255

10–1 Important financial crises 1637-1998   258
10–2 Viceroy tulip in Holland: equivalent value (in florins) 1636   260
10–3 Prices of Switser tulip (January - February 1637)   261
10–4 South Sea Company: spot and future prices 1720   263
10–5 Dow Jones index 1926-30   264
10–6 Gold and silver prices 1979-82 (monthly)   265
10–7 Mexico: stock market booms of 1979, 1984 and 1987 (monthly US$)   267
10–8 Over- and undervaluation of peso against dollar 1978-98 (annual)   268
10–9 Indonesian rupiah/US$ October 1997- March 1998 (daily)   272
10–10 Japanese stock market 1970-98 (monthly)   273

11 Investors   279

11–1 Psychographics of individual investor   281
11–2 Life cycle: return-risk   283
11–3 US households with stock investments 1983 and 1992   285
11–4 Global institutional investment (US$)   290
11–5 Total investment market and GNP of 27 countries   290
11–6 Institutional investment and total investment market in 27 countries   291
11–7 History of institutional investment in US: important dates   292
11–8 Money managers' assets 1975-March 1995 (US$bn.)   293
11–9 Growth of institutional investment in US 1975-95   294
11–10 Investment of 401(k) plans at December 31, 1994   295
11–11 Growth of managers and mutual funds 1985-94   295
11–12 Investments of US mutual funds 1975-95   296
11–13 History of institutional investment in Mexico: important dates   296
11–14 Institutional investment in Mexico 1992-97   297
11–15 Institutional investment: Mexico and US   298

11–16 Afores and Siefores (April, 1998)   299
11–17 Siefores investment (March 27, 1998)   299
11–18 Investment portfolios of Chilean AFPs 1997   300

12 Management   303
12–1 The investment management process   304
12–2 Model portfolio in US$ (January 1998)   305
12–3 Efficient portfolios and the efficient frontier   306
12–4 Investment benchmarks in pesos and dollars   306
12–5 Performance measurement with inflows and outflows   307
12–6 Stock mutual funds: annual return (in pesos) of top ten Mexican funds 1997 308
12–7 Stock mutual funds: top ten Mexican funds ranked by Sharpe ratio 1997   309
12–8 Stock mutual funds: return–risk 1997   310
12–9 Portfolio of Mexican stocks and eurobonds: return and risk   311
12–10 Investment management structure for typical company   313

Appendix A Investment   321
A–1 Combination of one risk-free and one risky investment   324
A–2 Combinations of risky investments   325
A–3 The securities market line   326

Appendix B Debt II   329
B–1 Equivalent rates for different maturities (20% return)   332
B–2 Sensitivity of debt securities to changes in interest rates   334
B–3 Calculation of duration   334

Appendix C Stocks I   337
C–1 Main Mexican stock market indices 1999   337
C–2 Stock series used for IPC of MSE (bimester XI-XII 1998)   338
C–3 Stock series used for INMEX (semester VII-XII 1998)   338
C–4 IPC and INMEX 1993-98 (monthly US$)   338
C–5 Mexican stock market indices 1991-98 (monthly US$)   339

Appendix D Stocks II   343
D–1 Risk premium between IPC (US$) and Brady bonds 1991-97 (monthly)   346
D–2 Fair value calculations for stock index (US$)   347
D–3 Fair value calculations for index: annual flows and sale price   348
D–4 Index forecasts for one year term   349
D–5 Fair value estimates for individual stock prices   350
D–6 Price forecasts for individual stocks for one year term   351

Appendix E Derivatives   353
E–1 Black-Scholes formulas for different underlying assets   353

Index

A

Academy of Stock Market Law, 163
Administradoras de Fondos de
  Pensiones. *See* " AFPs "
ADRs, 3, 19, 20, 163, 172–73, 180,
  199, 236
Afghanistan, 265
Afores, 114, 144, 286, 288, 298, 299,
  300, 313
AFPs, 288, 300
Africa, 262
Ajustabonos, 3, 35, 112, 119
ALFA, 205, 209
Alliance Insurance Company, 157
American Depositary Receipts. *See*
  "ADRs"
American Stock Exchange. *See*
  "Amex"
Amex, 175, 176, 230
Amortization, 116
Amsterdam Wisselbank. *See* "Central
  banks"
Anglo Mexican Mining Company, 160
Antwerp, 102, 155, 156
APASCO, 178
Arabs, 9, 101, 103, 125
Arbitrage, 44
Arbitrage Pricing Theory, 43–44, 327
Argentina, 54, 64
Asia Minor, 97
Asian crisis, 61, 64, 65, 83, 94, 204,
  257
Asset allocation, 46, 49, 191, 305
Asset class, 3, 42, 49, 59, 60, 66–67,
  123, 307
Athens, 9, 99
ATT, 213
Average life, 138

Aztecs, 104

B

Babylon, 98
Banca Serfin, 108
Banco de Avío, 107
Banco de Santa Eulalia, 108
Banco Mercantil Mexicano, 108
Banco Mexicano, 108
Banco Nacional de México, 108, 159
Banco Nacional Mexicano, 108
Bank acceptances, 111, 119–20, 130
Bank for International Settlements. *See*
  "BIS"
Bank of England. *See* "Central banks"
Bank of London, Mexico and South
  America, 108, 159
Bank of Mexico, 3, 85, 90, 92, 109–10,
  117, 119, 235
Bank of New York, 172
Bank of Rialto, 102
Bank of St. George, 102
Bank of Venice, 102
Barings, 107, 239
BARRA, 44
Basis points, 54, 146
Benchmark rate, 33
Benchmarks, 47, 210, 307
Berlin Wall, 5, 126, 270
Beta, 42, 251, 326–27, 354–55
BEVIDES, 217
Big Mac, 150
BIMBO, 145, 209
Binomial option valuation model, 247
BIS, 232
Black Monday, 267
Black Tuesday, 264
Black, Fischer, 230, 353
Black-Scholes model, 246, 353–54

Bloomberg, 10
Bolsa de México, S. A, 161
Bolsa de Valores de Mexico, S. A. de
   C. V., 162
Bolsa de Valores de Mexico, S. C. L.,
   162
Bolsa Mexicana de Valores, S. A. de C.
   V, 163
Bolsa Privada de México, 162
Bondes, 112, 114, 118
Bonds
   convertible, 121–22
   corporate, 111, 121–22
   fixed rate, 130–31
   floating rate, 131–32
   government (*prestiti*), 101
   indexed, 34–35
   inflation-linked, 3, 132–33
   liquidity cycle, 79
   zero coupon, 129–30, 241
Book value, 183, 185
Booms
   and financial crises, 257–59
   crash of 1929 (US), 264–65
   gold and silver, 265
   Mexican peso, 268
   Mexican stock market, 195, 266–68
   Minsky model, 269–72
   Mississippi, 262–63
   South Sea Bubble. *See* "South Sea
     Bubble"
   tulipomania. *See* "Tulipomania"
Bottom-up investment. *See*
   "Investment, bottom-up"
Brady bonds
   basic calculations, 335–36
   country risk, 54
   futures, 236
   history, 122–23
   index, 61, 64
   Mexico, 1, 3, 60, 64, 65, 66, 111,
     114, 115, 123–24, 146-47, 188,
     235
Brady Plan, 16, 122, 126
Brady, Nicholas, 122
Brazil, 11, 15, 16, 54, 64, 257
Bretton Woods, 225, 230
Britain. *See* "England"
Brokers, 2, 21, 29, 30, 91, 111, 163,
   164, 198, 199, 286, 298

Bruges, 102, 155, 156
Buffett, Warren, 50, 185
Bulletin B10, 220, 266
Burr Williams, John, 38

C

Canada, 290
Capital Asset Pricing Model. *See*
   "CAPM"
Capital Group, 10
Capital increase, 168
Capitalism, 7, 9, 15, 257
CAPM, 41–42, 326–27
CAPs, 267
CARBIDE, 171
Carranza, Venustiano, 109
Cash flow, 187
Caval. *See* "Standard & Poor´s"
CBOE, 230, 236
CBOT, 104, 229, 230, 231
CELANES, 171
CEMEX, 171, 172, 202, 209, 212
Central banks
   Amsterdam Wisselbank, 102, 156
   Bank of England, 102, 156
   Bank of Mexico. *See* "Bank of
     Mexico"
   Bolivia, 109
   Colombia, 109
   Fed. *See* "Fed"
   Riksbank, 102
   Uruguay, 109
Certificados de Tesorería. *See* "Cetes"
Cetes
   28 days, 33, 35, 117
   91 days, 1, 2, 133
   amount, 115
   basic calculations, 329–32
   description, 117–18
   futures, 236, 238, 242
   introduction, 111
   liquidity, 114
   trading, 112–13
   US$ returns, 66
   valuation, 130
   yield curve, 137
Charitable foundations, 282, 288–89

Charles V, 103
Chiapas, 95
Chicago, 21
Chicago Board Options Exchange. *See* "CBOE"
Chicago Butter and Egg Board, 229
Chicago futures markets, 229–30
Chicago Mercantile Exchange. *See* "CME"
Chicago Produce Exchange, 229
Chile, 12, 194, 288, 294, 299–300
China, 5, 12, 15, 94, 95, 262
CIE, 170
CIFRA, 171, 206, 210, 216, 217, 220, 221, 222, 350, 352
Citibank, 172
Civil War, 104, 157
Clearing house, 229, 239, 247, 261
Clinton, William, 76, 159
CME, 26, 29, 104, 151, 229, 230, 234, 236, 242, 248
Coca-Cola, 185, 211
COFAR, 169
Cold War, 9, 15, 125, 159
Collectivism, 5, 7, 9
COMERCI, 210, 216, 217, 220, 221, 222, 350, 352
Commerce Code (1884), 108
Commercial paper, 111, 120, 130
Commodities, 26, 79
Commodities Exchange Act (US), 230
Communism, 5, 9, 10, 104, 270
Community Chests, 104
Compagnie d'Occident, 156, 262, 263
Compagnie des Indes, 262
Compañía de Seguros La Mexicana, 162
Congress (Mexico), 115
Consensus forecasts
    earnings, 220
    economic, 93–94
Consols, 103, 137
Constant growth model, 343–44
Consumer Price Index. *See* "CPI"
Consumption, 25, 32
Contrary opinion
    economic assumptions, 276
    investment objectives, 276
    investment rule, 316–17
    specific investments, 277

trading, 277
Cortés, Hernán, 104
Counterparty, 239
Counterreformation, 103
Country funds, 287
Country risk, 51–69
    analysis services, 57–58
    debt, 52–59
    debt and stocks, 59–60
    definition, 51
    economic indicators, 55–57
    Mexico, 60–64
    premium, 140
    ratings, 52–55
    real rate, 34
    return, 51–52
    spread in US$, 146
    stocks, 59
CPI, 33, 119
CPO, 171, 172
Crash. *See also* "Booms"
    1929, 264–65, 291
    Minsky model, 271
    October 1987, 84, 90, 158, 163, 267
Credit quality, 143–45, 148
CrossBorder Capital, 77
Crowd, 273
Crusades, 101
Currency Hedging Contracts, 234
Cycles, 71–96
    economic, 74–76, 134
    emerging markets, 81
    government role, 75–76
    liquidity, 76–83, 134
    long, 71–74, 159
    Mexico, 83
    portfolio investments, 79–80
Cyclicality, 204

D

Dark Ages, 99
de la Huerta-Lamont Treaty 1922, 108
de la Madrid, Miguel, 84, 85
de la Vega, Joseph, 183, 227, 239
Debt, 97–127, 129–52
    country risk, 52–59, 61–63
    development of Mexican markets, 111–12
    global history, 98–104

global markets, 60–61, 60–61
    Mexico country risk, 64–66
    risk premium, 36
    sovereign, 52
Debt rating, 141
Debt securities
    corporate, 119–22
    dollars, 114, 122–27, 148–49
    government, 117–19, 117
    liquidity, 114–15
    pesos, 112–13, 148–49
    principal features, 115–16
    return ranking (dollars), 145–48
    return ranking (pesos), 140
    types, 129–33
DEC, 158
Deflation, 16, 95
Democratization, 5
Depositary, 172
Deregulation, 5, 16, 76, 85, 126
Derivatives, 225–54
    financial, 230–31
    forwards. *See* "Forwards"
    futures. *See* "Futures"
    global history, 227–31
    global market structure, 231–34
    main exchanges, 226
    Mexican market structure, 236–38
    Mexico, 21, 234–36
    options. *See* "Options"
    stocks and indices, 159
DESC, 205, 209
Devaluation. *See* "Peso"
Development banks, 109–10
Disclosure, 175, 199
Discount rate, 329
Disinflation, 95
Disney, 185
Displacement, 269–70
Diversification, 42, 316
Dividend discount model (DDM), 343
Dividends, 183, 212, 343
Dodd, David, 185
Dollar
    debt securities, 114, 122–27
    reference currency, 28
Donation, 282
Dow Jones. *See* "Index: Dow Jones"
Dreman, David, 274
Drucker, Peter, 22

Drugs, 95
Duff & Phelps de México, 141
Duration, 138–39, 333–35

E

Earnings, 218–20
Earthquake, 84, 85, 270
East India Company (England), 155
East India Company (Holland), 156, 227
Eastern Europe, 5
EBITDA, 144, 188
Echeverría, Luis, 83, 84, 110
Economic Solidarity Pact, 84, 85
Efficient frontier, 41, 306
Efficient markets, 44–46
El Niño, 90
ELAMEX, 176
ELEKTRA, 206, 216, 217
Emerging markets
    asset class, 3
    boom, 269
    Brady bonds, 122–23
    comparison, 19
    comparison with GDP, 164
    concentration, 177
    concept, 9–10
    crisis, 15–16, 65
    currencies, 259
    definition, 11–13
    derivatives, 231
    efficiency, 46
    flows, 11
    future importance, 23
    history, 9
    Kondratieff long cycle, 72
    liquidity cycle, 81
    Mexico, 19–21
    new issues, 169
    number, 11, 104
    potential, 13–14
    prospects, 15–16
    research, 11
    returns, 11, 37, 64
    US rates, 82
Emerging Markets Growth Fund Inc., 10, 339
England
    banks, 104

canals, 157, 259
companies, 155–56
debt, 102–4
East India Company, 155
empire, 9, 103, 158
foreign bonds, 259
Latin American mines, 259
railways, 157, 259
stocks, 157–59
Treasury bills, 104
Equivalent rates, 331–32
ERISA, 300
Euphoria, 271
Euro, 28, 90, 124
Eurobank, 125
Eurobonds
convertibles, 127
index, 311
international market, 124–26
Mexico, 114, 115, 126, 146
trading system, 29
types, 126–27
UMS 2026, 124, 190, 347
Eurocurrencies, 124
Eurodollar, 124
Euromarkets, 126
European Union, 28
Exchange rate. *See* "Peso".
Exchanges
Amex. *See* "Amex"
Amsterdam, 102, 156, 227, 230, 261
Antwerp, 102
Bruges, 102, 155
Buenos Aires, 160
CBOE. *See* "CBOE"
CBOT. *See* "CBOT"
CME. *See* "CME"
Comex, 26, 29
DTB, 231
history, 153–55
KCBT, 231
LIFFE, 231
Liverpool, 157
London, 104, 157, 230
Luxembourg, 125
Manchester, 157
MATIF, 231
Midam, 230
MSE. *See* "MSE"

NASDAQ, 29, 175
NYSE. *See* "NYSE"
PHLX, 230, 231
PORTAL, 173, 175
PSE, 230
Rio de Janeiro, 160
Santiago, 160
Sao Paulo, 3
SEAQ, 173
SIMEX, 231
SOFFE, 231
TIFFE, 231
External debt. *See* "Foreign debt"

F

Fair value, 185, 189, 196, 210, 347–49
Far East, 64, 101
Fed, 3, 76, 81, 94, 109, 137, 158, 257
Fed funds rate, 81
Federal Open Markets Committee, 81
Federal Reserve Board. *See* "Fed"
FEMSA, 209
FICORCA, 266
Financial crises, 257–59
Financial groups, 2
Financial market, 26
First Call, 220
Fitch IBCA México, 141
Fixed income securities, 97
Flanders, 155
Fleming, Robert, 291
Floating rate notes (FRNs), 126, 131–32
Florence, 102
Foreign debt
balance, 19
financing, 19
growth 1946-82, 110
history, 107–9, 110–11
offshore, 21
payments suspensions, 107
private sector, 19
value, 110
Foreign financial institutions, 3, 21
Foreign investment
stock market, 3, 18, 171–76
Foreign markets, 19–21, 181
Forwards, 227, 233, 239–43
France, 259, 262–63

Free float, 213
Fukuyama, Francis, 5
Futures
  Brady bonds, 236
  Cetes 91 days, 236, 238
  Chicago markets, 229–30
  cost, 242, 252
  coverage ratio, 354–55
  currencies, 231
  definition, 239–40
  eurodollars, 231
  GNMAs, 231
  history, 229
  MSE index, 3, 26, 236, 238
  payoff functions, 242–43
  peso, 3, 151–52, 234, 236, 238, 243
  petrobonds, 234
  South Sea Company, 229
  stock indices, 231
  stocks, 238
  strategy, 250–52
  Tbills, 231
  Tbonds, 231
  term, 251
  TIIE, 236, 238
  tulips, 261
  UDIs, 238
  underlying asset. *See* "Underlying
    asset"
  valuation, 240–42
Futurology, 88

G

Galbraith, John K., 256, 269
GATT, 16, 205. *See* "WTO"
GDP
  economic cycle, 72
  emerging markets, 164
  Mexico, 2, 83, 87, 346
  per capita, 12
  sectoral, 166
  US, 75
  world, 13
GE, 211
General Law of Credit Institutions, 109
Genoa, 101, 156
Germany, 90, 259, 290, 291
GIGANTE, 210, 216
Globalfinance, 199

Globalization, 1–23
  aspects, 5–7
    capital, 7
    goods and services, 7
    ideas, 5
    information, 5
    people, 7
  causes, 7–9
  definition, 5
  derivatives, 225
  history, 9
  Kondratieff cycle, 74
  Mexican markets, 18–19
  Mexico, 16–21
  social consequences, 21
  stock sectors, 207
GMEXICO, 218
GMODELO, 179, 209
Gold, 103, 259, 265, 270
Graham, Benjamin, 185
Greenspan, Alan, 76, 82
Gross Domestic Product. *See* "GDP"
GRUMA, 147
Guarantee, 115

H

Haarlem, 262
Hale, David D., 9, 286, 296
Hammurabi, Code of, 98, 99
Harvey, Campbell, 58
Hedging, 227, 239
History
  booms and crashes, 259–65
  emerging markets, 9
  global debt, 98–104
  global derivatives, 227–31
  global stocks, 153–59
  globalization, 9
  institutional investment US, 291–92
  Mexican debt, 104–12
  Mexican stock market, 159–64
  Mexico globalization, 16–18
  Mexico institutional investment,
    297–98
Holland
  derivatives, 227
  stocks, 156–57
  tulipomania, 259–62
Home country bias, 48

Homer, Sidney, 98
Hong Kong, 59
Howell, Michael, 51
Huerta, Victoriano, 109

I

I/B/E/S, 220
IBM, 158
ICA, 17
IFC, 10, 12, 339
IMF, 16, 257, 266
INDEVAL, 163
Index
    Bovespa, 3
    Brady bonds, 123
    Dow Jones, 1, 47, 67, 82, 158, 167,
        264, 267, 337
    EAFE, 60
    eurobonds, 311
    forecasting, 349–50
    FT/S&P, 340
    IFC, 339
    ING Barings, 340
    INMEX, 179, 338
    MEX, 236
    Mexican stocks, 337–40
    MMEX, 37, 210
    MSCI, 60, 340
    MSE, 1, 2, 37, 47, 67, 164, 167,
        308, 311, 337
    Standard & Poor's, 47, 337
India, 12, 15, 227, 262
Indicators of economic cycles, 74
Indonesia, 15, 271
Inflation, 133
    indexed bond, 34–35, 132–33
    Mexico, 2
    minimum return, 32–33
    US, 75
Infosel, 1, 2, 10
ING Barings, 107, 340
Inheritances, 284–85
Initial Public Offering (IPO), 167
Inside information, 46, 218
Institutional Investor, 57, 199, 200
Insurance companies, 103, 157, 159,
    289
Interbank Equilibrium Interest Rate,
    131

Interest Equalization Tax, 125
Interest rates
    antiquity, 98
    benchmark, 33
    derivatives, 232
    etymology, 99
    forecasting, 133–38
    futures, 231, 241
    liquidity cycle, 81–83
    options, 231
    term structure, 135
    US, 146
Internal rate of return, 39
International Country Risk Guide, 57
International Finance Corporation. *See*
    "IFC"
International Monetary Fund. *See*
    "IMF"
International Monetary Market, 231
International Quotation System (SIC),
    164, 170
Internet, 7, 72
Inventions, 72, 269
Investment, 25–50
    active management, 49–50, 52, 198
    advice, 314–15
    analysis, 304. *See also* "Research"
    bottom-up, 49
    correlation, 40–41
    definition, 25
    direct, 25–26
    five rules, 315–17
    global, 26–27
    liquidity, 29–30
    liquidity cycle, 79–80
    lonely activity, 277
    management, 303–17
        control, 307–12
        planning, 303–7
    passive management, 46–49, 52,
        191, 198
    portfolio, 25
    psychology, 273–77
    return, 27–29
    risk, 30–32
    strategic, 216
    styles, 46–50
    term, 30
    top-down, 49
    valuation, 38–44

Investment grade, 12, 64, 142
Investors, 279–301
  great, 50
  individual, 27, 280–85
    Mexico, 286
    organization, 314
    US, 285–86
  institutional, 27, 159, 287–89
    global, 289–91
    Mexico, 297–98
    organization, 312–13
    US, 291–97
  liquidity, 284
  psychology, 273–77
  term, 283
IPC. *See* "Index: MSE"
Iran, 125
Irrationality, 255–77
IRSA, 170
Issuers, 115, 341
Italy, 99–102, 155

J

Japan
  debt, 137
  devaluation, 94
  institutional investment, 291
  institutional investors, 290
  rice futures, 229
  stocks, 61, 67, 272
Jews, 103

K

Kahn, Herman, 88
Kennedy, John, 90
KIMBER, 171
Kindleberger, Charles, 257
Kondratieff cycle. *See* "Cycles:long"
Kondratieff, Nikolai, 21, 72
Kuwait, 90, 158, 268

L

Lagunilla Iñarritu, Alfredo, 104
Latin America, 11, 61, 64, 103, 104,
  164, 194, 207, 263
Latinfinance, 199
Law, John, 262
Lebon, Gustave, 273
Lekdyk Bovensdams Company, 102

Leverage, 239
Liberalization, 5, 16
LIBOR, 123, 126
Life cycle, 280, 282
Liquidity
  condition for booms, 270
  debt securities, 114–15
  definition, 26
  foreign markets, 181
  index of (MSE), 177
  INMEX, 178–81
  investor, 284
  organized markets, 29–30
  stocks, 177–78, 199, 213–15
LIVEPOL, 171, 206, 216
Lloyds, insurance market, 103
London Interbank Offered Rate. *See*
  "LIBOR"
López de Santa Anna, Antonio, 107
López Portillo, José, 84, 85, 110, 163,
  266
Luca Pacioli, 102

M

M4
  global, 78
  Mexico, 87, 192
Malaysia, 18
Manias, 256
Margin, 229, 242, 247, 252, 261
Market efficiency. *See* "Efficient
  markets"
Market-makers, 233, 289
Markowitz, Harry, 40
Maturity. *See* "Term"
Maximilian, 108
Mayeu, Filomena, 160
Medici, 102
Mediterranean, 9
Medium term commercial paper, 120–
  21
Merton, Robert, 225
Metallgesellschaft, 239
MexDer, 236, 238, 250
Mexican Association of Stock Market
  Intermediaries, 163
Mexican banking system
  foreign banks, 21
  history, 107, 108, 109

nationalization, 2, 163
privatization, 17
restructuring, 95
structure, 29–30
Mexican Brokers' Association, 163
Mexican Derivatives Market. See
"MexDer"
Mexican medium-sized company
market. See "MMEX"
Mexican Stock Exchange. See "MSE"
Mexican stock market
booms, 266–68
financing, 19
foreign investment, 171–76
growth, 167
history, 159–64
interest rates, 86
international indices, 339–40
issuers, 341
liquidity, 177–78
liquidity cycle, 192
main market, 168–69
national indices, 337–39
new issue booms, 169
primary market, 167–70
regulation, 29
secondary market, 168, 176–81
sectors. See "Sectors"
size, 18, 164–66
structure, 29–30
trading, 112
valuation, 18
Mexico
asset classes, 66–67
colonial period, 104–6
country risk, 60–64
debt history, 104–12
derivatives, 21, 234–36
development of debt markets, 111–
12
economic cycle, 83–84
economic forecast, 86–92
economy 1998, 96
elections 1998, 90
emerging market, 19–21
GDP, 2, 83, 87
global cycle, 83
globalization, 16–21
Independence, 16
individual investors, 286

institutional investment, 297–301
investment cycle, 86
liquidity cycle, 85–86
M4, 87
OECD, 12, 17
Revolution, 16, 108–10, 162
scenarios 1998, 92
Mexico Fund, 287
Middle Ages, 99
Middle East, 95
Miller, Merton, 343
Ministry of Finance and Public Credit,
30, 90, 92, 93
Minsky, Hyman, 269
MMEX, 3, 211
foundation, 164
index. See "Index:MMEX"
liquidity, 178–81
performance, 210
requirements, 169–70
Modern Portfolio Theory, 40–44, 305,
323–26
Modigliani, Franco, 343
Monetary policy, 33
Money market, 103, 111, 112, 129,
270, 329–31, 332–33
basic calculations, 331–32
Montes de Oca-Lamont Agreement
1931, 109
Moody's, 12, 53, 58
MSE, 1, 29, 30, 111, 121, 177. See
also "Mexican stock market"
derivatives, 236, 237–38
index, 37, 164
issuers, 341
liquidity index, 213
stock futures, 234
trading, 112
trading system, 29
Multiple
concept, 184–85
expansion and contraction, 188
historical comparisons, 193
individual stocks, 217
international comparisons, 194
price/book value, 60, 66, 189, 193,
217
price/flow, 186–88, 193
price/value, 185–86
sectors, 202–4

Mutual funds
  description, 287
  for retirement funds. *See* "Siefores"
  history, 291–92
  Mexico, 114, 286, 297–98, 308
  selection, 310
  stocks, 292
  US, 159, 285, 295–97

N

Nacional Financiera, 109, 115, 171
NADRO, 169
Nafin Trust, 16, 163, 171, 270
NAFTA, 17, 18, 64, 84, 164, 268, 270
National Bank of Agricultural Credit,
  109
National Bank of Ejido Credit, 109
National Bank of Foreign Trade, 110,
  111, 126
National Banking and Securities
  Commission, 30, 169, 175
National Banking Commission, 109
National Banking Convention 1924,
  109
National Bureau of Economic Research
  (US), 74
National Mortgage Urban and Public
  Works Bank, 109
National Securities Commission, 163,
  235
National Securities Dealers'
  Association (US), 29
Net earnings, 187
Net present value. *See* "Present value"
New York Stock Exchange. *See*
  "NYSE"
News, 45
Newton, Sir Isaac, 263, 272
Nicaea, Council of, 99
Nicolín y Echanove, Manuel, 161
Nobel Economics Prize, 42, 225, 344
Nominal value, 183
North American Free Trade
  Agreement. *See* "NAFTA"
NYSE, 17, 20, 29, 30, 90, 95, 157–59,
  164, 170, 172, 175, 176, 213, 229,
  264

O

OECD, 12, 17, 64, 78, 268
Oil, 76, 84, 85, 94, 115, 123, 158, 162,
  163, 265, 266, 270
OPEC, 269
Options
  American-style, 244
  cost, 247–48, 253
  currencies, 231
  definition, 243–44
  European-style, 244
  financial futures, 231
  indices, 231
  interest rates, 231
  intrinsic value, 244–46
  LEAPS, 236
  MEX index, 236
  Mexican ADRs, 235
  MSE index, 236
  payoff functions, 248–50
  peso futures, 236
  stocks, 230
  strategies, 252–53
  strategy, 253–54
  term, 252–53
  theoretical value, 246–47
  time value, 244–46
  underlying asset. *See* "Underlying
    asset"
  valuation, 244–47, 353–54
Orange County, 239
Ordinary Participation Certificate. *See*
  "CPO"
Organization for Economic
  Cooperation and Development. *See*
  "OECD"
Ottoman Empire, 155
Over-the-counter (OTC), 172, 175, 231

P

PANAMCO, 176
Panic, 271–72
Paper money, 270
Pawnshop
  Holland, 102
  Mexico, 106, 108
Payback, 184
Payments, 116
Payoff functions

futures, 242–43
options, 248–50
PEÑOLES, 171
Pension funds
  consultants, 315
  definition, 288
  history, 291–92
  US, 159
Pension plans
  401k, 293
  Chilean system, 299–300
  defined benefit, 288, 289, 293, 297
  defined contribution, 288, 292, 293,
    294–95, 313
Performance, 287
Performance measurement, 43, 307–11
Peso
  booms, 268, 270
  controlled rate, 3
  Currency Hedging Contracts, 234
  debt securities, 112–13
  depreciation, 2
  devaluation, 17, 85, 205, 266, 268,
    270
  exchange rate, 148–52
  futures, 3, 151–52, 234, 236, 243
  government debt securities, 117
  option on future, 248
  reference currency, 28
Petrobonds, 3, 111, 234
Petrodollars, 16, 125, 270
Petróleos Mexicanos (Pemex), 115
Philippines, 54
Phoenicians, 9
Policy
  fiscal, 75
  monetary, 75, 85
Political transition, 4
Porfirio Díaz, 107, 159, 162
PORTAL. See "Exchanges"
Portfolio
  construction, 305–7
  measurement of return, 323
  measurement of risk, 324–26
  performance measurement, 310–11
  theory. See "Modern Portfolio
    Theory"
Portfolio investment. See "Investment:
  portfolio"
Portugal, 12

Porvenir Online, 93, 216
Present value
  basic formula, 38–40, 322
  country risk, 51
  cycles, 71
  debt, 130, 132
  efficient markets, 44
  futures, 240
  individual stocks, 350
  interest rates, 77
  stocks, 189–90, 195–96, 220–22,
    343–45
  total market, 345–49
Price discovery, 239
Primary offering, 168
Private equity, 168
Privatization, 5, 16, 17, 85, 126, 195,
  270
Protectionism, 9
Psychographics, 280
Psychology, 273–77
Purchasing power parity, 149–51
Put and Call Brokers and Dealers
  Association (US), 230

Q

Q ratio, 186
Qualified institutional buyers (QIBs),
  173

R

Rate. See also "return"
  annualized, 28
  benchmark, 33
  compound, 28
  equivalent, 331–32
  fixed, 116
  floating, 116
  interest, 81
  internal rate of return (IRR), 39
  nominal, 28
  of return, 28
  real, 33–34
  reinvestment, 28
  risk-free, 33–35, 51
Rating agencies, 3, 12, 53, 120, 141–43
Reagan, Ronald, 9, 16, 76
Real rate, 33–34, 58–59, 119, 134

Reference currency, 27–28, 152, 190, 307
Rejection, 272
Renminbi, 94
Replacement value, 186
Repo operations, 113, 118, 331–32
Research
 bottom-up, 191
 departments of brokers, 198–200
 emerging markets, 11
 fundamental analysis, 185
 international brokers, 91
 report, 216
 techniques, 303–4
 top-down, 191
Retirement Fund Managers. *See* "Afores"
Return
 arithmetic mean, 321–22
 debt securities, 116
 definition, 27–29
 geometric mean, 321–22
 measurement for portfolio, 323
 Mexican investments, 27
 money market, 329, 330–31
 ranking. *See* "Return ranking"
 rates of, 28
 stock valuation, 346–47
Return ranking
 asset classes, 66
 benchmarks, 307
 debt securities (dollars), 145–48
 debt securities (pesos), 139–45
 investment, 32–38
 stocks, 190
Reuters, 10
Riksbank, 102
Risk
 definition, 2, 30–32
 measurement for portfolio, 324–26
 measurement for single investment, 323
 sovereign, 52
 tolerance, 32, 280–81, 286
 uncertainty, 44
Risk premium
 corporate debt, 36, 141–45
 country risk, 140
 definition, 35
 equity, 37

 large company, 37
 medium-sized company, 37
 spread in US$, 146
 stocks, 346
 term, 36, 140–41
Risk-free rate, 33–35, 119, 134, 309
Rome, 99, 101, 227
Romero de Terreros
 Pedro, 106
Ross, Stephen, 43, 247
Rostow, Walter, 12
Royal Dutch Shell, 88
Rule 144A, 173
Rupiah, 271
Russia, 95
 crisis, 11, 61, 64, 66, 166, 257
 invasion of Afghanistan, 265
 Revolution, 9, 16, 104
 Soviet Union, 125
 The Muscovy Company, 155

S

Saddam Hussein, 158
Salinas, Carlos, 84, 85
SAR, 3, 286, 294, 298, 300
Savings, 25, 32
Scenarios
 concept, 88
 generation, 89
 Mexico, 92–96
Scholes, Myron, 225, 230, 353
Schwartz, Peter, 88
SEAQ, 175
SEC, 30, 159, 162, 173, 175, 229
Secondary offering, 168
Sectors
 capitalization, 210
 comparison with GDP, 166
 concept, 198
 growth, 211
 international comparison, 205–7
 multiple analysis, 202–7
 rotation, 204–5
 stock market
  Automotive, 208
  Beverages, 201, 202, 203, 204, 208, 209
  Cement, 202, 203, 205, 206, 207, 208

Conglomerates, 166, 201, 205
Construction, 166, 202, 203, 204,
  208
Distribution, 201, 202
Durable Goods, 208
Financial Groups, 166
Financial Services, 201, 202, 210
Food, 202, 203, 204, 209
Food, Tobacco and Beverages,
  166
general, 201
Housing, 202
Media, 202, 203, 204
Steel, 203, 204, 205, 208
Stores, 166, 201, 202, 203, 204,
  205, 206, 207, 210, 216, 219
Telecommunications, 203, 204,
  210
Tourism, 202
Transport, 202
structural analysis, 207–10
stock market, 201
valuation, 198–213
value, 211–12
yield, 212–13
Securities and Exchange Commission.
  See "SEC"
Securities Laws (US), 30, 159
Securities Market Law, 30, 111, 163,
  176
Selection of investments, 47, 49–50
Settlor, 280
Sharpe ratio, 42–43, 308–10, 309, 310
Sharpe, William, 42
Short sale, 240
Siefores, 298, 299
Silk Route, 101
Silver, 103, 259, 265, 270
Singapore, 59
SITUR, 212
Slavery, 98, 99
Slim, Carlos, 50
Socialism, 5
Sokoloff, Kiril, 315
Solon, Laws of, 99
SORIANA, 210, 216, 217, 220, 221,
  222, 350, 352
Soros, George, 50, 312
Soukh-Al-Manakh, 268
South Sea Bubble, 157, 229, 263–64

South Sea Company, 156, 229, 263
Sovereign
  ceiling, 147
  debt, 52
  risk. *See* "Risk"
Spain
  empire, 16, 106
  financial system, 103
  payments suspensions, 103
Speculation, 49, 50, 226
Spread, 54
Spread over Treasuries (SOT), 146
Standard & Poor's, 12, 53, 58, 141,
  142
Standard deviation, 32, 41, 52, 59, 309
Stocks, 153–81, 183–224
  "variable income securities", 97,
    183
  country risk, 59, 63–64
  global history, 153–59
  global markets, 60–61
  liquidity cycle, 79
  Mexican history, 159–64
  Mexico country risk, 66
  return ranking, 190
  series, 213
  term, 67–69
  valuation, 343–52
Stripped spread, 54, 65, 146, 189, 335–
  36
Stripped yield, 146, 335–36
Styles of investment, 46–50
Suárez-Lamont Agreements 1942-46,
  109
Sumitomo, 239
Surprises, 90
Swaps, 233
Switzerland, 290
SYNKRO, 145, 212
Synthetic instruments, 254
System of Savings for Retirement. *See*
  "SAR"

T

Taiwan, 15, 18
TAMSA, 171, 172
Taxes, 284
TEAR2, 170
TECO2, 170

TELECOM, 178
Telerate, 10
TELMEX, 16, 19, 60, 121, 163, 171,
    201, 213, 235, 338
Tenochtitlán, 106
Tequila effect, 83
Term
    debt, 116
    futures, 251
    investment, 30
    investment rule, 316
    investor, 283
    options, 252–53
    return, 28
    risk premium, 140–41
    stocks, 67–69, 184
Term structure, 135
Tesobonos, 3, 112, 268
Thatcher, Margaret, 9, 16
The Economist, 58, 124, 150
TIIE. *See* "Interbank Equilibrium
    Interest Rate"
Timing of investments, 47, 49
Tobin, James, 186
Top-down investment. *See*
    "Investment, top-down"
Tories, 102
Treasury bills, 1, 33, 37, 54, 77, 82,
    137, 231
Treasury bonds, 2, 38, 54, 190, 231
Trustee, 280
Trusts, 280
Tulipomania, 156, 227, 259–62
Turkey, 12
Twelve Tables, 99

U

Udibonos, 3, 35, 112, 114, 115, 119,
    132, 332–33
UDIs, 119, 121, 133, 169. *See*
Uncertainty, 44
Underlying asset, 225, 230, 232–34,
    232, 238, 239, 250, 252, 353
United States. *See* "US"
US
    crash of 1929, 264–65
    debt, 103–4
    economic cycle, 74–75
    elections 1998, 90

GDP, 75
government, 76
individual investors, 285–86
inflation, 75, 265
institutional investors, 290, 291–97
Office of Management and Budget,
    76
railways, 259
stock market, 197–98
stock market history, 157–59
stock market sectors, 200
stocks, 61, 77
Treasury bills. *See* "Treasury bills"
Treasury bonds. *See* "Treasury
    bonds"
Treasury Secretary, 76
USSR, 5
Usury, 99

V

Valuation
    debt, 129–33
    futures, 240–42
    individual stocks, 220–22
    investments, 38–44
    options, 244–47
    stocks, 184–90, 213–24, 343–52
Value
    book, 183, 185
    face, 116, 183
    fair. *See* "Fair value"
    intrinsic, 244–46, 249
    par, 183
    present. *See* "Present value"
    principal, 97
    replacement, 186
    sectors, 211–12
    time, 244–46, 249
Value investing, 185
Value Recovery Rights, 123, 235
van Agtmael, Antoine, 10
Venice, 101, 156
Viceroy, 106
Vietnam, 74
Volatility, 2, 3, 32, 52, 59
Volcker, Paul, 76

W

Wack, Pierre, 88

Warrants, 3, 164
  counterparty risk, 235
  introduction, 235
  IPC, 235
  market capitalization, 237
Whigs, 102
White, George, 107
Wien, Byron, 92
William of Orange, 102, 156
World Bank, 10, 16
World Trade Organization. *See* "WTO"
World War I, 9, 72, 104, 158, 162
World War II, 7, 9, 16, 74, 104, 230, 291

WTO, 7, 16

X

XEROX, 158

Y

Yield curve, 134–37
Yom Kippur War, 265
YPF, 170

Z

Zedillo, Ernesto, 84